Globalization, Neo-conservative Policies, and Democratic Alternatives

ESSAYS IN HONOUR OF JOHN LOXLEY

EDITED BY A HAROON AKRAM-LODHI,
ROBERT CHERNOMAS,
AND ARDESHIR SEPEHRI

ARBEITER RING PUBLISHING • WINNIPEG

Printed in Canada by the workers at Hignell Printing.
Cover image and design: Mike Carroll   Layout: Tim Scarth

With assistance of the Manitoba Arts Council/Conseil des Arts du Manitoba.
We acknowledge the support of the Canada Council for the Arts for our publishing program.

Library and Archives Canada Cataloguing in Publication

Globalization, neo-conservative policies and democratic alternatives: essays in honour of
John Loxley / A. Haroon Akram-Lodhi, Robert Chernomas, Ardeshir Sepehri, editors.

Papers presented at the Conference: Governance and Adjustment in an Era of
Globalization held at the University of Manitoba, Winnipeg, Canada on November 8th,
2002.

Includes bibliographical references.
ISBN 1-894037-22-7

1. Conservatism. 2. Economic policy. 3. Globalization—Economic aspects.
4. Budget. 5. Economics. I. Loxley, John, 1942- II. Akram-Lodhi, A. Haroon (Agha Haroon),
1958- III. Chernomas, Robert IV. Sepehri, Ardeshir V. Governance and Adjustment in an Era
of Globalization (2002 : Winnipeg, Man.)

HC54.G65 2005   330.9   C2005-901106-8

CONTENTS

ACKNOWLEDGEMENTS

A Haroon Akram-Lodhi, Robert Chernomas
and Ardeshir Sepehri

THE origin of this book can be traced back to spring of 2000, when two of the editors were, under the auspices of the Vietnamese-Dutch Project for MA Programme in Development Economics, working in the University of Economics in Ho Chi Minh City, Vietnam. One morning they were talking about the personal and professional impact that John Loxley had had on them, and, as happens in such conversations, up came the idea that it would be interesting to get together a group of John's former students and have a conference. The downside was, of course, that this would neglect John's past and present colleagues. In this way, the idea developed of having a conference of John's current and former colleagues and students, who would come together to recognize the deep impact that John has had on them, both professionally and personally, and which would have, as its unifying theme, the intellectual ideas that had motivated his life and work. After 30 minutes a provisional list of possible contributors was assembled, and within an hour, a call for contributors was sent out via computer. Remarkably, within 24 hours more than half the contributors contained herein had agreed. It was a testimony to the impression that John Loxley has made.

Early drafts of this book were thus first presented at an international symposium in honour of John Loxley entitled "Governance and Adjustment in an Era of 'Globalization'" held on 8 and 9 November 2002 at the University of Manitoba in Winnipeg, Canada. Fletcher Baragar provided sage advice throughout the conference, and subsequently in the process that led to this book. Dean Bob O'Kell of the Faculty of Arts of the University of Manitoba made significant contributions to both the conference and the publishing of this book. The Department of Economics of the University of Manitoba provided support for the conference, and this assistance is acknowledged with thanks. So too is the support that was received from the Canadian Centre for Policy Alternatives, the Canadian Union of Public Employees, the Joe Zuken Memorial Society, and the Manitoba Federation of Labour. Special mention should also be made of the following people who devoted time and effort to ensuring that the conference was, in both academic and social terms, a success: Jean Altemeyer, Pete Hudson, Judy Ings, Si Kahn, Shirley Lord, Betty MacGregor, Shauna MacKinnon, Norah Richards, Nicole Ritchot, Anna Rothney, Nasreen Sepehri, Wayne Simpson, Neil Tudiver, and Jean Wilson. In addition, Greg Selinger, the Minister of Finance of the Government of Manitoba, took time off from his very busy schedule to deliver the opening remarks to the conference, and his contribution is appreciated. Mark Gabbert and Gregg Olsen of the University of Manitoba also facilitated a provocative roundtable that closed the conference on a theme close to John: "Whither Socialism?" Finally, special mention must be made of Bill Gerrard, who wrote and delivered a fine paper for the conference. This paper is not included in the book because of its subject matter, which is also close to John — soccer. Bill was a significant presence at the conference, and is very much a part of the collective effort that went into this book.

At various stages of this project Diane Elson, Sue Himmelweit, Stephen Gelb, Fred Nixson, and Marc Wuyts were all involved, and although they were not able subsequently to contribute to the conference or the book, their efforts are appreciated. At the Institute of Social Studies in The Hague, the Rural Development, Environment and Population Studies Staff Group provided financial support and a collegial atmosphere that allowed work on the conference and the book to continue unencumbered by the day-to-day minutiae of academic life. At Arbeiter Ring Publishing, Esyllt Jones has used her editorial flair to nurture the volume and at the same time greatly enhance the quality of the final product. Pat Sanders did a fine job copy-editing the final manuscript, while Carolynn Smallwood nursed the volume to life. Thank you also to Noeline Bridge for her hard work in preparing the index.

Salim, Camille, Raina, and Matthew Loxley have all, in their various ways, helped in making this work. A special word of thanks should, however, go to Aurelie Mogan, who assisted in the organization and logistics of the conference, and who played an active role in the conference itself.

Finally, Catherine, Cameron, and Róisín all put up with the work and the absences that went into making this book possible, and their contribution has been inestimable.

NOTES ON CONTRIBUTORS

ABDELLA ABDOU is an Assistant Professor in the Department of Economics at Brandon University, Manitoba, Canada. He was a student of John Loxley.

HAROON AKRAM-LODHI teaches rural economics and rural economic methodology at the Institute of Social Studies in The Hague, The Netherlands. His principal research interest is on the gendered political economy of agrarian change in Asia, with special reference to Pakistan, Vietnam and Fiji, and his work in this area has been published in numerous journals and books. He completed his PhD under John Loxley, whom he has known for 20 years.

Between 1998 and 2003 **SAMIA KAZI AOUL** worked on a variety of research projects in a number of institutions, including the Research Group on Mining Activities in Africa, the Centre of Studies on International Rights and Globalisation, the Centre of Human Science in Delhi, and the Institute of Sustainable Development and International Relations in Paris. Since 2004 she has been an Associate Expert in Social Protection in the Algiers office of the International Labour Organization.

JOHN KOFI BAFFOE is an Associate Professor of Economics at Nipissing University, North Bay, Canada. He obtained his PhD in Economics from the University of Manitoba, with John Loxley as his supervisor, and subsequently worked with John in evaluating the social and economic impacts of IMF and World Bank policies on Ghana and Zambia. Over the years John has been a very good friend and mentor.

Born and raised in Winnipeg, **FLETCHER BARAGAR** is an Assistant Professor in the Department of Economics at the University of Manitoba. He received a term position teaching economics in the mid-1980s during the early years of John Loxley's term as department Chair, and liked what he saw. Encouraged by John, he headed south, obtained a PhD from the University of Utah, and enthusiastically returned to Manitoba.

RAY BUSH teaches at the School for Politics and International Studies at the University of Leeds, UK. He writes on the political economy of underdevelopment, with special reference to the economic crisis in Egypt and the Egyptian countryside. John Loxley was a visiting Professor in the Department of Economics, University of Leeds in the late 1980s, and was his neighbour in Sheffield. They commuted together, watched Sheffield Wednesday, and inevitably discussed the positive possibilities for extricating Africa from the set of economic and political crises that it faced at the time.

BONNIE CAMPBELL is Professor in the Department of Political Science at the Université du Québec à Montréal. Throughout her career she has taught and researched in this field as it relates to Africa. She has recently been appointed to the Conseil scientifique of the Centre de coopération internationale en recherche agronomique pour le développement in France. She is the author of over seventy journal articles, and author, editor or co-editor of nine volumes, including, most recently, *Regulating Mining in Africa: For Whose Benefit?* and *Qu'allons-nous faire des pauvres? Réformes institutionnelles et espaces politiques ou les pièges de la gouvernance pour les pauvres.* In 1989 she and John Loxley co-edited *Structural Adjustment in Africa.*

ROBERT CHERNOMAS is a Professor in the Department of Economics at the University of Manitoba. He has published in both the academic and popular literature with respect to alternative macroeconomics, the history of economic thought, the political–economy of post-secondary education, health care economics and in the area of the socio-economic determinants of health. All of the above is connected to political activism. John Loxley and he are involved in each others' lives in everything from alternative budgets, to soccer, to government work, in the economics department, to family—the things that close friends do together.

LIONEL CLIFFE is Emeritus Professor of Politics at the University of Leeds. He and John Loxley worked closely together in Dar Es Salaam in the 1960s, and have been in and out of each other's lives ever since.

ROY CULPEPER was appointed President and CEO of The North-South Institute in Ottawa in 1995. He has written extensively on issues concerning international financial instability and global governance. Among his previous endeavours he is particularly proud of his work between 1975 and 1977 with John Loxley in the Resource and Economic Development (RED) Secretariat in Manitoba.

MARTIN DOORNBOS is a political scientist who has worked extensively on questions of governance, ethnic conflict, state building and state collapse in Uganda, the Horn of Africa and India. He has been for many years with the Institute of Social Studies in The Hague, The Netherlands. He was a contemporary of John Loxley during his time as a Research Fellow at the Makere Institute of Social Research in Uganda between 1965 and 1967.

MARIE-CHRISTINE DORAN is a researcher and lecturer in the Faculty of Political Science and Law at Université du Québec à Montréal and associate researcher at the Center for Research on Development in Paris. She is currently working on a research project on democracy, poverty and religion in Latin America, and has published many articles on the subject. John Loxley's work has been important to her in opening up the question of the impact of institutional reform on democracy and the democratic process.

ALEXANDER C. DOW is Professor of the Scottish Economy in the Division of Business Economics and Enterprise of Glasgow Caledonian University. His research interests and publications over the years have included the economic history of Canada, British economic performance and Scottish political economy. He obtained his PhD in Economics from the University of Manitoba in 1980, where he met and worked with John Loxley.

SHEILA C. DOW holds a Personal Chair in Economics at the University of Stirling, where she has taught since 1979. She has published widely in academic journals and contributed to monographs in the areas of monetary theory, history of thought, methodology of economics and regional finance. She is author of several books, the latest of which is *Economic Methodology:*

An Inquiry. In the 1970s she worked with the Department of Finance of the Government of Manitoba, where she got to know John Loxley.

AUGUSTIN KWASI FOSU is currently Director of the Economic and Social Policy Division of the United Nations Economic Commission for Africa in Addis Ababa, Ethiopia. He has published extensively in economic growth and development, and is co-editor of the *Journal of African Economies*. He feels privileged to have crossed paths with John Loxley, who was the first person to suggest that he consider the position of Director of Research of the African Economic Research Consortium, based in Nairobi, where he subsequently worked for nearly six years.

GERRY HELLEINER is Professor Emeritus, Economics, and Distinguished Research Fellow, Munk Centre for International Studies, University of Toronto. He has worked with John Loxley in Tanzania, South Africa, and the North-South Institute, among other places. He likes to think that he is at least partially responsible for John's coming to Canada.

PETER LAWRENCE is a former colleague of John Loxley's at the University of Dar Es Salaam and a fellow PhD from Leeds University in the UK. He has taught development economics for more than 30 years, principally at Keele University, UK. He has published widely on development issues and was a founding editor of the *Review of African Political Economy*, for which John Loxley has been a contributing editor throughout.

AURELIE MOGAN is an economist working on rural and community development in Canada. She has followed John Loxley's activities closely for over 20 years, as his partner, as mother to two of his four children, and as a companion in many adventures.

WICKY MEYNEN is a rural sociologist with wide experience in the field of gender issues, land reforms, fisheries and social movements. She has worked in Latin America (Colombia, Peru), Asia (India, Indonesia) and Africa (Tanzania), and for many years has been associated with the Institute of Social Studies in The Hague, The Netherlands. In Tanzania she was a contemporary and friend of John Loxley during her stay in Dar Es Salaam as a Research Fellow at the Economic Research Bureau between 1969 and 1972.

ARDESHIR SEPEHRI is an Associate Professor in the Department of Economics at the University of Manitoba, Canada. His research interests include international finance and international health care financing systems. He has done extensive field work in Uganda, Iran, Nepal, Vietnam, and in Tanzania, where he first worked with John Loxley in the 1980s.

JIM STANFORD is an economist with the Canadian Auto Workers in Toronto. He worked with John Loxley for several years on the Alternative Federal Budget and related progressive economic initiatives.

BRIAN VAN ARKADIE is a development economist who was assoicated with John Loxley in Uganda and Tanzania in the 1960s and worked with him in the Tanzania Advisory Group in Dar Es Salaam between 1981 and 1982.

ZELEALEM YIHEYIS teaches economics in the School of Business at Clark Atlanta University. John Loxley supervised his doctoral research in the late 1980s and early 1990s.

A BIOGRAPHICAL NOTE ON JOHN LOXLEY

Aurelie Mogan and A Haroon Akram-Lodhi

THIS book is a collection of essays on the themes that have shaped the life and work of John Loxley. John Loxley was born in Sheffield in 1942, the middle child in a family of 12 children, and it was the Sheffield of his youth that shaped who he would become. His father worked in the steel mills of Sheffield, and died at the age of 59 after suffering for several years with silicosis. John, at a very early age, was aware that the social services provided by Sheffield Council at the time—milk, education and housing subsidies—enabled the family to create a healthy environment in which all of the children thrived. With many other families in a similar economic situation, the community in which John lived developed a sense of spirit and mutual support. This setting helped form the basis for John's strong sense of social justice and community service.

Academically gifted, John was, thanks to the education policies of the Labour government of the day, able to study under Ken Woolmer and Walter Newlyn at Leeds University. While there, his concern for social justice within his own community became attached to an entrenched awareness that the issues facing his community were very similar to the issues facing developing countries, and in particular Africa. With a PhD in economics from Leeds, and with these intellectual and emotional commitments, John received a Junior Fellowship in African Economic Development in the mid-1960s, funded by the United Kingdom government. After lecturing at Makerere University in Uganda, he moved to Tanzania, where he held a variety of posts: Director of the Tanzania Sisal Corporation, Chief Economist at the National Bank of

Commerce in Tanzania, and Director of the Institute of Financial Management at the University of Dar Es Salaam, amongst others. During this period John was a key figure in Tanzania, both in terms of his work on monetary policy, and in terms of his contributions to the lively debates about African socialism that were so central to the political and intellectual milieu of Dar Es Salaam at that time.

In 1974 John was recruited by the incoming New Democratic Party administration to become Deputy Minister of the Canadian province of Manitoba's Research and Economic Development Cabinet Sub-Committee. While there, he made a significant input into the ambitious Great Northern Plan, which sought, in a fiscally responsible way, to promote the economic development of the more northern, poorer areas of the province. It was, not surprisingly, at this time that John began his long involvement with Aboriginal organizations in Manitoba and in Canada. However, at the same time he retained his international focus. On arriving in Manitoba John immediately became involved with the Manitoba Anti-Apartheid Coalition and, as a member of their Executive from 1975 to 1980, helped organize province-wide information campaigns and the voicing of grassroots Canadian opposition to the apartheid government in South Africa. John was also Chairman of the Western Board of Directors and member of the National Board of Directors of Oxfam Canada in 1976 and 1977. At the same time, he maintained his steadfast support of worker's rights and of the labour movement. In 1977, while still Deputy Minister, he joined the picket line and lent his support to the striking workers at the Griffin Steel Company in Manitoba.

In September 1977 John moved to the University of Manitoba. As Professor of Economics and later as Head of the Department of Economics, John was an instrumental figure in the development of one of the few diverse economics departments in Canada's universities, while at the same time teaching a generation of activist heterodox economists from within Canada and from around the world. John's extensive published work falls into three main areas: international money and finance, international development, and community economic development. His work is notable for its rigorous formulations, its accessibility, its very strong concern for social justice, his view that national and international policies should be analyzed for their impact on all segments of society, and his position that all people should have an informed voice in determining those policies. John shaped academic debates through his membership on the editorial boards of several journals, including the *Review of African Political Economy*, *Studies in Political Economy* and the *Canadian Journal of Development Studies*. His main areas of research, as well as his support for feminist analysis, and his recognition of the need for a political economy-based interdisciplinary analysis, have made him a sought after supervisor for a generation of graduate students.

While at the University John continued to work closely with several governments in Africa and other less developed countries. John was one of the earliest critics of the neo-conservative structural adjustment programmes being developed by the International Monetary Fund (IMF) and the World Bank, and to analyze and document the impact of such programmes. Thus, 1981 and 1984 John was an advisor to Government of Tanzania, dealing with macroeconomic policy and with negotiations with the IMF. John has worked as an economic advisor on macroeconomic reform or worked on structural adjustment policies and economic planning reports for the governments of Ghana, Zambia, Ethiopia, Mozambique, Madagascar, Guyana, Seychelles, St. Kitts and Nevis and the Mandela government in South Africa. During this period John also served as economic advisor on macroeconomic reform to international institutions such as the International Development Research Centre, the United Nations Development Programme, the International Labour Office, and the Commonwealth Secretariat. One of his more recent advisory roles was to act as a member of the Expert Group on Protecting Countries Against Destabilizing Effects of Volatile Capital Flows, appointed by the Commonwealth Secretariat to advise Commonwealth Finance Ministers, in 1998. In this light, it is not surprising that John also served on the Board of the North-South Institute in Ottawa. His approach in this various roles was always the same: to work with community groups and national governments, to analyze the impact of policies on all segments of the population, and to develop an alternative approach with people in mind. Indeed, John has some very unique skills, in that he is able to discuss and debate financial and economic policy with national leaders, finance ministers, chairmen of banks and international institutions, and then talk with equal effect to local community groups about the same issues.

John's work with community groups has occurred both outside and inside Canada. In Canada, he served as a member of the Board of Directors and Executive Committee of the Society for Manitobans with Disabilities from

1983 to 1987. While there he helped change the organization from the charity focussed "Society of Crippled Children and Adults" to a client-oriented and run organization. While doing this work, he concurrently served as an economic advisor to the Assembly of Manitoba Chiefs, as economic advisor to the Canadian Royal Commission on Aboriginal Peoples, as advisor to the Manitoba Métis Economic Development Corporation, and, most recently, the Alberta Métis Settlements. Since 1993 John has also been a member of the board of SEED Winnipeg, a primary instrument of community economic development. He has served as chair since 1999. John helped design and deliver two Aboriginal training programmes, one by the Manitoba Métis Economic Development Programme and the other by the All-Chiefs Budget Committee. These programmes have become templates for community economic development in Canada. Even while doing all this, John has been an economic advisor to the Credit Union Central of Manitoba. John has at the same time retained his work with labour unions and the labour movement, providing analysis, research papers, presentations and seminars, mediating, and commenting on behalf of union positions in the media, at policy commissions, and at public meetings. His analysis and positions while on the bargaining team or supporting the bargaining team of the University of Manitoba Faculty Association were always carried out with the interests of those earning the least pay and benefits and with the long term interests of the University in mind.

In 1991, in response to the devastating neo-conservative and uncreative policy decisions being made by the Winnipeg City Council and the Government of Manitoba, social activists in Winnipeg and Manitoba formed CHO!CES—A Coalition for Social Justice. John was one of the first co-chairpersons. With their grassroots and community organization and their analysis of options, CHO!CES reputation grew and spread throughout Manitoba and Canada, and was soon being replicated in other provinces. One of its major contributions to provincial, national and international forums was the development of 'alternative budgets'. Utilizing his abilities and understanding of the budgetary process and the results that it generated, John worked with other CHO!CES members and community groups to develop a fiscally coherent but more socially just alternative to the budgets that were being brought down by neo-conservative governments. These alternative budgets received a lot of media attention and forced governments to respond to the options with which they were presented, as well as recognize the political positions of their own budgets. As a consequence, between 1995 and 2000 John was the co-ordinator of the Canadian Centre for Policy Alternatives—CHO!CES Alternative Federal Budget. The Alternative Federal Budget brought together university scholars, labour representatives and members of community groups across Canada in a broadly consultative process. In addition to the budget documents themselves, the Alternative Federal Budget Group published several collections of essays on social and economic policy, published training materials on popular economic education, and ran workshops. John remains a board member for the Canadian Centre for Policy Alternatives.

John Loxley is defined by his spirit of generosity, in offering his time and expertise to diverse organizations and individuals. For his friends and family, it is a continual source of amazement that he is able to undertake and complete the amount of work to which he is committed. In this, he is proficient and efficient, practical and committed. John has always being willing to talk to student groups, summer camp programmes, community organizations and church meetings. He has supported numerous university students, taken public positions with no regard to his personal benefit, and enjoyed over 15 years of coaching children's soccer. Throughout it all John has consistently been concerned with public and community welfare, and in particular the welfare of the poorest segments of society. In 2000, John was honoured with the Joe Zuken Citizen Activist Award, for outstanding contribution to the social, political and cultural life of Winnipeg, in recognition of his exemplary community service.

Chapter 1

INTRODUCTION

NEO-CONSERVATIVE ECONOMIC POLICY, GOVERNANCE AND ALTERNATIVE BUDGETS

A Haroon Akram-Lodhi[1]

I. The purpose of the volume

THE essays in this book have been written to honour the professional and civic work of John Loxley, one of Canada's leading international development economists and a noted community activist. Running through John Loxley's public life are four interrelated themes: his concern for global social justice; his rejection of neo-conservative economic orthodoxies as a possible means of achieving global social justice; his view that national and international economic policies should be evaluated for their impact on all people in society; and his belief that all people should have an informed voice in determining the economic priorities and policies that shape their communities and societies. These themes are found in the essays that comprise this volume, which show that neo-conservative policies have not been mutually beneficial to all countries and all peoples, and that, as a consequence, there is a need to develop more democratic alternatives to economic policy making.

As Haroon Akram-Lodhi argues in Chapter 20, neo-conservatism is the intellectual foundation of the market-oriented ideology that has dominated the global economic system and the politics of economic policy-making around the world since the mid-1970s. Neo-conservatism fuses traditional conservative themes of morality, civil authority and hierarchy with a classical liberal emphasis on the need for a free economy. Neo-conservatism thus, in contrast to neoliberalism, articulates a free economy with a strong state (Gamble, 1988). The emphasis on the role of the state is seen, in particular, in the extent of economic regulation, the establishment of quasi-markets in health, education,

1

and other public goods, and the importance attached to the maintenance of internal and external security.

Neo-conservative economic policies have sought to overcome deep-seated problems in the way in which economies operate, both within countries and globally. Parts I, II and III of this book have as their central objective an examination of the impact of neo-conservative policies on economies and states. Neo-conservative efforts to reshape economies and the ways in which states operate have also faced opposition from within and across communities and countries. The essays in this volume touch upon several alternatives. One alternative in particular, explored in Part IV, goes by a variety of names, including alternative budgets, gender budgets, participatory budgets, and democratic budgets. Its central proposition is that there is a need to transform the politics of economic decision-making by placing it under popular and participatory democratic control. The essays in Part IV explore some of the implications of attempts to democratize the politics of economic decision-making.

Together, the essays collected here describe the dynamics of neo-conservative economic policies around the world. They are comparative assessments of attempts to alter the ways in which states work and popular efforts to democratize economic policy-making, based on material from Africa, Asia, Europe and North America. The reason that such a disparate set of regions, characterized, as they are, by very different levels of economic development, are used here is because all countries have, over the course of more than two decades, faced similar pressures to restructure their economies. In the 1980s and early 1990s this was done, fairly explicitly, to eliminate some of the social, economic and political gains that had been made in the 1950s, 1960s and 1970s. More recently, it was done because, as its proponents claim, globalization places an imperative upon all economies to continue to adjust the relative roles of the state and the market or risk being excluded from the global 'new' economy. This volume's exploration of adjustment and globalization demonstrates how more participatory and democratic economic policy-making options have emerged, with general and unique lessons capable of being learnt.

II. Neo-conservative economic policy

Neo-conservatism rose to prominence as an approach to economic decision making against a background of a slowdown in global growth. As Robert

Chernomas and Ardeshir Sepehri document in Chapter 2, between the 1960s and the 1990s "capitalism lost 60 per cent of its macroeconomic momentum." Chernomas and Sepehri, as well as Fletcher Baragar in Chapter 3, explain that the cause of this slowdown was a fall in the rate of profit in the advanced capitalist economies, as a result of costs of production rising faster than prices or productivity, an explanation that has wide empirical support (Woolff, 2003; *The Economist* 8 December 2001; Dumenil and Lévy, 2000; Brenner, 1998; Shaikh and Tonak, 1994; Armstrong, Glyn and Harrison, 1991; Moseley, 1988; Weisskopf, 1979). The response of policy-makers was, as Akram-Lodhi stresses in Chapter 20, to reestablish the dominance of the market through internal deregulation and privatization, external trade and financial liberalization, the opening up of economies to inflows of foreign direct investment, and the re-alignment of exchange rates in accordance with market priorities, while at the same time reshaping of the role of the state through lower corporate taxes, fiscal discipline, monetary rules, re-regulation, and the establishment of quasi-markets in public goods. Chernomas and Sepehri argue that these reforms were supposed to promote an internationalization of trade, production and finance, which together are the hallmarks of globalization. However, Chernomas and Sepehri demonstrate that the internationalization that has taken place since the mid-1980s has not been as significant as has been suggested by some, and that which has occurred has been predicated upon regionalization.

In Chapter 3 Fletcher Baragar presents a Canadian case study of the downward trend in overall profitability in Canada's business sector since the 1960s and of its relationship with a slowdown in the rate of growth of labour productivity, along with an examination of some of the elements of economic reform in Canada. Baragar demonstrates that reforms failed to bring about a recovery in the profit rate. As Chernomas and Sepehri note in Chapter 2, the anti-inflationary bias of neo-conservative economic policies resulted in restrictions on the availability of money and credit and thus the maintenance of high interest rates. The maintenance of high interest rates necessitated the restructuring of less efficient individual firms, which were forced out of business, and this affected the profit rate. Indirect business taxes also created a problem for less efficient individual firms, and this too lowered the profit rate. Thus, while one key neo-conservative policy prescription—strict monetary policies—brought some benefits to individual firms, it had a contradictory impact on the operation of market economies.

The impact of restrictive monetary policy was not felt just in the advanced capitalist countries. Increased interest rates at the end of the 1970s ratcheted up the costs of debt servicing in developing market economies and fostered a debt crisis (Loxley, 1986). The debt crisis allowed the International Monetary Fund (IMF) and the World Bank, the two premier international financial institutions (IFIs), to promote an economic vision in developing countries based on markets and incentives, placing particular emphasis on the role of the private sector and the need for state compression. As Abdella Abdou argues in Chapter 4, the structural adjustment programmes (SAPs) developed by the IMF and the World Bank attributed poor economic performance to an overextended public sector, a proliferation of distorting economic controls, and macroeconomic mismanagement. Abdou shows that SAPs have three policy dimensions that mirror reforms in the advanced capitalist countries. The first is macroeconomic, and involves fiscal restraint, tight monetary policy, and devaluation. The second is microeconomic, and encompasses trade, price, and financial liberalization. The third is institutional adjustment, and consists of policies such as privatization, improving the business climate and legal arrangements, and reforming governance and the civil service. Thus, economic reform in the advanced capitalist countries was followed first by reform in the developing and, later, transition economies, as the IFIs sought to use neo-conservative economics to integrate developing and transition economies into the world economy.

Two specific policy interventions have been considered particularly important by the IFIs for economies undergoing economic adjustment. The first intervention is devaluation. Reducing the value of a domestic currency relative to other currencies is designed to alter the relative prices faced by households and enterprises. In Chapter 5 Zelealem Yiheyis critically examines whether devaluation leads to an expansion of output, as orthodox economic theory suggests. Considering the evidence for Africa, Yiheyis finds that devaluation does not produce a consistent expansion of aggregate output. Rather, Yiheyis demonstrates that devaluation is neutral in its impact on output in Africa. The principal reason for this, according to Yiheyis, is that devaluation not only affects exports but also affects production in the non-exporting sector of the economy.

The second intervention that is important to the IFIs is financial liberalization. As Peter Lawrence notes in Chapter 6, according to the IMF the activities of the state have been, in general, to promote financial "repression." The principal form of repression has been the setting of ceilings on interest rates, while high reserve ratios and oligopolistic banking systems also contribute. Lawrence argues that the development of various forms of financial intermediation and of a range of instruments to maximize the uptake of domestic savings is an important part of economic growth, and thus it is easy to see why the IMF argues that growth follows financial development. However, in a thorough review of the theoretical literature Lawrence notes that there must be some pre-existing level of production and technology for financial markets and instruments to respond to the demands of producers and consumers. Moreover, in a review of the empirical literature Lawrence suggests that the relationship between finance and growth is conflicting rather than consensual. Lawrence suggests that in order to understand why the 'growth follows finance' argument is important for orthodox economic theory and the IFIs, it is necessary to stress the dramatic expansion of financial sector activities in most advanced capitalist economies over the past two decades and the role of finance in ongoing processes of globalization.

A key objective of economic reform in both the advanced capitalist and developing economies has been to reorient economies towards production for the world economy. Abdella Abdou notes in Chapter 4 that in Africa the push for export promotion is one that seeks to foster an economic reliance upon the production of primary products — cash crops and natural resource exploitation. In Chapter 7 John Kofi Baffoe provides a case study of structural adjustment in Ghana that explores the extent to which the economic model fostered by the IFIs is capable of producing sustainable agricultural growth. Under the tutelage of the World Bank Ghana introduced changes in the 1980s that brought about strict fiscal and monetary discipline, altered relative prices in favour of exports, and liberalized internal and external trade. However, Baffoe demonstrates that agricultural growth, while remaining a pivotal component of economic activity, was and remains erratic. The supply response of the agricultural sector to adjustment was not what had been promised. At the same time, shortages of foreign exchange under adjustment led to import strangulation, and reduced the capacity of the manufacturing sector, some of which had important linkages to the agricultural sector. In this light, the impact of structural adjustment in Ghana has been disappointing. While agriculture remains a mainstay of production, there are ongoing difficulties in increasing private sector investment, donor dependence has increased, and living standards have stagnated.

In Chapter 8 Ray Bush explores some of the contradictions of adjustment by examining agricultural reforms in Egypt. Bush demonstrates that, like Ghana, Egypt was, under the auspices of the IFIs, to adopt an agro-export-based economic strategy. Bush notes some of the key problems of this strategy. In particular, as Egypt is a food-deficit country, farmers need to continue to produce food for their self-consumption, and so agricultural diversification has been hampered, and agricultural export growth has not materialized. Yet, with liberalization the prices of agricultural imports have increased dramatically. Egypt's agricultural imports include staple commodities for which demand outstrips domestic supply, and this means that despite price increases people must buy, leading to a cut in real incomes. The result is that structural adjustment has brought about an acceleration of rural poverty amongst the majority, a finding that has also been made elsewhere (Lubker, Smith and Weeks, 2002). At the same time, Bush demonstrates that agricultural reform has strengthened the power of landowners and weakened the power of tenants, promoting a deepening socio-economic differentiation. Bush argues, however, that this is, for those pushing reform within Egypt, a welcome outcome. Larger landowners have been perceived by the state as having a better ability to benefit from market reforms.

With differentiation and poverty come increasing need for social provision. However, economic reform seeks to replace social provision with private provision through the market. One area in which social provision has been cut is education. In Chapter 9 Augustin Fosu examines the relationship between the levels of debt held by African governments and education spending. Fosu's analysis indicates that the level of potential debt service facing African economies adversely affects public spending on education. Indeed, removing the debt constraint would not only be good for growth, argues Fosu, but could also directly contribute resources into the all-important education sector of sub-Saharan African economies.

6

In a similar vein, in Chapter 10 Ardeshir Sepehri and Haroon Akram-Lodhi examine the impact of user charges and partial privatization of health care provision in Vietnam. Sepehri and Akram-Lodhi note that economic reform eroded the role of the public sector in the provision and funding of health care services and led to the rapid expansion of a private-public system, with serious consequences for the health care system. User charges were introduced that led to a rapid increase in fee revenues collected at public hospitals. As a result, hospitals and physicians became increasingly dependent on patient revenues from user charges. This change created a largely unregulated fee-for-service structure, which offered the potential risk of the over-provision of services to those capable of paying fees. If you are poor, adjustment can be bad for your health.

III. Neo-conservative policy and governance

The cases of agriculture in Egypt and Ghana, as well as the analysis of the education and health sub-sectors, all point to the negative impact that economic adjustment can have on social equity. Thus, economic reform has not brought growth, has not reduced poverty, and has not stabilized economies. The response to these conundrums by policy-makers has been disingenuous: the state as an institution has been held responsible for failure. It is argued that liberalization has not been sufficiently thorough and there has been a lack of national ownership of adjustment programmes, a consequence of poor governance. The way forward, it is argued, is further liberalization and the promotion of effective governance.

In Chapter 11 Brian Van Arkadie explores some of the issues surrounding the governance agenda. This agenda has two public faces. In the advanced capitalist economies, the crisis in corporate governance typified by Enron, WorldCom, Ahold and Parmalat has demonstrated the need for reform. In the developing economies governance is about fostering support for adjustment policies amongst local elites as a first step towards creating a degree of national 'ownership' of policy. However, elite support is not sufficient: the state beneath the level of the elite must be accepting of change. This requires, in turn, effective state capacity, and hence a change in public sector governance. With these two faces, governance can be taken to mean, as Van Arkadie argues, the practices guiding the formulation, implementation and oversight of the programmes, policies and activities of organizations in specific states. Of particular concern is the need to ensure that property rights are protected, that essential goods and services are provided, and that businesses are not over-regulated. Thus, as Van Arkadie writes, uncertainty about legal processes and property rights, capricious and arbitrary enforcement of rules, unpredictable licensing arrangements, ineffective tax administration, and rent-seeking officials together create a negative environment for businesses. In this perspective, then, it is clear that advocates of the governance agenda see corporate and state governance as a key determinant of growth.

Van Arkadie stresses that the meaning of governance is opaque. It was originally introduced in developing countries as a means of limiting the role of states and ensuring that adjustment was being implemented, while at the same time allowing discussion of more sensitive issues such as corruption. Corporate issues were not within its remit, with the exception of the need to privatize state-owned enterprises. More recently, in addition to corporate issues, it has come to mean trying to ensure that states do what they should do, well and efficiently. At the same time governance can also serve, according to Van Arkadie, a cosmetic purpose, making orthodox subjects such as public administration fashionable. Finally, Van Arkadie notes that the term, when it is used, often emphasizes the need for ethical behaviour, and hence has an element of morality.

Van Arkadie recognizes that for developing-country adjustment programmes to become nationally supported the IFIs face a contradiction: they want states to adopt policies that sustain reforms, but to do this they must allow states to have a modicum of control over the resources that are transferred. In Chapter 12 Gerry Helleiner presents a case study of these contradictions by examining the relationship between the Tanzanian state and the country's key donors, the Consultative Group (CG). It is a fascinating example of statements of intent by bilateral and multilateral donors failing to translate into changes on the ground, as donors require increasing control over domestic political and economic decisions. The key mechanism that allowed a modicum of progress in Tanzania was the establishment of an independent group that stood between the state and the CG, and which evaluated the performance of both players in meeting a predefined set of objectives that were predicated upon the Tanzanian state having greater control over its development cooperation programme. Helleiner's review of the problems that the new approach engendered leads him to express concern that the ongoing struggle over the terms and modalities of the independent monitoring process will continue.

The critical problem of the new relationship explored by Helleiner is that, as Van Arkadie cautions in the previous chapter, a key issue has been to try and shift indebted states towards a more technocratic approach to public affairs management. This impetus is explored, in the context of sub-Saharan Africa, by Bonnie Campbell, Marie-Christine Doran and Samia Kazi Aoul in Chapter 13. The authors note that the reform of governance, through the establishment of an agreed poverty reduction strategy, has been the basis upon which access to debt relief has been allocated to African states since the late 1990s. As a result, the commitment, feasibility and sustainability of political reform have become key areas of contestation between the IFIs and states. However, the authors argue that the institutional reforms propounded by the World Bank in particular offer a conceptualization of the working of the political process that emphasizes horizontal accountability in which state institutions check abuses by other state agencies. Vertical accountability, through which citizens and civil society seek to hold the state up to certain standards, is less important in this model because the state's capacity for self-restraint is a function of horizontal accountability. The authors argue that this type of emphasis represents a significant departure from a characteristic feature of representative democracies, namely the right of the electorate to express its will, and is predicated upon removing interest groups from the dynamics of power. Moreover, the approach is accompanied by the introduction of a technocratic and functional ethic into public affairs management, one that sidelines dissent, depoliticizes vital issues, and emphasizes the establishment of equilibrium between national and international interests. In the view of the authors, the governance agenda and the accompanying approach to the economic management activities of the state are predicated upon stability and system persistence.

The governance agenda has emphasised the need to decentralize state responsibilities as a means of bringing the state closer to the governed and thus increasing accountability and transparency. In Chapter 14 Wicky Meynen and Martin Doornbos examine some of the contradictions of decentralization, in this instance through the prism of possible implications for sustainable natural resource management. Meynen and Doornbos note that the decentralization agenda was first advocated by public choice advocates of a market-focussed agenda designed to achieve service delivery efficiency through privatization or through delegation. In this scheme participation implies market transactions, with people playing the role of consumers and possibly providers. However, Meynen and Doornbos stress that the test for meaningful decentralization is the extent to which lower levels of state administration are in a position to set their own priorities. Often, this ability is constrained. In addition, lower levels of state administration should have legitimate authority and adequate capacity to execute what they have been authorized to do. Often, this capacity is lacking. Finally, lower levels of state administration should have sufficient financial capability to carry out that which they have been authorized to undertake. This can be problematic.

Much of the decentralization agenda ignores these conditions for meaningful decentralization. Meynen and Doornbos argue that this is because lower levels of state administration often do not reflect democratic accountability but rather the importance of structural inequalities at the local level, and relations of power, patronage and privilege within and between communities. Certainly, it cannot be assumed that local communities are homogeneous, a point also made by Van Arkadie in Chapter 11. Decision-making processes and public resources can be captured by elites and interest groups at the local level even more readily than at the national level. Such realities severely constrain the possibility of devolving effective governance to the local level, and this is a problem of which the IFIs are aware. This means that decentralization, rather than making the state more local and more accountable, represents a much narrower and selective deconcentration of state functions that remain, nonetheless, under the control of the central state. This frees higher levels of the state from the financial and administrative responsibility for the activities that they decree. In this way, decentralization in developing countries becomes a cost-saving device, and not a democratic device, designed to be part of the general drive to reduce the role of central state.

In Chapter 15 Alexander Dow and Sheila Dow touch on a similar range of issues when they look at the possibilities for intermediate levels of state administration to implement policies designed to facilitate structural transformation. Dow and Dow's particular concern is the Scottish state, which, under a new constitutional settlement, decentralized some decision-making authority from London to Edinburgh. The architects of the new constitutional settlement argued that selective devolution would lead to an improvement in Scottish economic performance. Dow and Dow argue that in trying to understand the prospects for the Scottish economy globalization is still seen by some devolutionists as being the basis of a solution to problems, rather than being, at least in part, a cause of those problems. Dow and Dow also note that the dominance of finance in the Scottish economy has not fostered a rate of economic growth that is consistent with all-UK averages. They stress that dominant factors in the Scottish political economy are a net out-migration of people and increasing mortality rates for certain groups, both of which undermine attempts to raise productivity. Dow and Dow suggest that the cumulative impact of these factors implies an inability to promote the economic convergence of Scotland with the rest of the UK. Finally, there is an ethos of civic society, which sees a legitimate role for various groups to participate in and shape the changes of an evolving society. This ethos stands in contradiction to the prevailing orthodox understanding of the economy, which is predicated on atomistic individuals operating in markets, and technocratic management of the state.

IV. Alternative budgets

The emphasis on governance and decentralization has sought to remove politics from policy-making, leaving decisions to unelected technocrats subject only to horizontal accountability. Ironically, the attempt to de-politicize economic policy making over the past 15 years has triggered the development of a range of alternatives. These alternatives are predicated upon popular movements making a fresh commitment to create more participatory forms of democracy rooted in accountability, social equality, and giving people more control over their lives by "reclaiming the state" (Wainwright, 2003). One alternative in particular questions both the process and the outcomes of current modes of economic decision making and proposes economic democratization from below. This movement seeks to democratize the state budget.

In Chapter 16 Haroon Akram-Lodhi explains why state budgets have become an arena in which activists and partisan scholars have sought to confront the state. Akram-Lodhi argues that gender inequality, through its impact on the operation of markets and the distribution of assets, makes economies, in strictly economic terms, less efficient. Feminist activists and partisan scholars, over the past 10 years, have therefore sought to demonstrate how budgets can contribute to gender inequalities within particular settings. Commonly called the gender budgets approach, these demonstrations involve looking at who pays for public spending, who benefits from public spending, how intended beneficiaries perceive public spending, the impact of public spending on how people use their time, and the way in which the concerns of people, as women and men, are expressed in the policy-making process. Akram-Lodhi argues that as macroeconomic policy has become technocratic, it has become de-democratized, and, for many feminist activists and scholars, this de-democratization has reinforced gender-segmented participation in social, political and economic decision-making. This is, according to Akram-Lodhi, where the appeal of gender budgets for activists and scholars lies. By allowing women and men to enter into debates about the gendered impact of fiscal policy, gender budget initiatives have enhanced democracy in societies that, while often formally democratic, may be in reality less democratic than is commonly supposed because of gender-segmented participation in social, political and economic decision-making. Gender budgets contribute to the democratization of economic policy-making by assisting in the engendering of democracy.

Gender budgets use gender as a means of focussing on the need to construct economic policies that will eradicate poverty, reduce inequalities, and advance sustainable development. This is what Roy Culpeper, in Chapter 17, calls "the policy agenda of the real world." This agenda calls for greater democratic inclusion and popular participation in economic policy-making, and is seen in the rise of popular opposition to globalization. A democratic alternative will not be built upon universal rules and universal truths, Culpeper argues, but will rather be the result of a communicative and consultative process, through which a democratic consensus is built, democratic rules and customs are mutually understood and agreed, and the impact of performance for democracy is continually reviewed. Democratic economic policy-making will foster a return to economic planning, but, as Culpeper notes, now it will be planning from below.

Gender budgets can be considered one strand of what Jim Stanford, in Chapter 18, calls "the alternative budgeting movement," a movement with which John Loxley has been very closely associated (Loxley, 2003). This movement is discussed in Chapters 17, 18 and 19. In Chapter 19 Lionel Cliffe notes that the alternative budgeting movement has three core elements: the articulation of alternative policy premises based on core values; the working out of the financial implications of these policy options within a credible fiscal framework; and broad participation in this exercise. Cliffe notes that working within existing constraints to achieve a different set of outcomes offers a challenge to the orthodoxies of economic decision making, and moreover offers an alternative that demonstrates what can be credibly undertaken despite claims that "there just isn't the money," or "there is no alternative."

The alternative budgeting movement starkly reveals, as Stanford, Culpeper and Cliffe argue, a central and long-standing tension within popular movements about the need to be visionary by advocating and preparing for major changes in society, on one hand, and, on the other, the simultaneous immediate need to help people survive the difficulties of oppressive societies. Stanford notes that Rosa Luxemburg argued that both aspects are needed by popular movements. Similarly, in Chapter 19 Cliffe argues that there is a need for "radical pragmatism," and that this need has been long recognized. Cliffe, in a moving memoir, cites as an example the attempt to construct an African form of socialism in Tanzania in the late 1960s and early 1970s, a project with which John Loxley was deeply involved. In the mid-1970s a similar attempt was undertaken in Canada, where in the province of Manitoba the Research and Economic Development Secretariat of the provincial government, under the leadership of John Loxley, presented the Great Northern Plan, possibly the most comprehensive attempt at economic planning under social democracy (Loxley, 1993, 1990, 1981). The alternative budgeting movement globally could be seen as the latest, global, example of the need for radical pragmatism.

In his thorough case study of the alternative budgeting movement in Canada in Chapter 18, Stanford stresses the context. By the mid-1990s the Canadian state faced a serious and unsustainable fiscal situation. It was being pressured by politically powerful constituencies, including financial and business lobbyists, to restructure its budget. In this context the Federal Government in 1995 undertook an aggressive attack upon fiscal imbalances, in the form of a retreat by the state from many spheres of the economy. When the deficit-cutting agenda was launched, a coalition of labour and social justice groups built upon earlier initiatives in Winnipeg and in Manitoba more generally to come together to produce an Alternative Federal Budget designed to show that a better, more humane set of fiscal and social policies was fiscally feasible and economically sustainable. The Alternative Federal Budget also provided strong, and in some cases successful, arguments for activists seeking to resist immediate cuts. Stanford notes however some of the contradictions of the alternative budgeting movement in Canada. It placed more emphasis on incremental reform, and did not provide a critique of Canada's economy and society. The reason, as Stanford points out, was not a lack of interest. Rather, a chronic lack of resources combined with the overriding need to produce the alternative budget document explains why it was difficult for the alternative budget project to find a better balance between the incrementalist and the visionary.

In Chapter 17 Culpeper notes a different set of contradictions facing popular movements seeking to have greater access to and control over the state budgetary process in developing economies. The World Bank and IMF have sought to disconnect consultation processes between the local state, local civil society organizations, and the IFIs from core economic decision-making processes, including the budgetary process. Thus, developing countries do not consider alternative macroeconomic policy options under current poverty reduction arrangements between indebted developing countries and the IFIs. Culpeper suggests that the establishment of partnerships between civil society organizations in developing countries and the coalition behind the Canadian alternative budgeting movement could allow the former to adapt the Canadian experience to their own circumstances. A particularly important product of such a partnership could be to move core fiscal, monetary, and structural economic policies to centre stage of the consultation processes between the local state, local civil society organizations, and the IFIs, and in so doing open up the black box of the budgetary process in developing countries to, at a minimum, greater democratic scrutiny. Cliffe makes a similar point in his review of the experiences with and prospects for alternative budgeting in Africa in Chapter 19, arguing that alternative budgeting may be even more important in contexts where democratization is at an early and incomplete stage, such as Africa, if compared to the advanced capitalist countries.

Part IV thus concludes on a hopeful note: that alternative budgeting has the potential to assist, in many parts of the world, in a participatory democratization of the budgetary process that acts as a radically pragmatic means of bridging the divide between the visionary critique of existing structures and the immediate needs of those that have been disenfranchised by the forward march of globalization.

V. Conclusion

In pursuit of global social justice, John Loxley has, in his professional and civic life, sought to question the claims of neo-conservative economic policies and demonstrate the capacity of communities to reclaim control of the economic decisions that affect the daily life of societies. Neo-conservative economic policies have sought to use the state to undertake a set of structural economic reforms in both the advanced capitalist and the developing and transition economies. However, these reforms have been unable to improve economic performance. Therefore, efforts have been made to restructure the operation of the state itself. Using the language of governance there has been a shift towards a technocratic approach to economic decision making. However, as the scope for global citizens to exercise control over their own lives has diminished, popular movements of opposition have arisen. One form of resistance has been that in which John Loxley has been particularly active: the attempt to infuse popular participation into budgetary debates, using gender budgets, alternative budgets, and participatory budgets. John Loxley has made important contributions to the ideas that have informed alternative budgeting and has used his expertise and commitment to assist in a series of important experiments around the world.

John Loxley's professional and civic work demonstrates that alternative budgeting initiatives can contribute to more than just popular debate about underlying state strategies and priorities. Alternative budgeting initiatives can provide popular mechanisms for exposing corruption, dampening down political relationships predicated upon hierarchy and patronage, be a mechanism for resolving and preventing resource-based conflicts, and strengthening participatory democratization processes. At the same time, however, popular initiatives must balance long range goals and transformational demands along with realizable strategies for action that go beyond simple amelioration. Radical pragmatism has been an important means of addressing practical matters as well as big issues within popular movements for over a century. Alternative budgeting is a participatory democratic alternative to current neo-conservative policy making that is predicated upon radical pragmatism. It is an idea that can be very closely associated with the life and work of John Loxley. As these pages demonstrate, it is an idea whose time has come.

Footnotes

1 My thanks to Robert Chernomas, Ardeshir Sepehri and Peter Lawrence.

PART 1

Neo-conservative Economics and Globalization

Chapter 2

IS GLOBALIZATION AND ITS SUCCESS A MYTH?

Robert Chernomas and Ardeshir Sepehri

I. The "Great Stagnation": the historical context for globalization

IN the decade of the 1960s the world economy grew at the rate of 5.0 per cent (Thurow, 1996: 1-2). In the 1970s the real growth rate dropped to 3.6 per cent. By the 1980s the rate had dropped to 2.8 per cent, and continued this decline in the 1990s, when it fell to 2.0 per cent. In two decades capitalism lost 60 per cent of its macroeconomic momentum. Through the 1990s the overall European unemployment rate remained in double digits, and the Japanese economy has been stagnating for a decade. The recent capitalist convert, Russia, appears to be demodernizing to Third World levels, while much of the southern hemisphere has seen its social indicators deteriorating from already disastrous levels.

i. Theoretical context

A significant body of evidence suggests that capitalism entered into an economic crisis phase in the late 1960s, due to a fall in the rate of profit as a consequence of the costs of production rising faster than productivity and/or price (Brenner, 1998; Cherry et al., 1987). Crisis in this context does not mean catastrophic economic breakdown, or the end of capitalist social relations. Nor does it apply to capitalism in the usual sense of how it has operated since 1945. The difference between capitalism's business cycles and an economic crisis is that normal economic activity during a non-crisis phase of the business cycle is, within the context of prevailing social relationships, sufficient to restore prosperity (Gordon, 1980). By contrast, economic crisis undermines the stability of the institutional framework, because, as accumulation slackens, less profit is available to maintain those institutions whose relative stability and re-producibility permit the repeated fulfillment of an important socio-economic function.

Capitalism runs on profit. Without adequate profits, firms cannot invest in order to lower their costs of production, promote research and design in order to invent new products, produce new plants and equipment to meet increases in demand, or generate dividends for their owners. Without profits, the same firms will not be able to pay debts or advertize; they cannot compete and stay in business. Those firms with higher profits are better able to lower their costs of production, invent new products, and advertize their successes in produc-tion. Investments that generate less profit, because the costs of raw materi-als, machines, and/or labour are rising faster than productivity and/or price, diminish the capacity and incentive to invest again. If this situation becomes the average condition for firms in an economy, stagnation or depression is the expected result. It is, therefore, the rate of profit that provides the capitalist class with the product to invest, as well as the motive. As the rate of profit falls, investment, productivity, economic growth, and tax revenue tend to follow, while unemployment rises.

ii. Evidence

By standard accounting methods, between 1965 and 1973 the rate of profit in the US manufacturing and private business sectors fell by 40.9 per cent and 29.3 per cent, respectively. The profitability decline in the US economy did not bottom out until the early 1980s (Brenner, 1998: 95). The rate of profit de-clined in the other major capitalist economies as well (Brenner, 1998; Cherry et al., 1987), albeit not necessarily on the same precise schedule, resulting in global stagnation and the creation of a crisis far more serious and enduring than a normal cyclical downturn. Capitalism has been suffering from a quarter -century of economic slowdown, manifest by stagnation in all the advanced capitalist countries. While the crisis came earlier for some countries than for others, the profitability crisis is a global capitalist phenomenon.

The US appeared to be the first country to emerge from the crisis. However, as late as the period between 1989 and 1997, the US economy grew at an av-erage of only 2.3 per cent a year, which was less than Germany's 2.6 per cent and less than Japan's 2.4 per cent. Indeed, even in the period between 1994 and 1997, US growth of 3.0 per cent a year was not significantly higher than Europe's 2.4 per cent (*Left Business Observer*, 1998: 3). It was only in 1997 that the US appeared to emerge with signs of an apparently more vital macroeconomy, and recent economic events indicate that this vitality was largely illusory. The question that arises, then, is how has capitalism managed its profitability crisis?

iii. Corporate and state policy responses to the crisis of profitability

In the face of falling profits, corporations are compelled to find means of reducing their costs by lowering their wages and taxes and/or raising their productivity. Some of these methods represent advanced capitalism's "intensive" method of reducing costs through increases in productivity by means of mechanization. However, other methods of responding to profitability crises have included a return to "extensive" methods, including longer hours, lower wages, and deteriorating, low-cost working and environmental conditions. A generation of high national and international levels of unemployment and globalization has made labour more vulnerable. The real and threatened effects of unemployment and globalization, in the form of capital flight, tend to lower workers' expectations with respect to wages, benefits, and working conditions, as well as citizens' expectations with respect to health, education, and welfare.

During this period of crisis, the conditions of economic stagnation have given rise to a corresponding political response. The real or increased threat of capital flight due to competitive pressures imposed on governments the need to introduce attacks on labour in general and on state salaried employees in particular. This threat was enhanced by growth in the technological possibilities that could assist capital flight. Thus, attacks on the welfare state, in the form of the war on deficits, debt, wages, unions, and government in general, are, along with the socialization of private debt, arguably attempts by capital to restore profitability by using its increased influence over the state in its own interest.

Declining investment, in the form of an effective capital strike, is, along with increasing unemployment, increasing poverty, falling real wages, shortages in tax revenues, attacks on the welfare state, and qualitative social and institutional changes, part of the process of restoring profitability. For capital the resolution to the crisis requires restoring profitability.

A number of strategies have been employed to this end over the past quarter-century, the most marked of which is anti-inflation policy. Contemporary economic orthodoxy has failed to establish that inflation rates of up to 8 per cent have any negative impact on the economy or that zero inflation maximizes economic growth (Sarel, 1996). Nonetheless, the US central bank has, along with many other central banks, made the attack on inflation its prime goal over the past few decades. The war on inflation is accomplished by restricting the availability of money and credit, and, therefore keeping interest rates high. This discourages investment and makes it more difficult for low-profit firms, with their relatively inefficient capital, to stay in business. At the same time, this strategy facilitates the lowering of wages and reduces resistance to increases in labour intensity by increasing unemployment and lowering workers' expectations. This helps industry while preserving the value of the debt and, therefore, the source of profits of the financial industry.

In addition to anti-inflation policy, capital has other means to assist in the restoration of profitability. One obvious means is to use the threat of capital flight and capital strikes to pressure a largely sympathetic state to promulgate tax cuts for the corporate sector and the wealthy, which helps to redistribute income upwards to the capitalist class. The state can also assist in the restoration of profitability by reducing government-imposed regulations, which tends to lower prices in the affected industry and the wages of its workers. Finally, a strategic obsession with government deficits and debt, the corresponding attack on the welfare state, and lowering taxes on corporations and the wealthy can increase the insecurity and dependency of everybody else. The emphasis on the market, the minimalist state, and individual and family responsibility are thus all soldiers in the war against the welfare state, and reflected in declining state expenditures and the privatization of the public sector. Together, these neo-conservative state-focussed strategies assist in an institutional transformation that benefits capital, as firms are able to re-regulate industries so that they may better determine wages and benefits.

Such re-regulation is facilitated by corporate strategies that emphasize the threat of foreign direct investment (FDI) in non-unionized countries and in areas of developed countries where wages, taxes, and environmental regulation tends to favour business by offering lower costs and thus higher profits. Concurrently, the weeding out of all but the most productive and profitable means of production results in less capital available, as well as layoffs, wage reductions, benefit cuts, and speed-ups at work. Thus, the same profitability crisis that led to the downsizing process and the merger movement resulted in a massive number of bankruptcies and a destruction of capital not seen since the Great Depression. The general effect of this is that only more efficient and profitable capital is left standing.

II. Is globalization a myth?

It would be hard to exaggerate the degree to which the concept of globalization has penetrated our culture. It is treated at once as an economic tidal wave and as a paralyzer of the state. It has been used to justify deregulation, privatization, environmental degradation, free trade, deficit and debt mania, high interest rates, zero inflation targets, anti-labour legislation, and cuts to social spending and upper income and corporate taxes. These policies are, of course, executed by individual nation states. The rationale in defence of these policy changes is that the rules established by the now- dominant multinational corporations (MNCs) and the uncontrollable high-speed market highway they travel on must be obeyed lest you be run over and/or left behind. The trouble with this concept of globalization, whether it is explicitly or implicitly adopted, is that, objectively, it is largely a myth. However, it has considerable power to organize our thoughts as to how the world works.

Weiss (1997) identifies a spectrum of hypotheses with respect to the extent of globalization, ranging from strong to weak. The strong globalization hypothesis views the rapid growth of economic interdependence as a reflection of an emerging supra-national phenomenon. This is distinct from the three decades following the Second World War, when the expansion of world trade and finance was primarily led by the concerted efforts of nation states through the creation of an international financial system and successive rounds of multilateral tariff reductions under the General Agreement on Tariffs and Trade (GATT). According to this view, the era of state-led internationalism has run its course, giving way to a new phase of international political economy—a new globalism or borderless economy in which the internationalization of production is the driving mechanism of economic integration.

In such a borderless world, it is claimed, footloose MNCs, rather than nation states, are spearheading global economic interdependence, eroding national differences, and making domestic strategies of national economic management increasingly irrelevant (Hamdani, 1997; Horsman and Marshall, 1994; Ohmae, 1990; Reich, 1992). In this view, MNCs are claimed to be the dominant economic entities. Truly global MNCs own and control subsidiaries and engage in business alliances and networks in a number of countries. They engage in business alliances and networks in different locations of the borderless world. They source their inputs of labour, capital, raw materials, and intermediate products from wherever it is best to do so. Finally, they sell their goods and services in each of the main markets of the world (Dunning, 1997). Globalization is, therefore, according to this view, "triggering a process of systematic convergence in which all governments face pressures to pursue more or less similar policies to enhance their national (or regional) competitiveness, vis-à-vis other countries, as locations for international production'"(Hamdani, 1997: 3).

The erosion of state power is, however, contested by an alternate hypothesis of globalization, which holds that states never had the macroeconomic planning power that some claim before the emergence of globalization. However, those powers that it had and continues to have are significant (*The Economist*, 1995).

In contrast to the strong hypotheses of globalization, the weak hypotheses view the rapid expansion of cross-border trade, investment, and technological transfer, and the greater integration of national economies, not so much as a reflection of a globalized world, but, rather, as a more internationalized world where national and regional differences, including national institutions, remain substantial (Chang, 1998; Dymski and Isenberg, 1998; Hirst and Thompson, 1996; Weiss, 1997). From this perspective the external and internal constraints that strong internationalization tendencies impose on nation states are viewed to be relative rather than absolute, and they represent an evolving history of state adaptation to both external and internal challenges, rather than the end of state history. According to this view, many of the recent difficulties national policy-makers have experienced with macroeconomic management, such as balancing budgets, have more to do with internal fiscal difficulties caused by years of slow economic growth, prolonged recessions, and demographic changes, than with globalization tendencies. The available evidence demonstrates that the world is not becoming globalized so much as more internationalized—the impact of external and internal constraints remain relative, and thus national and regional differences remain critical.

III. Globalization versus regionalization in the world economy

To assess the extent and patterns of globalization, its limits, and its counter-tendencies, we follow the commonly used quantitative approach, with its focus on trade flows of goods and services, and capital flows. All interpretations of globalization recognize the sheer volume of cross-border flows of capital, goods, and services, and the growing interdependence and integration among the main world markets. However, the central issues in the debate are three: (i) do these trade and investment flows indicate an historically unprecedented trend? (ii) how substantive are these flows compared to their corresponding flows in earlier periods? and (iii) to what extent are these flows worldwide in scope?

i. Trade flows

Hirst and Thompson (1996) compare the history of the international economy and its regimes of regulation during the period between 1880 and 1914, when the gold standard structured international trade, with that of the international economy during the 1980s and early 1990s. They look at a wide range of measures of integration, including the share of merchandise exports and imports in output, defined as gross national product (GNP). Their results indicate that our highly internationalized economy is not unprecedented. Indeed, in

Table 1 Exports and imports as a percentage of GNP

	1913	1950	1973	1994
France	30.0	21.4	29.2	34.2
Germany	36.1	20.1	35.3	39.3
USA	11.2	6.9	10.8	17.8
Japan	30.1	16.4	18.2	14.6

Sources Maddison (1995); OECD (1998).

some respects, the current international economy is less open than the system that prevailed during the gold standard. Table 1 indicates the extent of internationalization, as measured by the sum of exports plus imports as a percentage of GNP of a number of advanced industrialized countries. In 1973, the share of exports and imports in GNP in most industrialized countries was lower than in 1913.

The degree of integration into the world economy has been even more limited for most regions of the developing world, with the exception of East Asia. For the developing countries as a whole, the share of exports plus imports in GNP rose from an average annual rate of 28 per cent during the 1960s to 34.4 per cent in the 1970s and 38.4 per cent in the 1980s (Hirst and Thompson, 1996: 28). When compared to the developed market economies, this is not a significant degree of integration. The only region of the developing countries that underwent a great deal of internationalization was East Asia, where the share of exports plus imports in GNP rose from 47 per cent in the 1960s to 69.5 per cent in the 1970s and 87.2 per cent in the 1980s. Africa's share actually dropped slightly between the 1970s and 1980, as did the Middle East's, where the downturn in oil prices reduced the region's share of exports and imports in GNP.

ii.   Geographic pattern of trade flows
The extent to which recent increases in trade flows have been global in scope is demonstrated by trade flows by region of origin and destination. Table 2 indicates that trade flows are highly concentrated among the rich Organization for Economic Cooperation and Development (OECD) countries in general, and in particular within the three, large, regional trading blocks of the European Union (EU), North America, and Japan. In 1996, export and imports by the OECD countries accounted for three-quarters of total world exports and imports. It is of interest to note that the EU as a trading block does not appear to be more integrated into the world economy. Intra-EU exports and imports have continued to account for almost 62 per cent of total of EU exports and imports. Thus, the growing importance of intra-EU trade indicates a clear trend towards "Europeanization," rather than towards globalization, as suggested by globalization theorists. At the same time, the growing importance of Japan's trade flows with the dynamic Asian economies also indicates

a trend towards "Asianization," rather than globalization. As Table 2 indicates, Japanese exports to the dynamic Asian economies more than doubled over the period between 1972 and 1996, thus reversing the traditional dominance of trade with the United States. Therefore, Table 2 suggests a growth in internationalization within regions of the world economy, which could be called "regionalization," rather than globalization. Japanese, American, and European states played essential roles in the regionalization of the world's major economies. The difference between globalization and regionalization is the degree to which already existing state institutions are able to regulate actual economic and environmental activity. The problem with the globalization myth is that policy changes supposedly take place outside the range of state powers as opposed to the current reality, where the state's fingerprints are all over free trade agreements and World Trade Organization documents.

iii. Net capital flows

There are various measures of capital mobility. According to one broad definition, net capital mobility is measured as the absolute value of the current account divided by gross domestic product (GDP) (Weiss, 1997). According to

Table 2 Geographical structure of OECD trade

Area/country	Source/destination	Source of imports			Destination of exports		
		1962	1972	1996	1962	1972	1996
OECD	OECD	72.5	77.7	74.7	72.0	78.5	75.0
European Union	European Union	49.7	59.6	61.5	54.3	61.5	62.2
Japan	United States	32.1	24.9	22.9	28.7	31.3	27.5
	DAEs[1]+China	10.2	12.8	29.3	15.5	16.5	33.2
	European Union	9.6	9.3	14.2	12.1	14.9	15.3
United States	OECD	64.6	77.0	68.0	60.3	73.1	70.1
	DAEs+China	9.0	6.3	19.1	2.4	4.3	12.9

1 DAEs are the Dynamic Asian Economies, and consist of Taiwan, Hong Kong, Malaysia, Philippines, Singapore, and Thailand.
Source OECD (1998).

this measure of capital mobility, current net capital flows are huge in terms of their absolute size, but they are not historically unprecedented. The peak peacetime years for net capital flows for 11 OECD countries and Argentina were between 1870 and 1889, followed by the period between 1890 and 1913, when international capital flows topped 3.7 and 3.2 per cent of GDP, respectively (Obstfeld, 1998: Table 1). The corresponding ratio for the period between 1990 and 1996 was 2.3 per cent.

iv. Foreign direct investment

If trends in trade cannot support the thesis of globalization, then it might be suggested that FDI would offer such support. After all, in a truly globalized economy, FDI might be expected to replace exports, as capital, free to move where it wants, locates in low-wage, low-tax countries. Indeed, one of the key structural changes in the world economy during the post-war period has been the change in the relative importance of trade and FDI. The total accumulated inward stock of FDI grew at an average annual rate of 18.2 per cent during the period between 1986 and 1990, and 9.7 per cent during the period between 1991 and 1995 (United Nations, 1998: 2). Over the same two periods the total nominal value of exports of goods and services grew at average annual rates of 14.6 and 8.9 per cent, respectively (United Nations, 1998: 2). Thus, there has been a decline in the relative importance of trade in the world economy since the early 1980s.

The rapid growth in FDI is often taken by theorists as proxy for the globalization of production in general and the dominance of MNCs in manufacturing production in particular. Instead of exporting goods, MNCs are serving foreign markets by building factories. However, a careful analysis of aggregate FDI figures reveals the inappropriateness of these proxies, and thus the misleading conclusions drawn from these figures (Weiss, 1997: 9). For a start, not all FDI flows are normally directed towards the establishment of new investment in manufacturing and other productive sectors of the economy of the host country. Non-productive and speculative ventures, such as real estate and the cross-border merger and acquisition activity of MNCs, are estimated to account for a major portion of aggregate FDI flows (Weiss: 8-9). Cross-border merger and acquisition activity alone accounted for over one-half of FDI flows in the second half of the 1980s, and as much as 58 per cent of FDI flows in

1997 (United Nations, 1998: 19). The dramatic expansion of merger and acquisition activity in the United States in the 1980s and 1990s should be conceptualized within this context. In 1997, merger and acquisition by foreign MNCs accounted for some 90 per cent of FDI flows into the United States (United Nations, 1998: 13). The corresponding ratios for the first and second half of the 1980s were 67 and 80 per cent, respectively (Hirst and Thompson, 1996: 71). The significance of cross-border mergers and acquisitions is that they are simply a transfer of ownership, as MNCs attempt to consolidate their

Table 3 Inward and outward foreign direct investment flows (as a per cent of gross fixed investment)

	Annual Averages	
	1986-1991	1992-1996
Total		
Inward	3.6	4.7
Outward	4.1	5.1
European Union		
Inward	5.7	6.0
Outward	8.4	8.6
United States		
Inward	6.5	5.0
Outward	3.4	7.4
Japan		
Inward	-	0.2
Outward	4.0	1.4
Developing Countries		
Inward	3.4	6.8
Outward	1.3	2.9

Source United Nations (1998).

positions within the three trading blocks, rather than the creation of new productive capacity.

The available evidence also indicates a redistribution of the stock of outward FDI from the primary and secondary, and towards the tertiary, sector over
the period between 1975 and 1990 (United Nations, 1992: 18). As it is not
possible to internationally trade many services, MNCs must invest abroad to
provide these location-specific services. With the growing importance of services in the high-wage economies, investments in services by MNCs can be
expected to grow in the future.

To judge the significance of, and recent trends in, the internationalization
of production, it is useful to look at the share of inward and outward FDI
flows relative to total fixed capital formation in building, plants, machinery, and
equipment. If the strong globalization hypothesis holds, the data should show a
large and increasing share of FDI in total investment. Taking the aggregate FDI
figures at their face value, Table 3 indicates that this is clearly not the case. FDI
accounted for a small share of investment in both developed and developing
countries and there is little indication that these shares are rising.

v.   The geographic distribution of foreign direct investment
Like trade flows, investment flows are also almost exclusively concentrated in
the advanced industrial states and in a small number of rapidly developing industrial economies. At the beginning of the 1990s, 75 per cent of the total accumulated stock of FDI was located in three trading blocks of North America,
the EU, and Japan (Hirst and Thompson, 1996: 63), a proportion that has not
changed much since the end of 1970s (Brandt Commission, 1980). This triad
also received approximately 70 per cent of worldwide FDI inflows in 1990, a
proportion unchanged from the average of the decade of the 1980s (United
Nations, 1992: 20). The dynamic Asian economies accounted for over 60 per
cent of investment in the developing countries by MNCs. This concentration
dropped only moderately in the early 1990s, as the major economies experienced a recession (United Nations, 1998: 5). This geographic distribution of
investment by the MNCs clearly contradicts the strong globalization hypothesis, according to which a growing portion of investment by MNCs should
be worldwide in scope, and the low-wage and low-tax developing economies
should attract an increasing share of investment by footloose MNCs. It is, how-

ever, consistent with the thesis of a growing internationalization predicated upon regionalization in the context of trade flows.

Several explanations are provided in the literature for the concentration of MNC activity, and especially core technological activity such as research and development, in high-wage and high-tax countries. First, concentration in the same country/region provides a pooled market for knowledge-intensive labour, which increasingly tends to be treated as a fixed cost. With new technologies placing a premium on fixed costs, including machinery, equipment, and specialized skills, the importance of raw material, wages, and other variable costs is reduced. Second, concentration allows for a close link between producers and specialized suppliers of inputs, especially in non-assembly operations. Third, locating within high-wage, high-tax OECD economies provides MNCs with a national institutional support system, including relationships with trade associations, training institutions, and, more importantly, with local and national governments. The latter supporting relationship is of particular importance because "(b)eing generally exclusive rather than open to all, support relationships of this kind constitute a competitive advantage" (Weiss, 1997: 10). Thus, in Hirst and Thompson's (1996: 96) examination of the home bias of US, Japanese, German, and British manufacturing MNCs, parent operations accounted for between 62 and 97 per cent of total assets, and between 65 and 75 per cent of total sales, in 1992 and 1993. Similar findings are reported by Tyson (1991), where US manufacturing parent operations accounted for 78 per cent of total assets, 70 per cent of total sales, and 70 per cent of total employment in 1988. This evidence suggests that labelling firms with international economic activity as "transnational" is a misnomer. The vast majority of corporations require state support, and a home base for labour, capital, and markets. It is more appropriate to call them multinational corporations.

vi.   Financial flows
In the case of money and capital markets, progressive internationalization has been dramatic, especially since the collapse of the Bretton Woods system in the early 1970s, and the subsequent liberalization of exchange and capital controls, as indicated in Table 4. The daily turnover on the world's major exchange markets rose fourfold between 1986 and 1993, reaching US$1.0 trillion a day, or

Table 4 Cross-border transactions in bonds and equities[1]
(as a per cent of gross domestic product)

	1975	1980	1985	1990	1995	1997
United States	4	9	35	89	135	213
Japan	2	8	62	119	65	96
Germany	5	7	33	57	172	253
France	-	5	21	54	187	313
Italy	1	1	4	27	253	672
Canada	3	9	27	65	189	358

1 Gross purchases and sales of securities between residents and non-residents.
Source Bank for International Settlements (1998).

about US$250 trillion a year (International Monetary Fund [IMF], 1993: 24), which is 33 times the total value of world trade.

The progressive internationalization of money and capital is a marked change that distinguishes the late 1980s and 1990s from the post-war period up to the mid-1980s. However, whether this progressive internationalization signifies a radical change, indicating a globalized financial market or a tendency towards a globalized financial market, is not clear, for at least two reasons. First, to assess whether the explosion in cross-border financial flows represents a new phase in the international economy, or simply a greater internationalization of finance, we need a clear model of a truly global financial market. Dymski and Isenberg (1998: 221) provide such as a rigorous model:

A financial market is internationalized when assets with idiosyncratic risk/return characteristics—that is, whose risks and returns are unique to the regulatory and banking structure of the country of origin—are sold offshore as well as domestically. A financial market is considered to be truly globalized when it involves the continuous exchange in financial centers around the world of assets whose risk/return characteristics are independent of national regulatory and banking structures....Globalization is, in effect, the end point of a process of the separation of financial asset characteristics (including prices) from the idiosyncrasies of their countries of origin.

Despite the explosion in cross-border financial flows during recent years, the penetration of foreign assets into domestic financial markets is still relatively light, and confined within the three trading blocks (Hirst and Thompson, 1996: 40-44). The available evidence from several large industrial economies also suggests that "home asset bias" — the tendency to invest in local assets — is strong even in financial markets. Investors in the United States have been among the least diversified, with the percentage of equity portfolio held in domestic equities equal to 98 per cent in 1987. The US is followed by Japan at 87 per cent, the United Kingdom at 78 per cent, Germany at 75 per cent, and France at 64 per cent (Cooper and Kaplanis, 1994). Moreover, whether internationalizing financial markets will lead to a globalizing financial market remains in dispute (Boyer, 1996; Wade, 1996).

Second, at least some of the recent growth in international financial flows and liquidity was brought about by policy-specific and conjunctural factors. These include the international recession, the growth in government debt through the 1990s, the abandonment of capital controls, the emergence of structural imbalances in payments for a number of large economies, and the liberalization and deregulation of financial markets by national governments. However, as these changes are policy-specific and conjunctural, they may be temporary (Hirst and Thompson, 1996). In this regard, it is important to recall that the classic gold standard years between 1889 and 1914 can be distinguished as a period with low interest-rate parity between the world's two financial centers in New York and London. Thus, when interest rate parity is measured by the standard deviation of the difference between one-year interest rates on sterling-denominated assets sold in New York and those sold in London, such parity was extremely low during this period (Obstfeld, 1998: Figure 1). Nevertheless, the shift in the policy regime and fresh conjunctural factors during the 1920s led to a marked retreat in the internationalization of financial flows and liquidity during the 1930s.

The progressive internationalization of money and capital markets acts as a double-edged sword. To the extent that cross-border financial flows spread risk across assets of various nationalities and redistribute savings across nations, such flows may enhance efficiency and capital accumulation. However, greater internationalization of financial markets also broadens the scope for financial speculation and the redistribution of income, wealth, and political power toward a growing worldwide rentier class. As the most recent Asian and Mexican crises indicate, the internationalization of "casino capitalism" not only makes national economies more vulnerable to short-term capital and money movements, but also contributes to greater interest-rate and exchange-rate volatility (Felix, 1998). As Keynes (1967: 159) reminded us in 1936, "Speculators may do no harm as bubbles on a steady stream of enterprise. But the position is serious when enterprise becomes the bubble on a whirlpool of speculation. When the capital development of a country becomes a by-product of the activities of a casino, the job is likely to be ill-done."

III. What would capitalism like to do to increase its profitability? The World Trade Organization in context

The changes that took place within the nation state as a response to capitalism's profitability crisis, in part, were justified as being made necessary by the forces of globalization. However, the internationalization of trade, production, and finance is not as great as has been suggested, and, in any event, that internationalization since the mid-1980s has been predicated upon regionalization. Together, these observations suggest that globalization is not by and large the way MNCs have responded to the economics of their profitability problem. However, if globalization is not an economic fact, but, rather, largely an economic myth that has been used to effectively reshape society in the interest of increasing capital accumulation, the data suggest that, as a political project, globalization has not, as yet, been successful, in that the rate of profit has not recovered to the levels of capitalism's golden age. The response to this contradiction has been the attempt to create a set of international rules to both further MNC interests as well as overcome domestic resistance to those interests. It is within this context that national governments have ceded economic power to the World Trade Organization (WTO).

In 1995 the WTO replaced the GATT. The WTO agreement is an extensive list of policies, laws, and regulations removed from the prerogative of national governments (Shrybman, 1999: 6). As a consequence, the WTO has extended the reach of trade rules into every sphere of economic, social, and cultural activity. Historically, trade agreements were concerned with the international trade of goods such as manufactured products and commodities. The WTO extended the ambit of international trade agreements to include investment measures, intellectual property rights, domestic regulations of all kinds, and services—areas of government policy and law that have very little, if anything, to do with trade, per se. It is now difficult to identify any issue of social, cultural, economic or environmental significance that would not be covered by these new rules of trade (Shrybman: 4).

Trade-related investment measures demonstrate the significance of the change. As a consequence of the WTO agreement, all sections of a nation's economy become open to foreign investment. This is achieved by preventing governments from favouring domestic corporations while, at the same time, establishing the pre-eminence of corporate rights and enabling foreign investors to enforce their new rights directly. Thus, the WTO agreement on trade in services in the area of health and education has the potential to effectively undermine the mechanisms with which publicly funded commitments to health care and education are made. This is because the agreement can be interpreted as requiring governments to provide the same subsidies and funding support to private hospitals and schools as it makes available to non-profit institutions in the public sector (Shrybman, 1999: 16).

These rules, of course, do not apply to any government or community that attempts to infringe on MNC rights.

> Here are some examples of typical US state laws or legal principles that conflict with the WTO: laws that promote investment in recycled material markets; that allocate public deposits or banking business based on community reinvestment performance or local presence; that impose 'buy local' requirements of preferences for state procurement; and that make state procurement contingent on certain social or human rights considerations, like the Macbride principles and Burma-selective purchase laws. Ninety-five laws have been identified as potentially 'WTO-illegal' in California alone, according to the Georgetown University Law Center. How do we know this? Japan, the European Union and Canada publish documents every year that list American laws they consider WTO illegal. (Borosage, 1999: 21)

In this light, it is hardly surprising that WTO rules have been described as international bill of rights for corporations (Shybman, 1999).

WTO authority stems from its powerful enforcement tools that ensure that all governments respect the new limits it places on their authority: trade sanctions that can cost hundreds of millions of dollars. While previous trade agreements allowed for similar sanctions, they could only be imposed with the consent of all GATT members, including the offending country. Now WTO rulings are automatically implemented unless blocked by a consensus of WTO members (Shrybman, 1999). In so doing, the WTO has the potential to greatly improve the profitability of MNCs by lowering their taxes and their costs of production through its effects on labour and environmental legislation. At the same time, the WTO expands the sphere of activities that MNCs can enter into, effectively commodifing much of what was out of the reach of the for-profit sector. As *The Economist* (2000: 9) has put it,

> Footloose capital is free riding on less mobile taxpayers, getting the benefit of services provided by governments in high-taxing countries while paying taxes in low-tax jurisdictions, if at all....Some EU governments also argue that tax competition makes it ever harder to tax mobile factors of production such as capital. Instead, they complain, they have to increase taxes on less mobile factors, notably labour, which may drive jobs away.

Of course, the WTO did not invent opportunities for footloose capital. However, it does provide footloose capital with a greater range of possibilities. Moreover, so-called globalization cannot explain the ability of MNCs to take advantage of this greater range of possibilities by extorting low taxes from the state or the effective privatization of the health or education sectors. These are quintessentially political acts, reflecting the relative power of capital at this juncture in our history. As Weiss (1999: 31) notes,

> while the external world of capital flows exerts real constraints on how governments can behave, so too does the internal world of regime orientations, institutions, and domestic politics. Failure to understand the power of path dependency and the pull of domestic pressures leads many globalists systematically to overstate both the power of globalization to determine domestic outcomes and its causal importance in constraining policy choice.

One significant implication is that the most important limitations on the scope of state involvement in the economy and what it can responsibly do to support productivity-enhancing growth and provide social protection may be self-imposed rather than externally induced. This is clear in the United States, where a two-decade-long self-imposed neo-conservatism has already exposed the acute contradictions of neo-conservatism to areas known for their spill-over effects and market failures, such as education and training (World Bank, 2003: Table 2.10).

Another clear example of the impact of neo-conservatism is in research and development activities in the US. The President's Information Technology Advisory Committee (PITAC, 1999) asks whether information technology research should be funded primarily by commercial interests. Their answer is no. The report argues that in the US, essential long-term, high-risk investments in the information technology (IT) sector are being sacrificed, in part because of near-term market pressures. This committee, made up of IT corporate executives and academics in related fields, explains it is the federal government that, since World War II, has provided the funding for IT research and has "trained most of our IT researchers" (PITAC, 1999:8). The effect of this is to have "seeded high risk research and yielded an impressive list of billion dollar IT industries." However, in both the public and private sectors, investment in technology research and development has, the committee argues, slowed to a relative trickle. American businesses, in an ever-shrinking and more highly competitive world, have devoted less of their resources to long-term research and development, directing their efforts instead towards reducing costs and getting new products into the pipeline today, at the expense of the future. The federal government has mirrored this trend because of dramatically increasing pressures on research and development budgets, with only modest increases in funding levels.

Lester Thurow (1999) has identified the necessity of recognizing capitalism's tendency to market failure with respect to long-term investment. He points out that private rates of return for research and development investment are, on average, less than half the rate of return accruing to society as a whole. There is powerful evidence of positive spillovers from research and development, but that left to themselves, firms will spend too little because they cannot capture all the benefits that flow from these investments. In addition to these disadvantages of self-interest in a competitive economy, there is also the issue of the time frame that often dominates the competitive firm's decision-making. The private sector, with its preoccupation with shareholder rates of return and competition, has a short-run time frame and therefore tends not to invest in advancing basic knowledge. Very few companies are able to invest for a payoff that is years away. Thus, as Thurow (1999: 291) writes,

> The only private labs that have ever focussed on anything other than short-run results are those such as Bell Labs and the IBM labs that were run by quasi-monopolies. The minute AT&T (forced by government) and IBM (forced by the market) joined the normal competitive capitalistic world, they cut long-term research out of their laboratory budgets.

In both the IT sector and biotechnology, it is the state that did the high-risk investment and then turned over the results to the private sector. "Moreover, many advances are broad in their applicability and complex enough to take several engineering iterations to get right, and so the key insights become public and a single company cannot recoup the research investment" (PITAC, 1999: 79). Governments tend to be more indifferent as to who reaps the benefits from investments in research and development, while firms tend to focus on their own rate of profit, and this plays an essential role in the long-term investment decision in capitalist economies.

What is true for research is, in varying degrees, also true for education and training, albeit different capitalist formations have different histories. Some capitalist private sectors invest more in education and training than do others. This does not change the basic role of the state with respect to research and training. Profit-maximizing firms prefer to train those already educated. As with research and development, the state, unlike the private sector, does not have to concern itself with losing an investment or training an employee for another firm.

The disadvantage of an unadulterated neo-conservative strategy is, therefore, that it can inhibit the production of basic research and the critical mass of workers with the vital skills required to ameliorate the accumulation crisis. Who, then, is going to do the inventing, problem solving, and symbolic analysis for the system? The corporate world is not becoming a simpler place, nor is its rate of change slowing. These examples of the essential role of the capitalist state with respect to capital accumulation are just that—examples. Similar cases could be made for the state's role in public health, the environment, and legitimation crises.

IV. Is there anything else going on beside the "race to the bottom"? "The climb to the top for a few"

The concentration of trade and investment flows among the three trading blocks and the small size of these flows relative to GDP in many countries suggest that these flows by themselves are likely to have a modest direct economic effect on the trajectory of the world economy. However, in their "race to the bottom," nothing has prevented MNCs and domestic firms from playing workers, communities, and nations against one another, as they demand tax, regulation, and wage concessions. Imposing the lowest environmental standards, wages, work and safety conditions, taxes, and social services, which has been referred to as social dumping, is an important part of MNC strategy to restore profitability. The problem for MNCs and the governments that serve them is that these strategies are only a partial answer to their problems. In reality MNCs and those governments serving their needs for accumulation often must follow a segmented strategy that incorporates both a race to the bottom and the climb to the top. While a climb to the top may induce governments to provide a well-educated labour force and high-quality infrastructure in order to retain and attract FDI, it falls short of, and is often inconsistent with, the needs of the environment, labour, and the citizenry.

Progressive economists find nothing inherently problematic with foreign trade or FDI as long as the interests of labour, the environment, and the citizens of all the participating countries are protected and enhanced. Given that the evidence suggests that the bulk of trade and production still takes place in the core economies, policies to ensure and improve this protection could, in part, be achieved by making use of already existing structures and laws. The most globalized of the factors of so-called globalization, short-term international financial flows, are also the most destructive and require a somewhat more unconventional policy response.

The character of regionalization of the world suggests ready solutions for the social service, environmental, and labour problems resulting from neo-conservative policies. A charter of economic and human rights, reflecting a climb to the top, could act as a counterweight to the WTO and could mean that Swedish and Japanese standards, rather than British and Chinese standards, would become the floor when trade and FDI take place. Foreign investors would have to comply with the highest standards prevailing in either their home or host jurisdiction, whichever is higher. All governments would have the right to regulate the activities of both foreign and domestic investors, to ensure their activities conform to the public interest. In the event of conflict with international environmental and labour agreements, these agreements should prevail over investment and trade agreements (Shrybman, 1999: 141). Instead of treating citizens' and labour rights and services and environmental issues as afterthoughts, as with the trade agreements in North America, regulation on a national, regional, and where necessary, global basis becomes integral to such agreements.

On the domestic front, central bank strategies must be broadened beyond the anti-inflation theme to include full employment and real investment strategies. These banks can become a source of credit for increased public investment, including community venture investment. Tax policy should be shifted away from promoting personal investment income and speculation, and towards tax credits for real investments by companies as well as by non-profit community investment activities (Stanford, 1999: 310).

On the international front, at least two sorts of policy directions need to be changed. The IMF's policy conditionality results in privatization, the opening up sections of the economy to foreign ownership, undermining labour arrangements regarding wages and job security, attacks on living standards, and the downsizing of government programs. As with central banks, these policies must be reoriented to focus on reducing unemployment and poverty, which history suggests is consistent with economic growth. The World Bank and the IMF would have to abandon their ideological attachment to free capital flows and uniform investment rules, leaving such issues to be determined democratically, by member governments (Loxley, 1999: 102).

Short-term financial movements that are often destabilizing and where the motivation is often speculation should be discouraged and/or penalized. A Tobin tax on short-term financial exchanges could discourage short-term capital movements by penalizing them without affecting long-term foreign investment. Borrowing countries could take the initiative by restricting certain capital inflows. Higher reserve requirements on banks borrowing abroad, especially on a short-term basis, and/or differential tax treatment on short- versus long-term borrowing, could also reduce the destabilizing effects of speculative borrowing (Loxley, 1999: 103-104).

Objectively, the conception of globalization is largely a myth, even while its conceptual power has real effects. Certainly the effects of the race to the bottom are genuine. They are the result of political-economic decisions, the product of capitalism's laws of motion. The engagement of MNCs and the governments that represent them in this process is both a problem and an opportunity for environmentalists, unions, anti-poverty organizations, and human rights activists. The same forces that provide the MNCs with their opportunities produce historically significant alternatives.

V. Conclusion

The context for so-called globalization is that capitalism entered into an economic crisis phase in the late 1960s. Crisis here does not mean catastrophic economic breakdown, nor does it mean capitalism as usual. In this conjuncture, normal economic activity is not sufficient to restore prosperity because as accumulation slackens, less profit is available to maintain those institutions whose relative stability and reproducibility permit the repeated fulfillment of an important socio-economic function.

Multinationals and their national governments have attempted to free themselves from constraints with respect to regulations, labour, and taxes. Old institutions are contracted and/or transformed while new ones are formed as the system struggles to restore accumulation. The WTO and other free trade agreements can be seen as a strategy to use international rules to overcome domestic resistance to multinational interests. However, this attempt at turning the world into a free enterprise zone has led to global legitimation problems for capital, as environmentalists, unions, and anti-poverty activists have coalesced to resist. They have abandoned parliamentary politics as the domain of capital and have declared their opposition in large numbers everywhere capital attempts to organize those rules, with the noteworthy exceptions of meetings in police states.

Interestingly, decades of neo-conservative rule do not seem to have restored a golden hue to capitalism. The period between 1948 and 1973 exceeded the 1995 to 2000 period, even in the United States, in every respect: productivity, inflation, unemployment, and profits. The only exception was stock market valuations, and recent scandals demonstrate the illusion of those valuations. The system's cheerleaders in the economics profession and mainstream media ignored this reality. As in the 1960s, we began to hear the triumphant end to the business cycle. Even if the so-called decade-long boom did occur in one country—and that, given recent revelations, may be open to doubt—all that was needed was to emulate the neo-conservative American model and all would prosper. Peruse the pages of *Business Week* or *The Economist* over the past few years and you can read the chorus in action.

The current world recession and the aftermath of September 11 have undermined faith in the market and brought the state back into management of the economy as governments promise subsidies to ailing sectors, use fiscal stimulus, and revert to military Keynesianism to mitigate the effect of crisis. Five years or so of apparent American economic success and decades of neoconservatism appear to have done little to restore global capital accumulation. What it may have done, however, is to resurrect political opposition—some of it reactionary, some of it progressive.

Chapter 3

THE CANADIAN ECONOMY IN THE 1990S: THE CHARACTER OF ACCUMULATION

Fletcher Baragar

I. Introduction

AS the ephemeral recession of 2001 recedes into the past, recent forecasts for the Canadian macroeconomy are, by conventional standards, rather encouraging. The July 2002 survey by Consensus Economics Inc. reported the prevailing view among 12 economic forecasters that Canada would experience growth in real gross domestic product (GDP) of 3.8 per cent in 2003 (*The Globe and Mail*, 19 July 2002: B5). This growth rate does not exceed the robust rates that were generated in the boom years of the late 1990s. However, they exceed the projected growth rates of the G7 countries, including the United States. This reverses the pattern of the 1990s, when US growth rates exceeded those of Canada in 7 of 10 years. Indeed, while stronger growth in the US relative to Canada characterized the 1980s as well as the 1990s, as shown in Figure 1 below, the evidence since 1999, when combined with the 2003 forecast, suggests a sustained improvement in Canada's relative macroeconomic performance.

The GDP figures are not, however, very likely in themselves to induce the conviction that the 21st century belongs to Canada. On the contrary, there has been and continues to be an extensive amount of research and discussion about Canada's poor economic performance and prospects relative to the United States. The issues of concern have included the emergence of a gap between Canadian and US unemployment rates, the "brain drain," the secular decline of the exchange rate between the Canadian and US dollar, and the widening productivity gap.[1] Much of this discussion carries the implication that capital accumulation in Canada is still encumbered by a number of structural and institutional constraints, and that further restructuring and policy measures are urgently needed.

Any assessment of the relative strength of the Canadian economy depends, at least in part, on the conceptual framework used to capture the character of the economy. This chapter's classical Marxist framework exposes the specific nature of capital accumulation in Canada in the 1990s. This approach, while using many of the standard macroeconomic variables and indicators, places primary emphasis on the class-based character of capitalist production. The framework yields a different, and arguably more incisive, picture of recent macroeconomic activity in Canada.

II. Accumulation in a classical Marxist framework

The foundation of the classical Marxist framework consists of the class-based character of capitalist production. Specifically, capitalists own the means of production and undertake the mobilization and coordination of these elements in the production process. Workers are hired by capital and are paid a wage. This labour activity, performed under capitalist relations of production, creates value. Newly created value in excess of the wage payment constitutes surplus value, which is the basis of profit. It is important to distinguish between the rate of surplus value and the rate of profit. The rate of surplus value, also referred to as the rate of exploitation, expresses the division of new value created between surplus value and the portion that accrues to the actual producers, the productive wage labourers, in the form of their total compensation package. The rate of profit expresses the net returns to capitalists as a portion of their total capital invested. As such, the rate of profit measures the degree to which surplus value is produced, realized, and appropriated by capitalists. From the perspective of capital, the rate of profit is the indicator of the overall health of the macroeconomy and is the best indicator of the rate of future accumulation.

Applying the classical Marxist framework to an analysis of the Canadian economy consequently implies a somewhat different focus from that associated with more orthodox treatments. In particular, primacy is accorded to the business sector rather than to the entire macroeconomy. The business sector can be defined along the lines offered by Statistics Canada (2002d) as "all of GDP except the output of general government, non-profit institutions and the rental value of owner-occupied real estate." Using this definition, the business sector "accounts for about 71% of gross domestic product" (Statistics Canada, 2002b). By excluding all non-commercial activity, the business sector essentially designates that portion of the economy for which profitability matters. Secondly, this is the sector that produces value, including surplus value. Consequently, all productive workers are located in this sector. In the Marxist framework, a productive worker is one who produces surplus value. All productive workers are located in the business sector, although not all workers in this sector are necessarily productive.[2] Furthermore, although mainstream macroeconomics does not make any distinction between productive and unproductive labour, or the productive and unproductive sectors of the economy, Statistics Canada, when attempting to provide data on value-added and productivity, explicitly confine their efforts to the business sector. This results in a de facto recognition that the productive-unproductive distinction, which has long figured prominently in classical economics, remains central to conceptualizing accumulation in the macroeconomy.

Accumulation in a capitalist economy, of course, implies the predominance of the two major classes, capitalists and workers, in the productive sphere. As defined by Statistics Canada, however, the business sector will also include non-capitalist enterprises. Particularly significant here is the category of the "own-account" self-employed worker, which is where the owner-operator has no paid employees. In the classical Marxist framework, these workers are referred to as "independent commodity producers." They are considered productive insofar as they produce value, but because they are not employed by capital, they do not produce surplus value. Their earnings appear as part of total labour compensation. As a result, the presence of the earnings of these own-account self-employed workers in the data for labour compensation in the business sector will understate the real rate of exploitation of wage labour.

Identifying the business sector with the productive sector, at least as a first approximation, still leaves open the issue of how to best conceptualize the non-business portion of the economy. As noted above, Statistics Canada's accounts attribute just under 30 per cent of GDP to this latter sector. A treatment consistent with the classical Marxist tradition would define this sector as unproductive of value. Its share of GDP would simply be a portion of the new value created in the productive sector but subsequently transferred to the non-business sector by such mechanisms as the tax system, subsidies, and unequal exchange. Thus, this sector's slice of GDP should be added to the value created by productive workers in the business sector. This treatment would augment the measured rate of exploitation of productive workers. The reclassification, however, although theoretically desirable, would entail a significant cost. Specifically, it would render unsuitable the extensive data that Statistics Canada has amassed concerning productivity and accumulation in the business sector itself, since Statistics Canada operates on the conventional non-Marxist premise that both the business and non-business sectors are productive of value and contribute to GDP. Thus, in order to utilize Statistics Canada's data sets, this paper's focus on the business sector will exclude that portion of GDP officially attributed to the non-business sector of the economy.

III. The rate of profit in Canada

There is a lack of consensus on how best to define profits and the profit rate. The emphasis in this essay on the business sector suggests that the appropriate concept would be that which best coincided with Marx's "profit of enterprise" (Marx, 1959: Ch. 23). The rate of profit would then be the ratio of business net revenues to the value of capital tied up in the production process. Defined in this manner, the denominator would include not only the stock of fixed capital—machinery, equipment, and buildings—but also the capital advanced for the purchase of raw materials, intermediate goods, and labour. Statistics Canada provides two ratios pertaining to rates of return on capital for business enterprises, but neither corresponds precisely to Marx's notion of profit of enterprise. These ratios are the return on equity (ROE) and the return on capital employed (ROCE). Statistics Canada (2001b: 94-5) defines the ROE as "after-tax profits, including a deduction for interest expenses (payments for lenders). It is the net profit available to the owners." The ROCE is defined as "the percentage return on total capital provided by the owners and lenders. The earnings figure is calculated before taking into account interest expense payments (payments to lenders) and dividends (payments to owners)." However, the ROE is not a good measure of the return on capital because the value of total equity is not equivalent to the value of capital advanced. Similarly, the ROCE differs from the profit of enterprise in that the numerator in the latter excludes interest payments on borrowed funds. Furthermore, as shown in Figure 2, although these two measures of profitability have moved in the same direction since 1988, they do not, in general, give comparable rates of profit. The ROE is markedly more pro-cyclical than the ROCE, and, on average, the ROE also gives a higher rate of return. The pronounced pro-cyclical character of the ROE shown in Figure 2 is due to the fact that the earnings of the owners of equity are residual insofar as interest on borrowed money capital is usually paid prior to valuation of firm profits and the payments of dividends.

A more serious limitation is that this data set only begins in 1988. Thus, whereas it comfortably covers the decade of the 1990s, and encompasses the most recent business cycle, which from peak to peak ran from 1988 to 1999, it does not provide a means by which profitability in the 1990s can be contrasted with that in previous decades. In order to benefit from the perspective that a longer time span can offer, an alternative measure of the rate of profit is needed.

Another, albeit somewhat cruder, indicator of profitability is expressed in the ratio of the value of corporate profits relative to the value of the fixed capital stock. Directing the analysis along this path, however, necessitates selecting an appropriate measure for the value of the capital stock. Fixed capital depreciates, and different methods of trying to capture this depreciation will yield different values. This essay opts for a geometric depreciation of fixed capital, with the value of the capital stock thus referring to the year-end net stock of fixed capital.

Proceeding on this basis, the rate of profit in the business sector for Canada can be constructed for a 40-year period beginning in 1961. The results are illustrated in Figure 3. As was noted in respect to Figure 2, the pro-cyclical nature of profitability is also evident in Figure 3. The three indicators of profitability exhibit similar movement throughout the 1990s, but their magnitudes vary. The period between 1988 and 1999 rather conveniently corresponds to the peak-to-peak movement of the most recent business cycle. Over this 12-year period, the average rate of profit, as calculated on the profit/capital stock basis, is 6.4 per cent. This is below the ROE average of 8.2 per cent for that period, but slightly above the ROCE average of 6.3 per cent.

Figure 3 also suggests that there is, at least since 1960, evidence of a downward trend in overall profitability in the business sector. This can be seen more clearly when the post-1960 period is broken into the three distinct business cycles that lie within this period, when the business cycle is defined in terms of the interval from peak to peak. The three cycles consist of the periods 1966 to 1973, 1973 to 1988 and 1988 to 1999, respectively, while the years 1961 to 1966 comprise the latter half of the cycle from 1955 to 1966. As presented in Table 1, the average rate of profit for each of these three successive complete cycles are just over 8 per cent, 7.9 per cent, and 6.4 per cent, respectively. This downward trend in profitability is consistent with recent empirical work on the trend in the rate of profit in the United States (Duménil, Glick, and Lévy, 2001; Moseley, 1999), and sustains the long-standing argument of both classical and Marxist economics that there is a tendency for the rate of profit to fall in capitalist economies. If, however, the last half of the 1990s are considered, along with 2000 and 2001, then the average rate of profit for the period between 1995 and 2001 rebounds back to a strong 8.2 per cent. This period does not encompass a full business cycle, but these are the years identified with the "new economy," in which the putative benefits of new technologies and economic restructuring are thought by many to have been realized. In order to ascertain, on the one hand, the extent to which capital accumulation in Canada in the 1990s reflects a secular tendency of the rate of profit to fall, and, on the other, the extent to which it ushers in the nirvana of the new economy, it is necessary to probe more deeply into the nature of the profitability of capital in Canada.

IV. Decomposing the profit rate

Using the ratio of corporate profits to the value of the capital stock as a measure of profitability, the rate of profit, r, can be expressed as follows:

$$r = \frac{\pi}{Y} \cdot \frac{Y}{L} \cdot \frac{L}{K} \quad (1)$$

where π = corporate profits
K = net year end capital stock
Y = gross domestic product
L = number of workers

The decomposition of the profit rate in equation (1) is useful since each of the three ratios on the right-hand side has a distinct economic interpretation. Specifically, π/Y denotes the profit share of output, Y/L gives output per worker, which is a measure of labour productivity, and L/K provides an indicator of the relative capital intensity of the production process, akin, in the Marxist framework, to the organic composition of capital.

Data is available for the Canadian business sector that permits the deployment of this particular decomposition with regards to the movements of the profit rate since 1961. The profit share of output is illustrated in Figure 4. As previously explained, output refers to the business sector only, and not to the entire economy. The movement of the profit share is virtually identical to that of the profit rate in Figure 3, with a slight but distinct downward trend over the period from 1961 to 1998. Thus, in terms of trying to explain this trend, very little additional insight is offered by this ratio. It still leaves open the question of whether the apparent decline in the profit rate and the profit share is attributable to a decreased ability of capital to marshal labour to increase the production of value, or whether it can be attributed to a relatively reduced capacity of capital to maintain its share of the value produced.

The second and third ratios speak directly to this question. It should be noted first, however, that whereas the profit share, as well as the profit rate, can be constructed using nominal values in both the numerator and denominators, this is not suitable for measures of labour productivity or for the labour-capital ratio. Since only the numerator in Y/L and only the dominator in L/K are expressed in price terms, movements in the aggregate price level will alter the magnitudes of these ratios. When the ratios are multiplied together, as in equation (1), these aggregate price effects cancel out, but they will be seriously misleading when the ratios are considered separately. This apparent difficulty can be easily resolved by using the same deflator to convert the nominal values of GDP and the capital stock to real values. As a result, the second and third ratios can then be understood respectively as real output per worker and the ratio of the number of workers to the real value of the capital stock.

Figure 5 shows the movement of the value of output, measured in terms of value added per worker in 1997 dollars. Over the period between 1981 and 1999 the trend is strongly upward, although there are significant year-to-year fluctuations. Unfortunately, the Statistics Canada data that converts the values to 1997 dollars does not cover the years prior to 1981. A different set of units are used in the Statistics Canada series that includes the decades preceding the

1980s, but this data can also be used to illuminate trends in labour productivity in the business sector.

A helpful way to explore some of these trends is to look at annual productivity growth rates, which are shown in Figure 6. The series here extends back to 1962. The widely discussed slowdown in the rate of growth of labour productivity is evident. The average annual growth rate of labour productivity is 3.77 per cent for the period between 1962 and 1973, but a rather meagre 1.22 per cent for the period between 1974 and 2000. However, these productivity growth rates are based on real output per hour worked. There was a secular decline in average annual hours worked by labour in the business sector from 1961 to 1982, although since then this annual average has been constant, as indicated in Figure 7. Consequently, the slowdown is even more pronounced when measured in terms of output per hour.

In much of the mainstream literature on productivity, this slowdown has been deemed significant because of its effect on real living standards. The effect on profitability has been less widely explored. Certainly, the post-1974 productivity slowdown is consistent with the secular decline in the rate of profit, but the channel through which productivity affects profitability is less direct. Specifically, the effect of productivity gains depends upon whether there are associated effects on the distribution ratio (π/Y) and/or on the labour-capital (L/K) ratio.

The extent to which workers are able to directly capture some of the pecuniary benefits resulting from the increase in labour productivity can be discerned by comparing the rate of increase of real wages with the increase in labour productivity. Figure 8 does this for the Canadian business sector over the last 40 years. The long-term trend of these two variables is similar, and both exhibit lower average growth rates for the post-1975 period. However, the data shows that, over the entire period between 1962 and 2000, the rate of growth in real wages has not kept pace with the rate of growth in labour productivity. Table 2 displays the difference between the average annual rate of growth of real wages and labour productivity for the three complete business cycles within this period, as well as for the pre- and post-1982 intervals. Over the real business cycle from 1966 to 1973, workers received real wages increases that, in percentage terms, exceeded the rate of productivity growth. This situation was dramatically reversed in the cycles from 1973 to 1988 and 1988 to 1999.

In considering the period from 1962 to 1982, annual percentage increases in real wages were only slightly below the average annual rates of productivity growth: -0.1 per cent. For the interval of 1982 to 2000, however, the gap was at -0.7 per cent, almost three quarters of a percentage point per year.

This real wage-productivity gap constitutes an increase in the rate of exploitation of labour. The rate of exploitation can be calculated as follows:

$$e = \frac{Y - W}{W} \quad (2)$$

where e = rate of exploitation, (Y) is nominal GDP for the business sector and (W) is nominal labour compensation in the business sector. The rate of exploitation, e, for the business sector is illustrated in Figure 9. This chart shows that despite considerable fluctuations, there was a marked increase in the average annual rate of exploitation in the 1980s and 1990s in comparison to the two preceding decades. Thus, despite the productivity slowdown, capital in the 1980s and 1990s was able to extract more unpaid labour from each of their workers than before. This increase in e would also, *ceteris paribus*, raise r, which would be at odds with the actual path of r over the period under consideration. Before drawing any conclusions, however, it is necessary to examine the third ratio in equation (1), the ratio of labour to capital.

Marx's organic composition of capital is analogous to the reciprocal of the L/K term in equation (1). Figure 10 depicts the organic composition of capital for the business sector over the last 40 years. The trend reveals an unambiguous increase, but again its actual trajectory has been uneven. In percentage terms, the ratio K/L increased almost 50 per cent between 1966 and 1982, but the total increase from 1982 to 2000 was only 15 per cent, and, for the last eight years, the ratio has been virtually constant.

Pulling together these various strands, a composite picture emerges, which permits a more informed description of the movement of the rate of profit in Canada. Beginning in the mid-1960s, falling rates of exploitation started to erode profitability of Canadian corporations. As depicted in Figure 11, this was the period when the wage-productivity gap was especially favourable to workers. Relatively high levels of employment combined with relatively high levels of unionization of workers in the private sector enabled workers to improve their relative position. This situation within the sphere of capitalist production, combined with a growing public sector and demands for expanded social programmes, constituted the early manifestations of the emerging crisis. A political response by capital was to induce the state to intervene more explicitly in tempering the wage demands of labour. The Trudeau government's anti-inflation policy of 1975 to 1978 and the 1975 announcement by the Bank of Canada of its "gradualist" monetary policy are two notable indications that federal economic policy was accommodating the needs of capital. In the workplace, however, capital's response included increased investment in capital goods. Measured as a percentage of GDP, total private investment in the 1970s exceeded the levels of the 1960s, 1980s, and 1990s (Stanford, 1999: Ch. 7 and 8). The surge in investment spending did not boost the rate of productivity growth. As noted above, that rate actually fell during the 1970s. In conjunction with a rising K/L, a neoclassical interpretation would invoke the principle of the diminishing marginal productivity of capital. Marx (1954: Ch. 15 and 25), however, emphasized that in addition to whatever productivity gains might result from equipping workers with more and better equipment, new investment is also an important weapon deployed by capital in the struggle with labour in the workplace. Various consequences, such as deskilling and the threat, whether realized or not, of replacing existing workers with lower paid workers or with machines, can effectively strengthen the relative power of capital in the workplace. This situation, in combination with the changing macroeconomic environment, raised the rate of exploitation in the 1970s. The result was that, despite a rising K/L ratio and declining rates of productivity growth, the profit rate in the business sector remained relatively robust in the 1970s.

In the 1980s profit rates sagged because of the recession of 1982. During the recovery they rebounded, but even at the peak of the cycle in 1988 they failed to attain the levels of the best years of the 1970s. The data shows that the K/L ratio continued to rise in the 1980s, but the rate of increase was less than that of the 1970s. On the other hand, the rate of exploitation was especially high. In terms of extracting surplus value from labour, capital had never done better throughout the entire period between 1960 and 2000. Workers were hit hard by the recession and the subsequent slow recovery of employment. Within the workplace, this was a decade in which considerable restructuring of the labour process occurred. This restructuring led to minimal gains in terms of labour productivity, but it also eroded the power of labour. Although there are difficulties involved in constructing the estimates, it would appear that unionization rates in the private sector fell (Meltz and Verma, 1997: 102-104). In the economy as a whole, the number of part-time workers as a proportion of total employment rose from 14.4 per cent in 1980 to 16.8 per cent in 1989 (Statistics Canada, 2001a: 31). The proportion of self-employed workers also rose from 12.6 per cent to 13.9 per cent over the same period. On average, the wages of these two categories of workers are below those of full-time employees. Restructuring within the workplace enabled firms to utilize this lower cost source of labour as well as to curb expectations of their full-time workforces. It is not coincidental that these initiatives occurred at a time when labour force participation rates were rising. By 1989, the labour force participation rate reached 67.2 per cent, a level that has not been exceeded before or since (Statistics Canada, 2001a: 34). Women and youth disproportionately constituted the new entrants into the labour force. Participation rates for women rose from 50.4 per cent in 1980 to 58 per cent by 1989. Youth participation rates reached 71 per cent in 1989, which is also an all-time high. Rising participation rates for women are partly due to a continuation of the long-term trend of rising female participation rates, but the acute economic exigencies experienced by many households in the 1980s also underlies the deepening labour market commitment of women and youth. These are, after all, the workers who disproportionately fill part-time and low-wage jobs.

Enhanced rates of exploitation combined with modest growth in the organic composition of capital imply that, within the sphere of production, the preconditions for full recovery of the profit rate were in place. The fact that the 1980s experienced only a modest recovery of profitability suggests that factors external to the sphere of production also played a role. As was pointed out by Marx in Volume III of *Capital*, the capitalist business sector as a whole is not, in general, able to realize in the form of profits all the surplus value that their workers produce (Marx, 1959). The channels through which this surplus value is transferred away from the capitalist class are numerous. However, with regards to the specific situation of the 1980s, evidence suggests that two of these sources of leakage were especially influential in depressing profit rates. The first are the indirect business taxes that are paid by businesses to the state. These show up in the national income accounts as taxes less subsidies on factors of production and products. Figure 12 shows indirect business taxes as a proportion of GDP over the period between 1961 and 2000. From 1975 to 1985, this ratio was below 11 per cent, a situation unmatched by any of the other years within this period. Beginning in 1986, this ratio rose dramatically and, as the decade closed, it had moved beyond 13 per cent. These unprecedented levels remained for most of the 1990s.

The second leakage occurred in the form of the high real interest rates that plagued the Canadian economy throughout the 1980s and the first half of the 1990s. Interest and miscellaneous income as a percentage of GDP peaked at 10 per cent during the recession of 1982, but this ratio exceeded 6.8 per cent for each and every year between 1977 and 1993. By way of comparison, the interest and miscellaneous income share was consistently below 4 per cent in the 1960s, and has also been under 6 per cent since 1997 (Statistics Canada, 2002c: CANSIM series V647783 and V649340). Undoubtedly, part of this increased interest/GDP ratio is due to the expansion of the public debt, but higher real interest rates also increased the cost of borrowing to firms and consequently placed an additional claim on the surplus value generated in the business sector.

V. The 1990s

As was pointed out earlier, business sector profit rates over the course of the business cycle from 1988 to 1999 fell short of the rates achieved in the two previous cycles. The severity of the 1991 recession pulled profit rates down to a level that had not been experienced at any time in the preceding three decades. As a result, annual average profit rates for the 1990s fared poorly compared to the preceding decades. The years between 1999 and 2001, however, were especially good in terms of profits, and the rise in the profit rate from its post-1961 nadir in 1992 to its second-highest level in 2000 suggests a very impressive recovery. Consequently, depending on one's vantage point, the movement of profit rates in the 1990s seems to imply a continuation of the secular decline in the rate of profit, as well as an alternative interpretation that supports the claim of a newly resurgent capitalism transformed by the "new economy."

The decomposition of the rate of profit, however, illuminates the character of accumulation in the Canadian economy in the 1990s. As shown in Figure 10, the K/L ratio rises in the years between 1990 and 1992, but then remains essentially constant for the rest of the decade. This failure of the organic composition of capital to rise must be a major contributing factor to the surge in profitability over the period. It should be stressed that this is not entirely unprecedented, since the period between 1982 and 1990, taken as a whole, constitutes a similar plateau. This slowdown in the rise of the K/L ratio, and its subsequent stagnation, can be attributed to two influences. First, the severe recessions of 1982 and 1991 precipitated decisions by firms to eliminate many existing but antiquated components of the capital stock. In the extreme case, bankruptcy is a particularly effective, if severe, means to economically destroy the value of fixed capital. This streamlining of the capital stock was further enhanced by the increased competition faced by Canadian producers in the aftermath of the Canada–US Free Trade Agreement of 1989 and the general round of tariff reductions in the 1990s. These developments, however, are of a specific, conjunctural, nature, unlikely to be able, in and of themselves, to permanently prevent the K/L ratio from resuming its historic rise. Secondly, technological change, especially the impact of new developments in the information and communication industries, has enabled the costs of various types of capital equipment to fall dramatically. The enhanced computational power of the latest generation of computers in conjunction with falling prices for much of this equipment serves as a well-publicized example. In this context, the technological aspects of the new economy are, in fact, playing a positive role in augmenting profitability, but here again it remains an open question as to whether the economic effects of recent developments can be sustained. The present global crisis in the information and communications technology sector suggests that limits may already be near.

On the productivity front, rates of growth of labour productivity in the 1990s have improved in comparison to the 1980s. A more telling factor, however, is that the real wage-productivity gap remained decisively negative over the decade as a whole. As was the case in the 1980s, in only three years was the gap positive. Consequently, as shown in Figure 9, the rate of exploitation remained high. From this perspective, there is nothing fundamentally different in the 1990s in comparison with the 1980s. The labour process has been transformed through the interplay of new technologies, new managerial strategies, the relatively weaker position of private sector unions, and less favourable labour market conditions and institutions. The crucial point, however, is that this transformation was initiated in the early 1980s and that it has characterized the regime of accumulation over the last two decades. It is not a peculiar feature of the 1990s. What was different about the 1990s was that there was an accentuation of some of the labour market and labour process developments that had already started in the 1980s. Thus, the 1990s should be understood in terms of an extension and consolidation of a new, neo-conservative regime of exploitation and accumulation.

Labour market data for part-time employment and for self-employment in the 1990s are two notable instances of the continuation and extension of developments that sprang to prominence in the 1980s. As was mentioned earlier, the ratio of part-time employment to total employment had risen to 16.8 per cent by 1989. The part-time rate continued to increase in the years immediately following, and peaked at 19.3 per cent in 1993. This rate hovered around 19 per cent for virtually the remainder of the decade, falling only to 18.5 per cent in 1999 (Statistics Canada, 2001a: 31). The trend of self-employment in the 1990s is even more striking. Beginning from a level of 13.9 per cent in 1989, the ratio of self-employed workers to total employment continued to rise throughout the first half of the 1990s and peaked at 17.7 per cent in 1997 (Manser and Picot, 1999). This rate has dropped slightly since its 1997 peak, but even in 2000, a year in which the unemployment rate fell to its lowest level in a quarter of a century, the self-employment rate remained above 16 per cent. Putting these developments together, Manser and Picot (1999: 43) claim that in the 1990s "most employment growth has been in self-employment and in part-time jobs" in Canada. Furthermore, in the 1980s, 40 per cent of the net new self-employment jobs involved own-account workers. In the 1990s, this percentage had risen to 90 per cent.

Increased reliance on part-time and self-employed workers is a means by which firms are able to contain labour costs and thereby contribute to the high rates of exploitation evident in the 1980s and 1990s. Part-time workers earn less per hour than do their full-time counterparts. Although some self-employed workers earn handsome incomes, those who earn more relative to paid workers tend to be those individuals who are also employers. Throughout the 1990s, own-account workers earned only about 70 per cent of the earnings of paid workers (Manser and Picot, 1999: 43). Although these own-account workers are not directly employed by capital, they contribute positively to capitalist profitability. The lower earnings of own-account workers suggest that capital can obtain various inputs and services at a lower cost from providers in this sector, thereby enabling capitalists to lower their own overheads. Secondly, the rapid growth of the self-employed sector, combined with their lower than average remuneration, opens the possibility that too much social labour has been allocated to production in those particular sectors, with the resulting devaluation of the value of the labour performed there. This overstocking of the labour pool is but one manifestation of the existence of Marx's reserve army of labour (Marx, 1954: Ch. 25). Part-time workers who would prefer to work full time is another. Taken together, they constitute a substantial portion of the Canadian reserve army of labour.

The existence of the reserve army plays a role that is functional for capital insofar as it acts to discipline labour in terms of the latter's wage demands and also in terms of their struggle over control in the workplace. Workers have resisted the efforts of capital to intensify its grip. Resistance takes various forms, some of which are subtle and localized, and which are therefore difficult to discern in terms of aggregate economic indicators. Work stoppages in the form of strikes and lockouts are visible, however, and are an overt measure of the intensity of the class struggle in the workplace. Overall, the incidence of strikes and lockouts, as well as an estimate of the percentage of working time lost due to these work stoppages, has fallen from the relatively high levels of the early 1980s. Labour disputes were less numerous and proportionally less disruptive in the 1990s than in the previous decade, which further supports the claim that the 1990s are best understood as a period of consolidation of a new neo-conservative regime of accumulation. This trend does not imply that labour has reconciled itself to and/or embraced the so-called realities of late 20th-century neo-conservative capitalism. Here, the assessment of Jackson, Robinson, Baldwin, and Wiggins (2000: 75) is astute: "today's workplace has become a leaner and meaner environment." It does, however, indicate that, in Canada at least, capital has forged an effective arrangement for the production of surplus value.

The positive effects of high rates of exploitation and a relative slowdown in the rise of the organic composition of capital in the 1980s on the rate of profit was somewhat offset by the decreased ability of capital to realize in the form of profits the surplus value created in the business sector of the economy. Real interest rates and indirect business taxes were identified as contributing to that realization problem. These two influences were also prominent in the 1990s. The Bank of Canada maintained relatively high real interest rates throughout most of the 1990s. Stanford (1999: 192) calculates that real short-term rates have averaged close to 6 per cent per year over the period between 1981 and 1998. The average for the real long-term rate exceeded 6 per cent over the same period. Short-term rates since 1993 have tended to be below this 20-year average, but only in 1999 was there any significant easing of this exceptionally tight monetary stance. As a result, monetary policy in both the 1980s and the 1990s impeded the ability of the business sector to realize surplus value, thereby depressing the rate of profit for the sector as a whole. Indirect business taxes, which soared as a percentage of GDP after 1985, continued to rise in the early 1990s, peaking at 13.7 per cent in 1993. As illustrated in Figure 12, this ratio was at or above the 13 per cent level for the entire period between 1991 and 2000. Overall, the combined impact of these taxes and interest rates was sufficient to depress profitability. As a result, the 1990s, despite a marked ascendancy of capital vis-à-vis labour, exhibited lower profit rates than the so-called crisis years of the 1970s.

VI. Conclusion

The 1990s can be characterized in Canada as a period of consolidation and expansion of a neo-conservative regime of accumulation initially established in the 1980s. Its effectiveness, from the perspective of capital, was based on the concerted efforts of capital, with some substantial assistance from the state, to restructure the workplace and the labour market. The relative balance of power between capital and labour was shifted in favour of the former. The overall result was a rise in the rate of exploitation. New technologies, the therapeutic effects of two recessions, and a new international trade and investment environment combined to alter the vintage and value of the capital stock, and this acted to offset the inherent tendency of the organic composition of capital to rise. These are the elements underlying the recovery of the profit rate in the 1990s and on into the early years of this century. Impressive as this recovery is, however, it has been constrained by the effects of high interest rates and indirect business taxes. These elements constitute an external claim on the surplus value produced within the business sector, with a consequent diminution of that sector's profits. Despite the direct impact that these particular components of Canada's fiscal and monetary policies have on business sector profitability, these components are not necessarily inimical to capital as a whole. The deleterious effect of high interest rates on growth and employment proved instrumental in creating and sustaining a favourable environment in which capital could orchestrate its assault on labour. The increased tax revenues, on the other hand, contributed in part to the funding of state activities, including the provision of various elements of the social wage. The latter is functional insofar as it softens some of the harsher features of the workplace and labour market restructuring. It also enables the state to continue fulfilling its legitimizing role by proclaiming allegiance to selective liberal values and programmes associated with the welfare state and the particular form of fiscal federalism found in Canada.

The impact of interest rates and taxes on profitability in the 1980s and 1990s suggests the possibility that further reductions in the levels of these variables could enhance profitability in the years ahead. The attendant ideological battle over the desirability and even affordability of Canada's social programmes has dovetailed nicely with the crusade for lower taxes, and it is not surprising that corporate interests line up unapologetically with those pushing lower taxes and leaner public amenities and programmes. As a result, the recent decrease in the ratio of indirect business taxes to GDP may be a harbinger of future developments in this area. The prospect for further sustained reductions in real interest rates is more problematic, given the preference of the financial community for price stability and high real returns for rentiers. Capital as a whole is also cognizant of the effectiveness of monetary policy in tempering wage claims of workers. Past and recent policy of the Bank of Canada has given priority to these concerns and, as a result, there is no indication that it views monetary policy as an instrument to directly increase profitability by pushing real interest rates down to historically low levels. Thus, on balance, future prospects for profit-enhancing tax reductions seem to be somewhat better than a profit-rate boost via the effect of low interest rates.

More generally, the prospects for accumulation in the new regime depend largely on developments affecting the rate of exploitation and the organic composition of capital. Labour has not yet mounted an effective challenge to the enhanced capitalist domination in the workplace. As a result, the current situation suggests that the high rates of exploitation may well persist through much of the first decade of the new millennium. The future path of the K/L ratio is more susceptible to movement that is inimical to the rate of profit. Recent recessions of marked severity, combined with implementation of new technologies, have restrained the secular tendency of the K/L ratio to rise. These are specific conjunctural occurrences, and there is no *a priori* reason to expect the next 20 years to demonstrate the same types of developments as have marked the previous two decades. Furthermore, although the rise in the K/L ratio has, for the moment, been contained, it remains at its highest level since 1960. Certainly, another severe and protracted recession would undermine pressures for the K/L ratio to continue its secular rise, but such an event does not appear imminent. Without a reduction in, or at the very least an effective restraint on, the organic composition of capital, profit rates in the first decade of the 21st century are unlikely to surpass the rates of the golden years of the 1960s.

Footnotes

1   On the Canada-US unemployment rate gap, see Riddell and Sharpe (1998). Recent perspectives on the brain drain can be found in the symposium in the September 1999 issue of *Policy Options* (Watson et al., 1999). Other contributions include Zhao, Drew, and Murray (2000) and Kesselman (2001). The Canada-US exchange rate seems to be a perennial topic in the media and the business press, and the secular decline has helped precipitate discussions about currency unions. See, for example, the debate in the December 1999 issue of *Canadian Business Economics* (Fairholm et al., 1999). On the productivity gap, see Baldwin, Harchaoui, and Maynard (2001), Rao and Tang (2001), Sharpe (2002), and the comprehensive collection of research papers in Rao and Sharpe (2002). Laidler and Aba (2002) is a recent entry into the debate on the connection between productivity and exchange rates.

2   Data limitations inhibit further efforts to distinguish between productive and unproductive labour in the business sector of the Canadian economy. Exploration of this important issue is beyond the scope of the present chapter, but for examples of work in this area in the United States, see Shaikh and Tonak (1994) and Moseley (1997).

Table 1 Average annual rates of profit, business sector

Period	Average annual profit rate, per cent
1961-1966 (incomplete cycle)	8.19
1966-1973	8.04
1973-1988	7.93
1988-1999	6.44
1999-2001 (incomplete cycle)	9.13

Source Statistics Canada (2002c): CANSIM series V1408125, V646928; and author's calculations.

Table 2 Wage-productivity gap, business sector

Period	Wage-productivity gap, per cent
1966-73	0.12
1973-88	-0.46
1988-99	-0.38
1962-73	-0.13
1973-82	-0.13
1962-82	-0.10
1982-2000	-0.73
1962-2000	-0.37

Note the wage-productivity gap is defined as average annual rates of change of real wages less average annual rates of change of labour productivity.
Source Statistics Canada (2002c): CANSIM series V716600, V717044, V717266, V737344; and author's calculations.

Figure 1 Growth rates of real GDP

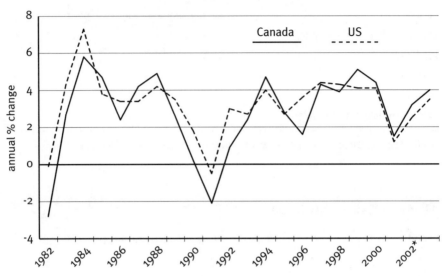

Source Statistics Canada (2001a): 6; U.S. Department of Commerce, BEA; Globe and Mail (2002).
*Note Growth rates for 2002 and 2003 are estimates.

Figure 2 Profit rates: All industries

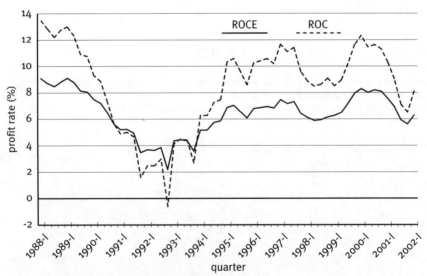

quarter
Source Statistics Canada (2002a): CANSIM series V634653, V634654.

Figure 3 Profit rates: Business sector

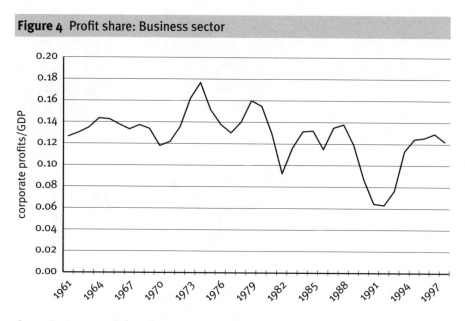

Source Statistics Canada (2002a): CANSIM series V646928, V1408425, and author's calculations.

Figure 4 Profit share: Business sector

Source Statistics Canada (2002a): CANSIM series V646298, V3860037 and author's calculations.

Baragar

Figure 5 Labour productivity: Business sector

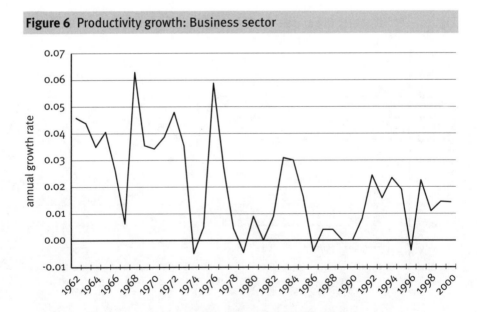

Source Statistics Canada (2002a): CANSIM series V2044291, V716378 and author's calculations.

Figure 6 Productivity growth: Business sector

Source Statistics Canada (2002a): CANSIM series V717266 and author's calculations.

64

Figure 7 Hours worked: Business sector

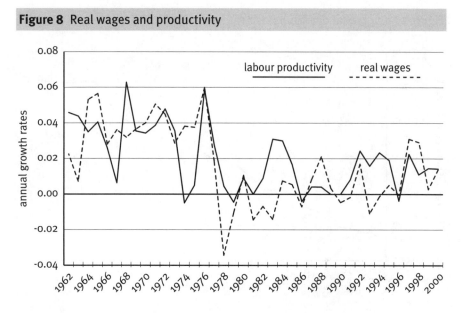

Source Statistics Canada (2002a): CANSIM series V716600.

Figure 8 Real wages and productivity

Source Statistics Canada (2002a): CANSIM series V717266, V717044, V716600, V737344 and author's calculations.

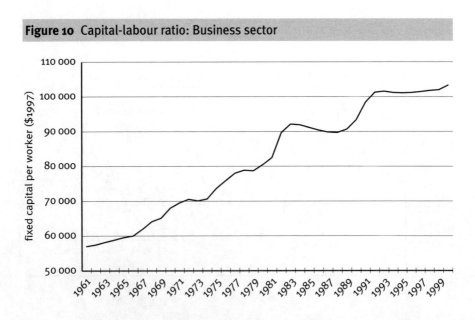

Figure 9 Rate of exploitation: Business sector

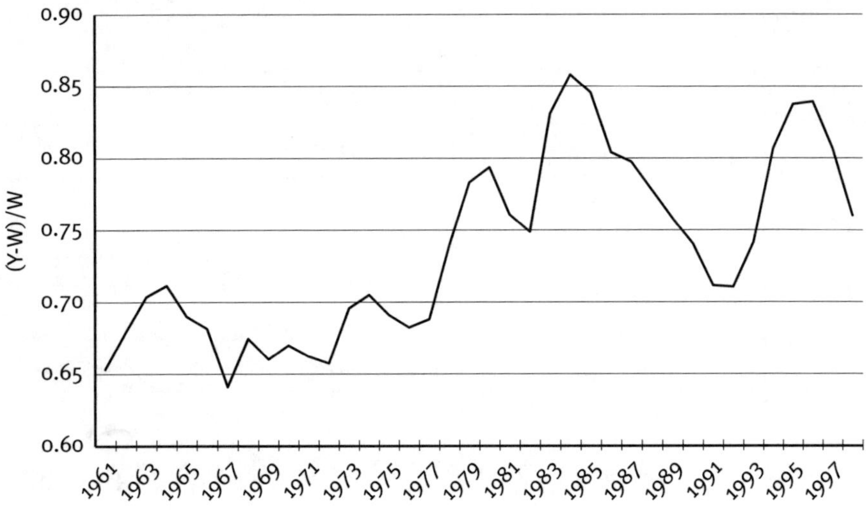

Source Statistics Canada (2002a): CANSIM series V717044, V3860037 and author's calculations.

Figure 10 Capital-labour ratio: Business sector

Source Statistics Canada (2002a): CANSIM series V1408373, V716378 and author's calculations.

Figure 11 Wage-productivity gap: Business sector

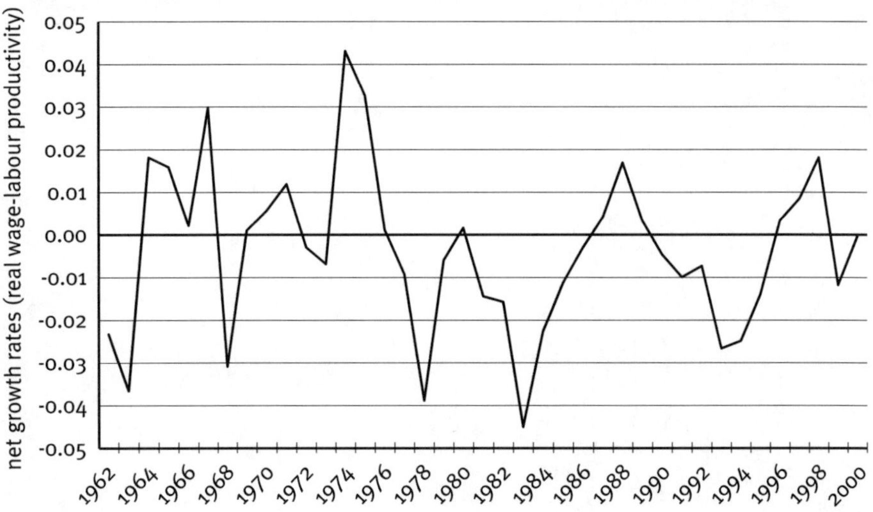

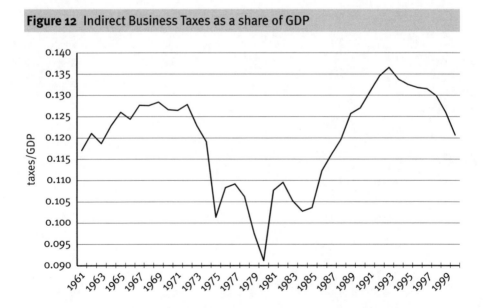

Source Statistics Canada (2002a): CANSIM series V717044, V716600, V716378, V737344 and author's calculations.

Figure 12 Indirect Business Taxes as a share of GDP

Source Statistics Canada (2002a): CANSIM series V647783, V647786 and author's calculations.

Chapter 4

ACCUMULATION IN AFRICA BEFORE AND AFTER ADJUSTMENT

Abdella Abdou

I. Introduction

TRADITIONAL development theory stressed the role of capital formation as one of the major themes in the process of economic development
(Nurkse, 1953). International financial institutions such as the World Bank
concurred, and financed numerous investment projects in developing countries. The emphasis on capital accumulation was unchallenged until the late
1970s, when the counter-revolution in development theory became prominent. Johnson and Johnson (1978) claimed that Keynesianism had led to a
misleading obsession with fixed investment and had distracted policy-makers
from attention to technical change and the importance of entrepreneurship.
Similarly, Bauer (1981) maintained that emergence from poverty did not require large-scale capital formation, and disputed the importance of investment
in economic development. His explanation of economic growth involved personal attitudes, social institutions, and political arrangements. The counter-revolution attributed poor economic performance in developing countries to an
overextended public sector, overemphasis on physical capital accumulation,
proliferation of distorting economic controls, and macroeconomic mismanagement. The International Monetary Fund (IMF) and the World Bank readily
accepted the main tenets of the neo-conservative counter-revolution. While
the IMF and the World Bank have not discounted the importance of investment to the same degree as Bauer, they have promoted a vision of growth
based on markets and incentives that places particular emphasis on the role of
the private sector (World Bank, 1985b).

This vision was made operational through structural adjustment programmes (SAPs), which were initiated in the 1980s and evolved into a fundamental shift in policy orientation in the economies of Africa and much of the
developing world. The programmes forced changes in the direction of these
economies, in their macroeconomic environment, resource-allocation mechanisms, institutional arrangements, and governance. Few events in African history have had such broad and wide implications on so many aspects of the
society, economy, and polity. The impact of SAPs on the forms of capital accumulation and the rate of investment in African economies is one of the main
aspects of this process of adjustment.

The economic and political changes wrought by SAPs are truly epoch-
making, and can, as a result, be used to divide the history of African countries since decolonization into two main periods: the pre-SAP period between
1960 and 1981; and the neo-conservative SAP period from 1982 to the present. The first period was dominated by questions of political independence,
while the second period has been preoccupied with the debt crisis and economic adjustment policies. However, the political and economic issues of each
of these periods are interwoven. In particular, in both periods the international
political and economic climate played a decisive role in fashioning the nature
of capital accumulation in Africa. Indeed, one of the main impacts of SAPs has
been a reconfiguration of the forms of capital accumulation. The role and mix
of public, private, and foreign enterprises and investment in Africa have been
recast.

II. Political independence and the Bandung project

The international arena after the Second World War was characterized by the
interplay of three forces. The first was that the centre of capitalism was organized under the hegemony of America, and Keynesian economic policies governed the process of capital accumulation. The second was that the Soviet bloc
was challenging the capitalist centre, under a state-owned, centrally planned,
economic mechanism. The third was that the rest of the world was emerging
from under colonial rule and was attempting to promote national development plans based on a mix of policies borrowed from the first two major forces (Amin, 1998: 21-22). The first two forces were the building blocks of the
international arena, while the third force, though significant, did not have the

coherence of organization, ideology, and alternative economic system needed to be an equal player. Nevertheless, the retreat of imperialism, the encouragement of the Soviet bloc, and the zeal created by liberation movements hurled new African countries onto the world scene.

However, from the perspective of African economic history, over the long run, decolonization may not have been as significant as colonization. Imperial partition opened internal African markets and established the tentacles of the international economic structure within which African economies functioned, while decolonization signified a change in formal control and not an alteration of the basic structure. Hence, political independence may not have constituted a major turning point in the broad historical trend of African economic development (Wallerstein, 1980). For this reason the economies of African countries, on gaining political independence, were dubbed "neo-colonial" by African liberation leaders such as Kwame Nkrumah. To change this condition, African leaders embarked on a number of initiatives on the international and national stages. In 1955, 29 newly independent Afro-Asian countries met for the first time in Bandung, Indonesia, to discuss anti-colonial struggles and to lend support to liberation movements. This meeting, known as the Bandung conference, signalled an attempt by African and Asian nations to demand consultation by Western powers on matters that affected them. In so doing, newly emergent African and Asian nations entered the world scene. The political and economic offshoots of this conference were the Non-Aligned Movement, formed in 1961, and the United Nations Conference on Trade and Development, formed in 1964. These movements fostered a policy of positive neutralism in the political field, and sought to promote policies that would effectuate some degree of disengagement from the world capitalist system in the economic arena.

At the national level decolonization recast the structure of ownership and investment in Africa. For most of the colonial era investment was monopolized by foreign companies, with some room for local entrepreneurs being opened up after 1945. The post-independence era provided a condition in which investment became a competitive arena for three forces: the state, foreign capital, and local entrepreneurs. The state has been prominent in post-independence African economies, due partly to state institutions inherited from colonial administrators and partly to the weakness of indigenous entrepreneurs (Austen,

1987). Additional reasons facilitated the push towards a state-directed econom-ic strategy. Although African countries remained within the Western capital-ist orbit, most avoided explicitly embracing capitalism as an ideology. On the political level, it was difficult to dissociate the anti-colonial nationalist struggle from anti-capitalist sentiments. Imperialism and colonialism were, after all, seen to be extensions of the capitalist system. While colonial powers manoeuvred to ensure that the African elites that replaced them were not communists, the ex-istence of East European, Chinese, and other socialisms still indicated the pos-sibility of an alternative route toward industrialization. Perhaps the most tout-ed alternative development route was what Soviet scholars called "non-capi-talist development" or the "socialist oriented" path (Popov, 1977). This strategy had a political and military component consisting of fraternal relations with the Soviet bloc. It also had an economic component consisting of restricting foreign corporations from dominating positions in the economy, giving state enterprises a leading role, placing an emphasis on heavy industry, and relying more on trade and aid relationships with the socialist world. Close to a third of African countries could have been counted as following this non-capital-ist path of development during its heyday in the late 1960s and early 1970s. Furthermore, even in Western countries this was a period in which the wel-fare state and Keynesianism were the norm. The field of economic develop-ment that took root at this time was dominated by Keynesian economists who were ready to assign a prominent role to the state in the development process. Moreover, Western countries were concerned with obtaining political and/or military alliances with developing countries, and consequently did not dictate to them about the role of the state in economic development. For all these reasons the state in Africa was bound to play a leading role in the accumula-tion process.

The prominence of the state was manifested through the nationalization of private firms, the formation of government partnerships with foreign owners, and the creation of entirely new industrial parastatals. The state was also in-volved in the economy through marketing boards, national trading companies, foreign exchange control, the licensing of different kinds of activities, and im-port substitution policies. The policies of nationalization, indigenization, and import substitution were used to try to increase African public and private ownership of enterprises, while at the same time avoiding domination by multinational firms and decreasing dependence on the metropole. However, the prominence of the state in the economy did not translate into a capacity to control the economy because of the administrative weakness of the state and underdeveloped economic forces. This may be indicated by the lower government expenditures of African states as compared to developed countries.

Table 1 shows central government expenditure as a percentage of gross national product (GNP) for selected low-income African countries and the G7 countries. The advanced countries tend to have a higher percentage of GNP devoted to government expenditures than do the African countries. Canada, the US, and Japan have low percentages. However, note that the data account for merely central government expenditures and that developed countries

Table 1 Central government expenditure as a percentage of gross national product

Low-Income African Countries	1972	1980	1993
Tanzania	19.7	28.8	...
Uganda	21.8	6.1	...
Malawi	22.1	37.6	...
Madagascar	16.7	...	16.1
Kenya	21.0	26.1	28.9
Ghana	19.5	10.9	21.0
Zimbabwe	...	35.3	36.2
G7 Countries			
United Kingdom	31.8	38.2	43.4
Italy	29.5	41.0	53.4
Canada	20.1	21.5	25.8
France	32.3	39.3	45.5
Germany	24.2	...	33.6
United States	19.1	21.7	23.8
Japan	12.7	18.4	...

Source World Bank (1985b, 1991, and 1995).

usually have federal structures with significant expenditure powers for lower levels of the government structure, whereas African countries usually are unitarian states. Including all levels of government makes the comparison of the role of the state between developed and developing countries even more dramatic. Using aggregated data the World Bank (1997: 2) has shown that for the years 1960, 1980, and 1990 the shares of total government expenditure in gross domestic product (GDP) for Organization for Economic Cooperation and Development countries was around 19 per cent, 44 per cent, and 48 per cent, respectively. The corresponding figures for developing countries were 15 per cent, 27 per cent, and 28 per cent.

Notwithstanding the limited capacity of African states, the policy environment they fostered during the first two decades following independence sought to reduce the relative strength of foreign companies in their economies. National political power introduced a new element into the relationship between the state and foreign corporations in Africa, and expropriation of foreign subsidiaries steadily increased from the 1960s to mid-1970s (United Nations Center on Multinational Corporations, 1988). At the same time, the availability of capital, in the form of aid and debt from multilateral institutions and socialist countries, strengthened the state in a relative if not absolute sense. As a consequence, despite limited capacity, African states became new and significant entrants into an economic space hitherto dominated by colonial companies. Apparently, even the state in a poor country may garner economic resources, compete, and negotiate with multinational firms better than a weak national capitalist class.

Some African countries, notably Kenya and Ivory Coast, were not enthusiastic about the nationalization of foreign companies. However, even among those that had a critical attitude to foreign firms, the door for foreign investment was not shut. Indeed, some African ruling elites may have found it easier both to control foreign firms and derive benefits from cooperating with multinationals than to deal with local entrepreneurs (Kennedy, 1988). That investment by multinational companies that African states did seek was not so much for capital as for employment creation, technology transfer, technical, and management skills, and access to the world market. Moreover, public enterprises, which tended to be capital-intensive, had to rely on foreign firms for inputs, technology, managerial skill and access to markets in order to be able to continue operation. Even Soviet economists did not see investment by Western capitalists in developing countries as being incompatible with the path of non-capitalist development (Popov, 1977). For their part, multinationals viewed their African operations as marginal to their global strategies, yet were interested in keeping their presence in African markets (Kitchen, 1983).

The role of African entrepreneurs in the post-colonial economy was conditioned by the attitude of the state. A long-term perspective suggests the national bourgeoisie would have had greater interest in the industrialization of African economies than in foreign capital, which lacks permanent roots in the continent. Domestic capital may also have been willing, to some extent, to promote national goals, participate in national politics, pay taxes, invest within the country and generally be more accountable to public interests (Kennedy, 1988). However, at the same time the national bourgeoisie may have been a weak collaborator with foreign capital, being unable to transcend its comprador, or service, role with regard to the metropole. The policies of African states toward the national bourgeoisie reflect these contradictory forces.

Indigenization policy was probably the main instrument employed to create favourable conditions for local capital. To support such policy, foreign capital was banned from certain sectors, and required to maintain a certain minimum level of capitalization, and to sell a specified share of equity to local investors. Government support for indigenous firms also came in the form of access to credit and foreign exchange, allocation of government contracts, and technical training. Given the weakness of African entrepreneurs relative to public enterprises and foreign firms, such supportive policies were needed for a substantial period of time, during which they would have to have been consistently applied. This does not seem to have been the case, with the possible exception of Kenya (Helmsing and Kolste, 1993; Leys 1978). According to Kennedy (1988) African states felt threatened by the prospect of a vigorous national bourgeoisie and were hesitant to allow it to flourish. In addition, the focus by many countries on large prestige projects enhanced dependence on foreign capital and expertise and allowed more room for foreign capital, against which local capital could not compete. While some African entrepreneurs were able to respond by forming partnerships with foreign capital, many remained compradors, and most were confined to the informal economy, which was and is characterized by petty commodity production. Certainly, other factors, such as the harsh

geographic environment of Africa, the influence of pre-capitalist social relations, the continued marginalization of Africa in the world capitalist system,
low urbanization, low per capita income, and what Nurkse (1953) described as
the human tendency to easily emulate the consumption habits rather than the
production habits of advanced countries, have all militated against the emergence of a strong national capitalist class. It is not yet clear whether state policy
or foreign investment played the decisive role in weakening the emergence of
an African capitalist class.

Has independence hurt the economic development prospects of Africa?
Jesperson (1992) maintains that African economies performed reasonably well
in aggregate terms during the 1960s and part of the 1970s. Austen (1987) un-
derscores the problems of the 1970s and the 1980s, and claims that the post-
colonial African economy has been characterized by a weakened position in
the international economy and by domestic failures in both the agricultural
and the industrial sectors. He suggests that "one lesson to be learned from historical contemplation might be that the continent should return to the less
pretentious development modes which prevailed before the unsettling events
of the Great Depression, the Second World War, and decolonization" (p. 258).
Does contemporary structural adjustment signal a return to the international
environment of the 19th century, in the shape of informal empire and colonialism? Is the new world order a repetition of history in a new guise?

III. Structural adjustment and globalization
The combination of the global recession of the early 1980s, the debt crisis, the
political and economic reforms initiated by Gorbachev in the mid-1980s, and
the information technology revolution destroyed the post-Second World War
order. The Soviet bloc collapsed, and the Non-Aligned Movement is defunct
in all but name. Amin (1998) claims that globalization is a euphemistic rendering of imperialism, and a new way in which the inherently imperialist nature
of the world capitalist system asserts itself. This assertion, in the form of contemporary neo-conservatism, expressed itself in developing countries in the
guise of SAPs.

Structural adjustment is a comprehensive and an evolving concept, of
which various definitions and perspectives exist, many predicated on the assumption that adjustment programmes are generated by changes in the inter-

national economic climate. Streeten (1987) defines structural adjustment as the essence of development. Here the concept is cast as "a problem of transition," of modernization and structural transformation. A less broad definition is that of Glover (1991: 174), in which structural adjustment is "a process of deliberately adjusting the structure of an economy to counter adverse shocks or to take advantage of new opportunities arising from internal or external economic shifts." The emphasis is on the response of a country to new economic conditions. He assumes that countries are free players in the global economy, and thus have a menu of choices with which to respond to changes. For Loxley (1986: 26), "the term 'structural adjustment' simply makes more explicit the fact that contemporary stabilization programs frequently imply substantial changes in the direction of the economy, in its sectoral priorities and in its institutional make up."

In practice, structural adjustment is made operational through specific economic policies that the IMF and the World Bank, working in close cooperation, require developing countries to follow in order to access their financial facilities. These policies have three prongs. The first is macroeconomic, and involves fiscal restraint, tight monetary policy, and devaluation. The second is microeconomic, and encompasses trade, price, and financial liberalization. The third is institutional adjustment, and consists of policies such as privatization, improving the business climate and legal arrangements, and governance and civil service reform. These neo-conservative policies are promoted "by the international financial institutions, and the northern governments which control them, to create new regimes of accumulation in the South based on the further internationalization of trade and payments" (Loxley, 1998: 48).

Adjustment programmes mediate the asymmetric relationship between the metropole and the dependent economies. By making local state elites act on behalf of global capital, SAPs have forced African states into the role of a comprador whose task is the provision of local security and markets for a worldwide neo-conservative capitalist order. This is part of a general trend in which the bourgeoisie of the Third World "have abandoned their national plan in 'the spirit of Bandung,' to accept compradorization" (Amin, 1990: 17). A similar view is expressed by Willoughby (1993: 66), who suggests a new institutionalist theory of imperialism. Using the concepts of leading new institutionalists, including Buchanan, Tulloch, and North, he maintains that government and economic elites of the periphery may have come to the conclusion "that the benefits of joining a common legal tradition outweigh the differential benefits they might obtain by discriminating against foreign (and domestic) capitalist agents...it is more rational to dismantle statist interference and share the surplus generated by relatively unrestricted capitalist enterprise" (1993: 66). With its emphasis on foreign investment flows and good governance, the New Partnership for African Development (NEPAD) seems to fit this line of analysis, and hence, is compatible with the neo-conservative agenda.

The issue of structural adjustment in Africa is marginal to the world system when compared to the retreat of Keynesianism in the West and the total reversal of the command economies in eastern Europe. Still, for Africa, the loss of the elbow room it had begun to establish in the international political and economic setting, a loss that emerged because of the demise of the Soviet Union, the decline of the economic left in Europe and North America, the detailed policy conditionalities associated with external indebtedness, and the state's shrinking role in the economy, constitutes a fundamental shock. These changes have important implications for the mix of enterprises and the level of investment in Africa.

Large external indebtedness, privatization, and loss of sovereignty are closely associated. Zeleza (1993) gives an example of one of the most dramatic episodes concerning the consequences of external indebtedness for a dependent economy. In the second half of the 19th century, Egypt found itself in dire financial straits and indebtedness. In 1875, foreshadowing the debt-equity swaps and privatization of the contemporary structural adjustment era, the Egyptian government sold its shares in the Suez Canal Company to Britain for a small fraction of what Egypt had actually spent on the project. The deal not only gave Britain an economic windfall, but also a political and strategic foothold in Egypt. Britain obtained cabinet positions in the Egyptian government, culminating in the colonial status of Egypt in 1882. While the present indebtedness of African countries seems to have been handled with leniency by bilateral lenders through rescheduling and other options offered by the Paris Club, the adverse implications of indebtedness for the sovereignty of African states and their ability to forge national economic policies are obvious.

Privatization and deregulation are perhaps the main institutional reforms that weaken the national state. They have significantly reduced the number of

Table 2 Number of privatization transactions in sub-Saharan Africa

	Up to 1989	1990	1991	1992	1991	1994
Annual	475	328	352	292	275	382
Cumulative	475	803	1155	1447	1722	2104
	1995	**1996**	**1997**	**1998**	**1999**	**2000**
Annual	485	426	241	129	86	67
Cumulative	2589	3015	3256	3385	3471	3538

Source World Bank (2000a, 2002a).

public enterprises, as well as weakened indigenization programmes in Africa. Table 2 shows the extent of privatization in sub-Saharan African countries in the 1980s and 1990s. During this period over 3500 public enterprises were privatized, of which 52 per cent were in the manufacturing and agricultural sectors, followed by services, trade, and finance. The effect of these changes on the configuration of state, local, and foreign investment has implications for the degree of control Africans have over their economies. In the absence of a dynamic African capitalist class, privatization involves the transfer of major national assets to foreign ownership. Such transfers pre-empt the opportunity of Africans to learn to operate large enterprises effectively, and thus diminish the potential for long-term development associated with indigenous entrepreneurs. While we must note the potential role of foreign investment in the transfer of technology, management, and marketing techniques, its contribution to African development has been minimal historically. This is because it has tended to focus on extractive industries with limited linkages to the rest of the national economy, has usually been import-intensive, and has been combined with a significant capital outflow.

What has been the impact of structural adjustment on the rate of capital formation? The World Bank and the IMF seek to decrease public investment in the hope that privatization and other components of adjustment policies lead to a surge in private investment that more than offsets the decline in public investment. The available data on domestic private investment and public investment in Africa are sparse and incomplete. Nevertheless, some observa-

Table 3 Average domestic investment as a percentage of GDP in sub-Saharan Africa, 1970-2000

	1970-1975	1976-1981	1982-1985	1986-1990	1991-1995	1996-2000
Private investment	12.64	12.76	9.75	10.28	10.0	11.4
Public investment	10.24	12.35	8.9	9.14	9.0	8.0˙
Total investment	22.88	25.1	18.6	19.42	19.0	19.12

Source Calculated from Everhart and Sumlinski (2002).

tions can be made from Table 3 about the trends in domestic investment for the period between 1970 and 2000. The table presents the averages of private, public, and total domestic investment as a percentage of GDP for 12 sub-Saharan African countries. The data indicate a declining trend in total domestic investment over the three decades. The average share of total domestic investment in GDP during the 1970s was 24 per cent, declining to 19 per cent in both the 1980s and 1990s. The corresponding values for private domestic investment in these periods are 12.7 per cent, 10 per cent, and 10.7 per cent. The figures for public investment are 11.3 per cent, 9 per cent, and 8 per cent. Clearly, the decline in public investment has not been replaced by sufficient increases in private investment. In fact, both have declined over the adjustment period, and the rates of investment in the pre-adjustment period are generally higher than those in the adjustment era.

Table 4 shows foreign direct investment (FDI) flows to sub-Saharan African countries, all developing countries, and the world for the period between 1980 and 2000. We can glean from the data that in absolute terms FDI flows to Africa have increased over time. However, Africa's share in overall flows is small and has declined over this period. Columns 6 and 7 in Table 4 show FDI flows to sub-Saharan Africa as a percentage of worldwide FDI flows and FDI flows into developing regions, respectively. Africa's share in total FDI flows declined from 1.8 per cent in the first half of the 1980s to 0.7 per cent in the second half of the 1990s. Africa's share of FDI flows to developing countries declined from 7.1 per cent to 2.7 per cent over the same period. The last two columns of Table 4 compare the share of FDI in gross fixed capital formation in sub-

Saharan Africa and in all developing countries. This share is consistently higher in Africa than in other developing regions. The data in Table 4 imply two apparently contradictory patterns. The first is that even though absolute FDI flows have an upward trend, the declining share of the flow to Africa points to the continued marginalization of Africa in the world capitalist system. The second is that, despite the marginalization of Africa, the relative role of FDI in capital formation in Africa has increased. This may be associated with the decline of domestic investment in Africa as shown in Table 3, as well as by the absolute increase in FDI flows to Africa as shown in Table 4. In an empirical investigation of the impact of FDI flows on domestic investment in developing countries, Agosin and Mayer (2000) found that FDI has a crowding-in effect in Asian countries, a crowding-out effect in Latin American countries, and the results for Africa were mixed. Of the 12 African countries included in their investigation, three experienced crowding in, and in the remaining nine countries the impact of FDI on domestic investment was either neutral or resulted in crowding out. The increased prominence of FDI in gross investment in Africa, relative to other developing regions, may indicate the fragility of African capitalists in the new environment created by structural adjustment. Domestic African enterprises may have lost out to foreign investment as governments abandoned Africanization programmes, and liberalization and de-

Table 4 Average FDI inward flow in billions of US dollars, and shares in per cent, 1980-2000

	US$, billions			per cent				
Periods	World	DCE	SSA	DCE/World	SSA/World	SSA/DCE	DCE/GFC	SSA/GFC
80-85	48.9	12.6	0.9	25.3	1.8	7.1	4.2	4.7
86-91	159.3	29.1	1.7	18.2	1.1	5.8	3.4	6.7
92-95	251.9	81.9	2.7	33.9	1.1	3.3	6.3	11
96-00	780.2	198.1	5.3	28.4	0.7	2.7	11.4	15.6

DCE = Developing Countries and Economies, SSA = sub-Saharan Africa,
GFC = Gross fixed capital formation
Source Calculated from United Nations (1992, 1998, and 2001).

regulation allowed multinational firms to use their long-established strengths to become prominent in African markets.

In the first two decades of the post-independence period, African states promoted nationalization and indigenization policies without abandoning close cooperation with foreign enterprises. The present circumstances, however, resemble the economic model that prevailed before the epoch of decolonization, a return to which Austen (1987) recommended. In the 19th century African economies were dominated by foreign firms and African petty commodity producers, while African states were non-existent or weak. Currently African states have been weakened due to both adjustment programmes (Riddell, 1992) and the narrowing of their manoeuvring room in the world system. However, the ascendant position of foreign investment in Africa could be beneficial if it results in the "fortification and diversification" of African economies (Warren, 1980). It remains to be seen if reinvigorated imperialism—the penetration of international capital into Africa—will end the marginalization of the continent in the world capitalist system. It is also possible that, instead of leading to sustained capitalist development, this reinvigorated imperialism will preserve non-capitalist modes of production and rigidify African countries into primary commodity-producing economies. Such an outcome will restrain the forces that could shoulder sustained capital accumulation—African entrepreneurs—by restricting them to comprador roles or confining them to the petty commodity-production sector.

IV. Conclusion

The degree of autonomy and dependency of African economies and the role of the forces of capital accumulation have fluctuated with the phases of world capitalism. African states and local private enterprises experienced the greatest autonomy in the immediate decades following political independence. The main economic aspiration then was to transform African economies from dependency on raw materials, and, therefore, vulnerability to fluctuations in metropolitan demands, to an economic structure with an appropriate balance among primary, manufacturing, and service sectors. During this period the strength of national liberation movements and the existence of a world socialist camp allowed African countries a space in which to build economies based on state capitalism and/or a national bourgeoisie by partially disengaging themselves from the world capitalist system. This period was not long enough nor the policies of African countries sufficiently conducive for the creation of strong domestic or regional economies. Contemporary structural adjustment is the repeal of the opportunity of partial disengagement from the world capitalist system, of state capitalism, and of import substitution. Structural adjustment calls for export promotion based on comparative advantage, and, therefore, reliance on the production of cash crops, mineral extraction, and natural resource exploitation. Under this neo-conservative economic model, the future of modern enterprise in Africa may be confined to the primary sector, as it was before the 1960s, and with greater room for multinationals than would have been imaginable during the years following political independence.

The current fear and hope of Africans with regard to foreign investment in particular and their relation to the capitalist core in general is perhaps best expressed by two initiatives that came into focus in the year 2002. In June of that year African leaders representing NEPAD met the leaders of the G7 countries and reached an agreement to work together. In July African leaders met in Durban, South Africa, to transform the 40-year-old Organization of African Unity into an African Union (AU). Even though all African countries were participants in both processes, the emphasis of the two initiatives differed in that the promoters of the AU stressed the need to strengthen African sovereignty and power in the world system, while NEPAD stressed economic issues and cooperation with the Western industrialized countries. The AU initiative was lead by African leaders who may be described as still belonging to the Bandung project era, while the promoters of NEPAD were African leaders who more or less accepted the neo-conservative new world order. In Durban the NEPAD agenda dominated the inaugural meeting of the AU, and the original promoters of the AU were sidelined. The meeting adopted NEPAD as a blueprint for Africa's economic development, thus signalling the official triumph of neo-conservatism over the Bandung spirit in the continent. The triumph of the NEPAD initiative is, however, countered by strong criticism by African academics and non-governmental organizations who see in NEPAD a futile dependence on external financial resources and a repeat of SAPs under a new name (Nkrumah, 2002). For now, most African leaders have decided to make the AU and NEPAD complementary rather than competitive institutions. They are, no doubt, hoping that NEPAD might just create the right mix of FDI, domestic investment, and state involvement that would help Africa open a new chapter in its history of development. The circumstances under which such a hope may materialize is a topic for further research.

Chapter 5

STAGFLATIONARY DEVALUATION IN SUB-SAHARAN AFRICA: A REVIEW OF THE EMPIRICAL EVIDENCE

Zelealem Yiheyis

I. Introduction

EXCHANGE rate adjustment, in the form of devaluation, has been increasingly included as one of the key policy measures in neo–conservative economic reform packages designed to better manage the balance of payments. This has been the case especially in those countries undertaking structural adjustment and stabilization programmes sponsored by the World Bank and the International Monetary Fund (IMF). Since the primary objective of devaluation is to regain or enhance external competitiveness and thereby strengthen the balance of payments in general and the trade account in particular, its effectiveness in the past has been gauged largely by the performance of the external sector. However, it has become increasingly clear that devaluation can have adverse consequences for domestic macroeconomic activity (Cooper, 1971; Krugman and Taylor, 1978; Lizondo and Montiel, 1989).

The possible adverse effect of devaluation on aggregate economic activity is known as the "contractionary devaluation" hypothesis. There has also been a growing concern that devaluation could engender inflation to the extent of undermining its effectiveness in promoting macroeconomic stabilization. The stagflationary hypothesis, which postulates a simultaneous occurrence of output contraction and inflation in the short run, emerges from models constructed in the new structuralist tradition (Bruno, 1979; Taylor, 1979, 1981; Van Wijinbergen, 1986). They support the stagflationary hypothesis under certain structural assumptions, including, but not limited to, sluggish supply response, real wage rigidity, dependence on imported inputs, and credit constraints. This

85

contrasts with the traditional view, which, under the assumptions of excess capacity and expenditure switching, shows devaluation to be expansionary (Kenen, 1985). In models that assume pre-existing exchange controls with active parallel markets, both the contractionary and inflationary effects of devaluation tend to be smaller (Kamin, 1995; Nowak, 1984; World Bank, 1994a; Younger, 1992).

The theoretical ambiguity of the effect of devaluation on domestic macroeconomic activity suggests that whether devaluation is stagflationary is an empirical question, to be answered by looking at the experiences of countries with respect to exchange rate adjustment. A growing body of empirical literature addresses this issue in the context of developing countries. The purpose of this chapter is to review the empirical evidence from sub-Saharan Africa (SSA). African economies are a fitting economic environment for testing the stagflationary hypothesis for a number of reasons. First, many countries in the region launched devaluations or otherwise adjusted their exchange rates over the last couple of decades. Second, many of the devaluing countries in the region share most of the structural features that produce, or enhance the likelihood of, a stagflationary outcome. Third, the region, which is otherwise similar in major structural features, comprises countries where the parity of the exchange rate was maintained for an extended period of time, such as the CFA Franc Zone, as well as countries where exchange rate adjustments occurred. The final reason is the backdrop against which devaluations were implemented in the region. In large part, changes in exchange rate policy in the non-CFA Franc Zone were increasingly instituted against a background of severe exchange controls and overvalued nominal exchange rates. They were introduced in response to, or during, economic stagnation and decline. Devaluations were also, of course, launched under external pressure, as a component of stabilization and structural adjustment programmes (Lipumba, 1992).[1] Therefore, examining and characterizing the effects of devaluation will also contribute to our understanding of the working and effects of structural adjustment and stabilization programmes.

The present review focusses on relatively recent and cross-country studies that examined the output and inflationary effects of devaluation at the aggregate level. The balance of the available evidence does not lend consistent and strong support to the stagflationary hypothesis. Inflation does indeed tend to follow devaluation, although the size and duration of the effect have been such that nominal devaluations were translated into real depreciation. Also, in spite of real depreciation, consistent expansion in aggregate output has not materialized, as was argued by the proponents of devaluation. At the same time, however there is little evidence that devaluation was contractionary. Devaluation thus appears to have been neutral in its effect on output performance in SSA.

II. Stagflationary devaluation: evidence from sub-Saharan Africa

An increasing number of sub-Saharan African countries launched currency devaluations in the 1980s and 1990s, mostly as part of neo-conservative stabilization and structural adjustment programmes (World Bank, 1994). The principal objective of the exchange rate adjustment was to improve the balance of payments. At issue here is not whether devaluation was successful in attaining the officially stated objective, but whether the empirical evidence indicates that in the process it adversely influenced domestic economic activity.

A variety of estimating approaches has been employed to generate the empirical evidence, including the before-after approach, the with-without approach, and more traditional econometric methods (Goldstein and Montiel, 1986; Khan, 1990). The before-after approach examines the effects of devaluation episodes and compares the performance of a given indicator before and after the policy change. The with-without, otherwise referred to as the control group approach, compares the before-after change in the behaviour of an indicator between the devaluing and non-devaluing countries. A variation of this approach compares the performance of devaluing and non-devaluing economies after controlling for each group's initial conditions. Econometric methods directly test the effect of exchange rate adjustments on variables of interest. Each of these approaches is used in the studies examined below.

i. Aggregate output

Various kinds of output indicators have been used to examine the effect of devaluation on aggregate economic activity, including the level of real gross domestic product (GDP), and the growth rates of real GDP and per capita real GDP. Table 1 summarizes the empirical evidence from a number of cross-country studies on the effect of devaluation on aggregate output. We consider first findings based on the before-after and control-group approaches. Kamin

(1988) examined devaluations that resulted in at least a 15 per cent depreciation in the nominal exchange rate. He calculated the time profile of performance indicators over three years prior to, and four years after, devaluation and
compared them—both over a short- and long-run horizon—with the average performance indicator of the entire sample for the corresponding comparison period. There was little evidence that significant contractions in output
followed devaluations. However, devaluations were typically preceded by recessions. Similarly, Yiheyis (1997b), constructing a seven-year time profile and
applying the before-after approach, found no consistent evidence of contractionary devaluation in his investigation of 24 episodes with a yearly cumulative
depreciation of at least 14 per cent in the nominal external value of domestic
currencies. Finally, Mosely and Weeks (1993) compared the growth rates of
real GDP in countries where the real effective exchange rate appreciated with
those where it depreciated over a 10-year period. They reported a differential
of 1.2 percentage points in favour of the 11 countries with depreciated real
exchange rates. The difference, however, was statistically insignificant.

Although the before-after approach is valuable to characterize the devaluation process and to identify the stylized facts surrounding devaluation episodes,
its results are questionable. When applied to historical data, the approach tends
to attribute changes in the behaviour of the response variable solely to variation in the exchange rate, without explicit and adequate consideration of the
evolution of other factors that may influence the outcome of devaluation. The
findings thus obtained would not necessarily correctly estimate the effects of
devaluation if, indeed, other determinants of output changed along with the
exchange rate. In fact, the outcome ascribed to devaluation might have been
obtained without a change in the exchange rate. This criticism is especially valid because devaluation is more often than not implemented as a component of
stabilization and structural adjustment programmes involving changes, among
others, in fiscal, monetary, and commercial policies, which reinforce or offset
the effect of devaluation.

To minimize the weakness of the before-after approach while retaining its
merits, Yiheyis (1997b) estimated a regression model and removed the combined effects of major, relevant, explanatory variables other than the exchange
rate. The results are broadly consistent with those based on the actual data,
pointing to little evidence of contractionary effect. However, larger devalua-

Table 1 Summary of Cross-Country Studies on the Output Effects of Devaluation

Author(s)	Coverage	Model and Method	Findings and Conclusions
Agénor (1991)	23 countries including nine from SSA: Burundi, Cameroon, Gabon, Malawi, Nigeria, Sierra Leone, Togo, Zaire, and Zambia. Pooled data, 1978-87.	Econometric model. Y: real GDP X: Unanticipated movements in the RER, the money supply, government spending, and in foreign economic activity, the actual RER, and time trend. Fixed-effect procedure. IV method.	An anticipated depreciation of the RER has a negative effect while unanticipated depreciation exerts a positive effect, the former at a higher level of significance than the latter. The contractionary effect persisted even after a year.
Bleaney and Greenaway (2001)	Botswana, Burkina Faso, Cameroon, Cote d'Ivoire, The Gambia, Ghana, Kenya, Malawi, Mauritius, Niger, Senegal, Tanzania, Togo and Zimbabwe. Pooled data, 1980-95.	Econometric model. Y: real GDP growth rate. X: lagged real GDP, TT, change in TT lagged, TT volatility, RER misalignment lagged, and RER volatility. Fixed-effect procedure. OLS estimates.	RER misalignment exerts a statistically significant delayed (once-lagged) negative effect. The impact of RER volatility is negative, but highly insignificant.
Cottani et al., (1990)	24 developing countries including six from SSA: Ethiopia, Malawi, Mali, Somalia, Sudan and Zambia. Pooled data, 1960-83.	Econometric model. Y: Per capita GDP growth rate. X: RER instability and RER misalignment indices.	Both RER misalignment and instability have statistically significant negative effects. This is interpreted to suggest that the two variables are empirically distinct as regards their relation to growth.
Dordunoo and Njinkeu (1997)	12 countries. Burkina Faso, Cameroon, Congo, Cote d'Ivoire, Gabon and Senegal from the CFA zone; Ghana, Kenya, Madagascar, Nigeria, Tanzania and Zambia from the rest of SSA. Pooled data, 1973-93.	Econometric Model. Y: Growth of per capita real GDP X: initial per capita real GDP—level and squared—terms of trade, total debt, investment, openness, exchange-rate regime, convertibility index, growth rate in neighboring countries. Results of the random-effects procedure presented.	The growth performances of the two groups of countries (CFA and non-CFA countries) are comparable. The exchange-rate regime variable is statistically significant only in a version of the model where currency convertibility index is included.

Note Y=dependent variable, X=Explanatory variable, TT=terms of trade, RER=Real exchange rate, IV=Instrumental variable, OLS=ordinary least squares, 2SLS=two stage least squares.

Table 1 Summary of Cross-Country Studies on the Output Effects of Devaluation (continued)

Author(s)	Coverage	Model and Method	Findings and Conclusions
Elbadawi and Majd (1996)	11 CFA Franc Zone countries versus 18 other SSA countries. Pooled data, 1973-89.	Modified Control Group approach. Compares the average annual growth rates of real GDP of the two groups of countries over two time horizons.	By short-run comparison (1986-89 vs 1982-85) non-CFA countries outperformed CFA countries in output performance. A long-run comparison (1982-89 vs 1973-81) reversed the relative performance, which, however, was statistically insignificant.
Faini (1994)	Ghana, Kenya, Malawi, Senegal and Zambia. Country-specific and pooled data, 1980-88.	Econometric model. Y: Real GDP X: Investment, RER (current and lagged), real GDP lagged. OLS and IV estimates supplied.	Although small in magnitude, contemporaneous devaluation has a statistically significant positive effect. The lagged effect is negative, albeit less significantly.
Ghura and Grennes (1993)	33 SSA countries. Pooled data, 1972-87.	Econometric model. Y: Per capita real GDP growth rate. X: RER misalignment and instability indices, investment to GDP ratio, population growth, TT growth. IV estimates supplied.	Misalignment of the RER exerts a statistically significant adverse effect. RER instability has a negative effect, but it is significant only when misalignment is not controlled for.
Kamin (1988)	Developing countries including 13 from SSA: Botswana, Burundi, Ghana, Kenya, Lesotho, Rwanda, Sierra Leone, Somalia, South Africa, Sudan, Swaziland, Tanzania, and Zambia. Selected years of devaluation, 1953-83.	Comparing real GDP growth between devaluing countries and the entire sample before and after devaluation episodes, by constructing a seven-year time profile—three years before and three years after devaluation. Sixty devaluations examined.	An increase in output growth in absolute terms in subsequent years, resulting in relative improvement. While recessions typically preceded devaluation episodes, little evidence that they were contractionary.
Khan (1990)	69 developing countries including SSA countries. 1973-88.	Modified Control Group approach. Compares the growth performance of IMF programme and non-programme countries.	Statistically insignificant negative effect on output growth rates.

Note Y=dependent variable, X=Explanatory variable, TT=terms of trade, RER=Real exchange rate, IV=Instrumental variable, OLS=ordinary least squares, 2SLS=two stage least squares.

Author(s)	Coverage	Model and Method	Findings and Conclusions
Mosely and Weeks (1993)	28 SSA countries. 1980-90.	Real GDP growth compared on the basis of the direction of change of the real effective exchange rate.	Countries whose real exchange rate appreciated averaged a growth rate of 2.2 per cent while those who had a depreciated exchange rate grew at 3.4 per cent. The difference was not statistically significant, however.
Nwanna (1987)	20 LDCs including 10 from SSA: Ethiopia, Ghana, Kenya, Malawi, Sierra Leone, Sudan, Tanzania, Togo, Zaire. Pooled data, 1960-85.	Econometric model. Y: Real GDP. X: Rate of change of nominal exchange rate-inflation rate (current and lagged), actual inflation rate- expected inflation rate, real GDP in industrial countries, lagged. 2SLS estimates.	Statistically significant negative contemporaneous effect. The decomposition of the sample into low-income economies (all of which are from SSA) and upper-middle income countries indicates that the negative effect is larger and persistent among the former. For the other group, the lagged effect was significantly positive.
Rouis, et al. (1994)	22 SSA countries. Pooled data, 1971-91	Econometric model. Y: Per capita real GDP growth rate. X : Initial income, investment rate, life expectancy at birth, rate of change in RER at past prices, inflation resulting from nominal devaluations. 2SLS estimates.	The coefficient of the RER is insignificantly positive while that of the 'inflation resulting from devaluation' is significantly negative. The null hypothesis that the sum of the two effects is zero was not rejected, interpreted to suggest a neutral effect of real depreciation when controlling for the effect of inflation.
Yiheyis (1997b)	Botswana, Burundi, The Gambia, Ghana, Kenya, Madagascar, Malawi, Mauritius, Sierra Leone. Selected years of devaluation, 1978-89.	Real GDP growth compared before and after devaluation episodes. Time profile of real GDP growth, both for actual and adjusted data, constructed over seven years—three years before and three years after devaluation. 24 episodes examined.	On average, little evidence of contractionary effect. However, the effect is susceptible, among others, to initial conditions and to the size of the devaluation. Devaluation was more expansionary where it was launched against a background of economic slack and more contractionary elsewhere. Larger devaluations tended to generate more discernable positive effects than smaller adjustments.

tions and those implemented during or following a recession were more expansionary than others. This approach is an improvement over the before-after method that uses unadjusted data except for the implicit assumption that the only relevant variable that the specified regression model excluded was the exchange rate.

In a similar vein, Mosely and Weeks (1993) demonstrated the importance of real exchange rate depreciation by controlling for trade liberalization and participation status in structural adjustment programmes. Those liberalizing countries with depreciated real exchange rates grew at the higher rate of 3.8 per cent than those countries without depreciation, which grew at 1.2 per cent. Grouping countries on the basis of their participation status in structural adjustment programmes, Mosely and Weeks found that the adjusting countries, which saw their real exchange rate appreciate and their public capital expenditure decline, grew at a much slower rate than non-adjusting countries with depreciated real exchange rates and increased public capital expenditure. The growth rate differential was 5.5 percentage points. They concluded that the depreciation of the real exchange rate was the key movement required for the success of adjustment and recovery in the region.

While the use of the control-group approach avoids the weakness of comparing before-after changes in historical data, it has its own limitations. Implicit in the use of this approach is the assumption that devaluing and non-devaluing countries experienced similar economic conditions prior to the devaluation so that the difference in economic performance between the two groups can be attributed to devaluation episodes. This assumption is valid if members in either group are selected randomly. However, as Khan (1990: 203) argues in the context of IMF stabilization programmes, of which devaluation is typically a part, programme countries "are adversely selected in the sense of having relatively poor economic performance prior to the program period." This argument can also apply to exchange rate adjustments that are independently administered. Thus, in the presence of systematic differences, prior to devaluation, between the control group and devaluing countries, the approach is bound to yield a biased estimate (Goldstein and Montiel, 1986; Khan, 1990). This recognition has led to the development of the "generalized evaluation estimator," which is the control-group approach modified to reflect possible differences in initial conditions between treatment and control groups.

Khan (1990) employed this method and found that the real effective exchange rate had no statistically significant effect on growth rate changes in one-year and two-year comparisons between IMF-supported and non-supported countries. The output effect of devaluation may also be inferred from a comparative assessment of the performance of CFA Franc Zone countries and other SSA economies, the former serving as the control group. Thus, Elbadawi and Majid (1996)—employing the modified control-group approach and correcting for bias in sample selectivity resulting from the non-random nature of zone participation—reported that CFA countries were outperformed by the rest of SSA where nominal exchange rates were adjusted, suggesting that devaluation was expansionary. This was, however, true only when the performance of the two groups of countries was compared over a period of three years. When the comparison horizon was extended to roughly seven years, the growth performance of the two groups differed in favour of the Franc Zone, although the differential was statistically insignificant.

In addition to the before-after and control-group approaches, econometric methods have been used to directly test the output effect of exchange rate changes. The econometric models specified and estimated differ not only in their lists of control variables and estimation methods, but also in their representations of the dependent and the principal explanatory variables of interest. For example, Faini (1994) specified the level of real GDP to depend on the contemporaneous and once-lagged values of the real exchange rate, with other two control variables. He reported a small, but statistically significant, positive short-run effect. The delayed effect was negative, although at a lower level of significance. Nwana (1987) estimated a Lucas-type supply function in which the level of real GDP depends, among other factors, on the current and lagged percentage changes of the real exchange rate. The estimating procedure postulates a differential response to economic shocks by low-income and upper-middle-income economies and the sample countries are categorized accordingly. It was observed that the short run effect of real depreciation is negative for the entire sample and appeared to have turned positive only in the long run. A comparative analysis of the effects on the two groups of countries seemed to indicate that the contractionary effect of devaluation is not only greater in magnitude but also tends to last longer in low-income countries, all of which are from SSA, than in the upper-middle-income economies. The differential response is attributed to differences between the two groups, *inter alia*, in the size and operation of financial markets, resource base, and agricultural productivity.

The output effect of devaluation was examined under explicit assumptions of macroeconomic equilibrium and rational expectations by Agénor (1991). He developed a model derived from aggregate supply-and-demand equations and estimated it by distinguishing between anticipated and unanticipated changes in the explanatory variables, including the real exchange rate. The author found that anticipated depreciation of the real exchange rate adversely affected real GDP, as opposed to unanticipated depreciation, which was expansionary. His results also suggest that the contractionary effect persisted beyond the first year of devaluation, as reflected in the statistically significant negative sign of the coefficient of a one-period-lagged real exchange rate.

In other models, the hypothesis of contractionary devaluation is tested with the growth rate of per capita real GDP as the response variable. For example, Rouis et al. (1994) specified an endogenous growth model augmented to include the rate of depreciation of the real exchange rate as a determinant of total factor productivity. The rate of real depreciation of the real exchange rate is comprised of two components: the change of the real exchange rate measured at past prices; and a component capturing inflation resulting from nominal devaluations. The estimated coefficient on the first component is positive, albeit statistically insignificant. On the other hand, the term that includes the domestic rate of inflation is significantly negative. A statistical test failed to reject, at the five per cent level of significance, the null hypothesis that the sum of the two coefficients was zero. This suggests that real depreciations are neutral with respect to the growth rate of per capita real GDP in the transition to the steady state, when controlling for the effects of inflation. However, the authors acknowledge that the exclusion of monetary and fiscal variables from the model makes it difficult to isolate the effect of real depreciation on the dependent variable. Applying the Granger causality test, the same study documents the absence of a causal relationship between output and devaluation.

The output consequences of exchange rate policy have also been evaluated by representing the latter by the extent of exchange rate misalignment, which is measured as a percentage deviation of the official exchange rate from its equilibrium counterpart. To the degree that devaluation removes, or reduces the extent of, exchange rate misalignment—which is a measure of the extent of overvaluation of the official exchange rate—a statistically significant association between output performance and the misalignment index would point to expansionary devaluation. In a model where the misalignment and volatility of the real exchange rate are the explanatory variables, Cottani, Cavallo, and Khan (1990) found both variables to have exerted a deleterious effect on the growth rate of per capita real GDP. Similarly, but controlling for more output-determining variables and using three alternative measures of real exchange rate misalignment, including the parallel currency premium, Ghura and Grennes (1993) found that real exchange rate misalignment and its volatility exerted negative effects when each variable sequentially entered the regression equation. However, when the model was estimated with the two variables included, neither turned out to be statistically different from zero, questioning the empirical distinctness of the two variables observed by Cottani et al. Utilizing more recent data, but with the growth rate of real GDP as the response variable and with an expanded set of controls, Bleaney and Greenaway (2001) documented that real exchange rate misalignment negatively influenced output growth, and real exchange rate volatility had no discernable effect.

An implication for output growth may also be drawn from the study conducted by Dordunoo and Njinkeu (1997). They estimated a growth equation on data drawn from CFA and non-CFA countries with a dummy variable representing the exchange rate regime of the two groups of countries. To the degree that one group maintained the parity of its nominal exchange rate while the other adjusted it, the effect of devaluation might be evident from the estimates of the dummy variable coefficient. In their study, the regime dummy was insignificant except in models with controls for the currency convertibility index, suggesting the neutrality of devaluation with respect to growth performance. The validity of this interpretation, however, depends partly on the plausibility of the implicit assumption that exchange rate arrangements and practices in the non-CFA countries are homogeneous.

Obviously, the econometric evidence presented above enables one to disentangle the *ceteris paribus* effect of the explanatory variable of interest. Equally plain, though, is the fact that the adequacy of the estimated coefficient in representing the *ceteris paribus* effect, both in sign as well as numerical and statisti-

95

cal significance, depends on whether the regression model was correctly specified and appropriate estimating procedures were employed. Given the fact that
devaluation in the region was, in large part, implemented as one of the components of reform packages, isolating the effect of exchange rate policy would
require controlling for as many relevant variables as possible. Further, econometric evidence based on the real exchange rate as the explanatory variable
is at best suggestive of the effect of discrete, large devaluation episodes. Real
exchange rates tend to fluctuate over time, although exceptional swings are
to be expected during devaluation. Moreover, since devaluations are typically
large and discrete events, "their influence, particularly, as regards expectations,
may differ qualitatively from slower, more routine exchange-rate adjustments"
(Kamin, 1988: 3). Even if the devaluations are small and periodic adjustments,
the real exchange rate, as an endogenous variable, reflects and represents the
outcome of the policy change and not the policy change itself. With the real
exchange rate as the explanatory variable, one cannot directly read off the output effect of nominal devaluation; rather, one would infer what the effect of
the policy change might be by supposing that the movement of the real exchange rate was caused by the nominal devaluation.

ii.   Real exchange rates and inflation

Whether nominal devaluation will be dissipated by induced inflation has been
a subject of controversy. In fact, one of the reasons why authorities in the region resisted devaluation in spite of overvalued exchange rates is said to be
the fear of inflation and scepticism about achieving real depreciation (Gulhati,
Bose, and Atukorala 1986; Helleiner, 1994; Kimei, 1992; Loxley, 1986, 1989).
By assessing the impact of nominal devaluation on the real exchange rate, one
can draw the implications of the policy change for output and price adjustment under certain assumptions. For a nominal devaluation to generate a favourable real effect, both on the competitiveness of the external sector and
on the economy as a whole, it should be translated into real depreciation.
Provided that output and real depreciation are positively related, a nominal
devaluation that induced the latter would be expansionary. Given the foreign
price level, the magnitude of price adjustment relative to nominal devaluation
can also be inferred from the evidence on real exchange rate effects. However,
the limitations of the various estimating approaches also apply to the empirical

Table 2 Summary of Cross-Country Studies on Price and
Real Exchange Rate Effects

Author (s)	Coverage	Model and Method	Findings and Conclusions
Canto and Greene (1991)	The Gambia, Ghana, Kenya, Nigeria, Sierra Leone, Somalia, Tanzania, Uganda, Zaire, and Zambia. Quarterly time-series data, 1978-89, for most countries.	Vector Autoregression model. Causality tests conducted in bivariate and trivariate settings, the latter including monetary growth in addition to the rates of change in the CPI and the nominal exchange rate. Decomposition of the variance of the forecast error of inflation and impulse response functions were also used to examine the relationships among the variables.	Statistically significant inflationary effect recorded (at the conventional significance level of five per cent) for Kenya, Sierra Leone and Zaire according to bivariate Granger causality tests. Fewer cases reported when monetary growth was accounted for (Sierra Leone, and Zaire). In most of the sample, neither the exchange rate nor money played a dominant role in explaining innovations in the CPI.
Elbadawi and Majid (1996)	11 CFA Franc Zone countries versus 18 other SSA countries. Pooled data, 1973-89.	Modified Control Group approach. Compares the average rates of inflation between the two groups of countries over two time horizons.	By short-run comparison (1986-89 vs 1982-85) CFA countries enjoyed a lower inflation rate than non-CFA countries. The differential persisted in the long run (1982-89 vs 1973-81) in favor of CFA, but it was statistically insignificant.
Elbadawi and Soto (1997)	Seven developing countries including four from SSA: Cote d' Ivoire, Ghana, Kenya, and Mali. Country-specific, time series data, 1960-94, where available.	Econometric error-correction model. Y: RER X: nominal exchange rate, current, lagged and lead; changes in openness, TT (current and lagged), long term capital inflows (current and lagged), government consumption, public investment, foreign interest rate and short term capital inflow.	The contemporaneous effect is significantly positive in Kenya and Cote d' Ivoire (0.37 and 0.43, respectively), but it is significantly negative in Mali (-0.65). In Ghana, anticipated devaluation exerted a positive effect while the contemporaneous and lagged effects were negative (as mentioned in the authors' discussion of results.)
Faini (1994)	Ghana, Kenya, Malawi, Senegal and Zambia. Country-specific and pooled data, 1980-88.	Econometric model. Y: Inflation X: Rate of change in the nominal exchange rate, wage rate, money supply, and capacity utilization, proxied by a deviation of output from its trend. OLS and IV estimates supplied.	Devaluation is inflationary, but its long-run impact is not large. The official exchange rate lost explanatory power when its parallel counterpart was included in the inflation equation for Ghana, where the author felt the inflation process was different from the rest of the sample.

Note Y=dependent variable, X=Explanatory variable, TT=terms of trade, RER=real exchange rate, CPI=consumer price index, IV=Instrumental variable, OLS=ordinary least squares.

Table 2 Summary of Cross-Country Studies on Price and Real Exchange-Rate Effects (continued)

Author (s)	Coverage	Model and Method	Findings and Conclusions
Ghura and Grennes (1993)	33 SSA countries. Pooled data, 1972-87.	Econometric model. Y: RER X: Rate of change in nominal exchange rate, TT, degree of openness, capital inflow, excess domestic credit.	Nominal devaluation has a statistically significant positive effect on RER, with a parameter estimate of .291, suggesting that nominal devaluation results in real depreciation.
Kamin (1988)	Developing countries including 13 from SSA: Botswana, Burundi, Ghana, Kenya, Lesotho, Rwanda, Sierra Leone, Somalia, South Africa, Sudan, Swaziland, Tanzania, and Zambia. Selected years of devaluation, 1953-83.	Comparing the inflation rate between devaluing countries and the entire sample before and after devaluation episodes, by constructing a seven-year time profile—three years before and three years after devaluation. 74 episodes examined. Differences in inflation performance were subjected to binomial-sign test and t-test.	Marked increase in the short run. More or less stable in the second half of the period relative to the comparison group, suggesting small long-run inflationary effect.
London (1989)	23 African countries. Annual data, 1974-85.	Econometric Model, Y: Rate of Inflation. X: Changes in the bilateral exchange rate, rate of monetary expansion, growth rate of real income, change in the expected rate of inflation. Methods include cross-sectional analysis of period averages.	Statistically insignificant positive effect for the study period as a whole. Statistically significant effect observed for the sub-period 1980-85.
Odedokun (1997)	32 SSA countries of which 10 are from CFA zone. Quarterly pooled data: 1980:1 to 1991:4.	Econometric Model. Y: Rate of inflation. X: Rates of depreciation of effective official and parallel exchange rates, effective import price inflation, monetary growth, lagged Y. Current and lagged values of X variables used.	Both the official and parallel exchange rates have a statistically significant positive effect on inflation in 13 of the non-CFA countries. The sum of the effects (current and lagged) is larger for the parallel rate than for the official (0.34 vs. 0.19). For CFA countries, the effect of the official rate is insignificant. The parallel rate has a positive effect but smaller than reported for the non-CFA group.
Rouis et al. (1994)	22 SSA countries. Pooled data, 1971-91	Granger causality test between devaluation and inflation.	Inflation Granger-causes devaluation, not the other way around.

Note Y=dependent variable, X=Explanatory variable, TT=terms of trade, RER=real exchange rate, CPI=consumer price index, IV=Instrumental variable, OLS=ordinary least squares.

Author (s)	Coverage	Model and Method	Findings and Conclusions
Rouis et al. (1994) Razzak (1995)	20 SSA countries. Pooled data, 1971-91.	Econometric model. Y: rate of RER depreciation. X: lagged Y (capital), rate of nominal devaluation, current and three times lagged, inflation tax, monetary growth at past prices, and interest rate, proxied by change in inflation, lagged. 2SLS estimates.	The contemporaneous effect is significantly positive. A 10 per cent nominal devaluation leads to an 8.8 per cent real depreciation. Lagged effects are negative, but small and all but one statistically insignificant. The combined effect is different from zero: a 10 per cent devaluation translated into a 7.7 per cent real depreciation in the long run.
Shafaeddin (1992)	60 developing countries including 25 from Africa. 1980-87.	Comparing inflation performance as well as the "effectiveness of nominal devaluation" index, which is the ratio of percent changes in RER and nominal exchange rate, across four income groups over two periods.	During the first year, nominal devaluation translated to real devaluation at a ratio of 30 to 74 per cent. It was most effective in the highest income group, followed by the lowest. With time, devaluation's effectiveness eroded, but relatively at a faster rate in the lowest income group.
Shafaeddin (1993)	58 developing countries of which 25 are from Africa. 1980-87.	Comparing inflation performance by classifying countries according to level of development and the extent of import shortages.	The inflationary effect of devaluation depends on the extent of import shortages. Those countries that suffered the most from import shortage had the highest inflationary effect.
Yiheyis (1997b)	Botswana, Burundi, The Gambia, Ghana, Kenya, Madagascar, Malawi, Mauritius, Sierra Leone. Selected years of devaluation, 1978-89	Inflation rate compared before and after devaluation episodes. Time profile of the inflation rate, both for actual and adjusted data, constructed over seven years—three years before and three years after devaluation. 24 episodes examined.	Roughly half of the episodes were associated with a rise in inflation, with the mean rate declining. Far more devaluations registered long-run improvement than deterioration in inflation performance. The effect turned, among others, on pre-episode inflation record, size of devaluation and on the size of the decline in the parallel currency premium.
Yiheyis (2000)	Burundi, Ethiopia, Ghana, Kenya, Malawi, Mauritius, Sierra Leone, Tanzania, and Zambia. Pooled data, 1971-89.	Econometric model. Y: RER X: Fiscal deficit, Openness, TT, net capital inflow, and rate of nominal devaluation. Fixed-effect procedure, OLS and IV estimates.	The rate of nominal devaluation exerted a statistically significant effect on the real exchange rate. The parameter estimate ranged between 0.24 and 0.28.

determination of the inflationary effects of devaluation.

According to the econometric evidence presented in Table 2, nominal devaluation induced, at least in the short run, real depreciations more often than not. Rouis et al. (1994) and Razzak (1995) documented a positive contemporaneous effect, which was significant both numerically and statistically. On average, a 10 per cent nominal devaluation resulted in roughly 9 and 8 per cent real depreciation in the short and long run, respectively, suggesting a small inflationary effect. Ghura and Grennes (1993) and Yiheyis (2000) also reported the effectiveness of nominal devaluation in inducing real depreciation, although the effectiveness ratio is lower. Elbadawi and Soto (1997) recorded a statistically significant effect for two of the SSA countries in their study. For the other two countries, however, the effects were found to be negative.

There is more direct evidence on the inflationary effect of devaluation. Applying the before-after and control-group approaches, Kamin (1988) found the rate of inflation to have risen in the year following devaluation. However, no conclusive evidence was offered whether the inflationary pressure persisted beyond the first year. Of the 74 devaluation episodes examined, 36 were followed by a sustained increase in inflation after the first year, but the aftermath of the rest of the episodes was characterized by disinflation. Compared to the control group, the devaluing countries saw their inflation accelerate through the year immediately following devaluation, but register a relative decline afterwards. In a related analysis, the author found the real exchange rates to have relatively depreciated in the devaluing countries over the long term. Yiheyis (1997b), comparing the before-after changes in historical and adjusted data, arrived at a similar conclusion. Roughly half the devaluation episodes investigated were associated with a rise in inflation, with the mean rate declining. Far more devaluations were followed by long-run improvement than by deterioration in inflation performance. The extent to which devaluation became inflationary was found to be susceptible to, among other things, the pre-episode inflation record, the size of devaluation, and to the size of the decline in the parallel currency premium.

Comparing inflation performances before and after exchange rate adjustments that resulted in more than five per cent nominal depreciation, Shafaeddin (1992) observed most developing countries to have experienced inflation subsequent to devaluation. However, nominal devaluations were translated into real devaluations at a ratio of 30 to 74 per cent during the first year. The stage of economic development of the sample countries influenced the magnitude of the inflationary effect and the effectiveness of devaluation. Developing countries at the lower end of the income spectrum suffered a higher inflation than their counterparts at the other end. A long-run comparison suggested that the effectiveness of devaluation eroded over time, at a relatively faster rate in the lowest income group. Exploring further what might determine the inflationary effect of devaluation, Shafaeddin (1993) classified the sample into four categories on the basis of the severity of import shortages encountered over the sample period. The comparative result suggested that countries that had the highest import shortage experienced the highest inflationary effect of devaluation, compared to those with low import shortages. No pattern was established for the middle two groups of countries. The countries at the lowest level of development with the most severe import shortages among the sample countries are mostly from SSA. While the susceptibility of the inflationary effect of devaluation to the level of economic development and severity of import shortages is plausible, it is difficult, without diagnostic test results, to determine whether the reported differences are systematic.

Khan (1990), using a modified control group approach, reported that the real effective exchange rate exerted a statistically significant positive effect on changes in the rate of inflation in a one-year comparison period and a neutral effect in a two-year comparison period. Elbadawi and Majid (1996) compared the average inflation performance of countries from the CFA zone and the rest of SSA, and documented the former to have enjoyed lower inflation rates than the rest of the sample, suggesting that the adjustability of the official exchange rate in non-CFA countries has contributed to their relatively poor inflation performance. Over a longer comparative period, the differential turned statistically insignificant.

Regression models were also estimated to isolate the effect of exchange rate changes on inflation. In a cross-sectional regression analysis based on period averages between 1974 and 1985, London (1989) found exchange rates to have exerted a statistically insignificant positive effect on inflation during the study period as a whole. However, dividing the observations into two sub-periods revealed that exchange rates were relevant in explaining inflation in the second half of the study period when changes in exchange rate policy were more frequent. In a model where the official exchange rate is one of the explanatory variables, Faini (1994) found devaluation to be inflationary, with a relatively smaller long-run effect. The official exchange rate lost its explanatory power when the parallel exchange rate was included as an additional variable in the inflation equation of Ghana, one of the sample countries. Odedokun (1997) explored more fully the role of the parallel market in the inflationary process on a dichotomized sample of CFA and non-CFA countries. Both the official and parallel exchange rates exerted a statistically significant positive effect on inflation in the non-CFA countries. The sum of the current and lagged effects of the parallel exchange rate exceeded that of the official rate. Further, the lag in the effect of the parallel exchange rate was longer than that of the official exchange rate. For CFA countries, the effect of the official rate was imperceptible, and, in certain cases, even negative. The parallel exchange rate was estimated to have a positive effect, but smaller than that reported for the non-CFA group.

Fielding and Bleaney (2000) assessed the implication of the exchange rate regime for inflation performance using a regression model by classifying their sample into two groups, depending on the type of exchange rate arrangement they adopted for most of the sample period. Their results indicate that countries that maintained a fixed exchange rate without devaluation had a lower inflation rate than those countries where the official exchange rate was flexible. They estimated the differential at 18.6 percentage points, of which 7.2 percentage points were accredited to the effect of price controls from the fixed exchange rate regime and the balance to the monetary discipline associated with the regime. By the logic of the control group approach, their findings imply that devaluation is inflationary. There is a caveat to this interpretation, however, given the variety of exchange rate arrangements among the members in each category, as well as differences in the degree of exchange rate adjustment in the flexible group over the sample period.

Using a vector autoregressive (VAR) model, Canetti and Greene (1991) examined the relationship between the nominal exchange rate and the consumer price index in bivariate and trivariate settings—the latter including the growth rate of the money supply. The Granger causality test in the bivariate setting suggested a statistically significant effect only in three of the 10 countries of the sample. Fewer cases of Granger causality were found when mon-

etary growth was included in the analysis. Their result, based on the decomposition of the variance of the forecast error of inflation, demonstrated that the
exchange rate played no dominant role in explaining trends in the consumer
price index. The results of a VAR model are, however, suggestive of long-run
relationships and may not describe short-run effects. Rouis et al. (1994) also
applied the Granger causality test and found inflation to have Granger-caused
devaluation, not the other way around.

III. Concluding Remarks

An overview of the stagflationary hypothesis suggests conflicting claims about
the nature and magnitude of the effect of devaluation on output and inflation.
Thus, the issue is largely empirical — the structural and institutional features of
the devaluing economy and the conditions under which the policy is implemented are important in characterizing its effects. The survey of the empirical
literature on the subject in the context of SSA, which is by no means exhaus-
tive, revealed that the cross-country evidence is relatively thin, largely indirect, but reasonably broad-based. With these caveats in mind, there exists little
conclusive evidence that devaluation was stagflationary in SSA in the 1980s
and early 1990s, in the sense that there was a simultaneous contraction of output and increase in inflation. To be sure, the evidence is mixed and appears to
depend partly on the estimating approach and the way the explanatory variable is represented. Consider first the output effect. The before-after and control-group approaches yielded mixed results, but none produced a statistically
significant contractionary effect. When a positive effect was recorded, it was
largely insignificant, or no diagnostic tests were applied. With regards to the
econometric evidence, based on the real exchange rate as a proxy for devaluation, devaluation appears to be neutral. The findings imply that devaluation
had negative, or insignificantly positive, contemporaneous and negative delayed effects. Where the effect was positive, its magnitude was small. Two of the
regression models (Faini, 1994; Nwana, 1987) which found significant positive
and negative effects, respectively, were estimated with fewer control variables,
rendering the magnitude and significance of the reported effects questionable
in cases where devaluation was accompanied by movements in other output-
influencing variables. On the other hand, the indirect econometric evidence,
based on the misalignment of the real exchange rate, implies that devalua-

tion would exert a favourable influence on the growth of aggregate output. However, whether such an implication is justified depends on the extent to which the improvement in the misalignment index can be attributed to exchange rate adjustments.

On balance, therefore, there is little evidence that devaluation was contractionary. At the same time, however, there is not strong, consistent, and corroborated direct evidence that it was expansionary, as the proponents of stabilization and structural adjustment have consistently suggested. The presence of the parallel market may provide a partial explanation for the observed non-contractionary outcome (Kamin, 1995). In addition to the now attenuated cost-push effect, the shift of exportable goods from the unofficial to the official market, in response to the induced reduction in the parallel currency premium, may have increased recorded output (Yiheyis, 1997a), offsetting the adverse effects possibly suffered by the non-export sector. Plainly, the importance of this factor varies from one country to another, depending on, among other things, the type of export items and the size and duration of the premium's decline.[2]

With respect to the inflationary effects of devaluation, the evidence suggests it was positive. However, the effect was neither large nor durable enough to dissipate the policy's influence on the real exchange rate. On the contrary, nominal devaluations on average resulted in substantial short- and long-run real depreciations. The finding that inflation did not rise as high as originally feared, in the sense of not achieving real depreciation, may be explained by some of the institutional and structural features of the region. In SSA the practice of wage indexation is uncommon, making the inflationary effect smaller (World Bank, 1994a). In addition, the implementation of devaluation against a background of exchange controls, in conjunction with the presence of active parallel currency markets, provides another explanation. The inflationary effect under such circumstances will be smaller, since the potential inflationary effect has already been felt through the depreciation of the parallel exchange rate and the rise in the price of traded goods (Nowak, 1984; World Bank, 1994a; Younger, 1992). Another reason for the small inflationary effect of devaluation is the possible favourable effect of the policy change on the fiscal deficit, as Chhibber and Shafik (1991) argue in the case of Ghana. However, the converse is also a distinct possibility if devaluation widens the deficit and the latter is monetized (Azam, 1999; Pinto, 1990).

In summary, the evidence on the stagflationary hypothesis is mixed and inconclusive. While it is clear that devaluation engendered inflation, the effect appears to be neither large nor persistent. Devaluation was not conclusively found to be contractionary, but it also contributed little to reverse the economic decline and stagnation that preceded it. To the degree that devaluation improved the performance of the external sector, the neutral effect on aggregate output coupled with the inflationary outcome might lead one to the conjecture that devaluation may have hampered economic activity in the non-export sector of the economy.

The implications of devaluation for output and inflation in SSA appear to be under-researched. More direct evidence, based on systematic and comprehensive studies, with expanded coverage, is needed to provide a definitive assessment. In addition, further empirical investigation of the channels of transmission from devaluation to aggregate output and inflation will give more insight into how devaluation works. Finally, more work also needs to be done in examining the output effect of devaluation at a disaggregated level and in empirically identifying the conditions under which its favourable outcome is magnified and its adverse effect minimized. Addressing these and similar issues in different settings will enhance our understanding of the devaluation process and the nature, magnitude, duration, and mode of transmission of its effect on domestic macroeconomic activity in the context of SSA and other developing countries sharing similar characteristics.

Footnotes

1 Polak (1995:753) observes that nearly 100 per cent of IMF-supported programs involved exchange rate action by the late 1980s.

2 In his assessment of the impact of devaluation in Ghana and Zambia, Loxley (1990b) points out the importance of the nature of the major export item (cocoa in Ghana and copper in Zambia) for determining the inflationary and output effects of devaluation in the presence of the parallel market. Accordingly, he found devaluation to have lessened the inflationary impact in Ghana and worsened it in Zambia.

Chapter 6

FINANCE AND DEVELOPMENT: FOUR DECADES ON

Peter Lawrence

I. Introduction

SINCE the early work of Newlyn and Rowan (1954) on the colonial African money and banking system, and of Loxley (1966) on the East African monetary system, there has been a shift in thinking about the finance-growth relationship.[1] The debate about whether financial development follows or induces growth has been replaced by an almost consensual, fundamentally neo-conservative, belief that sustained economic growth follows financial development. The World Bank tells us that financial development "contributes significantly to growth;" "is central to poverty reduction;" "directly benefits the poorer segments of society;" and "is associated with improvements in income distribution" (World Bank, 2001d: 75). These stirring statements contrast sharply with Joan Robinson's often quoted phrase: "where enterprise leads, finance follows" (1952: 6).

The relationship between financial development and economic growth is too complex to allow for generalized assertions such as those quoted above. There is now a great deal of data related to this relationship at the macroeconomic level, and analysis of these data has supported both directions of causation, but has also suggested bidirectionality. At the microlevel, there is also a substantial amount of information on the demand for, and use of, credit. Little is known, however, about the precise workings of policies to liberalize financial markets and expand the impact of financial services on decisions by economic agents to invest, and, by such investment, generate growth. Two central questions about the financial development-growth relationship should be addressed. The first is whether the consensus has as strong a basis as its proponents would like to think. The second is why it is so important to demonstrate that finance leads growth. Perhaps more important is an understanding of which policies are likely to support the expansion of existing real economic activity and to induce the growth of new activity.

II. Does finance lead or follow?

The literature on the relationship between financial development and economic growth has taken two roads. The first has tried to establish the importance of well-developed financial markets and institutions for economic growth (Fry, 1995; Goldsmith, 1969; Gurley and Shaw, 1960). The second has tried to demonstrate the negative effects of policies that repress the development of such markets and institutions (McKinnon, 1973; Shaw, 1973). It is not surprising that emphasis has been placed on the importance to economic growth of the development of financial markets and institutions. Growth fundamentally depends on investment. Investment is financed by borrowing, which, in turn, is made possible by deposits of various forms with banks and non-bank financial institutions. Modern growth theory has emphasized the importance of other factors such as education, but a well-functioning financial system is regarded as critical.

The development of various forms of financial intermediation and of a range of instruments to maximize the uptake of domestic savings is an integral part of the development process. As Newlyn and Rowan (1954: 207-208) observed in their seminal study of British colonial banking in Africa, financial institutions influenced and mobilized savings, channelled savings into investment, promoted the mobility of resources, generated the expansion of the market economy, and contributed to the diffusion of improved production techniques. The question is whether the importance of the financial sector is likely to arise organically out of the process of development, or is a requirement for that development process to begin and to accelerate. It is difficult to disagree *a priori* with Newlyn (1977: 1), who argues

> it is necessary to stress its [finance's] subsidiary role. Ultimately, economic development depends on decisions taken by individuals or groups in a political or social context resulting in the mobilization of human activity for the task of transforming traditional modes of production and the social relations associated with them.

The financial sector can be expected to take opportunities presented to it by the production and consumption decisions of economic agents, but those agents have to be engaged in significant economic activity. However, Newlyn (1977: 36) also cautions that "the imposition of institutions conditioned by the requirements of developed countries on financially unsophisticated economies leaves a very large gap in the financial system." Moreover, the existence of institutions that channel credit to productive use does not necessarily mean that all productive credit needs will be fulfilled. It is unlikely that such institutions will lend to agents without collateral; some accumulation will have to have taken place before financial markets can play a role in resource allocation.

All this seems like common sense, as does the general idea that as accumulation proceeds, financial institutions and instruments develop and, in doing so, assist the further accumulation of investment goods. The political context to which Newlyn refers plays a crucial role. The degree to which governments regulate and intervene in the financial system will determine the degree to which the latter will make a positive contribution to growth. As Loxley (1966: 1) notes,

> the monetary and financial system of any country will reflect the political, economic and even social structure of that country.... Because of the importance of the policies of monetary and financial institutions to the general growth and stability of the economy and to the distribution on income and wealth of society in general, some degree of government interference in the affairs of these institutions is now accepted.

Of course, interference can be for good or ill. Governments regulate even the freest financial markets to ensure the security of lenders. However, as the "financial repression" school has demonstrated, governments in many countries, especially developing countries, have over-intervened in the monetary and financial system, even if for good growth reasons. It is worth remembering the reasons why governments thought intervention in the financial system was necessary. First, in many ex-colonial countries, banks were owned by foreign companies and their primary interest was private profit and not investment for long-term development. Second, the banks' position as formal institutions lending only to proven credit-worthy customers at market interest rates excluded many potential borrowers, thus limiting investment and slowing growth. Third, as much of the initial development investment to build the infrastructure and to stimulate growth by setting up state enterprises would have to come from the state, governments would have to direct the financial sector towards this development objective.

In poorly developed economies the state may be the dominant economic actor and, if so, thus engages in a process of long-term development management. Effective, coherent, and realistic development management means directing investment funds to projects that may yield low returns in the short run, but high returns in the long run as external economies are generated. Thus, the reasons for state intervention were — and are — quite coherent. Nonetheless, if the quality of development management and its execution is poor, then low or zero returns may be both the short- and long-run outcome. Such problems are common in the execution of such interventions, and gave rise to theories, associated especially with McKinnon and Shaw, of financial repression. The principal form of repression was the policy of setting a ceiling on interest rates (Shaw, 1973: 81ff). Interest rate ceilings lead to an excess supply of securities, as borrowers' rates become low or even negative in real terms, after taking inflation into account. Low or negative real rates reduced or removed the incentive to save. Credit rationing is the typical result. However, such rationing does not guarantee that credit goes to its most productive use, an outcome that depends on the judgement of the decision-makers. Worse, it produces incentives to corruption as bank officials can arbitrage between market rates and low interest ceiling rates as their price for granting loans. Low interest rates favour low-risk, low-return projects. Moreover, loans on some projects are never repaid as maturities on them are continually extended as a result of favouritism by banks towards certain lenders, or because of the political clout of certain lenders (Shaw, 1973 82-87).

Other elements of financial repression are high reserve ratios and an oligopolistic banking system that offers high spreads between deposit and lending rates (Shaw, 1973: 87-88). Theories of financial repression fit beautifully into the neo-classical model and its critique of state intervention and government price controls in capital, commodity, and foreign exchange markets. The converse of financial repression is financial deepening. Under financial deepening, market-clearing interest rates correctly price the reward for foregoing current consumption. Competition in the banking sector reduces the interest rate spread, signifying higher levels of banking efficiency. There is a greater diversity of financial assets with different lengths to maturity, and the development of capital markets where these assets can be traded. Liberalization of other markets where prices are controlled is regarded as a key corollary to money-market liberalization. The result should be a higher savings ratio, stronger control over domestic credit expansion, higher investment productivity, and, consequently, greater inflows of foreign short- and long-term capital.

However, the banking system may fail liberalizers at the first hurdle. The Shaw-McKinnon argument rests on the view that markets allocate resources best and that state development management agencies are not better at plotting development paths. However, Stiglitz and Weiss (1981) famously proposed that lenders were more likely to favour lending at low interest rates to low-return, low-risk projects. This was because lenders did not have enough information on borrowers, and because in lending to high-risk borrowers they were likely to be subject to more loan defaults. The implications for developing countries are that rather than higher interest rates leading to moves away from credit rationing, they would lead to greater credit rationing by lenders because of asymmetric information and risk aversion on the part of lenders.

In a major review of the literature on financial development and economic growth, Levine points to five basic functions of financial systems (Levine, 1997: 690). They

- facilitate the trading, hedging, diversifying and pooling of risk;
- allocate resources;
- monitor managers and exert corporate control;
- mobilise savings; and,
- facilitate the exchange of goods and services.

The existence of intermediaries, whether capital market institutions, merchant banks and finance houses, or commercial and savings banks, reduces information costs for those parting with liquid assets, or those wishing to sell their financial assets. In his parable of Fred, who has designed a new truck, Levine points to the way financial intermediaries enable Fred to diversify risk and mobilize others' savings, which are then loaned to Fred. Levine also shows how the financial intermediaries acquire information about Fred's capacity to make his project a success and to give investors in the project a competitive rate of return. Without these intermediaries, Fred's project may not get off the ground, technological progress is held back, and growth is slower.

It is not difficult to see how theories of finance and growth point to the conclusion that finance leads growth. However, it is also not difficult to argue that without the pre-existence of some level of production and technology, financial markets and instruments can only respond to the demands of producers and consumers. In other words, finance follows growth. It is instructive that while Levine (1997) regards the link between finance and growth to be advanced enough to draw relatively firm conclusions, he also cites evidence that economic growth generates financial intermediation, which in turn promotes growth, thus proposing that "financial and economic development are jointly determined" (1997: 703). So, does finance lead or follow, or both?

Recent empirical work has given substantial support to financial repression theory and its implications. Of 20 studies reported by Kitchen (1986: 90-91), 13 give positive support to the hypothesis, four are either negative or inconclusive, while three give limited support. Of 21 studies analyzing the relationship between financial development and growth, reported by Fry (1995), 16 econometric studies find positive relationships, as do three non-econometric country case studies. Of the econometric studies, 10 use nominal or real interest rates as the independent variable indicating financial deepening, while the other, and later, six adopt one or more financial ratios, such as M2 as a ratio of gross domestic product (GDP), or private sector credit to GDP. Two of the later studies ran causality tests, one of which found causation running from financial development to growth in seven out of eight countries, while the other found causation to be bi-directional. One of the studies using real interest rates discovered an inverted U relationship, in which high, very real interest rates had a negative impact on growth where these rates had been raised to regain credibility or compensate for perceived country risk. More recently, Levine (1997) reports further studies, including historical ones, all of which support the hypothesis that financial development is growth inducing.

The study referred to by Fry (1995) that suggests a bi-directional relationship is that of Demetriades and Hussein (1993), which covered 12 countries. In a later version involving 16 developing countries over 27 years and four different econometric causality tests, these authors find that finance does not lead growth. In seven countries, they find a bi-directional relationship, in six countries they find that growth leads finance, and in three countries they find that one of their financial indicators causes growth. However, in one of those cases, one of the tests finds bidirectionality; in another, reverse causation; and in the third, causation running from finance to growth where the data was not cointegrated. They also conclude there is a country-specificity that may make dangerous the "lumping together in cross-section equations countries with very different experiences in relation to financial development" (Demetriades and Hussein, 1996: 407). Levine's survey does refer in a footnote to time series investigations that give conflicting results, but then claims that "many time-series investigations find that financial sector development Granger-causes economic performance." However, only one reference is offered to such an investigation (Wachtel and Rousseau, 1995), which appeared to be the only one at that stage that produced such a result.

Further work by Demetriades with Luintel (1996a; 1996b) has thrown doubt on the consensual story. In their study of banking sector policies in Nepal (1996a) and India (1996b), the authors find that policies that affect financial deepening also affect growth; that is, the two are jointly determined. However, in their country studies, there is strong evidence of the negative effect of repressionist policies on financial development (1996b; 1997). The story here seems to be that liberal financial policies will lead financial development, as is to be expected, but that greater financial development does not necessarily lead growth.

It is the work of Levine and his colleagues that has dominated the recent literature. For example, King and Levine (1993), using cross-country analysis, find that financial development, measured in various ways, is strongly correlated with economic growth. They then turn this into a causal relationship running from finance to growth by relating the values of financial development at the beginning of the period they analyze to growth over the subsequent period. They argue that the predetermined component of financial development is strongly associated with later growth and its sources. They control for growth and investment in the decade prior to the initial year but that does not change their conclusions, although they do not report the results. The key issue therefore remains: what has determined this predetermined component?

Beck, Levine, and Loayza (2000) report seven studies between 1996 and 2000 that show a positive relationship between financial intermediary development and economic growth. Notable omissions from the list of studies are those of Demetriades and his colleagues, who, as noted, do find associations between financial development and economic growth, but not the causal relationships that Levine and the seven studies find or deduce. Nevertheless, Beck et al. make a powerful case for financial intermediaries acting on economic growth via total factor productivity growth. This time they try to overcome the endogeneity issue by using the "legal origin" of each country as an instrument for financial intermediary development. The advantage of using legal origin is that for most developing countries, the legal system they developed depended on which country had colonized them. Thus, legal origin is exogenous, and explains cross-country variations in creditor rights, systems for debt contract enforcement, and corporate information disclosure standards (Beck et al., 2000: 262-4).[2] They are able to show in a cross-section instrumental variable approach and in a panel study comprising 77 countries over five time periods that financial development "exerts a large impact" on economic growth. Nevertheless, the issue remains of what drives financial development, and how far it and growth are jointly determined by prior policies and forms of development.

Recently published work continues to throw doubt on the consensus. One interesting study using a path analysis suggests a periodicity to the relationship between financial development and growth (Graff, 2002). Using a data set comprising 93 countries over five time periods, Graff finds a bi-directional relationship in the 1970s and that finance led growth in the 1980s. However, between 1975 and 1980, finance may have been detrimental to growth, although he can only speculate that the oil price shocks, and either financial repression or deregulation, could have been responsible for this. Two other recent pieces of reported research question the consistency of the consensus relationship between financial development and economic growth. Deidda and Fattouh (2002), using a threshold regression model and the data set of King and Levine (1993), show a non-linear relationship between financial development and economic growth. They find that there is no significant relationship between financial development and growth in low-income countries, but in high-income countries the relationship is positive and highly significant. Shan, Morris, and Sun (2001) conduct Granger causality tests on a VAR model for nine OECD countries and China. They find evidence of bi-directional causality in five of the countries and of reverse causation in another three.

Arestis and Demetriades (1997: 784) undertake a methodological review of the finance-growth literature, in which they point to the scepticism of researchers about the cross-country regressions employed by King and Levine and others. The authors note some of the econometric problems associated with this type of study, some of which suggest that the issue of causality is best addressed by time-series techniques on a country-by-country basis. This point is illustrated by two time-series econometric analyses. The first compares the relationship between stock market development in Germany and the US, finding that in Germany banking sector development causes growth, and stock market capitalization "affects real GDP only through the banking system" (Arestis and Demetriades, 1997: 790). In the US, on the contrary, they conclude, "there is insufficient evidence that…financial development causes real GDP. On the other hand, there is abundant evidence of reverse causality, i.e. real GDP positively contributing to both banking system and capital market development."

The second time-series analysis is concerned with the relationship between financial repression/liberalization and economic growth, taking the case of South Korea and using annual data over the period from 1956 to 1994. The analysis constructs a financial repression index. This incorporates Korea's policy of controls on interest rates, and its direction of credit and bank reserves. It controls for real interest rates, financial depth and capital stock per head. The econometric analysis finds a positive relationship between financial repression and economic growth. This turns out to be consistent with most stories, including that of the World Bank (Arestis and Demetriades, 1997: 796), about the benefits of mild repression with positive but low real interest rates. It also fits the theoretical story derived from the work of Stiglitz and Weiss (1981), in which high real interest rates result in financial crises because asymmetric information causes banks to invest in high-risk, high-return projects that fail. As the authors point out, this does not mean that financial repression has this effect everywhere. Much will depend on specific policies and the effectiveness of institutions, which can vary significantly between countries.

III. What does history show?

Intercountry variation in the relationship between finance and growth is also a feature of the historical evidence, some of which is surveyed in Levine (1997). However, Levine's conclusions are not necessarily those of the authors of the studies he cites in support of the consensus. One such is Cameron and colleagues' influential study of banking in early industrialization in some European countries and Japan (Cameron, Crisp, Patrick, and Tilley, 1967). This study shows a wide variation in banking experiences and degrees of success. Even in the case of Scotland, where he finds that "the superiority of its banking system stands out as one of the major determining factors (of growth)," he adds that there is only one other that can rank with it: Scotland's educational system. He further suggests that the relative decline of the Scottish economy compared with England has occurred as the two countries' banking and education systems became increasingly "assimilated" (Cameron et al., 1967: 97). However, it is not possible to deduce from Cameron's account any clear chain of causation. He appears to take both the view that Scottish banking "developed in response to the changing needs and circumstances of the Scottish economy," and that "innovations in bank policy and practice were made which account for much of the system's unusual effectiveness in promoting and facilitating economic growth" (1967: 75). This is not a surprising position, given the possibilities of simultaneity or two-way causation.

As far as the industrial revolution in England is concerned, Levine's survey refers to an alleged argument of Hicks that "capital market improvements that mitigated liquidity risk were the primary *causes* [Levine's italics] of the industrial revolution in England," and that "the products manufactured during the first decades of the industrial revolution had been invented much earlier. Thus technological innovation did not spark sustained growth" (Levine, 1997: 692). In fact, the passage in Hicks (1969: 143-145) to which Levine refers tells a different story. Hicks argues that what characterized the industrial revolution was the shift from circulating to fixed capital; that is, to large amounts of machinery and equipment. He argues that alongside this technical change was a financial development, "which...had been occurring at the same time, at more or less the right time." This was "not simply that rates of interest had fallen" but that there was a "greater availability of funds." People who wanted to invest in fixed capital either had to have their own financial resources, or be able to borrow "from someone else (it may be a bank), who is able to borrow or who has liquid funds" (Hicks, 1969: 144). Hicks then, in something of a leap, suggests it was the earlier development of financial markets that made liquid funds more easily available, and this was crucial to the financing of the shift to greater amounts of fixed capital. The evidence he presents for greater liquidity in the form of instruments such as South Sea or India bills does not make a clear link with the financing of the industrial revolution, and, indeed, he does then go on to argue that what really drove the shift to fixed capital was science. The steam engine followed a century after physicists discovered the principles underlying heat and pressure, although to construct an engine required knowledge of techniques associated with moving parts and of resistance to pressures. A range of skills had to be brought together. What eventually cheapened capital was not the lower interest rates deriving from greater financial liquidity, but the development of machine tools, "*the* [Hicks's italics] essential part" of the industrial revolution. This is quite the contrary of Levine's account of Hicks. It is possible that Levine's misinterpretation of Hicks is derived from a rendition by Bencivenga, Smith, and Starr (1995), to which Levine refers, who offer a similar interpretation.

Cameron's account of English industrialization, also referred to by Levine, makes two points about early industrialization that put the importance of the financial system in a different perspective from that of Levine's interpretation. First, the demand for capital for investment in manufacturing was small, relative to GDP; and second, capital investment was largely financed by reinvesting profits (Cameron et al., 1967: 36-39). Kindleberger, using a large number of sources across Europe, endorses this view and, referring to the work of Deane and Cole, and later Feinstein, adds that over the period of the industrial revolution, savings as a proportion of GDP rose by only one or two percentage points (Kindleberger, 1984: 196-201). The major demand for capital came from local authorities to improve infrastructure. Manufacturers who could not finance all their needs from their own resources borrowed from other manufacturers. Later industrialization accelerated by the railway boom had to be financed institutionally, facilitated by well-established capital markets and joint-stock banks (Kindleberger: 196-201). However, this was well into the 19th century, not the 18th, when, at least in Britain, the industrial revolution began in earnest.

There is no evidence here of the industrial revolution *waiting* for financial markets and every evidence that financial markets developed alongside industrialization and eventually played an important role in making credit available more easily. This was especially the case once the size of capital investments outgrew the retained profits of the family firm, and once the family firm grew to a size where it had to become incorporated. Nonetheless, the importance of the financial sector to promoting investment and in propelling growth at particular periods in history does not give rise to a general rule. What historical investigation confirms is that developed financial markets were increasingly important for industrialization, but that financing responded to economic development and particularly to the technological revolutions induced by science, more than vice-versa. The very idea of the industrial revolution *waiting* for financial markets suggests a process in which prior industrial development induces technological change that in turn induces further industrial and financial development.

In any case, an increase in financial services activity will always contribute to economic growth, given that this is measured by the growth in GDP and that the value added of the financial sector is a component of GDP. Indeed, it is surprising that growth has not been measured as the growth of GDP minus financial sector growth to avoid this accounting issue. The graph below shows how the share of the financial sector in GDP has grown over the period be-

Figure 1 Shares of the financial sector in GDP, 1965-94

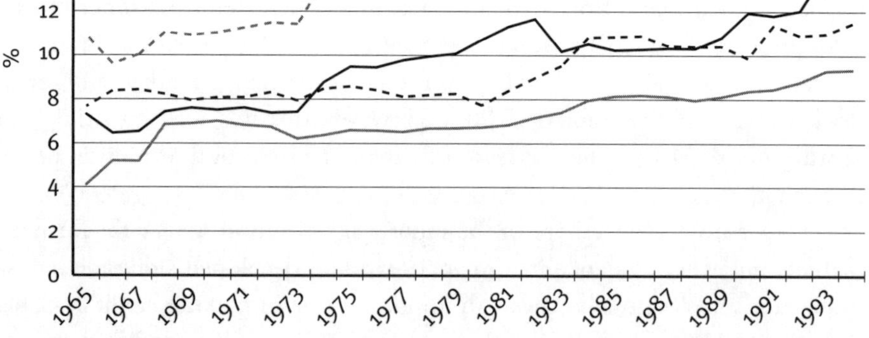

Source United Nations (2002).

tween 1965 and 1995, especially in the OECD countries and latterly in Latin America and the Caribbean. These are averages and cover 27 selected countries for which full data was available. They suggest there is an issue here to be addressed.

IV. Back to Africa

Recent empirical work on the finance-growth relationship is conflicting rather than consensual. Historical research puts the consensus on flimsier ground still. A sensible view that could constitute a consensus with better support is that the direction of causality might be different at different stages. It could be bi-directional over time, as Graff's study, quoted above, suggests, and certainly non-linear, as proposed by Deidda and Fattouh (2002). To illustrate this, it is worth going back to Loxley (1966: 76). Writing about the 1950s and early 1960s, he notes:

> The regional distribution of banking business naturally follows the pattern of economic activity within East Africa — those areas most integrated into the cash economy receiving most banking facilities.

Not only does he describe a strong association between finance and economic activity, but he clearly implies that finance follows — the development of the banking sector in different parts of East Africa reflected the level of economic activity.

However, this did not mean that banks were only reactive. Here is Loxley on the loss-making mobile banking units in east Africa: "banks tend to look upon these units more as mobile advertisements and hope that as the cash economy expands, people in these areas will become bank conscious" (1966: 78). Even banks did not believe that they led economic activity. Attempts in the early 1960s to increase deposits through advertising security to the non-bank public did not succeed as well as banks anticipated. In Loxley's account, high primary commodity prices in the early 1960s led to increases in economic activity and a concomitant expansion of banking activities. However, deposits did not grow as fast as lending. Banks believed that in the 1960s east Africa was overbanked. Increasing the number of banks would lead to a redistribution of existing business rather than growth of new business. Only with the expansion of the cash economy would banks expand and become more profitable. Finance follows again.

Of course, the main reason why banks would want to expand and gain more deposits was to lend on. But lend on to whom? Africans experienced difficulty in getting credit. They had little collateral except land, to which they did not usually have title. They suffered prejudice from those bankers who believed that Africans "had not yet developed a money mentality and respect for debt obligation" (Loxley, 1966: 99). It was not surprising, then, that the banks saw their major role as channelling credit to expatriate farms and other enterprises, although as political independence loomed they began to realize it was in their best interest to direct banking services to African farmers and traders.

Lack of collateral and risk of default deterred lending to Africans. Even if they granted loans, the banks could not be sure they would be used for the purpose lent and they did not have the resources to monitor the use of loans. Yet African farmers and traders needed credit to expand their activities. Information asymmetries could be overcome by channelling credit through cooperatives, and of course governments could intervene to establish organizations whose sole task was to channel credit for investment. Loxley documented early developments of this kind. In terms of the overall debate about the role of finance, it becomes evident here that the availability of investment credit is critical.[3] However, banks are less interested in pushing out loans than in ensuring that the purposes of the loan are productive and will guarantee the returns necessary to pay off the loan. Even here finance follows, responding to the demand for credit, but only where the risks of lending are covered by adequate borrower collateral.

The growth of curb markets and other forms of informal lending are a response to these features of the formal banking system. Loxley argued strongly that there was little informal financial activity in east Africa. There were some licensed moneylenders and pawnbrokers, but they were of little importance. Thirty years later, a case study of Tanzania confirmed that informal finance is not as extensive in Tanzania as in west Africa (Nissanke and Aryeetey, 1998). A recent case study of cattle and credit in Tanzania concludes that the absence of informal credit markets has prevented poorer people from buying cattle (Dercon, 1998). However, informal finance does not simply consist of borrowing in curb markets. There is lending among family, neighbours, and friends, often at zero interest rates, as well as lending between traders and farmers. Savings and credit societies of individuals with common ethnic bonds are also prevalent (Nissanke and Aryeetey, 1998).

Such informal markets have been expanded in the process of trade and financial liberalization in the 1990s. Instead of formal institutions crowding out informal agents, liberalization has enabled existing informal lenders to operate more openly and has encouraged new lenders to appear. In some sectors informal lending is an important source for the expansion of the activities of urban microenterprises and small farmers, providing up to 55 per cent of start-up investment funds in some cases (Nissanke and Aryeetey, 1998). The patterns of lending are quite specific to each type of lender. Thus, landlords and farmer lenders lend mainly to farmers, traders to traders and sometimes to small enterprise and farmers. Particularly interesting relative to the Asian literature (Lawrence, 2002) is the high level of interlinked transactions, which stands at between 70 and 90 per cent of informal commercial credit transactions. Increasingly, credit is used for productive/commercial as well as consumption activities. In one survey, 58 per cent of credit was used for productive and commercial purposes, and this rose to 63 per cent if housing was included (Nissanke and Aryeetey, 1998).

This brief review of African credit market experience suggests that the presence of formal financial markets is not necessary to the early economic development of the kind that is likely to generate higher rates of growth in economies where the majority of producers are small-scale and agricultural. Asian experience, too, has suggested that informal and semi-formal institutions will continue to be a source of credit for a large proportion of the population. The Grameen Bank is a much-quoted example. Even if the informal sector were to be included in measures of the financial sector as a whole, it seems evident from Nissanke and Aryeetey's survey that informal sector expansion is demand-driven, increased demand being derived from greater trading opportunities. In this sense the process of financial sector expansion is little different from that described by Loxley in the 1960s.

V. Concluding remarks

Two questions arise from consideration of the literature on finance and development. The first is: why is it so important to prove that finance causes growth? The second is: accepting that financial development is an important part of the process of economic growth, which policies are most likely to produce financial development and lead to economic growth?

The answer to the first question may lie in the realm of both ideology and political economy. Since in the consensual neo-classical orthodoxy, liberalization of all markets is critical, then to be able to show that liberalization of financial markets leads growth helps to confirm the status of the omniscient neo-conservative consensus. Second, the last two decades have seen an expansion of financial sector activities that has made this sector a critical part of most developed economies. Pushing policies that lead to financial sector expansion opens up possibilities for the global expansion of the major financial institutions. Even, or especially, in the wake of the Asian financial crisis, when more caution might have been expected, demonstrating the significance of financial development has appeared more than focussing on production of saleable commodities. To be sure, economists such as Stiglitz have urged caution and have pointed out that financial sector expansion should not exceed institutional capabilities to regulate it. However, there has to be some connection between the proselytizing of the International Monetary Fund and the World Bank, and the expansion of what we used to call "finance capital."[4]

As regards the second question, knowing that financial sector development generates economic growth does not indicate which financial policies specifically aid growth.[5] As we have seen for sub-Saharan Africa, it could well be that trade and financial reforms generate sufficient informal sector activities to satisfy and even initiate a considerable expansion of small- and medium-scale productive activity. Policies that increase the linkages between the formal and informal sectors, advocated by Nissanke and Aryeetey in their study, could slow down such expansion because of the different forms of collateral required by the formal institutions. Policies that increase financial sector regulatory capacity, which is clearly important for the formal sector, may drive informal agents underground. In the wake of the Asian financial crisis, attention has turned away from the issue of the relationship of financial development and growth to issues of the governance and regulation of financial institutions and markets. Financial liberalization may do more harm than good in the absence of adequately governed and regulated institutions and markets. However, it is difficult to see how such policy discussions can be conducted outside the consideration of economic strategies as a whole. Moreover, if industrial and agricultural strategy is to be eschewed in favour of a neo-conservative reliance on market forces, how are we to know what policies to pursue with respect to the financial sector, other than to foster its expansion because it promotes growth?

All this suggests that we need to reconsider the relationships between finance and production, looking at the financial and monetary sector as a lubricant of productive activity as well as a producer of financial instruments. Not only does that require us to return to case-study work such as that of Loxley (1966), but also to situate the current limited debate about finance and development in both its empirical and theoretical contexts. This means, finally, a reconsideration of the political economy of money and finance in the tradition of Marx and Hilferding as well as the more often quoted Schumpeter.

Footnotes

1 The work undertaken for this chapter derives from research into the effects of financial policy on household behaviour, funded by the United Kingdom's Department for International Development (DFID), Social Science Research, under contract R7968. The views presented here are those of the author and not of DFID. Thanks to participants in seminars at the University of Manitoba and the Institute of Social Studies, The Hague (and especially Haroon Akram-Lodhi, Martin Doornbos, and Marc Wuyts for very helpful comments on an earlier draft).

2 Although it could be argued that the legal system cannot be taken as exogenous because it could determine some of the rules of the financial framework.

3 The lack of adequate domestic savings was incorporated in the two-gap analysis originating in the work of Chenery and Strout (1966) in which foreign aid covered the investment-savings gap. This shaped the development of government financial institutions through which aid was channelled but did not increase the financial depth of recipient countries.

4 One connection is certainly the hegemonic position of IMF and World Bank staff (or staff trained by these institutions) in the finance ministries where financial policy decisions are made.

5 This point has also been forcibly made by Wachtel (2001: 357) in a review of the literature, which concludes "there is ample evidence to make a convincing case that financial sector development promotes economic growth."

PART 2

Neo-conservatism and Equality

Chapter 7

GROWTH, SAVINGS AND INVESTMENT UNDER STRUCTURAL ADJUSTMENT: THE CASE OF GHANA

John Kofi Baffoe

I. Introduction

AFTER a decade of steady progress during the early post-independence period, the Ghanaian economy started deteriorating in the early 1970s and developed into an economic crisis in the early 1980s. The government of the Provisional National Defence Council (PNDC), realizing that the decline could not be halted or reversed without a massive infusion of foreign exchange into the Ghanaian economy, approached the International Monetary Fund (IMF) and the World Bank for financial assistance. These multilateral institutions, along with other bilateral donors, agreed to provide assistance, but subject to conditions, which comprised a package of economic and financial reforms, and were introduced as an Economic Recovery Program (ERP) in 1983. Between 1983 and 1991 the government pursued the reforms in earnest, and to the admiration of the multilateral financial institutions. Following a brief hiatus, the reforms resumed in 1993 under a civilian government, and are continuing after the January 2001 election of a new government to administer the country.

II. The ERP in context

i.   The Ghanaian economy prior to the ERP
Following independence in 1957, the Ghanaian economy performed reasonably well. Economic growth averaged about 4 per cent during the 1960s, led by cocoa exports, which accounted for about 70 per cent of foreign exchange

Table 1 Ghana: selected economic indicators, 1970–1983

	1970	1971	1972	1973	1974	1975	1976
Real GDP (millions of 1975 cedis)	5349	5628	5488	5646	6033	5283	5097
Real GDP growth (%)	6.7	5.2	-2.5	2.9	6.9	-12.4	-3.5
Real per capita GDP (in 1975 cedis)	511	598	571	572	587	493	460
Gov't revenue and grants (millions of cedis)	486.2	421.9	396.9	583.5	810.6	869.8	1151.6
Gov't recurrent expenditures (millions of cedis)	378.3	430.7	449.1	569.2	875.4	997.4	1308.0
Gov't development expenditures (millions of cedis)	108.4	103.8	96.0	169.3	286.1	441.2	637.2
Gov't total expenditures (millions of cedis)	486.7	534.5	545.1	738.5	1161.5	1438.6	1945.2
Gov't total budget deficit/surplus (millions of cedis)	-0.5	-112.6	-148.2	-155.0	-350.9	-568.8	-793.6
Gov't total budget deficit/surplus as % of GDP	0.02	4.5	5.3	4.4	7.5	10.8	12.2
Growth in broad money supply (%)	-	3.5	3.7	21.9	24.3	33.4	39.0
Inflation (%)	3.5	5.1	20.3	1.7	24.3	41.2	41.1
Nominal lending rate (%)	9.0	9.0	12.0	10.0	10.0	10.0	10.0
Nominal savings rate (%)	2.5	7.5	7.5	5.0	5.0	7.5	7.5
Real lending rate (%)	5.5	3.9	-8.3	8.3	-14.3	-31.2	-111.2
Real savings rate # (%)	-1.0	2.4	-12.8	3.3	-19.3	-33.7	-113.7
Gross savings as % of GDP	11.2	8.3	12.1	13.9	9.6	13.8	8.3
Official exchange rate (cedis per US$1.00)	1.02	1.03	1.33	1.15	1.15	1.15	1.15
Parallel exchange rate (cedis per US$1.00)	1.69	1.52	1.68	1.50	1.73	1.99	2.91

Sources Alderman (1991); Aryeetey, Harrigan and Nissanke (2000); Central Bureau of Statistics, various issues; IMF, various issues a; IMF various issues b; Loxley (1991); May (1985); World Bank (1985a, 1987b).

	1977	1978	1979	1980	1981	1982	1983
Real GDP (millions of 1975 cedis)	5212	5654	5512	5576	5362	5036	4888
Real GDP growth (%)	2.3	8.5	-2.5	-1.2	-3.8	-6.1	-2.9
Real per capita GDP (in 1975 cedis)	459	504	478	467	439	399	391
Gov't revenue and grants (millions of cedis)	1393.1	2578.4	2949.4	3279.3	4855.3	5253.2	10241.0
Gov't recurrent expenditures (millions of cedis)	2322.2	3334.5	4076.8	6329.3	8602.6	8029.4	13403.5
Gov't development expenditures (millions of cedis)	695.4	759.8	594.7	1390.0	926.9	816.7	1354.5
Gov't total expenditures (millions of cedis)	3017.6	4094.3	4671.5	7719.3	9529.5	8846.1	14758.0
Gov't total budget deficit/surplus (millions of cedis)	-1624.5	-1515.9	-1722.1	-4440.0	-4674.2	-3592.9	-4517.0
Gov't total budget deficit/surplus as % of GDP	14.6	7.2	6.1	10.4	6.3	4.1	2.4
Growth in broad money supply (%)	44.5	71.1	30.5	38.6	27.6	39.6	47.4
Inflation (%)	121.2	73.2	54.4	50.1	116.5	19.2	128.7
Nominal lending rate (%)	10.0	10.0	14.0	14.0	14.0	10.0	10.0
Nominal savings rate (%)	7.5	12.0	12.0	12.0	18.0	8.0	11.0
Real lending rate (%)	-111.2	-63.2	-40.4	-36.1	-102.5	-9.2	-118.7
Real savings rate # (%)	-113.7	-61.2	-42.4	-38.1	-98.5	-11.2	-117.7
Gross savings as % of GDP	10.1	5.8	6.0	5.0	3.9	3.6	3.5
Official exchange rate (cedis per US$1.00)	1.15	2.75	2.75	2.75	2.75	2.75	30.00
Parallel exchange rate (cedis per US$1.00)	9.20	10.00	15.56	15.87	26.25	61.67	76.58

Baffoe

Table 1 Ghana: selected economic indicators,1970–1983 (continued)

	1970	1971	1972	1973	1974	1975	1976
Exports (millions of US$)	449	350	441	634	731	807	827
Imports (millions of US$)	481	434	307	458	821	791	863
Trade balance (millions of US$)	-32	-84	134	176	-90	16	-36
Current account balance (millions of US$)	-68	-146	108	127	-172	17	-74
Index price of exports (1968=100)	128.6	109.3	126.1	176.7	274.1	297.7	286.1
Index price of imports (1968=100)	122.6	134.6	174.8	197.2	272.1	311.8	359.2
External terms of trade (1968=100)	104.9	81.2	71.7	89.6	100.7	95.5	79.6
Minimum wage (cedis per day)	0.8	0.8	1.15	1.15	2.00	2.00	2.00
Average monthly earnings (cedis)	51.84	53.55	75.08	69.01	91.49	107.28	120.00
Real average monthly earnings (in 1975 cedis)	117.00	115.00	134.00	121.00	129.00	107.28	84.98
Cocoa exports ('ooo tonnes)	413	454	414	349	385.1	397.3	326.7
Gold exports ('ooo kilograms)	19.9	19.8	22.5	22.6	19.1	16.4	16.5
Cocoa producer price (cedis per tonne)	292.7	292.7	365.9	439.0	548.8	585.4	731.7
Real cocoa producer price (in 1975 cedis per tonne)	660.6	628.5	653.0	770.6	774.9	585.4	518.2
Maize output ('ooo tonnes)	481.6	465.4	402.4	426.4	485.7	343.4	286.4
Rice output ('ooo tonnes)	48.8	54.9	70.1	62.0	73.2	71.1	69.8
Cassava output ('ooo tonnes)	2387	2388	2840	2865	3696	2398	1819
Yam output ('ooo tonnes)	909.4	909.4	678.8	605.9	849.5	709.2	574.0
Plantain output ('ooo tonnes)	1641	1641	1670	2071	2024	1246	1257

Sources Alderman (1991); Aryeetey, Harrigan and Nissanke (2000); Central Bureau of Statistics, various issues; IMF, various issues a; IMF various issues b; Loxley (1991); May (1985); World Bank (1985a, 1987b).

	1977	1978	1979	1980	1981	1982	1983
Exports (millions of US$)	1014	575	995	1148	977	804	341
Imports (millions of US$)	1038	612	853	1129	1267	1012	368
Trade balance (millions of US$)	-24	-37	142	19	-280	-208	-27
Current account balance (millions of US$)	-80	-46	122	29	-421	-109	-174
Index price of exports (1968=100)	433.7	449.7	536.3	651.9	420.5	319.6	2113.5
Index price of imports (1968=100)	419.5	475.3	564.4	686.3	682.2	663.1	4197.4
External terms of trade (1968=100)	103.4	94.6	95.1	95.0	61.6	48.2	47.8
Minimum wage (cedis per day)	3.00	4.00	4.00	5.00	12.00	12.00	25.00
Average monthly earnings (cedis)	215.00	226.00	286.00	461.00	463.00	465.00	973.00
Real average monthly earnings (in 1975 cedis)	68.84	41.78	34.24	36.77	33.08	27.87	25.49
Cocoa exports ('ooo tonnes)	277.4	268.2	280.8	258	225	180	157
Gold exports ('ooo kilograms)	15.0	12.5	11.1	11.0	10.6	10.3	8.6
Cocoa producer price (cedis per tonne)	1333.3	2666.7	4000.0	4000.0	12000.0	12000.0	20000.0
Real cocoa producer price (in 1975 cedis per tonne)	426.9	493.0	479.0	319.0	857.3	719.2	524.00
Maize output ('ooo tonnes)	312.2	269.3	308.6	354.0	334.2	264.3	140.8
Rice output ('ooo tonnes)	62.9	60.8	63.0	64.1	43.6	37.1	269
Cassava output ('ooo tonnes)	2119	2334	2320	2896	2721	1986	1375.2
Yam output ('ooo tonnes)	497.1	517.1	550.4	523.1	462.8	374.1	354.3
Plantain output ('ooo tonnes)	776	902	784	931	835	763	754.7

earnings (Killick, 1978). However, problems in the Ghanaian economy surfaced in the early 1970s. The economy declined at an average rate of -3.3 per cent from 1979 to 1983 (Table 1). Real per capita gross domestic product (GDP) in 1975 cedis declined continuously from 504 cedis in 1978 to 391 cedis in 1983. The rate of inflation averaged about 80 per cent between 1977 and 1983, reaching a peak of about 129 per cent in 1983. The high rate of inflation resulted in the continuous erosion of the purchasing power of earnings. Real average monthly earnings in 1975 cedis declined from 107.28 cedis in 1975 to 25.49 in 1983.

Government budgets were imbalanced, with an average annual budget deficit of 6 per cent of GDP between 1978 and 1983 — annual figures are illustrated in Table 1. Merchandise exports fell from US$995 million in 1979 to US$341 million in 1983, a 66 per cent decline. The decline was due to lower outputs of virtually all the major tradeable commodities; in particular, near 60 per cent reduction in cocoa exports and about a 47 per cent reduction in gold exports between 1975 and 1983. The real producer price of cocoa, measured in 1975 cedis, declined from 857 cedis in 1981 to 524 cedis in 1983. This contributed to lower cocoa output. Lower export revenues also constrained imports. Table 1 demonstrates that the level of imports fell from US$853 in 1979 to US$368 million in 1983, a reduction of around 57 per cent.

Finally, the output of all major staple foods also fell. Between 1979 and 1983 maize output declined by 54 per cent, rice by 57 per cent, cassava by 41 per cent, yam by 36 per cent, and plantain by about 4 per cent. There can be little doubt that Ghana was facing a major economic crisis in the early 1980s, a crisis that came to a head in 1983.

ii. The causes of the economic crisis
The economic crisis in Ghana was the result of structural weaknesses in the Ghanaian economy, terms of trade deterioration, and economic mismanagement. Five examples of structural weaknesses can be highlighted. The first was the dependence on agriculture as the mainstay of the economy, without any conscious effort to increase agricultural productivity or diversify the structure of the Ghanaian economy (World Bank, 1985a). The average contribution of agriculture to GDP from 1970 to 1983 was 51 per cent, followed by services at 31 per cent, and industry at 18 per cent. Between 1979 and 1983, output of

all major staple food crops declined, while the population grew at an average of about 2 per cent per annum. This resulted in a food shortage that reached a catastrophic level in the early 1980s as a result of a severe drought.

A second structural weakness was the lack of diversification of exports from cocoa, which thus made the Ghanaian economy vulnerable to fluctuations in the world cocoa price (World Bank, 1985a). From 1970 to 1983 cocoa accounted for an average of 62 per cent of exports. Declining world cocoa prices combined with oil price increases resulted in a terms of trade deterioration from 1977 to 1983. Table 1 demonstrates that the terms of trade declined continuously from 103.4 in 1977 to 47.8 in 1983.

A third weakness also related to cocoa. The government had an overreliance on cocoa duty as the main source of tax revenue (Sowa, 1994). A decline in cocoa exports from 1979 to 1983 resulted in a reduction in cocoa duty, and contributed to government budgetary problems. Fourth, the economy had very large public and service sectors relative to the production and manufacturing sectors, and this imbalance meant that the economy lacked a dynamic growth engine (World Bank, 1987b). Finally, and related to this point, there was inadequate mobilization of domestic resources for capital formation (Kapur, Hadjimichael, Hibert, Schiff, and Szymczak, 1991).

Two examples of economic mismanagement stand out. The first was the large government deficits that resulted mainly from low cocoa duty, and which were mostly financed through borrowing from domestic financial institutions (Leechor, 1994). This caused an average monetary growth of about 42 per cent between 1978 to 1983, resulting in excess liquidity and high rates of inflation in the 1970s. The rate of inflation peaked at 129 per cent in 1983.

Second, the maintenance of a fixed and highly overvalued exchange rate discouraged exports and resulted in huge profits for traders of imported goods (Leechor, 1994). Despite the massive deterioration in terms of trade, and the high rate of inflation, successive governments failed to adjust their domestic policies on the exchange rate. The official rate was hardly adjusted, remaining at 2.75 cedis per US dollar from 1978 to 1982. However, Table 1 shows that the parallel exchange rate changed from 10.00 cedis per US dollar in 1978 to 61.67 cedis per US dollar in 1982. Cocoa producers were severely affected by the exchange rate policy. Despite periodic large increases in the nominal producer price of cocoa, the real value of the producer price in 1980 was about half the real value in 1970. Many cocoa farmers were unable to maintain and harvest their farms. Furthermore, most of the farms had exceeded their economically productive life. This contributed significantly to the decline in cocoa exports and a shortage of foreign exchange. The foreign exchange squeeze also affected local manufacturing industries that depended on imported inputs.

iii. *The impact of the economic crisis*

The major consequence of the economic crisis was a substantial reduction in the living standards of most Ghanaians (World Bank, 1985a). In urban centres real wages and salaries were so low that they were simply impossible to live on. Many Ghanaians had to supplement their wages and salaries by engaging in petty trading or small business. Most workers adjusted by producing more of their own food and other requirements. Illicit rent-seeking activities, known as *kalabule*, became rampant. At the same time, basic infrastructure fell into disrepair, and physical conditions in schools, hospitals, and health centres, as well as water supply facilities, deteriorated because of lack of maintenance. The need to resuscitate the Ghanaian economy became apparent.

The PNDC government quickly realized that the social and economic deprivation of Ghanaians could not be halted without a massive injection of foreign exchange into the economy. The government, therefore, approached the IMF and the World Bank for financial assistance. The multilateral institutions, along with other bilateral donors, agreed to provide assistance, but subject to conditions comprised in a package of economic and financial reforms, and introduced as the ERP in April 1983.

III. The ERP

By the adoption of the ERP, Ghana became the first African economy to introduce a structural adjustment programme. Between 1983 and 1986 the ERP aimed to arrest the decline in the Ghanaian economy through sound macroeconomic management. The emphasis was on adherence to strict fiscal and monetary discipline, the rehabilitation of the country's social and economic infrastructure, the realignment of relative prices in favour of productive activities and exports, and the liberalization of international trade (Aryeetey, Harrigan, and Nissanke, 2000). This period can, therefore, be considered the period of stabilization.

Between 1986 and 1992 the second phase of the ERP sought to adjust the economy by focussing on the removal of structural impediments from the Ghanaian economy, to promote increased output and growth, and on the liberalization of the economy, to encourage private sector savings and investment. Measures to mitigate the social cost of the ERP were also introduced (Aryeetey, Harrigan, and Nissanke, 2000). This period can, therefore, be thought of as the period of adjustment. From 1992 to 2000 the adjustment processes were broadened and deepened. Emphasis continued to be placed on the removal of structural bottlenecks to increase output and growth, the liberalization of the economy to encourage private sector savings and investment, and measures to alleviate poverty. However, the policies were pursued under a democratically elected government, and this period can be thought of as a period of continuing adjustment (Leite et al., 2000). Table 2 gives a broad overview of the policies and reforms introduced under the different phases of the ERP.

i. *Exchange rate reforms*
The authorities adopted a gradual approach in moving towards a unified, market-driven foreign exchange system. Between 1983 and 1986 a step-wise devaluation of the value of the domestic currency, the cedi, resulted in its depreciating from 2.75 cedis per US dollar to 90.0 cedis per US dollar.

A weekly Dutch auction system was introduced in 1986 in place of the administrative allocation of foreign exchange. Initially, a two-tier system was introduced, where a higher, officially determined, rate applied to cocoa exports, debt servicing, and the importation of petroleum and essential drugs, while a lower auction rate applied to all other foreign exchange transactions. The exchange rates were unified in 1987 and the auction rate applied to all foreign exchange transactions. Private foreign exchange bureaux were permitted in 1988. The auction system was replaced with an interbank market system in 1992.

ii. *Increases in the producer price of cocoa*
Various increases in the producer price of cocoa were approved under the adjustment programme, in line with the government's objective of paying cocoa farmers about 55 per cent of the long-run world market price for cocoa (Loxley, 1991: 17). The producer price of cocoa was increased periodically

Table 2 Policy measures and reforms under the EAP

Area of reform	Stabilization phase (1983-1986)	Adjustment phase (1986-1992)	Continued adjustment phase (1992-2000)
Pricing reforms	• Currency devaluation • Increases in producer prices,especially cocoa • Removal of price controls • Wage restrictions • Reduction of subsidies for agricultural inputs • Cost recovery measures • Rationalization/ deregulation of energy and utility prices	• Market-oriented foreign exchange auction introduced • Interest rates liberalization • Increased producer price of cocoa • Guaranteed minimum price for maize and rice increased • Bank fees and charges decontrolled • Licensing of foreign exchange bureaux	• Wage and salary increases • Increased producer price of cocoa • Guaranteed minimum price for staples abolished • Removal of subsidies for agricultural inputs
Monetary policy and reforms	• Tight monetary policy through credit ceilings	• Tight monetary policy through credit ceilings • Bank restructuring plan adopted • New banking law to enhance the supervisory role of the Bank of Ghana adopted • New management and board of directors for all banks appointed • Non-performing loans of the private sector and state enterprises in financially distressed banks replaced primarily with Bank of Ghana bonds • Requirement that banks lend for agriculture abolished	• Tight monetary policy through open market operations (mostly using T-Bills) • Repurchase Agreements (REPOs) introduced • Automated book-entry system introduced for trading and keeping record of holdings of T- Bills

Source Alderman (1991); Armstrong (1996); Aryeetey, Harrigan, and Nissanke (2000); Institute of Statistical Social and Economic Research, various issues; Loxley (1991); Tsikata (2001).

Area of reform	Stabilization phase (1983-1986)	Adjustment phase (1986-1992)	Continued adjustment phase (1992-2000)
Fiscal policy and reforms	• Tax reform to increase government revenue • Fiscal discipline	• Fiscal discipline • Medium-term expenditure planning framework introduced	• Introduction and withdrawal of Value Added Tax at 15% in 1995 • Tax Reform • Introduction of Value Added Tax at 10% in 1998 • Medium-term expenditure framework introduced
Structural policies and reforms	• Rationalization of tariffs and duties • Removal of import controls • Measures to increase cocoa production	• Financial sector reforms • Investment promotion • Divestiture of some State Owned Enterprises (SOEs) • Export promotion • Measures to increase agricultural output • Public sector investment programme	• AGC shares floated • Divestiture of additional SOEs • Procurement of agricultural inputs privatized • Private companies licensed to purchase cocoa on behalf of Cocoa Board alongside Produce Buying Company
Institutional reforms	• Establishment of the National Commission for Democracy	• Management reforms in SOEs • Financial sector reforms • Civil service reforms • Capacity building in core ministries • Reforms to enhance the planning process • Educational reforms • Establishment of PAMSCAD secretariat • Improvement in the statistical and information system • Presidential and parliamentary elections in 1992	• Establishment of a multi-sector regulatory agency • Coordination of donor support for public sector management • Establishment of measures and institutions for poverty alleviation • Presidential and parliamentary elections in 1996 • Presidential and parliamentary elections in 2000

from 20,000 cedis per tonne in 1983 to 2,428,000 cedis per tonne in 2000.

iii. Monetary policy and financial sector reforms

The monetary authorities attempted to use a tight monetary policy to reduce domestic absorption, eliminate balance-of-payments deficits, and reduce inflation. This was done through credit ceilings, credit controls, and increasing administrative interest rates. Interest rates were liberalized with an adoption of open-market operations, primarily through Bank of Ghana Treasury Bills. The government also realized that the banking system had failed in its primary objective of mobilization of resources for growth and development, and in its supporting role of the development of a monetary sector. The financial industry was, therefore, reformed to improve financial intermediation. Non-bank financial institutions, including credit unions, rural banks, and non-governmental organizations, were established to improve financial intermediation in the rural areas. A variety of special credit programmes were introduced to provide financial assistance to the private sector. Bank restructuring was also initiated in 1989, and new basic regulations were introduced, including minimum capital requirements, capital adequacy ratios, prudential lending ratios, exposure limits, and accounting and auditing regulations. The supervisory role of the Bank of Ghana over financial institutions was strengthened. Banks were required to submit accounts for off-site monitoring, and annual on-site inspections as well as off-surveillance were instituted to verify compliance with regulations. Bank of Ghana Bills were introduced in 1988 as interest-bearing instruments the banks could hold. Non-performing loans, which had reached about 41 per cent of total credit in 1989, were swapped for government-guaranteed, interest-bearing bonds issued by the Bank of Ghana, or were offset against liabilities to the government or the central bank in 1990 and 1991. The banking system was liberalized and a stock market established in October 1990. The Bank of Ghana introduced Repurchase Agreements in 1998 that involved daily reversible transactions in Treasury Bills with maturities of up to 14 days.

iv. Fiscal policy

The main objective was to reduce fiscal deficits in order to control inflation and prevent the crowding out of the private sector. Policies to achieve this objective included cost-recovery measures for public services, reduction and elimination of subsidies, divestiture of state-owned enterprises, retrenchment in the civil service, rationalization of the tax structure, mobilization of taxes, improvement in the efficiency of tax collection, broadening of the tax base, introduction of a Value Added Tax, and general fiscal restraint. At the same time, efforts were made to rehabilitate the economic and social infrastructure with increasing outlays for infrastructural development under a Public Sector Investment Programme.

v. Wage and salary reforms
After initial restrictions on wages and salaries in the civil service, the government established a national Tripartite Committee of representatives from the government, the trade unions, and the private sector to review wages and salaries. Various adjustments were recommended by the committee under the different phases of the adjustment programme.

vi. Liberalization of prices
Prices subsidies were abolished and full cost-recovery increases permitted on water bills, electricity bills, and medical services.

vii. Savings and investment
Policies under the adjustment programme aimed at shifting the focus from public investment to private investment, including foreign investment, and the replacement of administrative control over the allocation of resources with market forces. Reforms most pertinent to investment and savings included government efforts to increase public savings and reduce domestic borrowing requirements, including the tax measures noted above. Public infrastructural development to complement the production of marketable products by the private sector was promoted. Domestic price reforms and the liberalization of external trade provided incentives for private investment. In particular, the reduction in tariff rates from 30 per cent in 1985 to 10 per cent in 1990 would, it was hoped, promote private investment. Finally, tax reforms reduced corporate taxes.

viii. Trade liberalization and foreign investment
The import licence scheme was abolished in 1989, thus removing all restrictions on imports. Tariffs were rationalized with tariff rate often between 10 and 30 per cent. Export taxes were abolished, except for cocoa. Non-traditional exporters were not obliged to surrender their foreign exchange receipts to the Bank of Ghana. Barriers to the entry of foreign firms were, in large part, abolished.

ix. Structural reforms
In an attempt to improve productivity, various reforms were introduced to change the structure of the Ghanaian economy. Company income tax was reduced in the manufacturing sector. Favourable new investment and mineral codes were enacted. Measures were also taken to streamline investment procedures. Remittance of dividends overseas was allowed as an incentive to private sector investment. The banking system was reformed to restore confidence in the financial industry. A Private Sector Advisory Group was established to advise the government on how to encourage private investments. Some state-owned enterprises (SOEs) were divested and the Ashanti Goldfields Company privatized.

Procurement of agricultural inputs was privatized. Private companies were licensed to purchase cocoa on behalf of the Cocoa Board and the Produce Buying Company. Various programmes and projects were established to rehabilitate agricultural services and increase agricultural productivity. Guaranteed minimum prices for maize and rice were abolished and subsidies on agricultural inputs removed, most notably on fertilizer, insecticides, and fungicides. The International Fund for Agricultural Development also introduced a scheme to help small-holder farmers in the savanna region of the country.

x. Institutional reforms and capacity building
The government launched a civil service reform programme in 1987 to downsize the highly bloated and inefficient civil service, and, at the same time, to introduce capacity-building activities to improve the efficiency of various institutions. For example, Policy Planning, Monitoring, and Evaluation departments were created in some ministries, including the Ministry of Agriculture, the Ministry of Finance, and the Ministry of Trade. A Debt Management

Department was also established in the Ministry of Finance to monitor and coordinate donor support. Management reforms were initiated in SOEs, financial sector reforms were introduced, and the collection, analysis, and dissemination of statistical information by the Ghana Statistical Service improved considerably. A Program of Action to Mitigate the Social Costs of Adjustment (PAMSCAD) was introduced to address the social impact of the adjustment programme.

The National Commission for Democracy (NCD) was established in 1982 with responsibility for the political education of civil society, and to advise the government on how to develop a participatory democratic process. The NCD was also responsible for monitoring the government's performance in fostering a democratic process. In 1990, the NCD recommended the adoption of a multiparty democratic system, and in 1991 a 260-member Consultative Assembly began its proceedings. A new constitution was adopted in 1992, and presidential and parliamentary elections held in November and December, respectively. The second and third elections under the new constitution were held in December 1996 and December 2000, respectively.

In 1990, the National Development Planning Commission (NDPC) was established to formulate and implement an enhanced economic strategy for consolidating the achievements of the ERP. The commission was also responsible for laying the foundations for accelerated economic growth and poverty reduction. The NDPC developed a long-term programme of economic and social policies that became known as Ghana—Vision 2020 (Government of Ghana, 1995).

IV. The impact of the ERP

On the basis of the broad objectives of the three phases of the ERP, and the specific objectives of various measures and reforms, a number of benchmarks could be used to evaluating the ERP. However, three conventional benchmarks—growth, savings and investment—had a crucial impact on economic dynamism and structural change.

i.   The impact of the ERP on economic growth

Economic growth averaged about 4.6 per cent per annum from 1984 to 2000 (Table 3). Economic growth in the stabilization phase averaged 5.4 per cent

Baffoe

Table 3 Ghana: selected economic indicators, 1983–2000

	1983	1984	1985	1986	1987	1988	1989	1990	1991
Real GDP (millions of 1975 cedis)	4888	5158	5420	5702	5975	6312	6633	6853	7217
Real GDP growth (%)	-2.9	5.5	5.1	5.2	4.8	5.6	5.1	3.3	5.3
Real per capita GDP (in 1975 cedis)	391	416	426	437	446	459	470	474	486
Contribution of agriculture to GDP (%)	61.3	53.9	51.6	50.7	48.4	47.4	47.1	44.6	44.4
Contribution of services to GDP (%)	24.7	37.3	38.0	38.5	40.2	41.0	41.6	43.5	43.9
Contribution of industry to GDP (%)	14.0	11.5	13.0	13.3	14.1	14.4	14.0	14.5	14.3
Growth in agricultural GDP (%)	-6.9	9.7	0.65	3.3	0.04	3.6	4.2	-2.0	4.7
Growth in services GDP (%)	0.31	72.7	7.5	6.5	9.4	7.8	6.7	7.9	6.3
Growth in industrial GDP (%)	-11.9	9.0	17.6	7.6	11.5	7.3	2.6	6.9	3.7
Gross fixed capital formation (% of GDP)	3.6	6.9	9.5	9.3	10.4	10.9	13.5	12.2	12.7
Public sector investment (% of GDP)	0.7	2.5	4.1	7.2	7.9	7.6	8.0	4.6	4.6
Private investment (% of GDP)	2.9	4.4	5.4	2.1	2.5	3.3	5.5	7.6	8.1
Gross savings (% of GDP)	3.5	8.0	8.1	9.7	12.5	15.0	12.0	8.6	9.0
Average monthly earnings (cedis)	973	2287	3631	7433	10524	13805	24257	30056	35212
Real average monthly earnings (in 1975 cedis)	25.49	42.90	61.7	101.4	102.7	102.5	143.8	129.9	129.0

Sources Alderman (1991); Aryeetey, Harrigan, and Nissanke (2000); Central Bureau of Statistics, various issues; Institute of Statistical Social and Economic Research, various issues; May (1985).

142

	1992	1993	1994	1995	1996	1997	1998	1999	2000
Real GDP (millions of 1975 cedis)	7498	7873	8168	8535	8976	9433	9867	10305	10690
Real GDP growth (%)	3.9	5.0	3.8	4.0	4.6	4.2	4.6	4.4	3.7
Real per capita GDP (in 1975 cedis)	492	503	509	519	532	545	558	566	573
Contribution of agriculture to GDP (%)	42.5	44.1	40.8	36.3	36.5	36.6	36.7	36.5	36.0
Contribution of services to GDP (%)	45.5	30.8	31.3	28.1	28.0	28.7	29.0	29.2	29.7
Contribution of industry to GDP (%)	14.5	29.8	27.9	24.9	24.9	25.4	25.1	25.2	25.2
Growth in agricultural GDP (%)	-0.64	2.5	2.9	4.2	4.0	4.3	5.1	3.9	2.1
Growth in services GDP (%)	7.7	7.0	5.0	4.7	4.2	6.5	6.0	5.0	5.4
Growth in industrial GDP (%)	5.8	4.3	1.3	4.1	4.8	6.4	2.5	4.8	3.8
Gross fixed capital formation (% of GDP)	13.8	14.6	14.2	13.6	16.0	17.9	20.0	22.2	24.6
Public sector investment (% of GDP)	9.5	9.7	11.1	9.5	7.8	6.2	8.4	11.2	12.0
Private investment (% of GDP)	4.3	4.9	3.1	4.1	8.2	11.7	11.6	11.0	12.6
Gross savings (% of GDP)	8.0	5.5	9.6	10.6	13.5	4.2	15.0	17.0	18.1
Average monthly earnings (cedis)	39712	n.a.	n.a.	n.a.	n.a.	n.a.	n.a.	n.a.	n.a.
Real average monthly earnings (in 1975 cedis)	132.1	n.a.	n.a.	n.a.	n.a.	n.a.	n.a.	n.a.	n.a.

per annum, and growth in the adjustment and continued adjustment phases averaged 4.7 per cent and 4.3 per cent per annum, respectively. While there has been growth during the ERP, the momentum of growth has slowed, which helps explain trends in real per capita GDP. Real per capita GDP in constant 1975 cedis rose from 391 in 1983 to 573 in 2000, an increase of 46.5 per cent. However, despite this increase, real per capita GDP in 2000 was about the same as that of 1973. Not only has the momentum of growth slowed, but the impact of growth upon per capita GDP has been disappointing.

As Table 3 demonstrates, the contribution of the agricultural sector in GDP decreased from 61.3 per cent in 1983 to about 36 per cent in 2000. By way of contrast, the contribution by services increased from 24.7 per cent in 1983 to 29.7 per cent in 2000, and the contribution of the industrial sector increased from 14 per cent in 1983 to 25.2 per cent in 2000. Thus, the structure of the Ghanaian economy moved from a predominantly agricultural-based economy to a structure in which agriculture, services, and industry were all important, albeit with agriculture remaining "first among equals."

In terms of sectoral growth, agricultural GDP growth averaged about 3 per cent per annum from 1984 to 2000. However, growth fluctuated from 4.5 per cent per annum in the stabilization phase, to 1.65 per cent per annum in the adjustment phase, and to about 3.63 per cent per annum in the continued adjustment phase. Overall, agricultural GDP growth lagged behind overall GDP growth, reducing the rate of economic growth. This lag is explained by the weak supply response of various agricultural policies initiated under the ERP (Aryeetey, Harrigan, and Nissanke, 2000), including an increase in the domestic price of farm inputs resulting from the removal of agricultural subsidies. As well, the continued reliance of agricultural production on rains meant agriculture was very vulnerable to adverse climatic conditions.

Growth in services GDP averaged about 10.3 per cent from 1984 to 2000. Services GDP grew at an average of 28.95 per cent in the stabilization phase, 7.63 per cent in the adjustment phase, and 5.47 per cent in the continued adjustment phase. The slowdown in the services sector parallels that in overall growth, which was mainly due to transportation problems and infrastructural constraints. In particular, despite the numerous road-rehabilitation programmes, the country's roads were badly maintained.

Growth in industrial GDP averaged about 6.1 per cent per annum from 1984 to 2000. Industrial GDP grew at an average of 11.4 per cent in the stabilization phase, 6.3 per cent in the adjustment phase, and about 4 per cent in the continued adjustment phase. Once again, the slowdown in the growth momentum in the industrial sector parallels that of overall growth. However, there was wide variance in this growth pattern (World Bank, 2001b). The fastest growing industries were cement, petroleum, and metals. Mineral production also increased considerably because of the doubling of gold production by the Ashanti Goldfields Company. The construction industry was also very active during the ERP. Offsetting this was the major problem of insufficient electric power generation to meet the country's needs. This remains a major structural problem.

ii.   The impact of the ERP on savings and investment

The share of gross fixed capital formation in GDP increased steadily from 3.6 per cent in 1983 to 24.6 per cent in 2000 (see Table 3). Overall, the investment ratio was among the top 10 in sub-Saharan Africa (Leite et al., 2000: 18). The contribution of the private and public sectors towards investment, however, fluctuated during the period. Investment from the mid-1980s to the late 1980s was led by the public sector, an increase from its abysmal level of 0.7 per cent of GDP in 1983 to 8 per cent of GDP in 1989, while private sector investment declined from 5.4 per cent of GDP in 1985 to 3.3 per cent of GDP in 1988. During the period between 1990 and 1992, there were some fluctuations in the relative importance of public and private sector investment. However, private investment rose consistently from 8.2 per cent of GDP in 1996 to 12.6 per cent of GDP in 2000, while public sector investment declined from 11.1 per cent of GDP in 1994 to 6.2 per cent of GDP in 1997, before recovering to 12 per cent in 2000. As with the industrial sector, there was some variation in the investment record of the private sector (World Bank, 2001b). In the mining sector, for example, there was a substantial increase in private investment due to the expansion of the Ashanti Goldfields Company and the opening of several foreign-invested mining enterprises.

However, overall, private investment showed a weak response to the adjustment policies. Several factors explain this. First, the high lending rates resulting from the liberalization of interest rates in an era of high inflation made the cost of borrowed capital very expensive. For example, the average lending rates during the stabilization phase, the adjustment phase, and the continued adjustment phase were 15.75 per cent, 23.5 per cent, and 37 per cent, respectively. At the same time as interest rates were liberalized, the Bank of Ghana pursued a tight monetary policy, which produced a credit crunch even as interest rates soared. Second, the high domestic cost of imported raw materials, resulting from the massive depreciation of the domestic currency after the liberalization of the foreign exchange market, increased the cost of investing. Third, the inability of domestic companies to compete with the technologically advanced and economically efficient foreign companies after trade liberalization weakened the investment response of the domestic private sector.

The ratio of gross saving to GDP averaged about 7.3 per cent in the stabilization phase, 10.9 per cent in the adjustment phase, and 11.7 per cent in the continued adjustment phase. Annual figures are shown in Table 3. These savings rates were fairly consistently beneath the government's target, and the savings impact of the ERP was disappointing. Several factors contributed to the low saving rate. These included negative real saving rates resulting from the high rates of inflation, low real wages, large borrowing by the government to finance the deficits in the 1990s, and the lack of saving mobilization efforts by the major financial institutions.

V. Conclusions

After almost 20 years of structural adjustment policies, the growth record of the Ghanaian economy has been disappointing, not least of all to Ghanaians themselves. Following an initial boost to growth from stabilization and adjustment, the momentum of growth slowed. By 2000 the average Ghanaian was not better off, in terms of per capita income, than in 1973. Moreover, although the economy had become more diversified, agriculture remained, after almost 20 years of adjustment, the mainstay of the Ghanaian economy.

Agricultural growth was erratic under the ERP. Policy had sought to address structural problems by promoting private sector investment to increase productivity. However, the removal of subsidies on agricultural inputs was at odds with the objective of improving productivity and food security, because input use declined. As a result, the supply response of the agricultural sector to the ERP was disappointing.

A similar story can be told in the industrial sector. Policy was predicated on the view that the sector, and particularly the manufacturing sector, was hampered by distortions in prices emanating from exchange rate policy and the trade regime. The emphasis was, therefore, on liberalization, in order to make the industrial sector more efficient. However, the foreign exchange constraint led to import strangulation, and reduced the production capacity of the manufacturing sector. Getting the prices right was not enough to stimulate production; to compete effectively, some non-price production and investment constraints had to be addressed. That these were not is demonstrated by the private investment record, which remained disappointing. Exchange rate devaluation and high interest rates made the cost of borrowing extremely high, while the private sector continued to face constraints in domestic credit markets. National savings rates remained very low.

The services sector has increased its share of GDP, but following an impressive growth performance during the stabilization phase, the momentum of the sector has slowed. Retail and wholesale activities responded to the liberalized environment, and tourism activities and some financial services expanded to take advantage of the removal of controls. The role of the services sector is, in part, to facilitate the smooth running of the productive sector. Hence, if the productive sector does not expand as rapidly as the services sector, the future growth of the services sector might be further constrained.

In this light, the long-term sustainability of growth in Ghana might be called into question. The services sector, which has witnessed the most dramatic increase in its share of GDP, is linked to activities in the agricultural and industrial sectors, and thus requires growth in these latter two sectors. However, growth in both the industrial and agricultural sectors has been disappointing. In the industrial sector in particular, the growth momentum has slowed since the conclusion of the stabilization phase. The weak supply response indicates that the private investment response sought by policy-makers has not been forthcoming. This begs a question: what explains the growth that has occurred? The answer is that the growth that has occurred under the ERP has often been due to public investment (Loxley, 1991). Much of this public investment is donor-funded. Indeed, the Ghanaian economy is now more donor-dependent than at any time in its history, and is, as a consequence, very vulnerable to public policy in donor countries.

The impact of structural adjustment in Ghana has been one of disappointing growth, ongoing difficulties in increasing private sector investment, and increasing dependence on donors. Sustainable economic development in Ghana requires a change in economic strategy that addresses the constraints that hamper the development of a strong agricultural sector and that links agricultural production to the processing and manufacturing industries. The ERP has singularly failed to do this.

Chapter 8

AGRICULTURE AND ECONOMIC ADJUSTMENT: THE CASE OF EGYPT

Ray Bush

I. Introduction

THIS chapter reviews Egypt's experience of economic reform, particularly in the agricultural sector, in order to question the declared success of structural adjustment in Egypt.[1] Economic reform can be traced back to 1986, when agricultural liberalization was initiated by Deputy Prime Minister Yusef Wali. The process of reform deepened considerably when a structural adjustment programme was introduced in 1991. The reform programme of the Government of Egypt (GoE) had been intended to deliver economic growth and alleviate poverty, in large part by fostering greater proximity to international markets for Egypt's farmers while attempting to create a capital-intensive and export-oriented agriculture. However, the actual experience of reform has been very different. Citing a report in *Business Monitor International*, one of Egypt's main opposition newspapers reported in 2000 that "the effect of the policy of economic reform did not extend to the poor and that the distribution of the dividends of the economic activities was not fair" (*Al Ahali*, 22 March 2000). The paper noted that the share of gross domestic product (GDP) for the poorest 20 per cent of the population fell from 3.9 per cent to 1.7 per cent in the period between 1991 and 1995. During the same period the share of GDP for the richest 20 per cent of the population rose from 41 per cent to 46 per cent. The paper drew the implication that the social costs of economic reform have been harsh.

At the same time, the delivery of fundamental elements of the reform programme has been very slow. By the end of 1999 Egypt still had privatized only

131 of the 314 public sector companies originally identified for privatization (Economist Intelligence Unit, 2000) and the banking sector in particular remained under the control of the GoE. Relations with the major international financial institutions (IFIs), especially the World Bank and the International Monetary Fund (IMF), were, by mid-2002, fraught, as reform was not being delivered with sufficient rigour by the GoE. Although international donors had agreed in February 2002 to US$10.3 billion in support for the country over three years, the IMF refused the fast disbursement of US$2.1 billion. While the IFIs seemed to accept that the Egyptian economy was in a recession, the IMF was particularly unhappy that Egypt had not adopted a more flexible approach to the management of the exchange rate. Moreover, in general, the patience of the IFIs was running out more quickly than in the past. Despite the fact that the 900,000 young people who entered the job market annually had almost non-existent employment prospects (Fergany, 2002), the IFIs tended to disregard the social implications of such poor employment performance. Indeed, the IFIs viewed as a mere bargaining tool the argument of the GoE that it could not implement economic liberalization too quickly for fear of possible social unrest that could, in turn, lead to an Islamist uprising. The GoE, in fact, has used its policies of political deliberalization to create an atmosphere that it is under threat. The debacle over the imprisonment, twice, before a final release in 2003, of American university sociology professor and human rights activist Saad Eddin Ibrahim illustrates what the GoE thought it could get away with in terms of Egypt's still relatively independent judiciary and the criticism of the international community. Saad Eddin's prosecution followed a serious clampdown on opponents to the ruling National Democratic Party, when activities of the Islamist Labor Party were suspended in May 2000 and more than 200 members of the banned Muslim Brotherhood were arrested between October 1999 and September 2000 (*Middle East Times*, 2000).

Despite its slow pace of reform and despite the fact that Egyptians were involved in the attacks on the US in September 2001, President Hosni Mubarak gained some international sympathy, if not hard cash, for the consequences on the Egyptian economy of the World Trade Center attack. A decline in tourism after September 11 cost the Egyptian economy US$2 billion and thousands of hotel workers were made redundant (*Financial Times*, 26 June 2002). The more general decline in the world economy after September 11 had an impact on other key elements of Egyptian national income: remittances from transport through the Suez canal, remittances from migrant labour, and oil income.

Notwithstanding the negative social consequences of neo-conservative reform, one of the reasons the pace of change in Egypt has been slower than the IFIs would prefer is because of a contradiction at the heart of economic reform in Egypt, between actual state policy, and notably the persistence of state-sponsored projects, and the rhetoric of neo-conservative free market reform. The contradiction reflects the different perceptions of the role of the state borne by major office holders and by business and elite groups that have benefitted from the early phases of reform. The contradiction is reflected in the crude notions of agricultural modernization that have been used during the reform process, notions that assume that Egypt's farmers know little about markets and incentive structures, and, therefore, require some kind of "guidance."

II. Economic reform

Egypt's Economic Reform and Structural Adjustment Program (ERSAP) was signed in 1991, after three years of negotiation and following the collapse of an agreement with the IMF in May 1987. That earlier agreement was intended to reduce the foreign debt that had accrued during Anwar Sadat's presidency and the open-door policy of *infitah* that had been pursued by Sadat (Waterbury, 1983). The agreement collapsed because of IMF impatience at the pace of change and consequent demands for a further, deeper, opening up of the economy. However, Mubarak was wary of the changes proposed by the IMF in the mid- and late 1980s, such as a hike in interest rates to between 20 and 30 per cent and a large increase in energy costs (Seddon, 1990). He was, in particular, anxious not to generate the economic conditions that could recreate the street protests that had met Sadat's earlier attempt to raise the price of bread. Given this anxiety, it is indeed ironic that the programme to which Mubarak agreed in 1991 was one that went much further than any hitherto proposed set of structural reforms. Mubarak's willingness to accede to a more extensive reform agenda reflected the deep-seated nature of the economic problems facing Egypt at the start of the 1990s.

The 1991 ERSAP gave Egypt an SDR[2] 400 million standby credit agreement with the IMF, a US$300 million adjustment loan from the World Bank, and an agreement with the Paris Club for US$28 billion in relief for official government and military debt. In exchange, the GoE agreed to roll back the state from economic activity (Abdel Khalek, 2001; Niblock, 1993). In so doing, reforms were intended to open the economy to international capital, reduce inflation, and allow exchange rates to respond to market forces (United States Embassy, 1991). To that end, state subsidies were slashed, and there was a restoration of private currency dealing, a new sales tax, a relaxation of the licensing of external trade, and the commitment to reduce the budget deficit from 20 per cent of GDP in 1990-91 to 3.5 per cent in 1994-95 (Butter, 1992).

Egypt met most of its targets. The government deficit fell from 17.7 per cent of GDP in 1991 to 0.8 in 1997. In this, the GoE was helped by revenue from the new sales tax. Total tax revenue rose from E£7.8 billion to E£13.3 billion between 1990 and 1993, an increase of 71 per cent (Ibrahim and Löfgren, 1996: 171). At the same time, subsidies to goods and services fell by 16 per cent, from E£4.5 billion to E£3.8 billion in the 12 months following the introduction of the ERSAP. A new three-year IMF Extended Fund Facility was agreed in 1993, and a further agreement with the IMF for a standby loan was made in October 1996. This later agreement was intended to consolidate earlier reforms, keep the budget deficit close to 1 per cent, and accelerate the pace of privatization. It was also intended to usher in accelerated reductions in energy subsidies (IMF, 1997).

Nonetheless, protracted difficulties between the GoE and the IFIs continued regarding the pace of reform, for reasons that predate September 11. In large part this is because the GoE was never serious about implementing a number of key reforms stipulated by the IFIs. This is true of privatization in general, and especially the intransigence shown by the GoE regarding its removal from the banking sector. Simply, the GoE would never privatize such a valuable and strategically important sector. In this light, it might be asked why Mubarak agreed to the ERSAP in the first place. The answer is straightforward: the president sought a benefit from his alliance with the US during the first Gulf War. A major debt write-off was Egypt's reward for collusion with the "international community's" removal of Iraqi forces from Kuwait, but, in exchange for such a write-off Mubarak had to show that reform of Egypt's ailing economy would be swift. Stabilizing the economy was relatively easy, although the social costs of such action were harsh, and were not compensated by the

Egyptian Social Fund for Development (SFD) initiated by the World Bank and the United Nations Development Programme. The SFD only created short-term temporary employment, rather than implementing policies to address the country's structural employment crisis. Domestically, Mubarak's agreement to withdraw the state from economic production was intended to meet the class interests that supported his presidency, and which had been blocked by the years of Nasser and had not been given enough space by the capitalist zeal of Anwar Sadat. These interests are located in finance capital, construction, and services, groups that had benefitted from preliminary liberalization as long as the influx of foreign capital and competition was stymied (Mitchell, 1999). The domestic constituency also included the military, which receives US$1.3 billion annually from the US (Bush, 1999).

The unwillingness of the state to undertake the sort of deep structural reforms desired by the IFIs put the Egyptian pound under enormous pressure despite four devaluations in the 12 months to July 2002. The four devaluations in 2001 and 2002 led to an effective loss of 25 per cent of the value of the pound. Officially, the pound/dollar exchange rate was put in the range of E£4.50–E£4.64 in mid-2002. However, in mid-2002 the pound exchanged at E£5.10 on the black market, a black market that was said to account for up to 80 per cent of the total volume of trade (*Financial Times*, 26 June 2002).

Despite the pressures on the pound, Egypt's stabilization and reform programme has, in general, been deemed a success by mainstream commentators (Subramanian, 1997; United States Agency for International Development [USAID], 2000). However, more independent voices have demurred, including one of the country's leading economists. Abdel-Khalek (2002: 32) has argued that the reform package failed to note three important specificities of the Egyptian economy: that it was a food-deficit country, that it had experienced extensive "dollarization," and that it had significant idle capacity. To these specificities could be added the economy's overwhelming dependence upon income from three sources: rents from the Suez canal, labour remittances, and oil. With their emphasis upon the sequencing of reform, their concern with getting the exchange rate and interest rates right, and their preoccupation with trade, the IFIs and the GoE have failed to recognize these specificities. As a consequence, they have neglected the real economy. "In short," Abdel-Khalek (2002: 32) has argued, "issues of *exchange* appear to have taken *precedence* over those of production, with significant negative consequences." Nowhere is this more true than agriculture.

III. Reforming agriculture

Agriculture in Egypt accounts for about 19 per cent of GDP, 36 per cent of overall employment, and 22 per cent of commodity exports (USAID, 1999). More than half of Egypt's population of 68 million people lives in the countryside. Between 1981 and 1992 the average rate of real growth in agriculture was about 2 per cent per annum (Nassar, 1993). During the early part of this period, the most common explanation for Egypt's comparatively low agricultural performance had been the inheritance of price and marketing controls from the Nasserist era, and continued state ownership of major agricultural processing and marketing industries. These difficulties were recognized at an early stage of this period, and by the mid-1980s the GoE, with assistance from USAID, had initiated a reform programme (Bush, 1999). The core policy objectives of this neo-conservative programme included getting the state out of agricultural production, liberalizing input and output markets, promoting the adoption and export of high-value, low-nutrition agricultural products, including flowers and strawberries, and reforming land tenancy (World Bank, 1992b).

The agricultural reform package, which was initiated well before the 1991 ERSAP, has been trumpeted as a major success (Faris and Khan, 1993; Fletcher, 1996). There had been, for instance, an increase in crop production of 23 major crops between 1980 and 1990. Of notable importance, there was a doubling of wheat production, Egypt's key staple, between 1986 and 1992 as a consequence of a deregulation of cropping patterns, an expansion of the planted area, and an improvement in yields. This, in turn, facilitated an increase in farm incomes, further sustained by the decline in food subsidies initiated under the ERSAP. Yet underneath this apparent reform success rhetoric lie important caveats. The GoE had a growth target of 5 per cent per annum between 1981 and 1992. Agricultural performance failed to meet the targets set by the GoE. At the same time, USAID had provided, since the mid-1980s, about US$1.26 billion for the development of the sector. Given this volume of assistance, agricultural performance looks all the more disappointing. At the same time, while production increases were evident in the mid-1980s, production has slowed since 1990 (Mitchell, 1998). However, instead of concluding from this that the policies it has been promoting have been, at best, inappropriate, or, at worst, have further undermined the sector, USAID argued that "continued USAID support for the sector is essential" (USAID, 2000).

There are at least five reasons why the agricultural reform programme initiated in the mid-1980s has been, in many ways, a major disappointment. The first reason is that reformers have been relying on unreliable aggregate economic data. Economic accounting has undoubtedly improved in Egypt but ministries simply do not have accurate and reliable agricultural data upon which to make sweeping judgements about success. The second reason relates not so much to the quality of the data, but to the timeliness of the data. Fifteen years after USAID and GoE reforms began, liberalizers continue to rely on evidence of early increases in productivity, increases that have not been sustained over the life of the reform process (Bush 2002).

The third reason is that Egypt has been unable to benefit from the export-oriented strategy adopted by the GoE under the advice of USAID. The problem here is that most of the country's agricultural imports include staple commodities with low elasticities of demand, such as wheat, sugar, and edible oils. However, most exports are marked by high-demand elasticities. As a consequence, while agricultural exports may have increased from E£418 million in 1980 to just under E£1.9 billion in 1998, agricultural imports for the same period ballooned from E£1.2 billion in 1980 to E£11 billion in 1998. Agriculture thus contributed in 1998 to 33 per cent of Egypt's trade deficit (*Al Ahram Weekly*, 13-19 January 2000). This reflects the deep structural problem that Egypt is a deficit-food producer. Egypt produces about 6.5 metric tonnes of wheat, which amounts to about one-half of national demand, of which 3 million tonnes are used to produce *baladi* bread, which remains subsidized (*Financial Times*, 26 June 2002). Egypt's minister of supply, Hassan Khedr, noted in 2002 that the GoE spends E£3 billion per annum subsidizing bread, which accounts for an average of 52 per cent of the calorific intake for most Egyptians (*Financial Times*, 26 June 2002). The GoE has a long way to go before it meets its wheat production target of 13 million tonnes. As a consequence, Egypt is one of the top five global wheat importers (*Financial Times*, 26 June 2002)). By mid-June 2002 Egypt had imported about 1 million tonnes more than in the 2000-2001 period. Moreover, government subsidies for flour, edible oils and sugar remain untouched by economic reform. The need for farmers, and in particular small, land-holding peasants, to continue to produce food, has meant that agricultural diversification has been severely hampered, and, as a consequence, agricultural export growth has not materialized, despite the hopes of reformers. Thus, in 1998 Egypt produced an estimated 21 million tonnes of horticultural crops, of which only 5 per cent were exported (figures from Shura Council report, cited in *Al Ahram Weekly*, 13-19 January 2000).

The fourth reason that agricultural reform has been disappointing is because it has not only failed to deliver growth in employment, but it has, perversely, reduced rural employment opportunities dramatically, especially for women. According to Nader Fergany (2002), 700,000 jobs were lost in agriculture between 1990 and 1995. The impact of agricultural reform on tenurial relations accounts for at least some of this poor employment performance, the impact of which is all the more worrying because the urban growth that was meant to absorb the rural displaced has not happened. Even the Shura Council, which acts as Egypt's upper house, noted in 1996 that economic reform had so slowed employment growth that they were concerned with its continuation.

The fifth and final reason agricultural reform has been disappointing is that although some farm incomes have risen, poor agricultural performance, in particular in staple crop production, along with diminished employment prospects, has meant that rural poverty has generally accelerated during the reform period, as noted by the government's own statistical service (CAPMAS, 1998). Real incomes have fallen by 14 per cent in the cities and 20 per cent in the rural areas since 1991. If the measure of US$1 per person per day is used as a measure of poverty, and we assume E£500 is necessary for a family of five per month, then more than 80 per cent of Egyptians are poor. However, this result is not surprising; processes facilitating a deepening of poverty have been intrinsic to agricultural reform in Egypt.

IV. Modernizing agriculture and reforming tenure

In seeking to reform the agrarian sector, the GoE and the IFIs have explicitly pursued the modernization of agriculture. This pursuit has been seen as necessary to the liberation of rural productive forces from bureaucratic state power. Within the perspective of agricultural modernization, a number of policy instruments have been used, including the structure of land ownership and control, with tenure and reform issues, the role of technology, and the choice of particular technical solutions to agricultural productivity. The strategy to modernize agriculture has been to assert that changes in the policy environment will drive improvements in cash crop production and changes in rural property rights will improve rural incentive structures.

Probably the most significant reform measure undertaken by the GoE in the agricultural sector has been the reform of land tenure. Perhaps as much as 30 per cent of Egypt's agricultural land is tenanted, and tenants access their own family land too, renting in and sometimes renting out (Abdel Aal, 2002). There are probably about one million tenants in Egypt, of which probably 90 per cent rent in less than 5 *feddan*[3] (Saad, 2002). Reform of tenure took place with Law 96 of 1992, which revoked Nasser's Agrarian Reform Law number 178 of 1952. Law 96 emerged after a vigorous campaign by the GoE, in which it argued that farmers were wealthy and landowners were exploited as a result of Nasserist reforms. Nasser had given tenants rights of security of tenure and legal rights of tenancy. As a consequence, until 1992, rents for tenants were fixed at seven times the land tax, which was revised every 10 years and which was, on average, about E£20 per *feddan*. Moreover, the heirs of tenants under Nasser's legislation had de facto rights of inheritance and contracts held in perpetuity. In its campaign against Nasserist agrarian policy, the GoE argued that there was now a need for a return to "normalcy," in which, as an erstwhile military leader of the ruling National Democratic Party argued, justice would be done. In this instance, normalcy and justice implied landowners at last receiving a "fair" rent for their land.

Following the enactment of Law 96, a five-year transition period was established. However, many farmers did not think the legislation would actually be enacted. They were wrong, and when it was enacted on 1 October 1997 there were some immediate negative consequences. Those tenants who demanded delays in the implementation of the law or representation at a reconciliation meeting were threatened with expulsion. Many were, in fact, expelled and, as a result, lost crops in the ground (Land Center for Human Rights, 2002). This was especially the case in upper Egypt, where the sugar crop is cultivated over 12 months (Abdel Aal, 2002).

After the transition period all landowners could retake their land and charge tenants a market-based rent. As a consequence, with Law 96, rents in some cases increased to between E£1200 and E£2400 per *feddan*, depending on location and productivity—increases of between 300 to 350 per cent. Moreover, tenancies became annual, and tenancy agreements are seldom held by the actual tenants. Indeed, Law 96 allows landowners to dispose of land as they see fit, without notifying tenants at all, even if they have been farming land for very lengthy periods of time. Thus, tenant farmers became more insecure. That increase in insecurity had a further result. It undermined the access of farmers to new credit, because of both the loss of land that could be used as collateral as well as evicted tenants' failure to repay debts taken out before the loss of land to landowners.

There was opposition to Law 96 on the ground, although it was piecemeal. One striking exception, however, took place in April 1997, when 7000 farmers assembled in Cairo to oppose the legislation to be enacted in October. The Minister of Agriculture refused to accept a petition of 350,000 names collected over eight months, protesting against the bill. The minister did not believe the opposition could be so strong (Interview, Opposition Activist, Cairo, May 2000). Yet it was. Spontaneous and uncoordinated opposition was witnessed in around 100 of Egypt's more than 3000 villages. Indeed, violent protests against dispossession took place in the governorates of Dakhalia, Faiyum, Luxor, Qena, Sharkia, Menoufia, and Giza. In these areas security forces were used to enforce the interests of landowners before any attempts were made to use the courts to resolve legal issues. As a consequence, opposition was suppressed, with many tenants being forced off the land. One human rights organization specializing in rural issues, the Land Center for Human Rights (LCHR), estimated that between January 1998 and December 2000 there were 119 deaths, 846 injuries, and 1500 arrests in Egypt's countryside relating to the implementation of and subsequent conflict about Law 96 (LCHR, 2002). Sporadic rural unrest continued into 2002.

The GoE argued that the unrest was orchestrated by Islamists. In so doing, the government made the issue of farmer opposition to Law 96 one of law and order rather than of opposition to an unjust law. However, the depth and breadth of the opposition to Law 96, with the issues of control and access to land, as well as linked struggles over water rights and irrigation, indicate that rural Egypt is now more highly politicized than it was during the 1950s. The question that naturally emerges then, given this outcome, is why Law 96 was enacted at all, along with the related question of whether it met the demands of the IFIs on the GoE that land markets be liberalized.

V. The politics of Law 96

Although the reform of land tenure was not part of the ERSAP, it is clear that it was central to the proponents of neo-conservative liberalization and, hence, at the centre of the strategy of the IFIs. USAID noted, for instance, that "the new law is consistent with the privatisation and economic liberalisation policies of the GoE. It provides the basis for the development of a land market" (USAID, 1997: 1). In a similar vein, the Food and Agriculture Organization of the United Nations (FAO) argued that the reform programme recognized the need to adjust "the land tenancy system in order to achieve equity and efficiency in the agricultural sector" (FAO, 1999: 2). FAO did not elaborate on what "greater equity" meant in this context. Nor did it elaborate which, if any, social groups might particularly benefit from tenure reform.

The programme of economic reform agreed to in 1991 gave the green light to Mubarak to transform rural relations of production by changing tenure. Changes to tenancy had been muted earlier by Sadat in his strategy of "de-Nasserization," and Mubarak had arguably been looking for a suitable time to initiate change with the support of a parliament dominated by landowners. The GoE thus argued in the Egyptian parliament during the early 1990s that changes to the law were necessary to "regularize" relations between owners and farmers and to improve the returns to landowners (Saad, 2002). Similarly, for the bureaucrats of USAID, Law 96 established "a more normal and balanced relationship between tenants and owners" (GoE and USAID, 1999: 2). Indeed, USAID colluded with the GoE in downplaying the conflict that emerged during the land act's enactment.

That conflict did nonetheless emerge. Reconciliation committees were set up for the purposes of mediating disputes. Yet, when local people even came to know about them, these committees became arenas for the security services to work with local government officials and landowners to exact signatures from tenants to hand over their tenanted land. USAID wanted land titling, and used the reconciliation committees to that end, to the exclusion of other concerns such as security of access to land, the development of opportunities for rural labour and goods markets, and the development of rural infrastructure (Village respondents, Dakhalia, Giza, and Beni Suef). These issues were not seen as a necessary accompaniment to the process of land tenure change; where they were addressed at all, they were tacked on afterwards, and therefore effectively ignored. As a consequence, there has been little attempt to ameliorate the tremendous decline in living standards that Law 96 brought with it for many rural people.

The decline in rural living standards in the wake of Law 96 has been especially notable in female-headed households. Women who, before October 1997, had worked land based on inherited tenancies from deceased husbands were suddenly dispossessed of the basis of their livelihood (Bush, 2002). The consequences across the countryside have been that women have taken their children out of school because costs can no longer be met, diets have dramatically changed, budgets have been tightened, and household assets such as jewellery and other personal belongings have been sold, in order to meet daily living expenses (Bush, 2002a). Moreover, women have been driven into petty trading occupations, selling items like sweets and vegetables that have tiny margins (Bush 2002a; Bach 2002). Child labour has also increased, as labour hirers have used the new entrants to the labour market to work as day labourers on neighbouring farms. In short, there has been a return to near-indentured terms and conditions of labour service. The institutionalization of rural violence has sustained this deterioration in the terms and conditions of labour service. Such violence has also deepened the suspicion with which small farmers view government.

VI. Modernizing Egyptian agriculture: a critique

Efforts to modernize Egyptian agriculture, both through reform of the agrarian structure and through the facilitation of technical change in agriculture, have been seen, particularly by neo-conservative IFI policy-makers and the GoE, as a means by which the rural productive forces could be further developed. To that end, agricultural reform has strengthened the power of landowners and weakened the power of tenants. The inequality of Egyptian agriculture has been reinforced as a result of Law 96. A recent study by the Faculty of Agriculture at Menofia University has noted a shift in the structure of land ownership and a failure of government to invest in the agrarian sector during economic reform. The report indicated that only 6.9 per cent of owners owned 51.1 per cent of cultivated land and only 1 per cent possessed 8.5 per cent (*Al Waft*, 20 March 2000). By contrast, more than 69 per cent of owners possessed less than one *feddan* and 93.1 per cent owned less than three *feddan*. This suggests that socio-economic differentiation is deepening in the Egyptian countryside (Bach, 2002). This evidence contradicts GoE and IFI oratory that the reforms of land tenure and economic reform more generally have promoted greater justice. Indeed, it is precisely these larger landowners, that is to say those with more than 10 *feddan*, who account for about 35 per cent of Egypt's cultivable area but only about 2 per cent of landowners, who have been the target of reform. Larger landowners have been perceived by reformers as having the ability to accumulate capital and drive market reforms (Central Agency for Public Mobilisation and Statistics, 1991). Agricultural reform has thus been designed to enhance their ability to further accumulate capital and further drive market reforms.

There are two major flaws with the large landowner bias implicit in Egyptian agricultural reform. The first is that it misunderstands the ways in which production is organized and decisions are taken in the typical small rural household. Reformers have either been unable or unwilling to understand actual rural relations of production and social reproduction. Put crudely, reformers in USAID and the GoE have assumed that small Egyptian farmers know nothing about markets and price incentives (Bush, 1999; Hopkins, 1993). Reformers have, therefore, assumed that getting the state out of the control of agricultural production and marketing will *ipso facto* release market forces that can be used by large landowners to generate significant increases in the sector's output. However, the actual decision-making processes of small farmers and large landowners may be very different from the neo-classical textbook view, and, as a consequence, market reform may not be the universal panacea for raising productivity (Hopkins, 1993). In particular, small farmers do understand markets and price incentives, while the decision making of large landowners may be predicated upon attempts to sustain their social power. Indeed, as Mitchell (1998) has noted, there is little proof that the early increase in agricultural production resulted from the withdrawal of the state. Instead, he argues that improvements in production figures seem to be the result of previous under-reporting by farmers or inaccuracy in pre-1986 production figures.

The second flaw of the strategy is that it is based on a very simplistic view of state power. The characterization of agricultural modernization has been rather unhelpfully viewed as state against the market. Policy-makers in the IFIs and the GoE have simultaneously adopted the view that the state has been all-powerful as well as being inefficient and rent seeking. In relation to Egypt's agriculture, it seems there has been both too much state intervention and too little effective intervention. The conclusion drawn by international advisors in the Ministry of Agriculture is to get the state out of agricultural moderniza-tion—or, at least, to declare that this has been what has been happening since 1986. In so doing, the GoE and the IFIs have, in effect, sided with the large landowners, particularly as they have failed to provide effective safety mecha-nisms for the small farmers and the landless Egyptians who have suffered from economic reform. They have also conveniently forgotten the subsidies that have promoted and sustain US and European agriculture, and which, in so do-ing, contribute to the underperformance of Egyptian agriculture.

If agricultural reform has, in effect, been biased towards large landowners, it is worth stressing that the inequality that dominates the agricultural sector is but a pale reflection of the greater inequality that dominates Egypt. The ru-ral oligarchy is, in turn, subordinate to a dominant 40 or so families engaged in a mix of agricultural and non-agricultural assembly and importing busi-nesses. These families have benefitted from limited economic reform and from their close business links with government officials who have been unable, or are unwilling, to generalize their largesse (Sfakianakis, 2002). Thus, while the advocates of reform continue to stress reform efficacy, inequality increases. Indeed, my argument would be that the pattern of economic reforms has fun-damentally misunderstood the character of the Egyptian state, the way agricul-tural production is actually organized, and the impact of Law 96 in transferring resources from the poor to the rich.

VII. Conclusion

While neo-conservative economic stabilization may be seen to have been rel-atively successful in terms of its macroeconomic indicators for the Egyptian economy as a whole, there has been a failure to generate economic growth. This has been nowhere more stark than in the agricultural sector. The GoE has used the veil of economic reform to instigate changes in land tenure that have confirmed the interests of landowners and accelerated rural impoverishment. As a result, there can be little optimism that growth will return to the Egyptian economy and its rural sector. Indeed, criticism of Prime Minister Atef Obeid's handling of the economy has proved a useful cover for President Mubarak's much greater failure to understand the need to jettison the policy of the IFIs, and to seek an alternative development paradigm that concentrates on understanding the rural economy better and that seeks to diversify the national economy away from its dependence upon external rents and local spoils.

Footnotes

1 This chapter draws on *Economic Crisis and the Politics of Reform in Egypt* (Bush, 1999). The arguments are further developed in *Counter Revolution in Egypt's Countryside* (Bush, 2002).

2 An "SDR" is a "special drawing right." It is an internal account and reserve asset that was created by the IMF in 1970. For more detail, see Hoogvelt 1987.

3 One *feddan* equals 1.038 acres or 0.42 hectares.

Chapter 9

THE EXTERNAL DEBT BURDEN AND GOVERNMENT EXPENDITURE ON EDUCATION IN SUB-SAHARAN AFRICA

Augustin Kwasi Fosu

I. Introduction

DEBT service payments have been rising in sub-Saharan Africa since 1980. For example, as a proportion of exports, debt service payments increased from 7 per cent in 1980 to 15 per cent by 1995 (World Bank, 1999). Part of this trend is a consequence of the additional capital inflows that are the result of new loans and aid arising from structural adjustment programmes. More significant, however, is the fact that arrears as a proportion of total debt stocks increased dramatically, from 3 per cent in 1980 to 18 per cent in 1995 (World Bank, 1999a), signalling payment difficulties and, hence, the likely existence of a liquidity constraint for many sub-Saharan African countries (Fosu, 2001). However, there is large cross-country variance in both the debt service rate and arrears, which indicates disparities in the liquidity-constraint situation across countries. Thus, in 1998 the debt service rate ranged from 1 per cent or less in the Democratic Republic of Congo and Eritrea to 30 per cent or more in Angola and Zimbabwe. Similarly, arrears as a proportion of total debt stocks ranged from 1 per cent or less in Botswana, Eritrea, Gambia, Ghana, Mauritius, Senegal, Swaziland, and Zimbabwe, to 56 per cent in Ethiopia, 59 per cent in Nigeria, 67 per cent in the Democratic Republic of Congo, 68 per cent in Somalia, 78 per cent in Liberia, and 80 per cent in Sudan (Fosu, 2001).

External inflows of loans and aid affect government spending and revenues. A number of studies have examined the relationship between government spending and revenues in developing countries (Bleaney, Gemmell, and Greenaway, 1995; Lim, 1983), while others have focussed on the determinants of government expenditures (Dao, 1995; Fielding, 1997). However, much of the emphasis in the literature on the fiscal implications of external inflows in low-income developing countries, such as those of sub-Saharan Africa, has been on the role of external aid rather than of debt (Cashel-Cordo and Craig, 1990; Devarajan, Rajkumar, and Swaroop, 1998; Feyzioglu, Swaroop, and Zhu, 1998; Gang and Khan, 1990). While such a concentration reflects the historical importance of aid relative to external debt in these economies, a significant amount of aid is tied to loans, and, hence, the possibility of external debt. Existing studies generally have not sought to isolate the effect of external debt on government expenditures. A possible exception might be that of Cashel-Cordo and Craig (1990), which focusses on the impact of aid, but includes debt service among the variables explaining government expenditures and revenues. The study finds a negative effect of debt service; however, it does not separate out government expenditures.

Recent research suggests that the external debt burden has decreased economic growth in sub-Saharan Africa (Fosu, 1996, 1999). The basis of the relationship may be due, in part, to cuts in government spending resulting from liquidity constraints in many of the countries (Taylor, 1993). However, endogenous growth theory suggests a strong link between human capital investment, such as education, and growth (Romer, 1990). In sub-Saharan Africa the bulk of educational spending is by government—since the mid-1970s, an average of about 15 per cent of total public expenditure, or US$21 per capita (World Bank, 1988, 1989, 1992a, 1996a, 1999a). Education expenditure as a share of gross domestic product (GDP) has ranged from under 10 per cent in Nigeria, Somalia, and Sudan, to 21 per cent in Benin and Ghana. On a per capita basis, the range has been from less than US$5 in Benin, Chad, Ethiopia, Nigeria, Sierra Leone, Somalia, and Zaire, to as much as US$60, US$68, and US$88 in Mauritius, Ivory Coast, and Botswana, respectively. In light of the limited amount of work that has examined the effect of external debt on government spending, coupled with the figures on debt and education spending that have been presented, a question arises: might the debt burden in sub-Saharan Africa adversely influence development because of its impact on public expenditure on education?

II. Theoretical basis

A simple static theoretical model may serve as a basis for subsequent empirical estimation. The government is assumed to choose levels of education expenditure, E, and non-education expenditure, O, in order to maximize a social welfare function, U. However, this is not the usual individual utility function, where the functional arguments would be in the form of actual quantities of commodities. Instead, government spending can be viewed as consumption that may provide utility to society. In the public choice literature, government officials would seek to maximize the probability of being maintained in office. This could involve choices consistent with the preferences of the median voter, according to the median-voter model (Buchanan, 1989; Tullock, 1971), but such a model is probably unsuitable in developing countries where the democratic process is seldom at work. Instead, the social welfare function is likely to entail a weighted average of various political coalitions in the country. A more generic function is thus assumed to be optimized. That is, the government maximizes

(1) $U(E, O)$

subject to the budget constraint

(2) $E + O = R$

with R denoting government revenue, which may be represented as

(3) $R = T + N + A - D$

where T is tax revenue, N is domestic non-tax revenue, A is external aid, and D is debt service. With U_E and U_O as the marginal utilities of expenditures on education and non-education commodities, respectively, the first-order conditions are

(4) $U_E = U_O$

and

(5) $E + O = R = T + N + A - D$

Assuming that the social welfare function has the usual properties of strict quasi-concavity, then the second-order conditions that are satisfied are

Fosu

(6) $U_{EE} < 0, U_{OO} < 0$, and $U_{EE}U_{OO} > U_{EO}$

where U_{EE}, U_{OO}, and U_{EO} are the second–order partial utilities. Finally, by use of the implicit function theorem, we can write the demand function

(7) $E = E (R)$

where R is assumed to be exogenous.

We can now explore the response of expenditure on education, E, to revenue, and particularly the change in E following a change in debt service, D. Assuming that E is a normal good, then from equation (7)

$dE/dR > 0$

while from equation (5)

$dR/dD < 0$

Therefore, using the chain rule,

$dE/dD < 0$

so that we expect the partial effect of debt service on E to be negative.

There are caveats associated with these results. For example, government action can determine revenue levels, and thus revenue may be endogenous. However, debt servicing may be endogenous. Granted, if servicing reflects past borrowing decisions, and borrowers honour previously established contracts, then D would be exogenous (Cashel-Cordo and Craig, 1990). Should governments decide to repay all or some of their debt obligations, however, then D becomes endogenous. The degree of endogeneity would depend on the size of the penalty governing default. Where such penalty is sufficiently high, this potential problem is minimized. Moreover, if governments were able to trade off spending and debt servicing payments, then D would constitute an argument of the above utility function.

III. The empirical model
An appropriate specification of equation (7) would entail the institutional framework for government decision making, so a structural model might be preferable (Shepsle, 1979). For example, Heller (1975) and Mosley, Hudson and Hornell (1987) use structural equations to examine the implications of

external aid for developing countries. However, the estimation of structural models can be very sensitive to the nature of their specification. Moreover, the process of scrutinizing government budgetary decisions is not well understood, especially in developing countries where political processes are seldom embedded in a democratic framework. The available structural models thus all have non-trivial problems (see Inman, 1979, for a review). Consequently, several studies have relied on reduced-form models (Cashel-Cordo and Craig, 1990; Feyzioglu et al., 1998). Results emanating from these models can be relatively robust across different types of public choice mechanisms (Craig and Inman, 1986). Consequently, we adopt an essentially reduced-form specification here, though debt service payments will be endogenized.

Consistent with preference aggregation, income and level of development are assumed to shape the government's social welfare function and, hence, the demand for education expenditures presented in equation (7). Experiments performed with other variables have shown them to be inconsequential (Cashel-Cordo and Craig, 1990). In addition, factors determining total government revenue, R, will have an impact on E. These include external aid, debt service, and other forms of revenue, such as domestic resources. One way to address this potential omitted-variable problem is to estimate a domestic resource equation and augment the expenditure model with the residuals, as in Devarajan et al. (1998). Alternatively, one could use an instrumental estimation of a revenue model and include the predicted revenue in the expenditure model. However, choosing appropriate instruments can be difficult. For instance, Fielding (1997) employs as an instrument in the revenue equation the value of imports as a proportion of nominal GDP. Yet it is not exactly clear how well this variable can serve as an appropriate instrument, given that imports may themselves be endogenous.

In an attempt to circumvent this potential problem of endogeneity, the share of education expenditure in the government budget is used. The underlying assumption is that the relative allocation of the budget does not depend on domestic resources. Thus the estimated version of equation (7) is of the form:

(8) $\quad e = b_1 + b_2 D + b_3 F + b_4 Q + b_5 A + u$

where e measures the share of government expenditure on education, D is the external debt service rate, F is foreign aid, defined as Official Development Assistance (ODA) as a proportion of GDP, Q is income, measured as gross national product (GNP) per capita, A is the share of the population engaged in agriculture, intended to reflect the structure of the economy, and u is the stochastic disturbance term.

The above discussion suggests that the debt service effect is negative. However, the dependent variable in equation (8) is the education share of the government budget. Thus, for the coefficient of D to be negative, the positive effect of a change in R on education expenditure, E, must exceed the effect on other commodities, O. Whether this is the case depends on the Engel properties of education in the government budget. However, if other expenditures, such as non-education wages and salaries, are relatively fixed in the government budget, then a reduction in revenue due to an increase in debt service will result in a decrease in the education expenditure share. Hence, the coefficient of D, b_2, would be negative.

The remaining variables in equation (8) are for control purposes. The effect of foreign aid, F, for instance, will be contingent on the relative degree of responsiveness within the government budget, which will, in turn, depend on the nature of the external aid. Higher ODA should increase revenue and, hence, education spending. However, whether the education expenditure share increases depends on the nature and extent of the conditionality placed on the ODA. For example, if the aid is non-sector specific, then no special impact on the education expenditure share should be anticipated. As an income variable, higher per capita GNP should raise education spending. Whether the education share increases, however, depends on its Engel properties. Dao (1995), for instance, finds that the income elasticity of education is roughly unitary in developing countries. If so, then the Q coefficient, b_4, should be zero. The level of development is denoted, in part, by the share of the population in agriculture, A. The assumption here is that a larger agrarian population generates less demand for education, and, typically, less spending on education. However, the level of development need not lower the share of education in government spending. If the total budget is small within an agrarian economy, the required critical mass of education spending may constitute a relatively large part of the budget, so that the education share of the budget might not be lower for more agrarian countries, *ceteris paribus.* Thus, the sign of b_5 is likely to be ambiguous.

IV. Data and Estimation

Data used here are primarily from the World Bank's *African Development Indicators* (World Bank, 1992a, 1996a). Debt data are from the *World Debt Tables* (World Bank, 1988, 1989) and from *Global Development Finance* (World Bank, 1999a). The sample consists of 35 sub-Saharan African countries,[1] and the period is from 1975-1994. Five-year panel data are used. As is well understood in the literature, this type of data is preferable to pure time-series or cross-sectional data, for it combines important cross-country differences with possible inter-temporal dynamics. In addition, averaging over five years is likely to minimize non-systematic errors in the data.

The main explanatory variable of interest deserves special attention. As discussed above, debt service is likely to be endogenous in the sense that countries with pressing needs for government expenditures, such as on education, may adjust their debt service payments accordingly. Hence, actual debt service payments may reflect their ability to pay rather than prevailing debt levels. Debt service payments could also be lower for a given debt stock due to greater concessionality, which should show up as higher ODA. In any case, the actual debt service payment may not reflect the degree of the liquidity constraint (Fosu, 1996, 1999). Hence, a predicted debt service estimate is obtained by regressing actual debt service on net debt, defined as the debt stock less international reserves. In this instance, net debt is considered as the best indicator of the external debt burden, while predicted debt service is taken to be the best indicator of the binding nature of the debt service constraint (Fosu, 1999).

Table 1 presents summary statistics of the main variables used to estimate equation (8). The education expenditure share averages 15 per cent, and varies from 1.8 per cent to 24.5 per cent. The debt service rate averages 19 per cent. While the actual debt service rate ranges from 1.4 per cent to 56.7 per cent and has a standard deviation of 13 per cent, the predicted debt service rate varies from a minimum of 15 per cent to a maximum of 33 per cent and has a standard deviation of 2.7 per cent. Thus, as expected, the predicted debt service rate minimizes the stochasticity in the debt variable. Official Development Assistance averages 11 per cent of GDP. However, it displays large variabil-

Table 1 Summary statistics for debt and education expenditures

Variable	Mean	Standard Deviation	Minimum	Maximum
GEE	15.01	4.58	1.80	24.5
DSR	18.86*	12.89	1.45	56.69
PREDSR	19.31*	2.67	14.93	33.01
ODAGDP	11.14	8.79	0.10	52.80
AGCON	32.59	14.06	4.29	67.58
PCGNP	511.61	503.88	118.00	3154.00

Notes * The difference between the two means is due to rounding; GEE is the percentage of government expenditure on education; DSR is the debt service ratio, defined as debt service payments as a per cent of exports; PREDSR is the predicted debt service ratio, as defined in the text; ODAGDP is Official Development Assistance as a per cent of GDP; AGCON is the percentage of the population in agriculture; PCGNP is per capita GNP, expressed in 1987 US dollars.
Data Sources World Bank (1988, 1989, 1992a, 1996a).

ity, going from a minimum of 0.1 per cent to a maximum of 53 per cent, and with a standard deviation of 9 per cent. Similarly, the share of the population in agriculture, which averages 33 per cent, ranges from 4 per cent to 68 per cent. Per capita GNP, with a mean of US$514, also varies quite widely, from a minimum of US$118 to a maximum of US$3154. The rather large variability of the variables suggests that the sub-Saharan African sample spans a wide set of countries.

Equation (8) is now estimated, first using the predicted debt service rate and then, for purposes of comparison, the actual observed values. Results are reported in Table 2 for both the (pooled) Ordinary Least Squares (OLS) and Random Effects (RE) estimation procedures. The Fixed Effects model was also estimated, but, based upon the Hausman Test, the RE model was preferred. The main result of interest is the coefficient of the debt variable, which is observed to be negative and statistically significant when predicted debt service is employed, as in equations I.A and I.B. By contrast, the use of the actual debt service rate results in statistically insignificant coefficients in equations II.A and II.B. In addition, on the basis of the R^2 and the standard error of the estimate, the equations with the predicted debt service display better fit than their counterparts involving the observed debt service. Thus, on both

Table 2 Regression results for debt and education expenditure in sub-Saharan Africa

Variable/ Equation	I. Predicted Debt Service		II. Actual Debt Service	
	I. A (OLS)	I. B (RE)	II. A (OLS)	II. B (RE)
CONST	37.330[a]	35.567[a]	19.321[a]	19.26[a]
	(7.24)	(6.52)	(6.33)	(6.36)
DEBT	-0.931[a]	-0.854[a]	-0.008	0.003
	(3.99)	(3.36)	(0.16)	(0.07)
ODAGDP	-0.087	-0.077	-0.095	-0.104
	(1.50)	(1.19)	(1.48)	(1.47)
AGCON	0.013	-0.002	-0.051	-0.058
	(0.31)	(0.04)	(1.14)	(1.14)
PCGNP	-0.002	-0.001	-0.000	-0.000
	(1.22)	(1.05)	(0.19)	(0.25)
D7579	-5.117[a]	-4.191[a]	-1.933	-1.594
	(3.08)	(2.82)	(1.09)	(1.07)
D8084	-3.208[b]	-2.904[b]	-1.407	-1.497
	(2.17)	(2.27)	(0.91)	(1.20)
D8589	-2.002	-1.776	-1.220	-1.252
	(1.33)	(1.39)	(0.74)	(0.95)
R2	0.240	0.517	0.083	0.497
SEE	4.168	4.347	4.579	4.439
C2(df)	—	2.23(4)	—	3.75(3)

Notes – Models OLS is the pooled Ordinary Least Squares model; RE is the Random Effects model.
Test statistics [a] Significant at the .01 two-tailed level; [b] Significant at the .05 two-tailed level;
Absolute values of the t ratio are in parentheses; R^2 is the coefficient of determination; SEE is the
standard error of estimate; $C^2(df)$ is the Hausman chi square test statistic, with the degrees of freedom in
parentheses.
Variables CONST is the constant term; DEBT is the debt service ratio, either actual or predicted; D7579
is a time dummy variable that assumes unity for 1975-79; D8084 is a time dummy variable that assumes
unity for 1980-84; D8589 is a time dummy variable that assumes unity for 1985-89; other variables are
defined in Table 1.
Data Sources See Table 1.

theoretical and econometric grounds, equations I.A and I.B are preferable to equations II.A and II.B. This difference between the two sets of equations may be attributed to the aforementioned argument that the actual debt service rate is likely to be endogenous and not properly reflect the debt burden. On the other hand, as already noted, predicted debt embodies the binding nature of the constraint. One possible interpretation of the result is also that, when faced with a debt-servicing liquidity constraint, countries might choose to default rather than reduce certain expenditures, such as on education.

The remaining major variables display little significance in the regression. For example, though negative, the coefficient of the external aid variable is insignificant. This result suggests that ODA does not change the share of education expenditure in the budget. Similarly, the coefficient of per capita income is not statistically significant, though it tends to be negative. This suggests that the share of the budget devoted to education spending has very little relationship with per capita income. Similarly, the share of the population in agriculture has minimal effect.

The results for the time dummy variables suggest that a larger share of the budget was devoted to education expenditure in the 1990s, when compared to previous periods. Relative to the 1990s, the lowest education share was in 1975 to 1979, followed by 1980 to 1984, and then by 1985 to 1989. Thus, the net trend in the relative budget allocation for education appears to be positive as of the 1980s.

Equation I.B of Table 2 is selected as the "best" model, on the grounds of both theory and goodness of fit. Granted, the measures of goodness of fit are not strictly comparable between the two models. Within the two models, however, the measures of goodness of fit are comparable. Moreover, the results for the coefficient estimates and the measure of statistical significance are quite close between the two models. Therefore, Table 3 summarizes the results of the impact of the main regression variables using equation I.B. In particular, Table 3 reports the partial elasticities for the variables, as well as the partial effects. It is apparent that, among the explanatory variables, debt service is by far the most important. Not only are the partial effects insignificant for the other variables, according to the respective t ratios noted in Table 2, but also the partial elasticities indicate practically non-existent responsiveness of the education share to changes in these variables.

Table 3 Partial effects and elasticities for debt and education expenditure in sub-Saharan Africa

Variable	Partial Effect*	Partial Elasticity**
DEBT	-.854	1.10
ODAGDP	-.077	0.057
AGCON	-.002	0.004
PCGNP	-.001	0.034

Notes * Respective regression coefficients from equation I.B, Table 2.
** Computed as the absolute value of b(x/y), where b is the respective partial effect, x is the mean value of the explanatory variable, and y the average value of the education expenditure share.
Variables are defined in Table 1 and Table 2.
Data Sources See Table 1.

Using equation I.B as the best model, we can now assess the implications of "binding" debt service on education spending. As shown in Table 3, the partial effect of debt service on the education expenditure share is -0.854. Hence, a one-percentage-point increase in the predicted debt service ratio would, on average, translate into approximately a one-percentage point decrease in the share of education expenditure in the budget, *ceteris paribus*. This implies a decline of 5.7 per cent of the sample mean education expenditure share. Furthermore, with a sample mean total government expenditure of 25.2 per cent of GDP, the implied reduction is 0.215 per cent of GDP. Given a mean GDP of US$350 million in 1987 dollars across the countries in the sample in 1997, this reduction represents an average of some US$752,000 per country. Thus, a country with a binding debt service rate of just 22 per cent of exports, which is one standard deviation above the sample mean predicted debt service ratio of 2.7 percentage points, could suffer a decrease in education spending of about US$2 million. Indeed, if the analysis can be extended toward the predicted debt service maximum value of 33 per cent, a country could face a potential loss of nearly US$30 million in education expenditure.

V. Conclusion

This chapter sheds light on the impact of potentially binding debt servicing on government expenditure on education in sub-Saharan Africa, using five-year panel data over 1975 to 1994. The estimated model is a multiple regression equation with the share of education expenditure in the government budget as the dependent variable, and the predicted debt service ratio, external aid, per capita income, the share of the population in agriculture, and dichotomous time variables as explanatory variables. It appears potential debt service adversely affects public spending on education. Moreover, this debt variable is observed to be the most potent explanatory variable in the education expenditure equation. By contrast, the actual debt service rate is observed to be inconsequential. This outcome suggests that governments succeed in circumventing their external debt obligations when faced with a binding liquidity constraint.

An increase in the "binding" debt service ratio of one percentage point could reduce education expenditure by nearly US$800,000 per year on average. This is 6 per cent of the mean education budget. Indeed, with some countries facing potential debt service rates of over 30 per cent, the impact on such above-average debt-service countries could approach US$30 million per country. It is now widely accepted that there is a strong correlation between education and economic growth. In this light, and despite the usual caveat associated with econometric studies such as the present one, removing the debt constraint might not only be good for growth, as other studies have uncovered, but also could directly contribute resources into the all-important education sector of sub-Saharan African economies.

Footnotes

1   The countries in the sample are Benin, Botswana, Burkina Faso, Burundi, Cameroon, Central African Republic, Chad, Congo, Côte d'Ivorie, Democratic Republic of Congo, Ethiopia, Gabon, Gambia, Ghana, Kenya, Lesotho, Liberia, Madagascar, Malawi, Mali, Mauritania, Mauritius, Niger, Nigeria, Rwanda, Senegal, Sierra Leone, Somalia, Sudan, Swaziland, Tanzania, Togo, Uganda, Zambia, and Zimbabwe.

Chapter 10

ADJUSTMENT AND TRANSITION IN THE PROVISION OF HEALTH CARE: VIETNAM'S EXPERIENCE

Ardeshir Sepehri and A Haroon Akram-Lodhi

I. Introduction

VIETNAM implemented a series of economic reforms in the 1980s, which have collectively become known as *doi moi*, or renovation. The common principle underpinning many of these reforms was an emphasis on microinstitutional change. Markets became increasingly accepted as the principal mechanism of resource allocation, and there was, as a consequence, a steady erosion of the role of central planning and its two main institutions, agricultural production cooperatives and state-owned enterprises (SOEs). Among other things, reform sought to redirect industrial policy by enhancing the role of the private sector, while at the same time vigorously pursuing external trade liberalization and internal deregulation, including changes in agricultural markets, public sector restructuring, and financial sector reform. By 1989, reform was well advanced and had gained legitimacy (Fforde and de Vylder, 1996: 19). More specifically, by that time "prices mattered and autonomous capital had been accumulated outside as well as within the state and cooperative structures." Moreover, at several critical points in the reform process, the state undertook macroeconomic stabilization. In 1989 in particular, the collapse of the centrally planned economies of eastern Europe and the impending termination of Soviet aid demanded the rapid restoration of internal and external balance. As a consequence, in 1989 macroeconomic imbalances were effectively attacked through an unleashing of reform measures that sought to stabilize the economy and simultaneously build upon earlier microinstitutional reforms by encouraging a wholesale shift to a market economy. Central planning was abandoned. The authorities hastily implemented an orthodox neo-conservative stabilization programme, albeit without the financial support of the International Monetary Fund (IMF) and the World Bank. The programme undertook, among other measures, a tight monetary policy, a reduction in government spending, deeper market liberalization, the broadening of the tax system, the unification of multiple exchange rates, a dramatic devaluation of the Vietnamese currency, and the introduction of user fees for publicly provided services (Fforde and de Vylder, 1996; Ljunggren, 1993).

The neo-conservative reform programme was, on the face of it, a huge success. During the 1990s the average annual rate of growth of gross domestic product (GDP) per capita was 7.6 per cent, exports soared, while macroeconomic balance was maintained (World Bank, 2001c). Poverty rates fell dramatically, and indeed it was claimed that "almost no other country has recorded such a sharp decline in poverty in such a short period of time" (World Bank, 1999b: iii). As a consequence of this performance, until the onset of the east Asian crisis in 1997, Vietnam appeared to be on the verge of entering the ranks of the "tiger" economies of the region.

Stabilization and adjustment were, as a general rule, successful in those areas where institutions had developed that were capable of effectively implementing policy before the actual policy measures were introduced. Adjustment was less successful in areas where policies were introduced prior to the establishment of effective institutions. The social sector in general and the provision of health care in particular are, in this regard, a good case in point. In health care the government implemented a set of orthodox reform measures. These included the privatization of medical practices, the liberalization of the pharmaceutical industry, and the introduction of a user charge system. These measures signified a radical shift in government health policy. However, the reforms were introduced without putting in place a regulatory framework to monitor and control the quality and appropriateness of the health care services provided by the public and private sector. Moreover, an effective safety net that could protect the poor and vulnerable and, in so doing, ensure equitable access to public health services was not created (Sepehri, Chernomas, and Akram-Lodhi, 2003). As a result, reform effectively eroded the role of the public sector in the provision and funding of health care services and led to a rapid expansion of unregulated private medicine, private pharmacies, and drug vendors.

II. The health care sector in transition: a general overview[1]

i.   The structure of the public health system
Prior to onset of the 1989 economic reforms, the provision of health care services was dominated by public health facilities providing preventive, curative, and promotional care that was, in principle, free of charge. Delivery of publicly provided health services was organized along a four-tiered pyramid. At the bottom of the pyramid was Vietnam's extensive network of commune health centres (CHCs), which provided primary care and limited preventive outreach programmes at the village level. In 1998, 98.5 per cent of communes had their own CHC, serving on average about 7000 people, a coverage ratio comparable to that of Thailand, a country with a per capita income four times higher than the per capita income of Vietnam (Deolalikar, 2000: 91). Within the network of CHCs, brigade and hamlet nurses also provided first aid and promotional health services at the village level. The CHCs were financed partly by rural farm cooperatives and partly by local authorities. The former were responsible for the salaries of health personnel and drugs, and funding for investment in buildings and equipment were provided by the local authorities.

Above the CHCs was the district health system, with its intercommunal polyclinics and district hospitals acting as a higher level point of referral for the CHCs. In addition, district health centres provided outpatient services, and preventive medicine brigades managed and implemented public and preventive health programmes and services. These included, among other things, childhood immunization and malaria control. In the third tier of the pyramid were general and specialty provincial hospitals, and at the top of pyramid were central government hospitals as well as specialized hospitals and institutions providing mostly tertiary health referral, professional training, and medical research.

ii.   Health care services during transition
The public health sector came under increasing pressure during the transition, especially during the second half of the 1980s. Poor overall economic performance and the steady erosion of the two main institutions of the central planning system, SOEs and agricultural cooperatives, made it difficult for the state to sustain its vast network of health facilities. Years of low growth and

declines in the supply of highly subsidized drugs from eastern Europe led to widespread shortages of drugs, medical supplies and equipment, poor maintenance of medical equipment and buildings, and the demoralization of health professionals (Guldner, 1995; Prescott, 1997; Witter, 1996). By the late 1980s Vietnam's health care sector was in a serious crisis. The average number of consultations per person dropped by more than half, from 2.3 in 1984 to 1.2 in 1989, and the rate of inpatient admission dropped from 110 per 1000 population in 1984 to 79 in 1989 (Prescott, 1997). At the same time, poor economic performance and a steady decline in foreign aid led to the complete collapse of local production and distribution of pharmaceuticals (World Bank, 1992d). The health budget as a share of GDP dropped from 0.82 per cent in 1984 to 0.38 per cent in 1988, and by 1989 health expenditure per capita was equivalent to US$0.83, which was the lowest in Asia (World Bank, 1992d). By 1989 health care spending constituted only 3.3 per cent of total government spending (Witter, 1996: 161), and government could only meet 40 per cent of its most urgent health care spending needs (Guldner and Rifkin, 1993).

The adverse effect of transition on the health care sector was most pronounced in the provision of primary care. The economic reforms of the early 1980s and the eventual replacement of farm cooperatives by family farms deprived the CHCs and community nurses of their sources of financing. With the demise of farm cooperatives, the Commune People's Committees (the lowest tier of government administration) took on the responsibility of running and financing the CHCs. However, few Commune People's Committees agreed to finance community nurses (Dung, 1996: 62). As a consequence, while there was little change in the total number of CHCs, total commune health workers declined sharply from 58,665 in 1985 to 39,701 in 1990 and 37,733 in 1994 (Ministry of Health, 1990, 1997, cited in Nguyen et al., 2000). When combined with a drastic decline in the supply of subsidized drugs from the former Soviet Union, these changes in financing and staffing made it increasingly difficult for many CHCs to function and provide basic preventive care services (Dung, 1996). This was especially the case for those poor communes that had a limited tax base and thus limited public resources. The provincial governments' decision to pay the salary of approved health workers at the CHCs in 1994 may have rectified some of the problems of poor communes, in terms of their ability to pay their health workers. However, other problems, such as a lack of equipment and materials, a lack of medicine, and inadequate maintenance and repair, have continued to adversely affect the perceived quality of care provided by many CHCs (General Statistical Office, 1998: Table 3.11.4).

Steady erosion in the quality of public health services led health care consumers to increasingly seek to obtain health care services and drugs at open market prices (Fforde and de Vylder, 1996: 232). As the shadow private health sector expanded, pressures increased for the legalization of non-publicly provided medical services (Witter, 1996: 161). At the same time, the health care crisis threatened to undermine the impressive health outcomes of the 1970s. Therefore, the government moved to reform the financing and delivery of health care in Vietnam.

*iii.	The stabilization and adjustment programme and health sector reforms*
In 1989 the government, with technical support from the World Bank and other donors, implemented a series of health policy reforms. These included the legalization of the private provision of health services, the liberalization of the pharmaceutical industry, the introduction of user charges at higher level public health facilities, and the promotion of health insurance. These policy measures effectively transformed Vietnam's near universal, publicly funded and provided health services into a provision system based upon an unregulated private-public mix (Sepehri et al., 2003, 2002).

Since the legalization of private medicine in 1989, there has been a rapid growth of private health services including drug commission sellers, private pharmacies, general practitioner clinics, nursing homes and an expansion of traditional medicine. By 1993 private health spending per capita reached US$7.27, accounting for 84 per cent of total health spending. Between 1989 and 1993 public health spending per capita rose from US$0.83 to US$1.42 (Quan 1999: 383). Given the poor state of many public health facilities in the late 1980s and early 1990s, the increase in public health spending helped prevent further deterioration in the health infrastructure.

The relationship between the public and private health care sectors is ill-defined, and much private care lies beyond the influence and control of government authorities. Many of the doctors and assistant physicians working in public health facilities also run their own private practices before and after their working hours in public health facilities, to top up their low official salary (Witter, 1996). Indeed, in some public hospitals, physicians and nurses are alleged to run their own private practices using hospital facilities and equipment during working hours (Dung, 1996).

There is no professional oversight or regulation of the activities of private clinics. The state has a limited role in steering the development and direction of the private health care sector, and the regulation of private practice is unclear, weak, and heterogenous (Gellert, 1995; Lonnroth, Thuong, and Diwan, 1998). Granted, there are a few general guidelines for private practice. These include having a minimum of five years of clinical experience before doctors are eligible for private practice, minimum standards for equipment and premises, and the prohibition of selling drugs and medicines directly to patients. However, these guidelines and requirements are rarely enforced. According to a 1992 survey, only one-third of the doctors who saw patients privately were licensed private practitioners (Dung, 1996). It is also common practice for private physicians to dispense drugs in their own medical rooms (Lonnroth et al., 1998).

A user charge system was also officially introduced in 1989. In this system the three higher level government health facilities—those at the district, provincial, and national level—were allowed to charge a basic fee ranging from the equivalent of US$0.07 to US$0.25 per consultation. A more detailed fee structure was issued by the Ministry of Health in 1995, in which it set out the range of fees each type of hospital and clinic could charge for each type of consultation, diagnostic test, and procedure. At the same time, for the most part, patients became liable to pay for drugs. Depending on the type of services provided and drug or other supplies consumed, health facilities were also allowed to charge supplementary fees. However, the fee structure was—and is—applied differently in different parts of the country and the actual fee charged to the patient is often decided at each level of the health care system (Dung, 1996). Thus, central hospitals normally apply the ceiling price indicated in the fee schedule while lower level hospitals charge the floor price. Fees also tend to be higher in the south of the country than in the north for comparable services (Deolalikar, 2000).

Patients also make various forms of informal payments, in addition to official user charges, that are often not reported to the Ministry of Health (Ensor and San, 1996; Oxfam [GB], 1999; Segall, Tipping, Dao, and Dao, 1999;

Tipping, Troung, Nguyen, and Segall, 1994). Similarly, and more specifically, in the case of hospital visits it is also common practice for richer patients to pay higher hidden fees in order to receive better care (Dung, 1996). According to one recent study, gifts and rewards to health care providers accounted for as much as 20 per cent of total hospital bills for patients receiving better quality inpatient care, and 7 per cent for standard treatment services (Tran, 2001).

In constant 1994 prices, revenue from user charges increased threefold between 1992 and 1998, from just under 100 billion Vietnamese dong to 300 billion dong (Deolalikar, 2000). The growth in fee revenue was more pronounced during the period between 1994 and 1998, when real aggregate revenue from user charges grew at a compound rate of 29 per cent per year as compared to 6.4 per cent per year over the period between 1991 and 1994. The contribution of user charges to total public health expenditure has been quite modest, amounting to 7.4 per cent of total public health spending in 1998. However, since user charges are largely collected at the hospital level, this modest cost-recovery rate greatly underestimates the significance of user charges in financing hospital activities. The share of user charges in total hospital revenue rose dramatically, from 9 per cent in 1994 to as much as 30 per cent in 1998 (World Bank et al., 2001). The combined revenue from user charges and health insurance in 1998 amounted to 45 per cent of total hospital revenue. With a rising share of patient revenue in hospital revenue, the share of the state health budget in total revenue shrank considerably, from 76 per cent in 1994 to 47 per cent in 1998 (World Bank et al., 2001).

The rapid growth of revenues from user charges and insurance enabled hospitals to improve medical equipment, drugs, and other supplies. It also allowed them to improve staff morale by increasing bonuses. There are guidelines on how revenues from user charges can be used, especially in hospitals. Seventy per cent is supposed to be used for improving medical equipment, drugs, and other supplies such as chemicals and x-ray materials; 25 to 28 per cent is supposed to be used to reward health workers, in the form of a bonus; and 2 to 5 per cent should be used to build a supporting fund for the hospital (Deolalikar, 2000). However, according to an extensive survey of public hospitals in 1996 by the Ministry of Health, staff bonuses, which are entirely financed out of patient revenue, doubled in real terms each year from 1994 and 1996 across all hospitals. Indeed, for some categories of hospitals, bonuses paid were larger than the salaries. In 1996 bonuses accounted for 30 per cent of total staff income across all hospitals (Ministry of Health, 1996, cited in World Bank et al., 2001:81). Although the salaries of public health care providers have been increased several times since the inception of health reforms in 1989, such salaries, like the salaries of many other employees in the public sector, remain low, both in absolute and relative terms. In 1998 salaries of public health care providers accounted for only about 29 per cent of the total recurrent central and local state health budget (Deolalikar, 2000: Table E.2).

The increasing reliance of public hospitals on patient revenues has changed the incentive structure under which providers operate, with serious consequences for efficiency and equity. The rising share of patient revenues from user charges and health insurance in total hospital revenue, combined with utilization-based staff bonuses, has shifted the incentive structure towards an unregulated fee-for-service system, and away from a salary system and a centrally determined global budget. It is well known that a fee-for-service system under asymmetric information between provider and the patient, along with an incomplete agency framework, generates perverse incentives (Evans, 1984). This is because providers have little or no influence, at least in theory, on the level of fees. With limited influence there is a potential risk that services will be overprovided, in the form of longer hospital stays, the overuse of diagnostic tests, and the provision of relatively expensive drugs. Overprovision will be directed at those who can afford to pay official fees and generous "gifts" as providers direct the use of their own services, and of the cooperant hospital, to increase their income.

This problem of provider's moral hazard has not received much attention in the literature on user charges. The arguments in support of user charges often rest on an implicit assumption that treatment decisions are taken by the patient, or by the provider in the presence of asymmetric information between patients and providers. In the case of the latter, it is assumed that providers act as perfect agents, using their medical knowledge in the best interests of their patients. In other words, perfect agency holds. Following this assumption, the introduction of user charges or raising the level of fees is argued to encourage the rational utilization of services among users. It does this by limiting the use of services for frivolous or unnecessary reasons, by reducing patients' inappropriate use of referrals, and by curbing moral hazard on the part of households (de Ferranti, 1985; Griffin, 1987; World Bank, 1987a). However, the assumption of perfect agency has been questioned by some authors, who argue that the provider's influence on the utilization of medical services will, in general, respond to some blend of the patient's and the provider's interest (Evans, 1984). The proportions in the blend will be strongly influenced by how providers are financed and by the regulatory and administrative environment within which they operate. In a weakly regulated market, providers tend to overprovide costly services for those who can afford to pay and to neglect the needs of the rest of population (Evans; Hsiao, 1994; Preker and Feachem, 1994).

The perverse effect of fee-for-service systems on utilization is well documented for developed countries (see McGuire, 2000). The problem of overutilization and the escalation of costs have also been demonstrated for the transition economies and, in particular, for China. In China the transition from a centrally controlled public health system to a poorly regulated fee-for-service system has led to profiteering by providers working in both the public and private health facilities (Barr, 1994; Bloom and Gu, 1997; Bloom, Lucas, Gao, and Gu, 1995; Bogg, Hengjin, Keli, Wenwei, and Diwan, 1996; Chen, 1997; Liu and Hsiao, 1995; Preker and Feachem, 1994; Sidel, 1993).

The problem of the overprovision of services, especially in the case of inpatient care, is also evident in Vietnam. There, a user charge system was implemented without putting in place an effective regulatory mechanism to protect patients against potential abuses by providers, as well as to protect the poor and vulnerable against the undue cost burden of illness.

III. Utilization of health services

i. Utilization of curative services

Following the introduction of user charges and the legalization of the private provision of medical services in Vietnam, the utilization of public health facilities continued its declining trend. The average number of consultations per person dropped steadily from 1.8 in 1988 to as low as 0.93 in 1993 before starting to partially recover. The average number of consultations per person in 1998, the latest year for which the data are available, reached 1.7, which is far below the 2.3 recorded in 1984 and 1985 (Ministry of Health, 1998).

Using data from the 1998 Vietnam Living Standards Survey (General Statistical Office, 1998), Table 1 displays the distribution of health service contacts by sample households across providers and expenditure quintiles over a four-week reference period. Largely unregulated drug vendors were the most commonly used providers by all income groups. Of those poor households with illness that sought treatment, almost 70 per cent of contacts involved self-treatment with purchases of non-prescription drugs from pharmacies. Visits to public health facilities and private clinics accounted for 13 and 15 per cent of total health service contacts, respectively.

Table 1 also shows that the share of contacts with public hospitals and with private clinics and physicians in total household service contacts tends to vary positively with income. The share of contacts with public hospitals for the richest 20 per cent of the population was almost 2.9 times the share of the poorest quintile. The share of total service contacts with private clinics and

Table 1 Distribution of health services contacts by providers and per capita expenditure quintiles, 1998*

| | | Per capita expenditure quintile | | | | | |
	Average	Q1 (poorest)	Q2	Q3	Q4	Q5 (richest)	Q5/Q1
All public providers	13.0	12.5	11.7	12.9	13.1	14.2	1.14
Public hospitals	6.3	3.6	3.9	4.8	6.9	10.3	2.86
Commune health centres (CHCs)	5.8	8.3	7.4	7.0	5.3	2.8	0.34
Other public providers	0.9	0.6	0.4	1.1	0.9	1.1	1.83
Private clinics & physicians	16.6	13.2	14.2	17.1	16.0	20.0	1.51
Drug vendors	67.4	71.6	71.5	67.7	67.6	61.6	0.86
Traditional healers	3.1	2.7	2.5	2.4	3.3	4.2	1.55
Total	100.0	100.0	100.0	100.0	100.0	100.0	

* Home visits are assigned to hospitals, CHCs, private clinics, and traditional practitioners as reported by the respondents.
Source General Statistical Office (1998).

physicians by the richest 20 per cent of the population was 1.5 times that of the poorest quintile.

Not only do the poor visit public hospitals and private clinics less frequently than the non-poor, but when they visit they are most likely to receive a lower quality of care than the non-poor. The quality of services provided by public hospitals and private clinics and physicians is generally perceived by patients to be of a higher quality than that provided by the CHCs (Lonnroth et al., 1998; Pham, 2002; Tipping et al., 1994). Moreover, as Table 1 demonstrates, contacts with the CHCs accounted for a far larger share of total health service contacts by low- and middle-income groups than for high-income groups. These differences in quality are partly reflected in the cost of accessing various providers. As Table 2 shows, average cost per contact varies greatly across providers. Depending on the type of provider contacted, the richest 20 per cent of households spent somewhere between two to three times more per service contact than that spent by the poorest 20 per cent of households. This higher spending per contact by non-poor households reflects partly a higher quality of care and partly an over provision of services provided to non-poor households, especially in visits involving admission to hospital (World Bank et al., 2001).

Table 2 Average cost per contact by providers and per capita expenditure quintiles, 1998 (000 dong)*

		Per capita expenditure quintile					
	Average	Q1 (poorest)	Q2	Q3	Q4	Q5 (richest)	Q5/Q1
Public hospitals	169	82	143	169	186	193	2.3
Commune health centres (CHCs)	20	14	20	19	21	37	2.6
Private clinics & physicians	33	22	28	24	39	42	1.9
Drug vendors	15	9	9	12	16	27	3.0

* Home visits are excluded in the calculation of average cost per contact.
Source General Statistical Office (1998).

The data does not distinguish between outpatient and inpatient contacts with public hospitals over the four-week reference period. However, the survey provides separate data on inpatient contacts over the preceding year prior to the survey. Table 3 displays inpatient service contacts with public hospitals in 1993 and 1998 by per capita expenditure quintiles over a 12-month reference period. Table 3 reveals three important findings. First, inpatient admission rates for households in 1998 were far greater for non-poor households than for poor households. The average rate of admission was also far greater for the insured than for the uninsured, with the insurance enrollees having a rate of admission nearly twice the rate for the uninsured population.[2] The relationship between the admission rate and income is, however, less clear in the case of the insured. The insured are generally more affluent than the population in general, as demonstrated in the last row of Table 3. Second, not only are more non-poor than poor patients admitted to hospitals, but they are also

Table 3 Utilization of public hospitals (inpatient) by the insured and uninsured, and by per capita expenditure quintile, 1998

		Per capita expenditure quintile				
	Average	Q1 (poorest)	Q2	Q3	Q4	Q5 (richest)
Admission rate (per 1000)	50.4 (104.7)	33.9 (70.8)	43.5 (84.5)	49.3 (111.9)	61.9 (122.7)	63.3 (133.7)
Uninsured	44.0	33.3	36.7	42.0	53.8	59.2
Insured	87.2	42.3	107.3	96.1	94.0	73.2
Length of hospital stay (days)	14.3 (7.8)	10.3 (7.7)	10.9 (8.5)	13.9 (7.9)	14.6 (7.9)	18.8 (7.1)
Uninsured	13.0	10.4	9.5	13.7	11.9	18.3
Insured	17.8	8.7	15.3	14.4	20.8	19.7
Distribution of aggregate hospital days (%)	20.0 (20.0)	9.7 (13.4)	13.2 (17.7)	19.0 (21.8)	25.1 (23.8)	33.0 (23.3)
% of individuals with health insurance	16.1	6.2	9.8	13.4	18.9	28.7

Note Figures inside parentheses are for 1993.
Source General Statistical Office (1993, 1998).

more likely to be kept longer. As Table 3 shows, the length of hospital stay varies positively with income, with patients from the richest expenditure quintiles having, on average, a one-week longer hospital stay than those from the lowest expenditure quintile. Third, a comparison of the admission rates and length of hospital stays between 1993 and 1998, as reported by households in the 1993 and 1998 Vietnam Living Standards Surveys, indicates a substantial decline in admission rates across all economic groups but an increase in the average length of hospital stays. The length of hospital stay rose from 7.7 days in 1993 to 14.3 in 1998.[3] Moreover, the length of hospital stay, which was more or less identical for all income groups in 1993, shows a strong income gradient in 1998. Variation in the length of hospital stay is more pronounced for the insured than for the uninsured.

Apparent class differentiation in hospital admission rates, when combined with apparent class differentiation in the length of hospital stay, suggests that the distribution of aggregate hospital days worsened between 1993 and 1998. As Table 3 indicates, the richest 20 per cent of the population accounted for about 33 per cent of aggregate hospital days in 1998, up from about 23 per cent in 1993. In contrast, the share of the poorest 20 per cent of the population in aggregate hospital days dropped from 13.4 per cent in 1993 to 9.7 per cent in 1998. The second and third poorest expenditure quintiles experienced a reduction in their share of aggregate hospital days of a magnitude similar to that of the poorest population quintile.

This pattern of utilization, skewed as it is towards the better off and the insured, is not consistent with the pattern observed in the developed countries, where the poor tend to use health services more frequently than the non-poor (van Doorslaer and Wagstaff, 1992; van Doorslaer et al., 2000). It is also not consistent with self-reported patterns of the incidence of illness and its severity in Vietnam. In such reporting the patterns of illness and its severity closely follow the poverty map, according to which most of the poor are found in the rural areas and among minorities (Desai, 2000; General Statistical Office, 1998). Consistent with the poverty map, there is a great deal of regional variation in the incidence of illness, with some of the poorest regions such as the Central Highlands experiencing an illness incidence rate as high as 50 per cent (General Statistical Office, 1998).

As Figure 1 indicates, although there is little variation in the incidence of

Figure 1 Incidence and severity of illness, by per capita expenditure quintile, 1998

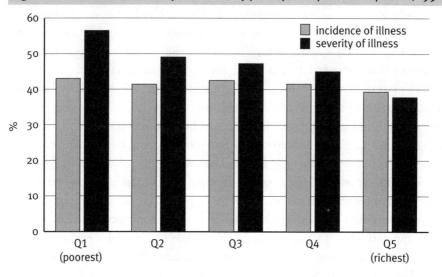

Source General Statistical Office (1998).

Figure 2 Average out-of-pocket expenditure per hospital contact as a proportion of annual per capita non-food consumption expenditure, by per capita expenditure quintile, 1998

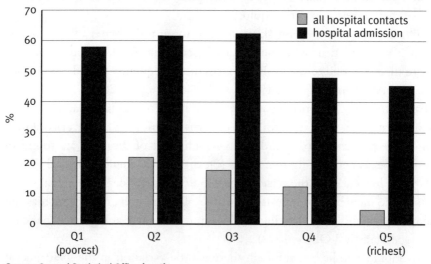

Source General Statistical Office (1998).

illness across various economic groups, the income gradient of the severity of illness, as measured by the person's inability to carry out usual daily activities during the preceding four weeks, is more pronounced. According to one study the burden of disease as measured by disability-adjusted life years among the rural poor is more than four times the rate experienced by the urban population and more than three times the rate for the rural population as a whole (Dunlop, 1999).

ii. The financial burden of hospital service contacts

Although the government is the largest provider of health care services, its role in the financing of health expenditure is very small, accounting for 20 to 24 per cent of health spending (Deolalikar, 2000).[4] With more than three-quarters of total health spending being met by out-of-pocket household payments, health care costs, and especially the cost of inpatient care, have become substantial for many low- and middle-income households. In order to assess the affordability of health care costs, average health care costs per hospital contact are compared in relation to annual household non-food consumption expenditure per capita. Figure 2 displays the ratio of health care cost over per capita non-food consumption expenditure, which can be called the affordability ratio, for various economic groups.

Even though poor households use hospitals far less frequently than non-poor households, whenever poor households had hospital contacts, each contact imposed a heavy financial burden on the poor. The cost of a single service contact with a public hospital takes up about 22 per cent of non-food consumption expenditure for a year for a person from the bottom two quintiles, while it takes up less than 5 per cent for a person from the top expenditure quintile. The cost burden per hospital contact is even greater if it involves admission to hospital. Indeed, as Figure 2 shows, a single admission to a public hospital accounts for over 60 per cent of non-food consumption expenditure for a year for a middle-income person, and for about 58 per cent for a person from the bottom quintile.

Vietnam Living Standards Survey 1998 data on hospital service contacts provide a snapshot of household out-of-pocket expenditure per hospital contact. An examination of hospital revenues from user charges and total hospital contacts over the period between 1995 and 1998 suggests a rapid increase in household out-of-pocket expenditure on hospital visits. After the introduction of a comprehensive system of user charges in 1995, hospital revenues per capita from user charges grew at annual rate of 28.7 per cent over the period between 1996 and 1998. Since the level of fees remained constant during the period, the rapid increase in user charge revenue per capita reflects the increase in the volume of care provided by public hospitals. A further decomposition of changes in the volume of services into changes in the utilization rate—defined as the number of service contacts per capita—and the intensity of servicing per capita—defined as the number of laboratory and radiology tests and other procedures performed—suggests that the latter accounted for almost 60 per cent of the increase in per capita user charges (Sepehri et al., 2002). Changes in the intensity of servicing were even more pronounced in the case of hospital admission, where intensity of servicing grew by as much as 20 per cent per annum. Although total hospital admissions remained constant over the period between 1995 and 1998, the length of hospital stays alone grew by as much as 15 per cent per year.

The increase in the intensity of hospital care can be seen as, among other things, an attempt on the part of providers to increase patient revenues in the face of a shrinking share of public resources allocated to hospitals, and low wages and salaries (Sepehri et al., 2002). The problem of provider's moral hazard has been viewed as being at least partly responsible for the escalation in insurance reimbursements paid to public health facilities in Vietnam (Dunlop, 1999; World Bank, 2001c). The rapid increase in the volume and intensity of hospital services provided to the Vietnamese population with health insurance has already endangered the financial integrity of several provincial health insurance funds. As a consequence, some measures, including the introduction of co-insurance and ceilings on reimbursement, have been taken to contain cost escalation (Dunlop, 1996; World Bank, 2001c). However, to the extent that utilization decisions, especially those regarding hospital admissions and the length of hospital stay, are influenced by providers, it is doubtful that changes in incentives aimed at inhibiting moral hazard on the part of insurance enrollees will curb utilization by themselves (Liu and Hsiao, 1995).

The increase in the intensity of hospital servicing may also reflect deterioration in the health status of individuals seeking hospital care. To the extent that user charges prevent individuals, and especially those from low-income households, from seeking early treatment, those individuals may wait until their illness is serious before getting admitted to a hospital. There is some evidence from Vietnam and other low-income countries that indicates that user charges delay utilization of health services, especially by the poor (Alderman and Lavy, 1996; Ensor and San, 1996; Gilson, 1997; Yoder, 1989). However, while the high cost of access may prevent uninsured individuals, and especially the poor, from seeking early treatment, it still remains unclear why the length of hospital stay in 1998 was far greater for patients from higher expenditure quintiles, a phenomenon that was less evident in 1993. Nor is it clear why the length of hospital stay is greater for the insured population, who face a far smaller out-of-pocket expenditure per hospital contact than the uninsured population (Sepehri et al., 2002).

The high and growing cost of accessing public hospitals can lead to long-term impoverishment of households. According to a recent participatory poverty assessment in Vietnam's Tra Vinh province, of the households that became poorer over time, 57 per cent cited illness as the cause of the decline (Oxfam [GB], 1999). A recent study of the financing of inpatient care in one of the poorest provinces of Vietnam also indicates that almost half of those in the lowest four quintiles relied solely on selling assets, and 19 per cent on borrowing, to finance the cost of their hospitalization (Pham, 2002). By contrast, over 60 per cent of households in the richest quintile relied solely on their own savings to finance the cost of their hospitalization. Similar results have been reported for China (Hossain, 1997; Yu, Cao, and Lucas, 1997).

There are formal mechanisms in place for exempting certain groups of people from user charges, including war veterans, the disabled, orphans, ethnic minorities, and the very poor, provided they are able to produce a certificate of indigency from their neighbourhood or village people's committee. Patients suffering from certain ailments such as malaria, tuberculosis, leprosy, and sexually transmitted diseases also receive free treatment, including drugs. However, the exemption mechanism works quite poorly in practice, at least in terms of protecting the very poor. According to the 1998 Vietnam Living Standards Survey, to the extent that patients were exempted from paying for consultation and treatment at public hospitals, higher income groups obtain a level of exemption only marginally lower than the poor. This reflects possibly the weaker position of poor households either to negotiate an exemption or simply not to be able to afford to pay a hidden fee. Ensor and San (1996) also found no correlation between fee exemption and household income, or between the number of offered fee exemptions and the general affluence of the commune. Health providers' incentive to give eligible patients exemptions has been further hampered by the rather low level of compensation provided by the central government. The share of subsidies and transfers via user charges and free health cards in total recurrent health expenditure by all levels of government was only 4 per cent in 1998, down from about 6 per cent in 1991-92 (Deolalikar, 2000).

The government has recognized the negative impact of health reforms on accessibility to health care services (Ministry of Health, 1996), and has issued several decrees and regulations, including the provision of free of charge medical cards to the poor, over the past several years. The purpose of such changes has been to improve access to care (Do, 2000). However, these policy initiatives have either yet to be implemented or to be extended to the entire country (Malhotra, 1999; Segall et al., 1999). More recently, the World Bank has initiated a provincial health system modernization project, which seeks, among other things, to build a policy framework and institutional capacity for improved quality of hospital care and develop mechanisms for financing catastrophic curative care for the poor.

IV. Conclusions

The transition from a centrally planned economy to a market-based one in the 1980s, combined with a neo-conservative stabilization and adjustment programme in 1989, led to a radical shift in the financing and delivery of Vietnam's near universal, publicly funded and provided health services. The legalization of private medical practices, combined with the liberalization of the pharmaceutical industry and the introduction of user charges, effectively transformed Vietnam's health services into a highly unregulated, mixed private-public system, with serious consequences for equity within the health care system

The introduction of user charges led to a rapid increase in fee revenues collected at the public hospitals. By 1998, revenues from user charges accounted for 30 per cent of public hospital total revenues, up from 9 per cent in 1994. The combined revenue from user charges and health insurance amounted to 45 per cent of hospital revenue in 1998. Higher patient revenues allowed hospitals to increase staff bonuses. With a dwindling share of the state health budget in hospital revenues, and with a declining share of official salaries in providers' total earnings, hospitals and physicians have become increasingly dependent on patient revenues. This change in the method of financing the public health care sector has shifted the incentive structure towards an unregulated fee-for-service system, and away from a salary system and centrally determined global budgets. The potential risk of overprovision of services under a fee-for-service system is well known, especially in a poorly regulated environment such as Vietnam, where providers are poorly paid and where there is no professional oversight or regulations to monitor the utilization and quality of services provided by hospitals.

An examination of hospital service contacts in 1993 and 1998, and across various income groups, highlights three points. First, people in higher expenditure quintiles receive not only more health care in the form of longer hospital stays and more intensive resource use during those stays than people in the lower expenditure quintiles, but also more than they did before. Second, the existing pattern of utilization, skewed as it is towards the better off, is not consistent with the self-reported pattern of the incidence of illness and its severity in Vietnam, where the pattern of illness and its severity closely follows the poverty map. The poor who are sicker now receive proportionally less health care. Third, the distribution of aggregate hospital days worsened between 1993 and 1998, with the share of the poorest 20 per cent of the population in aggregate hospital days dropping from 13.4 per cent in 1993 to 9.7 per cent in 1998. In contrast, the share of the richest 20 per cent of the population accounted for about 33 per cent of aggregate hospital days in 1993, up from about 23 per cent in 1993. The second and third expenditure quintiles also experienced a reduction in their share of aggregate hospital days of a similar magnitude as the poorest population quintile.

Even though poor households used hospitals far less frequently than non-poor households, these fewer visits imposed a heavy financial burden on the poor. The cost of a single service contact with a public hospital takes up about 22 per cent of non-food consumption expenditure for a year for a person from the bottom two quintiles. The financial burden on the poor of a single service contact with a hospital is far greater if it involves admission to hospital. A single admission accounted for over 60 per cent of the non-food consumption expenditure for a year for a middle-income person, and for about 58 per cent for a person from the bottom quintile. Although there are formal exemption mechanisms in place for protecting the poor and vulnerable, these mechanisms do not work well in practice.

To improve efficiency and equity in the health sector, policy-makers and health planners should consider strategies to deal with the problem of pro-vider's moral hazard. These could include the introduction of prepayment schemes, the establishment of state and professional regulatory bodies to for-mulate and implement standards and guidelines for clinical practice, and the development of strategies for assessing and approving both the importation and promotion of medical equipment and essential and non-essential phar-maceuticals. Moreover, the experience of countries with an efficient and eq-uitable health care sector suggests that to achieve improvements in efficiency and equity requires a strong, publicly funded, health care system or alternative methods of financing that avoid the pitfalls of user charges and their burden on the poor.

Footnotes

1 This section draws on Sepehri, Chernomas, and Akram-Lodhi (2003).

2 Insurance provision is very limited, covering only about 12.5 per cent of the country's population in 1998 and financing about 11 per cent of total expenditure on health (Ministry of Health, 1998). The scheme consists of two separate parts, one compulsory and one voluntary. The former is targetted at current and retired civil servants and the employees of SOEs, as well as those of private enterprises with more than 10 employees. It covers the cost of inpatient and outpatient treatment in state health facilities. The voluntary scheme is for the reminder of the population.

3 The 1993 and 1998 household surveys use a four-week and a one-year reference period, respectively, in obtaining information on hospitalization, and are thus subject to differing recall errors. Since the recall errors are larger with a longer recalling period, the 1998 length of hospital stay is more likely to underestimate the actual length of hospital stay. Facility-based data show that the length of hospital stay rose from 4.2 days in 1993 to 8.2 in 1998 (Ministry of Health, 1998).

4 The data on private health spending are only available from the 1993 and 1998 Vietnam Living Standards Surveys, and consistent data series for public spending is only available for the period between 1991 and 1998. The reported data on public health spending tend to vary by sources and coverage. The higher range estimate of the share of private

health spending is based on household health expenditures data from the 1998 Vietnam Living Standards Survey and total public spending on health. The latter includes spending from the state budget as well as from other sources, such as user fees, health insurance reimbursements, and donors (Deolalikar, 2000). The lower estimate of the share of private health spending is calculated by the authors using the data from 1998 Vietnam Living Standards Survey and government budgetary data on health spending.

PART 3

Neo-conservatism and the Crisis of Governance

Chapter 11

GOOD GOVERNANCE, MARKETS AND DONORS

Brian Van Arkadie

I. Introduction and definition

THIS chapter addresses weaknesses and ambiguities in the recent focus on governance in the donor-African aid dialogue, which in turn raise questions about the governance of the aid process itself. Nevertheless, the central importance of governance in development is obviously to be recognized. The introduction of governance issues and the increased awareness of the importance of institutions are obviously advances over the preceding period of structural adjustment, in which donors concentrated on a rather mechanical approach to economic policy issues.

From what is now a huge literature, a straightforward definition of the term "governance" can be found in a recent United Kingdom government policy document on governance and the poor, published by the Department for International Development (DFID, 2001). This document uses the term governance to mean

> how the institutions, rules and systems of the state—the executive, legislature, judiciary and military—operate at the central and local level and how the state relates to individual citizens, civil society and the private sector. We use *government* to mean the executive function at central and local levels. The *political* system and *politics* is the way power in the state is acquired and how groups inside and outside government influence the use of that power. (p. 11)

This definition, and the further discussion in the document, present "political governance" in terms of both the managerial capability of state bodies and the responsiveness of those bodies to the needs of citizens and of key actors in the economy.

Interestingly, governance is also widely used now in relation to the behaviour of corporations. Corporate good governance relates to the effectiveness of management in running business in conformity with established accounting and legal rules, and in responding to the views and interests of parties concerned with the operation of the organization: shareholders, workers, consumers, and the community at large. In both this and the development context, then, governance is more than a positivistic, value-neutral, technocratic term. Its use typically incorporates strong normative views about expected behaviour. In the development context, governance tends to incorporate a vision of an honest and efficient state that is both responsive to the public in general and, in the case of the DFID document quoted, the poor in particular. Good governance is also seen as incorporating an ability to implement the macroeconomic and microeconomic requirements for market-based growth.

Given these strong normative elements, it is not surprising that the use of the term in relation to both corporate governance and political governance often involves an element of moralistic exhortation about the need for ethical behaviour and greater social responsibility. However, good governance is also seen as being instrumental in achieving effective economic performance, both by corporations and governments. Thus, governance is not only seen as desirable as a social goal in itself, but also as a means to the achievement of economic goals.

Given the proliferation of literature, a discussion of governance could touch on a wide range of issues related to the inter-play between political processes and economic policy. In this chapter, the main focus is on the attention being given to governance in the contemporary discussions of economic policy in developing countries, and particularly in the context of the dialogue between donors and African governments. The chapter is concerned with governance issues as they relate to the pursuit of established economic development goals. To that end, and for the purposes of this discussion, the DFID definition will be paraphrased, and governance will be taken to mean the practices guiding the formulation, implementation and oversight of the programmes, policies and activities of organizations, and in particular of governments.

II. Why governance?

Why does governance feature so prominently in contemporary discussions of economic policy? It was not the case 15 years ago—indeed, at that time, the term was not commonly used in the economic development literature. Governance has emerged as a prominent feature of policy discourse in recent years.

An obvious reason for the emergence of the use of the term is the perceived consequences of poor governance. For example, in 2002, better corporate governance re-emerged[1] as a crucial issue in light of the reaction of stock markets to corporate misbehaviour. The popular current usage of corporate governance introduces new dimensions to the assessment of business management, in reaction to the discredited business fashions of the last boom. Similarly, in the development discourse, governance has emerged as a central theme partly as a response to the continuing poor performance of a large number of economies, which, in turn, has been associated with the poor performance of governments.

Governance is used to extend the discussion of the appropriate exercise of power and the ethics of managerial behaviour into new areas, and, in particular, to address aspects of the political process that are crucial to development but that were neglected by mainstream development economists in the recent past. It is evident that the nature of governance is likely to be a determinant of economic performance and the distribution of the benefits of growth. Thus, the widespread contemporary use of governance concepts reflects a heightened awareness of the instrumental importance of political and administrative factors conditioning economic performance.

However, the governance discourse is also concerned with specifically political agendas and objectives, incorporating visions of desirable political models. Inevitably, the instrumental and the normative are inter-twined. As a result, good governance practice is sometimes justified for the economic benefits it will generate, and at other times it is seen as a political end. This creates no problems when arguments drawing on either of these approaches work in the same direction. However, the discussion becomes more difficult when evidence suggests that politically desirable concepts of good governance are not a necessary condition for fast economic growth and may even be inconsistent with it. In such circumstances, a choice may have to be made between governance and growth objectives.

III. Governance as a development fashion

At one level, the popularity of governance may be considered largely a matter of fashion, if "fashion" merely involves changes in vocabulary and adornment as distinguished from "innovation," which involves the creation of new ideas and techniques. Fashion is a characteristic of most human activities and fashions in development policy are a significant exogenous factor influencing policy. The dynamics of fashion in development policy respond to a number of influences, such as changes in the political climate in the developed countries, the returns to be reaped by practitioners from apparent innovation, as well as, in the African context, the continuing failure to make an economic development breakthrough.

The defining influence on development policy thinking in the 1980s was the emergence of the Washington Consensus, espousing the maximum use of market instruments and a minimal economic role for the state. While the consensus reflected a shared analysis of the poor performance of government economic policies within the developing countries, it was, in the developed economies, more a response to political shifts. Thus, under the Reagan administration in the United States and the Thatcher administration in the UK, the earlier hegemony of Keynesian and moderately interventionist approaches to policy were displaced by a new orthodoxy, somewhat inaccurately described as "monetarism" and more recently labelled "neo-conservatism."

Given the rather poor institutional memory in development agencies, the cyclical nature of fashion sometimes goes unrecognized. Thus, the concept of "basic needs" appeared for a while on the development menu, and then was taken off for some years, before much the same issues re-emerged under the guise of "poverty alleviation." "Development plans" came and went, to re-emerge as "comprehensive development frameworks" while a "partnership in development" was unsuccessfully floated by Lester Pearson at the end of the 1960s, to be resuscitated—in this case with no change of label—30 years later. Likewise, many of the themes that now appear on the governance agenda enjoyed an earlier currency in discussions of nation building and the politics of development in the early post-colonial years.

Unpredictable shifts in donor fashions have become one powerful source of exogenous instability affecting policy-making in heavily aid-dependent countries. Currently, this is particularly evident in the changing attitudes of donors to poverty programs. In the early 1970s, propelled by the International Labour Organization's World Employment Program, and by work in the World Bank by such economists as Hollis Chenery, Muhbub ul Haq, and Paul Streeten, basic needs and poverty-focussed development became the flavour of the period. Then, with the oil shocks, economic crisis, and the decisive political shifts in the US and UK, structural adjustment, the retreat of the state, and belief in the market became the order of the day. Now poverty alleviation has again become the focus of aid agencies. For officials in developing economies, the changing views of donors are almost as powerful a source of uncertainty as fluctuations in international markets. For example, in a country such as Tanzania, it may seem somewhat ironic that officials are now lectured on the need to emphasize poverty alleviation. This is because poverty alleviation had long been the established priority of Tanzanian policy. Moreover, such lecturing has been done by the same institutions that had pushed policies that had led to a downgrading of basic needs priorities in the not-so-distant past.

IV. Governance as a component of economic policy

i.   *Governance and the economic role of the state*
Approaches to governance are most straightforward where good governance is seen as a component of, or prerequisite to, effective economic policy. Indeed, one route by which the term entered the discussion of economic policy in developing and transition economies initially was in the context of the evolution in approaches to economic reform. Mainstream approaches to economic reform can be described, in a simplified form, as follows. Advocates of market-based reforms in the 1980s and early 1990s focussed on the alternative ways market tools could implement effective policies and explored different transitional routes from controlled to liberalized economies, giving rise to debates about the comparative merit of "big bangs" in relation to gradual transitions to the market in formerly centrally planned economies (World Bank, 1996c). In the African context, the role of government was discussed largely in terms of appropriate economic policies and of minimizing the role of government by

reducing government budgets and interventions in the economy (World Bank, 1981). This set the stage for the World Bank's promotion of structural adjustment in Africa in the subsequent decade and a half.

Economists most committed to market-based solutions saw as their main tasks the advocacy of the efficiency of the market and the promotion of the broadest extension of market solutions. Attention to government as such largely focussed on the need to reduce state ownership and government controls, trim public expenditure, and, in particular, to reduce the size of the allegedly bloated civil service. Within that context, the political agenda was very much a matter of limiting the role of government to what it could manage effectively, preventing the government from generating fiscal and monetary instability, and eliminating what economists described as "economic distortions."

One reason for the introduction of governance as a dimension of the economic reform debate was the increasing recognition that such an approach to policy was not sufficient. An economic agenda defined largely in terms of dismantling important parts of the state apparatus easily neglected consideration of areas where the role of the state continued to be crucial. Experience demonstrated that when liberalization stimulated market responses, an inadequate supply of public services and ineffective operation of public institutions constrained growth. In a number of countries, an initial impetus to private investment after liberalization ran into the constraints resulting from poor and deteriorating public services — roads, water, and power. Pro-market economic doctrine had always recognized that there were many needs that would not be met by the market, requiring effective government intervention, but that concern was downplayed in the drive to dismantle the apparatus of government interventionism. Indeed, even those who thought that the main task of policy was to unleash the "magic of the market" eventually had to accept that the effective operation of markets required critical state inputs, including establishing an appropriate institutional environment and providing a range of services (public goods) not supplied effectively by the market. If the state was to continue to play an important role, the effectiveness of political processes could not be ignored.

In Africa, the introduction of structural adjustment reforms coincided with a decline in the capacity of governments to carry out required tasks. During the pre-reform period, government capacities had eroded as a result of the impact of such external shocks as the oil crises; from the effects of governments trying to do too much, taking on management tasks that overstretched bureaucratic capacity; and as a result of dysfunctional and failed control systems. Scarcities and bureaucratic controls created rent-seeking opportunities that provided income to needy public servants, just when their real incomes were eroding as a result of economic crisis. This was, to use the Tanzanian term of that time, the era of "technical *know-who*." At the same time, bureaucratic inefficiency and corruption greatly increased the transaction costs of business. Finally, and perhaps most critical for long-term development, deteriorating educational systems resulted in a decline in the quality of the workforce.

Structural adjustment was intended to render the economic role of government more manageable, but in the early stages of structural adjustment, the feedback of austere economic policies on the effectiveness of government was itself neglected. Fiscal austerity and the removal of policies that protected state employees contributed to a further severe deterioration in the capacity of governments to deliver even the most basic services. Initial efforts, crafted as they were by the Bretton Woods institutions, made a crucial blunder in promoting liberal reforms without addressing the prerequisites for the effective administration of those functions that necessarily remained the responsibility of the state. In fact, structural adjustment in its early applications further demoralized the public service, as sharp devaluations and budget tightening drastically reduced the real value of public service salaries, while at the same time many perquisites of office derived from the state's management role also disappeared. African governments in the 1970s had already made the mistake of assuming that if you did not pay farmers, they would nevertheless produce. Structural adjustment programmes made an equally dangerous error, assuming civil servants would continue to work despite a collapse in their incomes. This created the civil servants' response—"the government pretends to pay us and we pretend to work" (Van Arkadie, 1986).

From the late 1980s, there was an increasing awareness of the negative consequences of the erosion of government capacity, which generated a range of capacity building initiatives, now subsumed as a set of activities within the more general governance framework. At the theoretical level, the shift in emphasis was supported by renewed attention to market failure, which weakened the doctrinal foundations for the support of the minimalist state. At the empirical level, one reason for the revival in emphasis on the importance of the role of the state was the recognition that a key characteristic of the successful economies of east Asia was that their buoyant private economies were supported by coherent and effective state action. If government was seen, as a result, as central to the development process, good governance could then be seen as having a crucial instrumental role in achieving economic development goals. In this respect governance issues were no more than concerns that government should play its necessary economic role effectively. From that point of view, governance incorporated more traditional approaches to public administration and to the formulation of economic policy, while adding a political economy dimension that explored the political conditions that make for effective policy implementation.

The recognition that, even if the reforms of the past two decades involved a considerable retreat of the state, the state remained a crucial economic actor, is an important part of a newly emerging consensus. There is, of course, considerable debate over what the precise role of the state should be, but there is wide support for the view that the state should provide certain services, particularly economic infrastructure and investment in human capital. As a consequence, efforts to restore the capacity of government institutions—to raise the efficiency and probity of the public service to effective levels—have been high on the policy agenda, in Africa and elsewhere, for the past decade. The importance of government capacity for effective development is evident, but the efforts of the past decade have also demonstrated the great difficulty in achieving progress. In particular, it has proved difficult to use external assistance as a vehicle for promoting government reform. This is, in part, because aid modalities have themselves been a source of erosion of coherent public administration. Faced with weakening administrative capacity, donors were unwilling to fund the public service in general, but sought mechanisms to ensure the operation of those bits and pieces of the system that they took to be important, or that were seen as necessary for implementing their own programmes. This was done by such devices as project management units, special secretariats created to take on key tasks, and the use of national consultants on more attractive terms than the civil service. The result was that aid-supported activities became an important source of distortion in the public-sector salary structure and demoralized those officers not benefiting from donor projects. In those many cases where aid became the major source of development finance, the dysfunctional impact became a serious source of capacity erosion. Moreover, aid-supported administrative reform projects have often incorporated precisely those modalities that have disrupted the smooth functioning of civil service incentive systems. Aid dependence thus became part of the problem, rather than the means to a solution.

ii.   Governance and the recognition of the importance of institutions
Another critical factor propelling the intrusion of governance issues into the pure world of the economist was the recognition of the importance of institutions for the effective operation of markets (Van Arkadie, 1990). Many economists working in established market economies neglected the importance of institutions because they implicitly assumed the existence of the institutions conditioning markets in their own economies, without bothering to analyze their origins or functioning. However, while markets in economic models are abstractions, in reality they are institutions, governed by rules and influenced by the behaviour of various actors. Moreover, effective legal institutions are not only a matter of the enactment of laws, but also the administration of the law. The effectiveness of the state in setting up the "rules of the game" and ensuring their predictable and transparent application emerged as a key, and far from simple, issue. It became evident that effective governance, seen as the fashioning and implementation of the rules that provide the context for the market economy, is of crucial importance for the effective operation of a market economy.

The scholarly impetus to study the role of economic institutions came from economic historians (Gerschenkron, 1963), but the critical importance of institutions became recognized in the context of the transition economies. When planned economies began the transition to the market, it was clear that many important institutions were absent. In transition economies, there was an urgent need for company law, commercial law, bankruptcy laws, banking laws, and the like. Land tenure arrangements were a crucial factor in rural development and land law reform a crucial step in the reform process. The legislative task was enormous, although even more challenging has been the development of all the other components that make legal systems work—the judiciary, the legal profession, and a popular understanding of the law.

In transition economies, a key issue for proponents of reform is the degree to which laws and other public institutions are biased in favour of the public sector—the standard metaphor is to argue for a level playing field between private and public sectors. However, even more important for the creditability of reform process was the manner in which property rights are created (Van Arkadie and Karlsson, 1992). Property is obviously a key institution in the market, and market reform resulted in, and required, new patterns of ownership. The way in which property is acquired not only affects efficiency, but also the perceived fairness and legitimacy of a market system. It also affects politics—the appearance of crony capitalism and economic mafias results from the use of political power to accumulate illicit wealth by those with political access, and, in turn, the use of that ill-gotten wealth to influence the political process.

In most developing economies, although the institutions required for effective markets may have existed in principle—institutions such as systems of commercial law and secure land tenure—they may not have functioned adequately in practice. Thus, in the African context there is not the need to create a formal institutional fabric from scratch, as was the case in the former centrally planned economies, but similar issues are of crucial importance in relation to the way the rules of the game are administered. Uncertainty about legal processes, insecure property rights, capricious and arbitrary enforcement of regulations affecting business activities, unpredictable licensing arrangements, ineffective tax administration, and rent-seeking officials together create a negative environment for business activity.

iii.   Governance, ownership, and the process of policy-making
There has been a useful recognition that the implementation of an effective economic policy regime is not solely a matter of professional economic analysis and design, but also of political commitment. Even if economists believed they had the right policies to sell, they also had to be concerned with factors that determined governments' willingness to buy. The commitment to policies is as important as their substantive content.

Thus, the approach to policy-making as mainly being about identifying optimal economic solutions had neglected a number of issues central to effective economic policy. This became evident when the initial acceptance of reforms and policy packages as aid conditions was not sustained, where there was no commitment to persist with reforms in the face of setbacks, or no effective constituency supporting the reform process. This led to increasing attention to the political preconditions necessary for effective reform. In particular, donors became concerned with finding mechanisms to transfer the "ownership" of their agenda to their clients. It became evident, even to donors, that economic analysis backed by aid conditionality was not sufficient to ensure effective policy implementation. To carry a difficult package of reforms through, a high level of local commitment was required. There had to be a national constituency to support policies, which could back up the programme and sustain it in the face of opposition. All serious reforms threaten some vested interests, and in some cases are perceived to place burdens on the majority of the population. Thus, to carry through a difficult reform agenda, it was not enough to push the bitter medicine down the throats of unenthusiastic national authorities; there had to be a national basis of support for policies to be effectively implemented and sustained, a "national ownership" of policies.

How could the national ownership of policies be achieved? This is an issue very much subject to continuing debate. Some have sought the solution in charismatic leadership — a man on a white horse — or, as in east Asia, authoritarian or quasi-authoritarian regimes. In other cases, support is sought from a small technocratic elite. However, where political governance comes into its own is through the recognition that the most durable support for reform comes from building a consensus among a sufficient group of interests within the political system. Within a democracy, this is likely to imply building support and understanding in the ruling party as well as among the larger public. This is not to say that democratic processes necessarily lead to broad support for good economic policies, nor that effective consensus building in support of economic reform is not possible in a one-party state. In Vietnam, an aggressive program of market reforms was carried through via a consensus crafted by extended discussion, negotiation, and careful consensus building within the one-party system.

If policies promote change, there will always be some groups whose interests are threatened. Compromises may be necessary to put together coalitions of interest that see change as consistent with their perceived interests. This is not primarily a matter of selling policies, but rather of crafting an effective political process whereby policies are developed. Support is more likely for a policy package that has emerged from a formulation process based in the national decision-making structure in which the concerns of a potential constituency are addressed, and least likely if the policy package is crafted by external experts. This has implications for the aid relationship. Over long periods of aid dependence, donors have become accustomed to taking the initiative in defining policies, not only through conditionality mechanisms, but also by taking the initiative in identifying, preparing, and appraising projects, producing reports defining sectoral policy options, and, in effect, determining the development budget. This process shifts responsibility from national authorities, who can hardly feel responsible, or be held accountable, for programs initiated and designed by others. In effect, it has been a process of infantilization, which has drained initiative and responsibility away from national governments. It is not surprising that the result has been the lack of national ownership of the resulting programs. Accountability, ownership, and responsibility imply control. If programs are not controlled by the national authorities and, in a fundamental sense, do not emerge from the national decision-making process, then national governance is a sham. This reality will not be changed by a process of consultation, orchestrated and funded by donors, with outcomes largely pre-determined by donor priorities, and with donors thus effectively playing the role of a ventriloquist, managing and on occasions even drafting statements on both sides of the discourse.

In this regard, the shift being made by donors to budgetary and program support mechanisms and away from project support could provide the base for greater national control and real decision-making, the necessary preconditions for more effective national allocation mechanisms. However, the effect could be reversed if donors use the shift to program aid as an occasion for introducing more general policy conditionality to replace the loss of control previously exercised at the project level. For program support to become the vehicle for national ownership, donors would need to take the gamble of allowing national governments to control the disposition of the pocket money they are allocated.

V. Governance as a political agenda

In the development literature, the current emphasis on governance has been heavily promoted by donors, both as a response to perceived limitations in traditional approaches to economic policy and as a vehicle for promoting donor political agendas. In addition to effective government being seen as an *instrument* for the achievement of economic growth objectives, governance concerns were also increasingly promoted as *ends* in themselves. The donor community became increasingly assertive in promoting new social and political goals as cross-cutting issues motivating their approaches to external assistance. The distinction is not clear-cut: gender awareness, participation of civil society, decentralization, and multi-party democracy have been promoted as desirable in themselves and as necessary components of a successful growth strategy. Thus, such key governance concerns as anti-corruption were emphasized because corrupt practices were perceived as socially objectionable, and were also argued, on the basis of convincing evidence, to be a barrier to economic progress.

i.   Contradictions in the donor agenda

The use of aid to promote strategic and commercial interests has long been recognized as compromising the development impact of aid programs. However, there may also be contradictions in the use of aid as a vehicle for the promotion of a more benign agenda, in that the assertion of goals that incorporate the prevailing values of donors has real dangers. One problem is the susceptibility of donors to development thinking that responds to changes of opinion in the state, and to pressure from lobbies in the donor countries, rather than relating to the specific conditions in recipient countries. Apart from any larger philosophical questions regarding the use of the aid relationship for the promotion of political values, at the very practical level political ideas, whatever their intrinsic merits, are most likely to take root when they respond to the current needs and balance of forces in the society where they are being planted, rather than reflecting the factors conditioning thinking abroad. Even if goals such as political freedom and gender equality can be defended as universally applicable, their successful pursuit is more likely when initiatives have deep national roots. Moreover, the changing donor governance agenda, as it becomes loaded with politically correct items, may be of questionable viability when it places strong pressures on fragile political institutions. As countries struggle to make the institutions of multi-party electoral democracy work, a new donor rhetoric gains currency, advocating decentralization, local empowerment, and the engagement of "civil society."

However, there are risks of confusion in the proliferation of objectives. Over the past two decades, governments in Africa have received a mixed message from the donor community. On the one hand, in the 1980s they were advised in quite clear terms that the capacity of government was severely limited, and that, therefore, the extent of government intervention in the economy should be severely curtailed. Subsequently, they have been requested to incorporate a whole range of social engineering and political goals, carrying the implication that the state can fine-tune its interventions to achieve quite sophisticated objectives (Van Arkadie and Mule, 1996). A judgement is required about how much can be achieved, or else, in this arena, as in earlier economic management failures, the attempt to do too much too fast may become a recipe for failure.

Even more worrying is the inherent contradiction in the donor role—what might be called the "governance of governance" issue. This arises because the very intrusion of donors into political processes itself poses controversial issues of governance. This not only relates to the now widely recognized contradiction outlined above—the conflict between the donor compulsion to design and enforce policies, and the desirability of establishing ownership by national government—but also to ambitions to promote broader ownership, with governments being held accountable to its citizens. One route to political accountability is through governments being answerable to representative political institutions. This explains the promotion of credible multiparty electoral processes. However, how are elected representative bodies to be included in policy-making processes constrained by donor conditionality? When there is a conflict between the views of such bodies and the packages promoted by the donor community, how is that conflict resolved? That there is deep potential for conflict becomes clear when, having encouraged the election of representative government bodies, donors find the resulting decisions are not very consistent with "good" economic policy, and quickly find themselves trying to constrain and even bypass the elected representative bodies.

ii.   "Civil society" and the role of representative institutions

Having supported the opening up of electoral processes, donors sometimes seem to have little faith in the outcomes. The current fashion is to downplay the formal political process in favour of a broader, and ill-defined, concept of consultation, encapsulated in the term "civil society." In the aid community, the need for consulting civil society is now the accepted conventional wisdom, and at first sight and in principle it would seem to be a good thing. However, what consultation should be in practice remains unclear. For example, in the current Poverty Reduction Strategy process that many countries have been undertaking in relation to the Heavily Indebted Poor Countries process, there is a good deal of consultation of civil society. It is not clear, however, in what terms civil society should be defined, and who will be invited to the table. There has been a shift in emphasis from consultation with elected representatives in an effort to make formal political institutions work, to subjecting policies to informal consultations with representatives of concerned groups. There are risks of such donor-sponsored consultative processes becoming a parallel and competing system to that of formal political accountability through elected political bodies, perhaps particularly unfortunate at a time when the critical importance of electoral processes is also being promoted. Moreover, the criteria by which those to be consulted are selected is unclear, subsumed under the nebulous concept of civil society.

Recently, during an evaluation of the Poverty Reduction Strategy Paper (PRSP) process in Tanzania, it was made quite clear that one evaluation criterion should be the effectiveness of government's consultations with civil society. However, there was an astonishing lack of clarity among representatives of the donor community regarding what civil society was. Was it the citizenry at large, or was it organized interest groups such as trade unions, farmer associations, chambers of commerce or the like? The obvious weakness with focussing on such groups is that the main intended aid beneficiaries, the poor, are precisely the least organized, with their interest least represented by organized interest groups.

While to some the only plausible consultative process is through the electoral system—unless that is proposed to be displaced by referenda, opinion polls, or even focus groups—this has not been the way donors have decided to solve the problem. Their chosen way is to identify non-governmental organizations (NGOs) as the appropriate voice of civil society. It can be argued that although national NGOs can rarely demonstrate the sort of broad base that would justify a claim to represent a large constituency, they typically seek to serve the interests of the poor and underprivileged, or a more general community interest. Such claims may be merited by many NGOs, but their role remains ambiguous. Many NGOs are themselves sustained by donors, and are largely made up of small groups of middle-class development activists, often astute at assessing donor preferences. Indeed, given the resources at the disposal of donors, it is only too easy to create an apparent constituency for the donor reform agenda; for example, through the funding of NGOs, which are then only non-governmental in the sense that they are independent of the national authorities. Such NGOs are, in effect, donor organizations, responding to the powerful stimulus of donor funding.

The role of international NGOs in the governance of aid is also subject to ambiguity. Those international NGOs able to use leverage with development agencies to push their own agendas are caught in a contradiction. Although their objectives may be admirable, the use of donor leverage to further them is in conflict with the goal of national sovereignty for developing nations, a goal to which most progressive NGOs would also subscribe. No doubt it is preferable that donor agencies are influenced to promote progressive objectives, rather than being mainly subject to commercial influences or strategic concerns. However, ultimately a process in which donors set the policy agenda, desirable in content or not, infantilizes national political processes, resulting in donor paternalism obscuring accountability for decisions.

iii. Consultation as a means and an end

With the introduction of new approaches to governance, there is also confusion between means and ends, so that the actual purpose of development interventions becomes unclear. If the main objective of consultation is to draw on local knowledge in programme design, consultation has an instrumental role and is justified or not justified insofar as it contributes to the better adjustment of a programme to local conditions and preferences. However, there seems to be a sense in which consultation is valued irrespective of any instrumental outcome. If decentralization and consultation become ends in themselves, expenditures and interventions can be justified because they promote such activity, irrespective of whether they contribute to an intended outcome. The emphasis on what, in an earlier age, would have been described as a "community development" approach may have merits; however, consultation is time-consuming, involving real economic costs to participants. Those who participate may do so expecting a material return and may not be persuaded of the intrinsic merits of meetings. Moreover, the proliferation of governance-related objectives in project design may obscure the appraisal and evaluation of the intended material outcomes.

VI. The need for a deeper analysis: some examples

The following examples are based on personal observation of how governance issues seem to be used in practice in the aid dialogue in the African setting. Observation suggests that to meet the legitimate concerns for the social and political dimensions of development programmes, there may need to be a more careful specification of intentions and more profound investigation of social reality than is typically attempted in most public programme formulation. The subsections below offer some examples of areas where greater clarity is required.

i. The political model

The model of the "good society" informing the good governance dialogue is typically left implicit. It seems to involve a vision of a pluralistic society, with formal political processes that are democratic, a public service that operates effectively and honestly, and that is subject to consultative processes engaging organizations representing various legitimate interests in society. Insofar as formal political institutions are concerned, although there is controversy, a coherent body of doctrine is emerging about what constitutes proper process—there should be more than one party, and political power should be transferred through elections that are free and fair, according to emerging international criteria. This is, of course, an attractive vision of the prerequisites for democratic process. However, such an approach rules out of court any possible merits of one-party rule, although a number of the development successes of the 1970s, 1980s, and 1990s were implemented under *de jure* (China, Vietnam) or *de facto* (Singapore, colonial Hong Kong, Korea for extended periods, Taiwan) one-party regimes.

There are obviously great difficulties in incorporating the political governance agenda, as described above, into approaches to development policy if comparative studies suggest that the democratic, pluralistic society may not be always compatible with the requirements for fast growth in poor countries. The difficulty becomes greater if, in particular situations, it appears that higher levels of economic welfare may be a prerequisite for the stable political institutions with the desired governance characteristics. The historical record of a number of countries seems to have incorporated a sequence of authoritarian government and high economic growth, leading only later to a process of democratization. Such a model might even suggest the awkward possibility that authoritarian regimes may, in some cases, be the precursor for subsequent democratic good governance. This should not be taken to argue that authoritarian regimes have, in general, been consistent with economic growth. There have been more cases of kleptocratic dictators than authoritarian developmental states. However, it does suggest that in addition to exploring why systems are more or less democratic, it may be of equal interest to explore why some authoritarian regimes have promoted economic growth and others have been quite economically dysfunctional.

The view that a particular model of good governance is viable and consistent with economic growth and poverty alleviation cannot be adopted as axiomatic and applicable to all countries. The model has to be established by analysis and evidence. The underlying difficulty is that donor political doctrines are more axiomatic than evidence-based.

ii.   *Decentralization as a goal*

One donor axiom that seems to have gained widespread currency in recent years is that decentralized development will be more responsive to grassroots' needs, and, therefore, that political decentralization should be promoted, particularly in the context of the pursuit of poverty alleviation. The potential merits of decentralization derive from the premise that local government, being closer to the people, will be more responsive to their needs. However, difficulties arise from the anodyne vision of society implicit in some of the approaches to decentralization and bottom-up decision-making. For example, it cannot be assumed that local communities are homogeneous. The donor vision of rural society seems to be of a village community based on equality and shared interests that acts as a building block for a democratic participatory process. However, this vision was and is flawed in its failure to reflect critical potential conflicts of interest such as those between bureaucrats and villagers, or landowners and farmers, or those between family and village. Indeed, it is more than ironic that this donor vision is rather similar to Julius Nyerere's now widely discredited vision of the *ujamaa* village.

An additional axiom of donor thinking seems to be that the more local is the decision-making process, the more egalitarian, participatory, fair, and free from corruption it will be. Under some circumstances this may be true, but it is not universal. Decision-making processes and public resources can be captured by elites and interest groups at the local level even more readily than at the national level. Experience suggests that local government is as likely to be captured by local interest groups, such as landowners, local business people, and local party machines, as to reflect grassroots concerns. The realities of economic inequalities, social differentiation, and patron-client political networks are ignored in the appeal to bottom-up, participatory processes.

At the same time, available electoral evidence does not suggest that constituents typically feel that local government is closer to their concerns than national government. It is an almost universal experience that participation in local elections is less than in national elections, and often very much so. In light of these realities, and given that decentralization is demanding in the use of personnel and can be fiscally expensive, there needs to be a strong case made that it is likely to meet expectations.

iii. Who and what are the "stakeholders"

In addition to the concept of consulting civil society at the policy-making level, there is also a new emphasis on involving "stakeholders" in project and programme preparation and implementation. "Stakeholder" is, like "civil society," another popular but ill-defined term in the governance vocabulary. Indeed, it is rare that any effort is made to define the term or identify who are the stakeholders in question. This was recently demonstrated when I examined a donor's portfolio of agricultural projects in Tanzania. In addition to including references to the already noted fashion for bottom-up approaches, the empowerment of farmers, the engagement of civil society, and the promotion of decentralization, most projects included references to procedures to ensure the participation of stakeholders in decision-making. However, it was not noted who were the stakeholders. In an agricultural project, are they the farmers, or landlords, or consumers, or traders, or processors, or all or some of these groups? Moreover, when differing stakeholders' interests conflict, as they surely must at certain points, how is the conflict to be resolved? Insofar as the economic interests of these groups are in conflict, is consultation, rather than competitive market transactions, the appropriate means of resolution? Granted, some conflicts can be resolved through consultation, particularly where there is a positive sum game. However, economic decisions more typically involve choices between meeting competing interests, which require resolution either through a central allocative mechanism such as the national budget or through the market.

Beyond the woolly verbiage, the emphasis on consultation of stakeholders seems to imply two things: that collective decision-making by the various interest groups is usually a good thing; and that the interests of the various stakeholders can be conciliated through a consultative process. However, Adam Smith, in *The Wealth of Nations*, pointed out how a gathering of interest groups such as traders was more likely to lead to collusion in the particular interest, rather than the promotion of the public good. It is certainly not difficult to think of instances where the stakeholders are also the rent-seekers.

iv. Good governance and equity

A particular sense in which good governance is now seen as more than just an instrument to economic policy goals, but also as an end in itself, is in relation to issues of distribution, equity, and poverty reduction. A responsive and just system of government is important as a social goal and for its instrumental role in promoting an equitable pattern of growth. Indeed, it seems to be increasingly recognized that good governance implies a willingness of the state to promote economic equity. This means that even though market instruments are used, they are not worshipped. There seems to be increasing recognition that, where necessary, the state should intervene to protect the weak and promote the interests of the poor. That is all to the good.

This is not to say that market solutions are necessarily unresponsive to the needs of the poor. Rapid market-based growth can lead to poverty alleviation. The strong case that poverty alleviation and market-led economic growth can go hand in hand draws on the evidence of east Asia, where market-based, export-led strategies resulted in high rates of growth associated with remarkable reductions in poverty. This was true under a range of different political regimes, in Taiwan, Singapore, and South Korea, as well as the People's Republic of China, and now Vietnam. However, before celebrating the east Asian experience as demonstrating the absence of the market-equity dilemma, a number of points should be noted about characteristics of the east Asian experience in addition to the commitment to the market-based, export-led strategy. The first relates to initial conditions. The successes generally started with a reasonable degree of rural equality in terms of access to land, whether as a result of communist revolution or American-sponsored post-war land reforms. Property relations were changed by forceful state action. Second, all the east Asian successes involved a strong commitment to investment in the human capital stock, not only through universal primary education but also through massive investments in higher education. Third, the range of tactics adopted in relation to state intervention has been broad and heterodox. These have ranged from Korean support for big business, to Singapore's version of the welfare state, to the continuation of the leading role for a partially reformed state owned sector in China and Vietnam.

All this suggests a wide range of economic governance mechanisms in the east Asian experience, in the sense of state interventions in the economy and in the nature of the political regimes. However, although they differed, they were all responsive to the needs of economic growth and ensured the reasonable diffusion of benefits, particularly through education and access to land, throughout society. Market, yes, but with policies sensitively crafted to reflect local political and economic realities, and with a political economy that makes it plausible that there will be a diffusion of the benefits of growth.

There have been other experiences where growth has not been associated with such a broad diffusion of benefits, with negative social consequences and also, arguably, where unequal patterns of growth have contributed to economic stalemate. This is one possible interpretation of the history of many Latin American countries, and in Asia, Pakistan and Indonesia enjoyed periods of high growth that were neither sustained nor led to broad diffusion of benefits. Indeed, where systems of intervention and control have been used to bolster the interests of better-off groups, liberalization is unlikely to benefit the poor.

However, even much-criticized structural adjustment programmes, with associated devaluations and decontrol, in many countries initially shifted the terms of trade in favour of the peasantry. Thus, attention must be paid to the special conditions governing particular growth experiences.

VII. A concluding comment

From an Africa-wide perspective, the key question that now needs to be addressed is whether models of governance now being promoted (e.g. through the PRSP process) will make the state more responsive to the potential for broad based development, or whether it will be another instance of donor rhetoric promoting approaches that fail to root in local realities. The fundamental difficulty for the outsider is to come to terms with political and social realities as they exist, and to judge what is appropriate and what is possible given those realities, rather than promoting images of society largely based on an idealised interpretation (typically not very deep) of the Organisation for Economic Cooperation and Development (OECD) experience.

Footnotes

1 Corporate scandals and calls for the improved surveillance of corporate governance become big news during periods of deep market downturns. This was not only the case in 2002. It was also the case following the crash of 1929.

Chapter 12

LOCAL OWNERSHIP AND THE MONITORING OF DONOR PERFORMANCE: NEW AID RELATIONSHIPS IN TANZANIA? [1]

Gerry Helleiner

IN the early 1980s Tanzania was working on an ambitious but ultimately unsuccessful effort to develop a locally owned adjustment programme that could carry the support of the International Monetary Fund (IMF) As part of that effort, John Loxley wrote an unpublished memorandum on aid donor commitments and coordination in that country at that time. To establish the overall resource constraints, he examined what the prospects for official external finance might be, so that Tanzanian plans could be realistically based. However, like many others before him and after him, and in many other aid recipient countries, he found it extremely difficult to collect useful information from the aid donor community. This data problem was symptomatic of a much deeper, and remaining, problem in the aid relationship between recipients and donors: the extent to which there is a genuine common cause between the collaborators in the aid relationship. Much has changed with regard to the degree of collaboration in this relationship, although, of course, socially significant progress is typically slow and fraught with periodic setbacks. Nonetheless, the government of Tanzania (GoT) and its aid donors have recently led the world in important elements of its reform. This recent experience is not yet widely recognized. It deserves to be.

Early in 1994, during the administration of President Ali Hassan Mwinyi, the immediate successor to Julius Nyerere, perceptions of poor administration, corruption, the inadequacy of democratic processes, and budget mismanagement in Tanzania, together, it seems, with the somewhat prickly personality of Kighoma Malima, then Finance Minister, led to an unprecedented degree of mistrust of the government on the part of the aid donor community. At the same time the government of Tanzania saw aid donors as inappropriately intrusive and demanding, and unable or unwilling to deliver on promises. Finance Minister Malima had publicly blamed Tanzania's poor macroeconomic performance, including an inflation rate of over 30 per cent in 1993-94, upon the failure of donors to deliver on their promises, infuriating the donors who perceived it, rather, as the product of his own mismanagement. Despite the Tanzanians' return to relative IMF/World Bank respectability via orthodox stabilization and structural adjustment policies from 1986 onwards, the aid relationship was in a perilous state. Despairing of this situation, the government of Denmark initiated discussions with the government of Tanzania with a view to possible mediation efforts. The immediate outcome was the creation of a five-person independent group, the membership of which was to be agreed by the government of Tanzania, to investigate the problems in the aid relationship and their solutions. The group was made up of two Tanzanians, neither of who worked for the government, and three non-Tanzanian academics, including a Briton, a Dane, and a Canadian chair. Their terms of reference were broad, including such overall objectives as ascertaining "how cooperation efforts could be made more efficient," identifying "constraints which...could be reduced by GoT, the donors, or by the partners in common," and assessing "the relevance and effectiveness of the totality of aid programmes" (Helleiner, Killick, Lipumba, Ndulu, and Svendsen, 1995: i–ii). It is noteworthy that the terms of reference made specific mention of the need to clarify the concept of "ownership," which, the terms said, was "now widely accepted as a cornerstone in the relationships between African countries and their donors."

The "ownership" question acquired greatly increased salience in discussions of development problems and practices during the mid-1990s, not least in the African context where successes with IMF and World Bank-driven structural adjustment programmes and donor-driven projects seemed so scarce. A new consensus emerged, which the World Bank itself summarized in a report on aid effectiveness.

> Typically, assistance programmes that the recipient country perceives as being imposed end in failure or have only a small development impact. Governments and beneficiaries do not feel they have a stake when they have not contributed to the development of a programme. Furthermore, "home-grown" programmes may be more effective in incor-

porating institutional capacity, reflecting the needs of different domestic constituencies, and addressing constraints (World Bank, 1995a: 6).

In the words of the chairman of the Organization for Economic Cooperation and Development's (OECD) Development Assistance Committee (DAC) at the time,

> If donors believe in local ownership and participation, then they must seek to use channels and methods of cooperation that do not undermine those values. External support must avoid stifling or attempting to substitute for local initiative...The principles of self reliance, local ownership and participation which underlie the partnership approach are inconsistent with the idea of conditions imposed by donors to coerce poor countries to do things they don't want to do in order to obtain resources they need. That view of conditionality was always of dubious value. Treating development cooperation as a partnership makes clear that it is obsolete (OECD, 1995: 7).

Yet these widely recognized research results and high-level statements of aspirations towards new forms of development partnership between aid donors and recipients seemed, paradoxically, to be accompanied by ever-increasing degrees of external intrusion into domestic political affairs and economic policymaking in African countries (Helleiner, 2000a). Particularly sensitive in the African context was donor intrusion and subsequent failure in the form of so-called "technical assistance" (TA), which had been, by all accounts, ineffective in the creation and development of indigenous capacity (Berg, 1993; World Bank, 1996b). In this sphere too, impressive new principles for "new orientations in technical cooperation" that emphasized the need for long-term capacity building and for local control at all stages by the intended beneficiaries had been agreed to within the DAC (OECD, 1994: 21). Yet little seemed to be changing on the ground at the level of individual country aid programmes.

The Tanzanian initiative to explore the reasons for the breakdown in aid relationships and the particular mandate to investigate ownership questions was thus extraordinarily well timed. Members of the independent group were conscious of the broader international context within which they were working, and thus the potential for much wider ramifications from their assessments beyond the bounds of the Tanzanian specifics. The group delivered its report, with 21 specific recommendations for both the government of Tanzania and the donors, in June 1995 (Helleiner et al., 1995). The government of Tanzania was, among other things, to significantly tighten and strengthen the operations of the Ministry of Finance. It was to develop clear priorities in its investment and expenditure systems, based on a clear medium- to long-term development strategy that would give it a "vision for the future." Finally, it was to acquire and retain leadership in its own development efforts. As for the donors, substantial changes were needed, the report stated, in their "operational culture" at the country level, so as to reduce the vast gap between the rhetoric of "ownership" at DAC and/or donors' headquarters and country-level reality. The report argued that as soon as possible after Tanzania's first multi-party elections in 1995, there should be major improvements in Tanzanian economic management. These improvements were to be of a "second generation" character, which were much more difficult and required much more time than sheer macroeconomic stabilization. In order to do this, the report called for a significantly altered relationship between the government and the donors (Helleiner et al.).

Following the election of President Benjamin Mkapa later in 1995, the new government moved quickly to restore the faltering macroeconomic situation. At the same time, both the government and elements in the donor community undertook to begin to respond to the report's many recommendations for reform in Tanzania's longer term development efforts and aid relationships. Thus, in the first half of 1996, the government restored fiscal control through the introduction of a cash management system that left no room for expenditures beyond the limits set by revenue collections. Before the year ended, the government had also agreed to a three-year Enhanced Structural Adjustment Facility programme supported by the IMF. Concurrently, in September 1996 the government of Tanzania met with the Nordic countries to begin to rebuild previously cordial aid relationships and restructure them in such a way as to strengthen Tanzanian ownership of its own development programmes, using the independent group's report as major input. The meeting between the government and the Nordics reached a significant degree of agreement as to the appropriate way forward in aid relationships, and paved the way for the much broader and more significant donor-Tanzanian agreements that followed.

The key breakthrough in the improvement of aid relationships came in January 1997. At a government donor workshop in Dar Es Salaam, in which all the donors participated, participants drafted a set of "agreed notes" toward a new way of doing business. The agreed notes relied heavily upon the independent group's report and upon the prior Tanzania/Nordic agreement, and demonstrated a remarkable consensus on the common objectives to be pursued in the new aid relationships and on a number of specific first steps to be taken. The new partnership between the donors and the government of Tanzania would imply, say the notes, "a radical change of rules and roles between the partners in development." The guiding principle was to be that "Tanzania takes the lead" and that "Tanzania fully owns the development cooperation programmes in terms of planning, design, implementation, monitoring and evaluation" (Helleiner, 1999: Appendix II). The new aid relationship was also to be based upon a longer-term vision of Tanzanian development, incorporating such traditional objectives as improved governance; political participation, and macroeconomic stability; strengthened financial management and the capacity building needed to sustain it; open and honest dialogue; and, perhaps most significant of all, independent stocktaking that would monitor and evaluate progress towards the agreed objectives. The agreed notes included 16 specific points on which progress could be objectively monitored. Contributing significantly to this remarkable agreement was the happy coincidence of the previous arrival in Tanzania of a number of key reform-oriented donor representatives, notably the representatives from the Nordic countries, the Netherlands, the World Bank, and, a little later, the United Kingdom. Each of these arrivals carried with them newly decentralized authority to move forward in aid relationships, without waiting for broader systemic reforms. These donors were able, as a group, to set standards and to exert pressure for change upon their peers, both at this critical time and, as it turned out, also in the subsequent period.

All this planning for a minor revolution in the aid relationship in Tanzania was accomplished, it should be noted, some years in advance of the formulation of the concepts of Poverty Reduction Strategy Papers (PRSPs) in the IMF or Comprehensive Development Frameworks (CDFs) in the World Bank. Also ahead of the times in this respect, and attributable in part to the recommendations of the 1995 independent group, was the government's development of two policy documents, with widespread stakeholder consultation and thus a broader degree of "ownership" than had been characteristic of earlier policy documents. The first was the *Tanzania National Development Vision 2025*, which was finalized in 1997 and printed in 1999 (United Republic of Tanzania, 1999). The second was the *National Poverty Eradication Strategy*, issued in 1998, which sought to move forward an important component of the agreed vision (United Republic of Tanzania, 1998).

It was a particularly significant accomplishment to agree in January 1997 on specific and monitorable first steps to be taken in pursuit of the agreed aid relationship objectives. These included such steps as the following:

- the provision of data by donors, when asked, on actual and planned aid flows, including those to entities other than the central government, technical assistance and in-kind expenditures;

- the orderly exit by donors, in consultation with the Government, from development expenditures inconsistent with its declared priorities;

- the making public of the latest Policy Framework Paper, and initiation of consultations relating to the next one with representatives of the private sector and civil society;

- the review of the number of meetings between government and donors, and rationalization to increase effectiveness and reduce duplication;

- the rationalization and mainstreaming of project management through agreement on management responsibilities, staffing arrangements and remuneration;

- the review of technical assistance in support of more effective capacity building, improved use of local human resources, and local control of selection and management, as well as explicit consideration by all parties of its opportunity cost.

Similar or related objectives have frequently been agreed at high-level international meetings at the level of broad rhetoric, without serious effort to translate them into specific required actions. Specific undertakings of the kind agreed at the January 1997 donor–Tanzania meeting have many advantages over the more typical pronouncement of highly general agreed objectives or targets. First, they provide an important reality check as to what exactly the parties are actually agreeing upon. Second, when specific next steps are addressed, it is possible to generate genuine dialogue on concrete issues and there is potential for the negotiation of compromises where necessary. Third, specification of the details of agreement can make explicit the areas in which experimentation is proposed and in which all parties acknowledge, in advance, that there may be some risks and need for learning by doing. Lastly, as already implied, the listing of specifics facilitates a clear process of monitoring and evaluation. Agreement on specific first steps was critically important, then, for the successful operation of the new objectives of a new form of partnership between the donors and the government of Tanzania, a partnership based upon firm national ownership.

It was recognized from the outset that significant changes in the aid relationship were likely to be difficult to achieve. Some expressed scepticism, and many still do, about the possibility of any kind of genuine partnership between powerful donors and financially dependent governments anywhere (for one early and much quoted such assessment, see Patel, 1971: 305). However, problems en route to a new partnership-based aid relationship can arise from both sides of the emerging relationship. Among the most serious of such potential problems are the following five.

1. There may be confusion or disagreement as to what exactly is meant by "ownership" of national programmes. Some donors seem to believe that "ownership exists when recipients do what we want them to do but they do so voluntarily" (Helleiner, 2000a). In some conservative donor circles, the rhetoric of the transfer of programmes to local ownership may also be regarded as shorthand for their efforts to increase self-finance of programmes and thus reduce aid flows. On the other hand, recipients may naïvely assume that transfer of ownership amounts simply to turning over the money to the local treasury with few further questions asked. If there is no agreement as to what national ownership actually means in practice, there are likely to be continuing problems in achieving it. Indeed, that is why specific monitorable steps, such as were agreed in the Tanzanian case, are so potentially important.

2. There is always a danger that immediate pressure and short-term needs overwhelm the agreed longer-term objectives. Both sides of the aid relationship are vulnerable to this potential difficulty. Even those with the most sincere

commitment to the ultimate objectives may find it necessary, at times, to address urgent problems directly and thus to postpone resolution of the real and ongoing issues of ownership. Both donors and recipients must understand and accept the fact that there may be some short-run costs and risks as the longer term ownership objectives are more vigorously pursued and given higher priority. Any productive investment involves a gestation period during which there are no returns and, indeed, there are costs. Real change takes time.

3. The recipient government, in this case Tanzania, may fail to establish those minimum administrative and political conditions sufficient to establish its credibility with donors as to its capacity to lead and/or to take effective ownership. As aid flows decline and donors become more selective in their choice of countries to support, the government of Tanzania will have to continue to inspire donor confidence and trust. Bedevilling the Tanzanian image in the donor community in recent years, for instance, has been the political situation in Zanzibar. It would be tragic if the complexities of Zanzibari politics came to impede the significant progress that the Tanzanian government and its aid donors have been making on the development cooperation front.

4. The aid-recipient government is sometimes set up for failure by over-optimistic forecasts and expectations, both on the part of donors and of the government. Assessments of prospective performance have almost invariably been biased upwards in the African context; certainly this has been the case in Tanzania. Performance and policy reform targets for African countries are often too numerous, too onerous, and inappropriately phased. Development programmes can thus easily be overloaded and when the country fails to reach its targets, its government risks being categorized as a failure and, therefore, as undeserving of further assistance. It is incumbent upon both donors and recipients, as they work to construct new forms of partnership and aid relationships, to work at being realistic about the prospects for economic performance and for policy change, and to take adequate account of unforeseen contingencies, both in their planning and in their evaluations.

5. The normal bureaucratic incentives and imperatives within aid agencies may simply overwhelm the new partnership/ownership objectives. Aid bureaucrats must move their money, meet their own organizational deadlines,

and answer to their own political masters. In the words of the independent group in Tanzania,

> each donor has its own aid policies and "agenda," and is anxious to pursue its own ob-
> jectives even when these are not shared by the government. Constitutional, parliamen-
> tary and accounting requirements, aimed at ensuring proper accountability for the use
> of taxpayers' money, may also increase donor intrusiveness, a tendency that can only be
> enhanced by the perception...that corruption is a large and growing problem... It is also
> likely that agency staff will be under pressure to ensure that they spend their budgets,
> even if it requires a degree of bulldozing to achieve this result, and they may well see
> it as in their own career interests to secure a high level of aid giving or lending. They
> are also under pressure to show quick results and short-term efficiency. There are few
> rewards for those who are prepared to sacrifice short-term performance for the sake of
> slower but more sustainable progress (Helleiner et al., 1995: 15).

Thus, perhaps the greatest risk of all—and the greatest potential impedi-
ment to change—is that mere lip service is paid to the newly agreed objectives while bureaucratic ways are found by the staff of aid agencies to continue
with business more or less as usual.

By now it should be clearer than ever how critically important it is that forward motion towards the agreed objectives should be regularly, systematically,
and independently assessed. The government of Tanzania, with the particular support of the Danish International Development Agency and the World
Bank, worked quickly to develop a means for achieving the agreed stock-tak-
ing of progress in the implementation of the first steps agreed to at the January
1997 donor government meeting. Responsibility for this monitoring and evaluation of progress, especially towards the effective transfer of ownership of development programming from donors and international financial institutions
to the government of Tanzania, which was the core of the agreement to pursue
a new form of partnership, was initially assigned, at the invitation of the latter
government, to the former chair of the original group of independent advisors. As agreed, his stocktaking report was made to the next Tanzania donor
Consultative Group (CG) meeting in late 1997. However, by this time it was
still too early in the change process for very much to have transpired. In March
1999, though, again at the invitation of the government of Tanzania, and with
the full and frank participation of all the donors, a more comprehensive as-

sessment of progress towards the agreed objectives and implementation of the agreed first steps was requested by the government. This was undertaken once again by the independent assessor. Qualitative grades ranging from A to F were assigned by the assessor to the progress achieved on each of the now 18 agreed steps. The report of the assessor was presented to the 1999 CG meeting for discussion (Helleiner, 1999). The independence of the assessor and his familiarity with the Tanzanian development context were critically important elements in the achievement of both frankness in the report and broad acceptability of the assessment process. This is not to suggest, however, that all parties agreed with all the assessments. In particular, the IMF resident representative took strong exception to some comments on IMF practices in the report.

The 1999 report was mixed in its assessment of progress towards new aid relationships and ownership transfer in Tanzania. It recognized a significant shift towards Tanzanian leadership, particularly in the sphere of macroeconomic management, and most notably in the preparation of its own Policy Framework Paper and Public Expenditure Review. It also noted that aid donor attitudes and practices had changed significantly, and that much more genuine dialogue between donors and recipients was taking place. Several donors were also contributing to sectoral-level "basket funds" in some sectors, the uses of which were determined collectively, under Tanzanian leadership. Tanzanian budget and financial control systems had been strengthened, and corruption, while still a serious problem, was being more aggressively addressed.

It is important to note, however, that progress in the reform of TA was assigned poor marks. The agreed notes of January 1997 had set ambitious targets. In order to be effective, it was stated therein, TA should:

- establish appropriate modalities for integrating TA in the overall human resource endowment available in the country;

- institute modalities for effective capacity building and enhance the capacity-building role of TA;

- enhance complementarity between TA and local human resource utilization and development;

- enable the opportunity cost of TA to be considered explicitly by all the partners;

- ensure that selection and management of TA is the responsibility of the government of Tanzania. (Helleiner, 1999: Appendix)

The independent report noted that many donors did now provide more data, hire more local firms and individuals for technical and professional tasks, and try to involve the government of Tanzania more than before in the selection of TA personnel. Nevertheless, among other comments on this topic, it observed that TA expenditures

> contain large elements that are not cost-effective so far as Tanzanian development is concerned and frequently serve other (donor) objectives... Much of the technical assistance expenditure in Tanzania is perceived by the Government as an unnecessarily wasteful use of scarce aid resources, contributing little either to local human resource use (employment) or to capacity-building which together are the among the Government's top priorities... They are also perceived by the Government as positively detrimental to the development of local ownership of Tanzanian programmes... Despite some progress, technical assistance expenditures...remain among the most sensitive issues in the jointly agreed effort to transfer ownership to Tanzanians. (Helleiner, 1999: 19)

World Bank assessments of African performance and prospects have offered similar assessments of technical assistance elsewhere on the continent (World Bank, 2000b). The proportion of total development assistance made available to Tanzania in the form of technical cooperation has dropped in the past few years; and this is seen by most Tanzanians as a sign of progress in the aid relationship.

Finally, it is worth mentioning that the 1999 comprehensive report also recommended that an ongoing process of independent monitoring of aid relationships and emerging problems therein, no longer reliant on only one person, should be instituted by the government of Tanzania and its external development partners. This was agreed, in principle, at the 1999 CG meeting.

Between that meeting and the subsequent CG meeting in April 2000, the government of Tanzania developed its newly required PRSP and, unique to Tanzania, a Tanzania Assistance Strategy (TAS) to govern its ongoing relationship with the aid donors. At the 2000 CG meeting, the government and the donors reached a new agreement, in principle, that in the implementation of the TAS, and therefore implicitly also in the PRSP and CDF processes, donor performance would continue to be independently monitored and evaluated, as well as Tanzanian performance. This would create better balance in aid relationships, and give concrete expression to the stated and agreed aspirations toward genuine partnership and open dialogue between donors and the government of Tanzania in poverty reduction and development efforts. Debate took place at this meeting over the appropriate elements for future monitoring of donor performance, based in large part on a discussion paper written by the former independent assessor and circulated by the government of Tanzania. Most donors, but not all, seemed to accept its recommendations that donor performance monitoring should include the following elements, among others:

- the degree of compliance with governmental requests for timely and standardized information about aid expenditures and plans;

- the degree to which aid expenditures are incorporated within the government's budgetary system;

- the degree to which donor projects and programmes are coordinated, integrated into governmental expenditure frameworks and recognize governmental priorities;

- the extent of shortfalls in aid disbursements relative to previous aid commitments;

- the degree to which aid is untied with respect to country of procurement and/or available for local procurement;

- the degree to which the timing of aid disbursements is responsive to exogenous shocks that have an impact upon the Tanzania economy;

- the degree to which aid commitments are made for time periods longer than those that were the norm in the past;

- the share that procurement-tied technical assistance makes up in total aid expenditures; and

- the degree to which aid disbursement is for humanitarian rather than developmental purposes

Detailed argument for the use of such performance indicators in the monitoring of aid donor performance may be found in Helleiner (2000b).

Donor agreement on these elements was not complete. Japan, for instance, argued vigorously that its projects deserved assessment purely upon their developmental effectiveness. Nonetheless, they were incorporated into Tanzania's draft terms of reference for the independent group to be charged with responsibility for monitoring progress in aid relationships. The government's draft terms of reference also called explicitly both for an updating of progress made with respect to the 18 points of earlier agreement, upon which the 1999 report had commented, and for the development of further donor performance indicators for which the assessors could provide estimates.

There followed extensive discussion between the donors and the government of Tanzania, discussion already initiated at the 2000 CG, over the detailed terms of reference for the independent report on progress towards achieving the agreed new form of development partnership. In particular, the modalities of such an institutionalized independent monitoring and evaluation system were developed. Agreement was easily reached that the group should be balanced and independent. The agreed plan was that the report group would be made up of two Tanzanians not in the employ of the government, one non-Tanzanian African, and two experienced and non-governmental professionals from donor countries. Responsibility for assembling and supporting the team, it was also agreed, would rest with the independent Economic and Social Research Foundation of Tanzania (ESRF).

An early casualty of the discussions concerning the group's terms of reference was the CG discussion paper's recommendation that donor performance indicators should be recorded and assessments made with respect to each of the major sources of external support to Tanzania. In the previous independent reports of 1995, 1997 and 1999, naming individual bilateral donors was avoided, although there were some specific references to the IMF and World Bank. The bilateral donors now agreed that only collective donor performance monitoring should be attempted. More significantly, as discussions continued, emphasis shifted, under donor pressure led by Japan, and buttressed by the US, Germany, and France, away from the previous primary concern with the transfer of ownership and toward the more traditional, not to say old-fashioned, concept of aid effectiveness. To some degree this may have reflected a perception on the part of some donors that the government had failed to consult sufficiently broadly, at the earliest stages of its development, the terms of reference for the group's monitoring activity. In particular, there was concern that the draft terms of reference placed undue emphasis upon donor behaviour, and, indeed, upon particular forms of donor behaviour. Perhaps also contributing to the shift in emphasis was the initial absence, this time, of an independent "honest broker" to help in the achievement of agreement. With respect to this last point, once the independent ESRF entered the process, movement towards agreed terms of reference proceeded more quickly and smoothly. However, the terms of reference finally agreed for the independent monitoring group, although still within the framework of the new TAS, no longer included the development of new donor performance indicators and efforts to measure them. Local ownership now appears as only one of five explicitly mentioned broadly agreed means of increasing aid effectiveness, and, rather than being seen as the cornerstone of development partnerships, the objective is now only its promotion. The other broadly agreed objectives are reducing transactions costs in aid delivery, enhancing predictability of aid flows, consolidating accountability requirements and results orientation, and making technical assistance more supportive of local capacity building needs. The group is also mandated to establish a fresh baseline for the development partnership that takes into account contextual changes since the January 1997 agreement. These changes include the emerging transaction costs and potential ambiguities surrounding new experiments in collective decision making and the associated complexities of appropriate assignment of responsibility and accountability. This mandate seems entirely reasonable as long as, in the current context, it does not imply a relative downplaying of the previously central issue of ownership. More ominously, perhaps, the independent group is also requested to assess the utility of its own exercise and provide a case for "continuing with it or otherwise." Clearly the Government of Tanzania conceded some ground in this discussion. But far more significant than any such concessions are the facts that it took place at all; that, in the end, agreement was reached; and that a solid, independent assessment of progress in aid relationships will again be presented to the next Tanzania CG meeting. The terms of reference will still leave plenty of room for the independent group to develop its own potentially innovative assessment methodologies, make critical assessments, and offer fresh proposals for improvement and change.

No doubt the struggle over the terms and modalities, and even the very existence, of this innovative independent monitoring process in Tanzania will continue. Certainly nothing achieved thus far has been written in stone. There is bound to be considerable further learning by doing as the process evolves. What is indisputable, however, is that the Tanzanian experience in the reform and monitoring of aid relationships has been of a pioneering character and deserves both worldwide attention and worldwide support.

Footnotes

1   I am very grateful for insightful comments on an earlier draft by Benno Ndulu and Samuel Wangwe, neither of whom bears any responsibility for the contents of this paper. Although this chapter was originally prepared for this volume, a shorter version was published, by mutual consent, in the *Journal of Human Development* 3,2 (2002).

Chapter 13

GOOD GOVERNANCE, INSTITUTIONAL REFORM, AND POVERTY REDUCTION IN AFRICA

Bonnie Campbell, Marie-Christine Doran and Samia Kazi Aoul

[T]he "black box" of governance in some way affects public-sector performance, which in turn affects poverty or other outcomes. This is an important achievement that has helped to dramatically alter our perspectives on the process of development, but it does not offer us any firm prescriptions about what should be done. We have no firm grounds on which to assert, for example, that decentralization or improved budgetary arrangements will improve some particular aspect of public-sector performance...the limited coverage (of data) over time makes it more difficult to convincingly demonstrate causal relationships between governance and measures of well-being. Studies using these indicators confirm that development has occurred where there is now good governance—but it does not necessarily follow that they reliably point to where development will occur in the future (Holmes, Knack, Manning, Messick, and Rinne, 2000: 29-30).

I. Introduction

ACCORDING to the World Bank's *World Development Report 2000/2001: Attacking Poverty,* "Aid should be directed to countries with high levels of poverty. But that should be only part of the criteria for allocating aid. Also essential is having the right policy and institutional framework in place to make poverty reduction a success" (2001: 40-41).

One would be hard pressed to disagree with this statement, but the question that it clearly leaves unanswered is which policies and which institutional frameworks are the right ones?[1] In striving to build greater cohesion among the actions of multiple external agents—in itself a laudable objective—the World Bank is now taking the lead in the design and promotion of institutional reforms that are prerequisites for access to poverty alleviation funding of all kinds, be it bilateral or multilateral. This action is based on the consensus that has been generated among donors in the Bank's development of its Comprehensive Development Framework (CDF), released in 1998.

It is important to situate the World Bank's new role in context.[2] When, with the introduction of the concept of governance, the Bank explicitly ventured into the domain of institutional reform, it specified that it would not address the political dimensions of such reforms, considering them to fall outside its mandate. This position was set out in its first comprehensive paper on the subject, *Governance and Development*, which states that the issue of "the particular form of political regime (parliamentary or presidential, military or civilian, and authoritarian or democratic)," which is also an aspect of the notion of governance "clearly falls outside the Bank's mandate" (World Bank, 1992c: 58, note 1). The position was reiterated in a 1994 document (World Bank, 1994b).

The Bank shifted its position in just a few years, with the appearance of the *World Development Report 1997: The State in a Changing World*, and reversed it in the *World Development Report 1999/2000: Entering the 21st Century*. Moreover, this reversal was tied to the institution's commitment to poverty reduction, since the introduction of specific institutional reforms later became a condition of access to multilateral funds in this crucial area. Thus, following a joint proposal of the executive director of the International Monetary Fund (IMF) and the President of the World Bank, the Development Committee of the Bank and the Interim Committee of the Fund agreed, at their respective meetings in September 1996, on a programme of action that became known as the Heavily Indebted Poor Countries (HIPC) Initiative. Developed market economy governments soon reached an overwhelming consensus on the benefits of the HIPC Initiative. The purpose of HIPC was straightforward: "deserving" countries would be reimbursed for a portion of their debt, under certain conditions. In particular, reductions in the external debt of the most indebted poor countries would be framed within a broader long-term poverty reduction programme. The programme would, in turn, be embedded within a Poverty Reduction Strategy Paper (PRSP), a joint Fund-Bank innovation, that would specify a set of economic and institutional reforms agreed among a debtor, the Fund, and the Bank. The PRSP would be formulated with the assistance of the Fund and the Bank.

In September 1999, a joint meeting of the World Bank Development Committee and an IMF Interim Committee (subsequently renamed the International Monetary and Finance Committee) adopted a new, reinforced version that became known as the Enhanced HIPC Initiative (Culpeper and Serieux, 2000). Its general objectives coincide with those of the 1996 proposal, but it offers multilateral debt relief arrangements in addition to existing bilateral and private ones. Countries wishing to participate in the Initiative must have a poverty reduction strategy already in place, and their decision to participate commits them to making substantial progress on its implementation within a stipulated time frame. However, not just any strategy will do. In the PRSP of those countries that qualify for the Enhanced HIPC Initiative, the Bretton Woods institutions prescribe and propose to monitor a specific and elaborate set of structural, social, and macroeconomic reforms that are posited as conducive to rapid and sustained economic growth. Such reforms, it is asserted, are a necessary condition for durable poverty reduction. In short, access to debt relief funds becomes conditional upon a poverty reduction strategy in which certain institutional reforms are a *sine qua non*. In this way, donor support has become tied to institutional reform, and the World Bank and the IMF have come to be increasingly concerned with the political dimensions of reform.

It is rarely remarked that in becoming so concerned, the Bretton Woods institutions are in *de facto* violation of their own statutes. However, this reality is masked by the depiction of the reforms, and notably the striving for good governance and poverty reduction in general, as matters of sound administrative management, and therefore outside the realm of politics. The reforms are presented as "depoliticized," although they clearly have major political implications regarding the legitimacy of the political processes upon which they depend, and regarding the extent to which they contribute to a constrictive reconfiguration of local political space.

In order to discern the implications of these reforms, it is helpful to begin by considering the arguments advanced in their favor and the mechanisms through which they will be introduced. As well, one must examine their content and assess the likelihood that the funds released by their introduction, particularly through debt relief mechanisms, will actually make possible a significant measure of poverty reduction. To this end, we have divided this chapter into four sections. First, we analyze the documents of the multilateral agencies in order to discern the relationships that are asserted to exist among institutional reform, good governance and poverty reduction. Second, we examine the ways in which it is proposed to build legitimacy for these reforms within local societies. Third, we analyze the particular conception of the political process underlying recent institutional reforms, which is characterized by such concepts as the "self-restraining state," "horizontal accountability," and "effective governance." We analyze certain potential consequences of these recommendations for political space and democracy in the societies in which such reforms are proposed for implementation. Finally, we tie these theoretical ideas to recent field research on poverty reduction in Africa, with reference to the new debt relief mechanisms prescribed by the Enhanced HIPC Initiative. This is done in order to illustrate how such strategies appear to have become an instrument for "locking in" African countries to a world order over whose rules they have little say.

II. The justification for institutional reform

The links between institutional reform and poverty reduction are alluded to in various contexts, and spelled out more clearly and elaborately in two background papers to the World Bank's 2000/2001 *World Development Report*.[3] *Governance and Poverty Reduction*, for example, states that "good governance—through its impact on growth—alleviates poverty" and that "there exists a strong presumption that good governance improves health" (Holmes et al., 2000: 27-8). If governance is inadequate, goes the argument—that is, if property rights are not protected, essential goods and services are not provided, if industries are overregulated—investment and long-term growth prospects are dimmer, and the poor suffer disproportionately. As the background paper robustly claims, "recent empirical work corroborates these theoretical arguments, quantifying the costs of over-regulation, corruption, and other manifestations of bad government in terms of foregone investments and growth" (Holmes et al.: 27). The emphasis is thus on strengthening property rights, since these are considered fundamental to an environment favourable to investment and the development of the private sector. Moreover, the reference to "over-regulation" in the same phrase as "corruption" suggests that state involvement in managing the economy is not regarded as salutary, but rather as a cause for concern.

Within this general framework, it is suggested that institutional reforms seeking to produce favourable outcomes for the poor should be directed toward empowering the poor. To that end, there is a need to improve the capacity to provide basic public services as well as enhanced economic opportunities by increasing access to markets. Finally, institutional reform needs to provide security from economic shocks, corruption, crime, and violence. However, where the paper goes further is by clearly and directly suggesting that such reforms are predicated upon a reorganization of the state:

> There is reason to assume that the architecture of the state, including the relationships between the executive, legislative, and judiciary branches and other institutional arrangements for the transfer of power between governments, including voting arrangements and electoral laws, affect the performance of the public sector in responding to poverty (Holmes et al., 2000: 28).

The desired restructuring is seen to result from reforms that shift debtor governments toward a more technocratic approach to public affairs management. The best insurance against poor macroeconomic performance, it is asserted, lies in the implementation of sound monetary and fiscal policy (Holmes et al., 2000: 5).

A second World Bank background paper presents an analysis of why bad governance is believed to hurt the poor, and proposes very specific reforms. *Addressing Governance and Institutional Issues in the Poverty Reduction Strategy Process* (Girishankar and Levy, n.d.), asserts that weak governance finds its reflection in weak property rights, which are a disincentive for the accumulation of capital assets by the poor. It is further reflected in discriminatory practices in labour and credit markets, which cause missed opportunities for wealth creation. Finally, it is reflected in the misallocation of public resources away from high-return, poverty reduction activities such as investments in primary education or basic infrastructure. The paper therefore suggests there is a need for institutional reforms favouring pro-poor governance, and that the Bank can help bring them about.

One obvious role for the Bank in facilitating this process is to assist in diagnosing the quality of governance arrangements that affect their ability to undertake collective actions to reduce poverty. Equally important is the need to help borrowers and their PRSP partners identify reform options and decide on a critical reform pathway for achieving pro-poor governance (Girishankar and Levy, n.d.: 1).

In another formulation of the background paper, the Bank's role is described as "helping clients define institutional reform strategies" (Girishankar and Levy, n.d.: 2). The measures recommended to clients include expanding poor people's access to labour and credit markets, which is fairly standard, as is restructuring public sector personnel and financial management. It is also common to recommend the decentralization of the responsibility for the delivery or the favouring of the co-production of services. What is still not common is a recommendation to encourage a more autonomous fiscal administration through the institution of a more technocratic management scheme. Nor is it common to recommend measures to improve political participation, primarily by revising electoral rules for greater fairness, arranging power sharing among ethnic groups, and developing parliamentary oversight mechanisms. It is certainly not standard to recommend measures to disseminate information about governance, so that a better informed public steps up demands for accountability. Finally, it is not standard to recommend the deregulation and promotion of an independent judicial system.

The background paper is clear about the implications for changes to the legal framework made necessary by such institutional reforms:

> In this case, a reasonable strategy for achieving pro-poor governance would involve administrative reform and restructuring…to improve core public management functions, in combination with legal, judicial, and regulatory reforms that strengthen the incentive framework for commercial activity and the protection of persons and property (Girishankar and Levy, n.d.: 8).

It is useful to underline as suggested in the introduction that the proposed institutional reforms are central components of the CDF, put forward in the autumn of 1998 (Wolfenson, 1999; World Bank, 2000c). The overall objective of the CDF is to serve as a framework for the coordination of efforts to help countries move from centralized planning to a market economy. In this instrument, the emphasis is on the need for holistic partnership-style reforms designed to eliminate weak governance and thus contribute to poverty reduction. Recommended reforms include the liberalization of markets, prices, and trade; public sector reforms, and particularly privatization of public enterprises; decentralization of public services, accompanied by infrastructure reforms; the reform of the judicial system; and regulatory reform. Recommended reforms are presented as indispensable stages in the implementation of a poverty reduction strategy. Finally, the CDF framework serves as the cornerstone of the increasingly shared agenda of various agents—multilateral donors, bilateral donors, NGOs, and the like—that we return to below.

III. Domestic legitimation of the reforms

The preliminary thinking to the World Bank's 2000/2001 World Development Report in *Governance and Poverty Reduction* evinces an awareness of the need to ensure domestic legitimacy for reform, to secure the support of the different branches of government, and to locate possible sources of opposition or obstruction in advance. The term "veto gates" expresses this last concept in the following passage:

> To bring about institutional change, government decision makers must be able to ensure the support and cooperation of other parts of government, which are critical to approving and implementing the reform project—for example, legislature, bureaucracy, judiciary, etc. Assessing the strength of opposition to reform is important. It entails identifying the critical "veto gates," or institutional junctures, at which particular players can block the government's reform initiative. Who within the government needs to approve the proposed reform for its enactment? Who might be opposed to the reform project and why? What change in the design of the reform might win their support? Which groups outside of government are known to be opposed to the reform? (Holmes et al., 2000: 22)

The CDF's approach should be examined in light of this recognition. The CDF seeks to be holistic, and "is not a menu from which certain elements can be selected, while others are ignored" (World Bank, 2000d: 20). The CDF states that "to be credible, the long-term vision should be realistic and should ideally derive from a process of open national consultations. Involving domestic stakeholders will help to sustain this vision, especially when governments change" (World Bank, 2000d: 1). The stakeholders in question should include religious institutions, academics, workers, and bilateral and multilateral funding agencies. Nonetheless, it is worth stressing a crucial caveat: "Ultimately, the Bank and other major players must reserve the right to support only those proposals with which they agree" (World Bank, 2000d: 22).

Most probably because setting objectives and strategizing are postulated to be driven by external agencies, in these documents a clear concern for the domestic legitimacy of reform is very much in evidence. This concern is made operational in a third document, which takes the form of a survey questionnaire designed to provide "a structured method to assess client governments' readiness for reform" (World Bank, 2002b).[4] The survey is divided into three parts, which assess a client's commitment to reform, the political feasibility of reform, and the sustainability of reform. To gain the support of the bilateral and multilateral lending agencies, the client must be able to generate a consensus, implement the reform, and overcome opposition: indeed, the questionnaire scores the client's success in doing so. If the conditions are not fulfilled, the Bank may make proposals designed to render the environment more propitious.

The Bank suggests the questionnaire be used to gauge the political feasibility of the reform process. In particular, it can determine whether "new legislation with parliamentary approval will be required" (World Bank, 2002b). It can evaluate whether, in this light, a project should be redesigned to avoid the need for legislative approval. It can assess whether the opponents of a project are in a position to obstruct reform. Finally, it can examine whether there is any risk that future governments could reverse reform. As the questionnaire's protocols state, "we expect that policy reversal is less likely if there are a set of institutional constraints that reduce the ability of subsequent governments to undo reforms" (World Bank, 2002b).

If one considers the above not merely from the standpoint of administrative efficiency in implementing reforms but rather in terms of the implications of this kind of intervention for domestic political processes, certain serious questions arise. One is naturally led to wonder whether what is proposed does not amount to a significant departure from a characteristic feature of representative democracies—the right of the electorate to express its will in regard to public policy by voting in a government that promises to act in accordance with its wishes.

IV. Implications of reform

In this section, we shall discuss the potential implications of the reforms for political processes in the societies where they are proposed for implementation. We divide the discussion into three subsections. The first subsection explores the multilateralization of thinking and strategizing about poverty reduction. The second subsection examines the impact of technocratic approaches to poverty reduction on political processes. Finally, the third subsection evaluates the discourse that interlinks poverty reduction and institutional reform, and evaluates such discourse for the political spaces in the societies concerned.

i. Multilateralization of poverty reduction strategies

The *World Development Report 2000/2001* argues that aid should be apportioned to countries that have implemented the right policies and have the institutional framework necessary for success in their poverty reduction programs. The purported consensus concerning these issues justifies making poverty reduction funding, as well as poor countries' access to debt relief initiatives, conditional upon institutional reform. Thus, under the PRSP process, funding agencies would proceed in two stages. The first would be to undertake an analysis of the causes and dimensions of poverty. The second would be to use the analysis to describe the macroeconomic, structural, social, and institutional obstacles to growth and poverty alleviation. These two steps would then allow a description of the priority objectives and policies of the poverty reduction strategy.

Starting from the widely accepted general premise that durable poverty reduction demands rapid economic growth, the Bretton Woods institutions propound a quite specific model of growth and one that involves a complementary division of roles between the IMF and the World Bank. The role of the IMF is twofold. First, it must promote sound macroeconomic policies. Second, it must promote structural reforms in areas such as exchange rate regimes, fiscal policy, and the management of the public finances, including budget execution, budgetary transparency, and tax and customs administration. For its part, the World Bank has two key responsibilities. The first is to perform diagnostic tasks concerning poverty assessment, sector strategy formulation, reforms that lead to more effective institutions, and the establishment of social safety nets. The second is to consult on how to improve the efficacy of public spending, privatization, and regulatory reform. At the same time, the World Bank and the IMF intervene in a complementary manner in the areas of trade liberalization and development of the financial sector. This division of roles reflects a hierarchical reordering of policy priorities, not just institutions: macroeconomic adjustment under the aegis of the IMF takes precedence over sector adjustments under the World Bank.

Other stakeholders form another level of the hierarchy. This includes the bilateral funding agencies, which increasingly subscribe to the trend of multilateralization. The following passage is from the Canadian International Development Agency (CIDA):

> This comprehensive development model enjoys wide acceptance among international organizations—international financial institutions (IFIs) and the UN—and bilateral donors, as well as the developing world. Efforts are now being made by some bilateral donors, UN agencies, and IFIs to put the model into practice within their project portfolios, as well as through a number of new program approaches, such as the World Bank's Comprehensive Development Framework (CDF) and Poverty Reduction Strategy Papers (PRSPs), and the UN's Development Assistance Framework, as well as in programming instruments like sector-wide approaches (SWAPs).
>
> For example, the Comprehensive Development Framework draws together the principles of effective programming and is based on a holistic approach to development. PRSPs also create comprehensive frameworks for development that complement the CDF process, contribute to improved donor coordination, and help strengthen local ownership. Programming instruments, like sector-wide approaches, offer donor agencies a specific way to translate these holistic approaches into practice by allowing for investments across a broad programming sector, rather than in individual projects. SWAPs, and similar approaches, are also based on the principles of effective programming, particularly local ownership and development coordination (CIDA, 2001: 13).

Even before CIDA's new orientation became official, its commitment to this approach was not in question, as a World Bank document indicates:

> Pilot country teams understand that implementing the CDF is expected to be budget-neutral since the CDF approach is about a new way of doing the Bank's business. Some adjustments in administrative budgets have been necessary, but in most cases where country teams have made trade-offs within country programs, they have put more em-

phasis on sector approaches instead of projects, as well as being more selective in the defining Bank interventions [sic]. More recently, there has been incremental support from bilateral partners: Canadian International Development Agency (CIDA) has provided support for the CDF in Ghana; similarly, the Government of Japan has offered support for CDF work in the Kyrgyz Republic and Ghana, with a few more countries under consideration (World Bank, 2000).

Multilateralization suggests that the IMF and the World Bank have not only been increasingly able to set the development assistance agenda, but have also been able to establish a remarkable degree of consensus within the donor community that their version of the development assistance agenda is the correct one.

ii.   The impact of technocratic approaches to poverty reduction on political processes
In a background paper to the *World Development Report 2000/2001*, certain authors question whether it is correct to conclude that "globalization reduces the scope of governments to attend to poverty alleviation" (Moore and Putzel, 1999: 3). Other sources, though, such as the report of an international conference organized by the United Nations Research Institute on Social Development (UNRISD), respond categorically in the affirmative:

> Financial globalization and the dominance of neoliberal ideas in multilateral financial institutions and the G-7 countries…are narrowing the choices in economic policy making to a limited set of objectives. Described in some circles as the 'Washington Consensus', these objectives can be summarized as conservative fiscal policies, privatization, and open trade and capital accounts, all of which reflect an acceptance of price stability as the primary concern of macroeconomic policy… Pressure to standardize macroeconomic objectives encourages governments to restrict policy making to experts and insulate key economic institutions from democratic scrutiny (UNRISD, 2000: 1).

This, the authors contend, may affect democratization in two ways.

> First, it may distort the structure of accountability by encouraging national authorities to be more responsive to financial markets and multilateral institutions than to fledging parliaments and citizens. Second, social policies, which were crucial in consolidating Western democracies, may be treated as residuals of macroeconomic policy, and democ-

ratization that does not conform to neoliberal economic orthodoxy dismissed as populism (UNRISD, 2000: 1-2).

The potential results of this process, according to the same source, are significant. There may be an erosion of public confidence in the legitimacy of domestic institutions if their actions are dictated by external agents. It is possible that international investors would come to act as a constraint on democratic institutions, by withdrawing their capital if interest rates and other economic variables did not meet their requirements. In so doing, investors would prevent governments from implementing reflationary policies in periods of recession for fear of capital flight. It is also possible that the growing trend towards the creation of autonomous public authorities that check the discretionary powers of governments in key areas of policy-making might accelerate. Institutions that are potential candidates for autonomization include central banks, trade and finance ministries, tax administration offices, independent courts, electoral bodies, and ombudsmen.

It is a matter of prime importance to discover how these trends affect political processes. As UNRISD (2000: 3) notes, "[t]echnocratic approaches to making economic policy may affect the way governments respond to the concerns of citizens and elected representatives on such issues as employment, social protection and poverty eradication." As an illustration, it points out that if the fiscal authorities are independent, there is a risk they will be more responsive to market dictates than to the needs of the electorate, or, indeed, the electoral cycle. Redistributive pressures may directly conflict with the social policies favoured by technocrats as they seek to control expenditures, meet multilateral loan obligations, and attract private capital. In the same vein, the independence of central banks is not criticized per se, but the importance of raising official awareness to the need for policy objectives beyond the pursuit of price stability is stressed. Similarly, new public management reform promotes an improvement of public sector accountability, primarily by increasing managers' freedom to manage. To achieve this, it is commonly argued, policy-making must be kept separate from service delivery, "which becomes the responsibility of executive agencies" (UNRISD, 2000: 4). Finally, the costs of technocratic regulation itself must be taken into account. The UNRISD report argues that in a technocratic political process, technocratic groups are insulated from external pressure. One potential consequence is that the content of policies will be determined by rules that are context-indifferent; that is, policy-making will be separate from policy implementation. In health care systems in Africa, for example, it is argued that this type of technocratic regulation, so often associated with economic liberalization, has always had harmful effects. Thus, "economic crisis and liberalization in the 1990s produced major problems for users of Tanzania's health sector: high fees; social exclusion; erosion of exemption mechanisms for vulnerable patients; overprescription and use of expired drugs; misdiagnosis; and patient-managed referral practices" (UNRISD, 2000: 5).

Among the study's conclusions is the following:

> …technocratic decision making has resulted in the "technification" of social and political problems. In other words, poverty and social inequalities have been transformed into technical terms, with emphasis on targeting and safety nets… There are increasing demands for expertise in the social sector. However, there is less participation in the administration of targeted social programs, with the World Bank and national technocrats setting the agenda and maintaining overall control (UNRISD, 2000: 6).

Debates over the relationship between technocracy and political process are not new, and there is every reason to suppose they will continue. What is of particular concern here is that differing viewpoints about the role of each may be marginalized or even muzzled when technocracy is imposed from outside, for then the parameters of domestic debate about institutional reform are set in advance. The outcome is a depoliticization of social issues and a technification of terms like "poverty" and "social inequality." As a consequence, references to "targeting" and "social safety nets" replace "social welfare" in multilateral discourse.

Finally, the introduction of functionalism and technocracy into public affairs management appears to be aimed at sidelining dissenting views and depoliticizing the issue of resource distribution. However, it may also have the impact of shielding a growing number of areas from democratic scrutiny. At the same time, the exclusion of certain societal groups from management and participation in public affairs may impair legitimacy, elicit resistance, and ultimately render the application of the policies ineffective.

iii.   Poverty reduction, institutional reform, and political spaces

As to whether it is possible to determine what new models of national politi-cal processes are embodied in the proposed reforms, or the manner in which the policy process is, in fact, being "repoliticized," the position of the *World Development Report 2000/2001* in this regard is instructive. The report argues that "pro-poor coalitions that link the interests of the poor and the non-poor are important for poverty reduction. Improving the capacity of poor people to participate productively in economic activity also helps lay the foundation for faster growth" (World Bank, 2001: 108). However, beyond proposals as to how the state may encourage pro-poor coalitions, we are particularly interested in the conceptual model of political processes that informs the proposed institu-tional reforms. This model emerges from schools of thought that, as one might expect, are functionalist and instrumentalist in nature, with the guiding eco-nomic objective of providing "an enabling environment for the private sector" (World Bank, 1994b: 56). Such currents of thought have given rise to corner-stone ideas such as "the self-restraining state," "polyarchy," and "neo-constitu-tionalism." These ideas are presented as politically neutral. As a consequence, the particular conceptualization of notions such as "accountability," "participa-tion," and "effective governance" in these models has not received the atten-tion these notions deserve, even though they have major implications for the functioning of representative democratic systems as we know them.

The analysis in *Governance and Poverty Reduction* is, in this regard, interest-ing in several respects. It illustrates the application of a functionalist method-ology and an economistic approach to politics. Thus, the object of knowledge production is to contribute to system stability or persistence. Political space is then viewed as a market, and the important thing is to create the conditions for competition among more or less equally powerful stakeholders. A diagram in *Governance and Poverty Reduction* provides a particularly useful summary of this conception of politics: it depicts "horizontal accountability" as dependent on the equilibrium resulting from checks and balances created among the dif-ferent branches of government (Holmes et al., 2000: Table 1).

The centrality of horizontal accountability as a key concept in current Bank discourse calls for a brief examination of the texts from which it emerges. *The Self-Restraining State: Power and Accountability in New Democracies* (Schedler, Diamond and Plattner, 1999) is representative of this much broader literature, which provides the arguments in favour of a new democratic tradition applicable to developing nations, or "third-wave democracies." The authors state:

> ...we are witnessing today a growing awareness that liberal democracy requires governments that are not only accountable to their citizens but also subject to restraint and oversight by other public agencies. In addition to being restrained from below, the state must subject itself to multiple forms of *self*-restraint (Schedler et al., 1999: 1).

The analytical point of departure for this school is the concept of accountability: "...scholars now tend to perceive public accountability as a key attribute of both democracy and democratic quality" (Schedler et al., 1999: 2). This concept is deployed in answer to the now widespread criticism that elections reflect only one aspect of formal democracy. As well, the focus on this concept permits these theorists to develop a new distinction between horizontal and vertical accountability.

The authors define horizontal accountability as "the capacity of state institutions to check abuses by other public agencies and branches of government" (Schedler et al., 1999: 3). Its locus is in the interactions among the judicial, executive, and legislative branches. "[H]orizontal accountability complements but is to be distinguished from 'vertical' accountability," which they define in singularly restrictive fashion as the means "through which citizens, mass media, and civil associations seek to enforce standards of good conduct on public officials" (p. 3). Horizontal accountability is explicitly considered to be the more central of the two concepts since the state's capacity for "self-restraint" depends upon it. Mechanisms of restraint and oversight among various state institutions are seen as the best means to check tendencies to abuse power, to counter tendencies to gain more, and, hence, the best approach to ensure democratic procedures.

The potential implications of such an approach for the functioning of democratic systems are enormous. First, because of the emphasis on horizontal as opposed to vertical accountability, public control over political processes is very much marginalized, as is any reference to public participation through the formulation of demands and the exercise of power to have them addressed. A more comprehensive approach to accountability would include civic participation in policy-making; what we have here instead is a proceduralist approach that merely emphasizes the role of citizens in enforcing standards of good conduct. Second, there is no mention of the vehicles, such as social movements and political parties, whereby democratic demands are relayed. The reason is that horizontal accountability is asserted to depend on the existence of "independent, nonelective, specialized bodies of oversight (which may form part of any of the three branches). These autonomous institutions of accountability are typically insulated from state officials and from the people as well. Clearly, such institutions may come to clash with the principles of vertical accountability" (Schedler et al., 1999: 3).

Third, and particularly important, is the need to identify how the proponents of these ideas define the concept of "democratic procedures" as well as the assumptions on which they base their definition. The point of departure for authors like O'Donnell (1999) is the concept of "polyarchy," which is borrowed from Robert Dahl (1989). For Dahl, the characteristics of polyarchy are as follows: "(1) elected officials; (2) free and fair elections; (3) inclusive suffrage; (4) the right to run for office; (5) freedom of expression; (6) alternative information; and (7) associational autonomy" (p. 221). To these O'Donnell adds "(8) elected officials (and some appointed ones, such as high court judges) should not be arbitrarily terminated before the end of their constitutionally mandated terms; (9) elected officials should not be subject to severe constraints, vetoes, or exclusion from certain policy domains by other, nonelected actors, especially the armed forces; and (10) there should be an uncontested territory that clearly defines the voting population" (p. 46). Polyarchy, according to O'Donnell, is presented as vastly preferable to other types of rule, which are based on only one of its main component traditions.

This conclusion arises from a set of assumptions prevalent in certain trends in American political thought, and whose influence over the World Bank's contemporary analyses is undeniable. These trends are characterized by a great distrust of the state, arguing that the less it intervenes, the better for the people (Moore, 1993: 39-49). This type of argument serves to legitimate the importance assigned to horizontal accountability in the new polyarchies, for it is warned that the executive "will seek to maximize its power" (O'Donnell, 1999: 41), be it through usurpation or corruption.

Interestingly, these authors do suggest that "political authority comes from each and every member of the demos: if this is the case, those citizens who temporarily—by rotation, lot or election—happen to be in charge of public affairs must make their decisions having in view the good of all" (O'Donnell, 1999: 42). However, this discussion is detached, both conceptually and analytically, from the concepts of horizontal and vertical accountability. In fact, when more classical conceptions of democracy are referred to, these are redefined to serve specific procedural objectives. The same passage states that "even though these democratic expectations do not bear directly on horizontal accountability, they have the consequence of demanding a high degree of transparency in political decision making, which has at least a potential anticorruption implication" (p. 42). The result is the introduction of an instrumentalist conception of "democratic expectations" that serves to justify the emphasis placed on horizontal accountability. The omnipresence of corruption becomes important not only in legitimizing this form of accountability, but also, according to O'Donnell, in suggesting that institutional energies should be devoted more to it than to vertical accountability: "The point is that, insofar as some forms of corruption become highly visible and are generally condemned by public opinion, they can provide a handle for thinking more positively than I have done so far about how to enhance horizontal accountability" (p. 43).

Perhaps most critical for the conceptualization of political processes is the fact that the institutional arrangements proposed as the basis for the operation of the self-restraining state increasingly distance us from the forms of participation typical of classical popular democracy. In the initial World Bank document on governance, participation is restrictively redefined as enabling the public to "influence the quality or volume of a service through some form of articulation of preferences or demand" (World Bank, 1992c: 22). Thus defined, participation simply refers to a means of securing local support and cooperation as well as a means of claiming popular legitimacy, but only for those who implement reforms, not for those who resist or oppose them (see Beckman, 1992: 92). The introduction of such a limited notion of political participation works as the counterpart of the fact that these approaches consider the polyarchic systems that Dahl puts forward as the most relevant basic model. Seen to be composed of a complex and changing mix of elements, these systems are said to represent "the really existing democracies of the modern world" (O'Donnell, 1999: 34). The absence of what the author calls "properly authorized state agencies" (O'Donnell, 1999: 30) in the countries targeted for reform justifies the institutional changes necessary to establish horizontal accountability in the new polyarchies (O'Donnell, 1999: 42). Moreover, although elections are presented as the main factor making for vertical accountability, O'Donnell expresses an important caveat about them:"it is not clear to what extent this facet of vertical accountability is effective" (p. 30).

One is confronted here with a very circumscribed idea of democracy. By contrast with a model in which civic participation expands rights (Alverez, 1997: 15-40), this model of democracy offers only the opportunity to elect those who will govern and the right to formulate demands. Yet O'Donnell goes even further: he restricts demands to those actions that "denounce and/ or demand restitution or punishment for allegedly wrongful actions by public authorities" (O'Donnell, 1999: 30). This restricted sense of the term "demand" must be situated in a context where, as discussed above, the prime objective of the political model is stability. However, a variety of demands that do not meet this definition may get in the way of governments' attempting to implement reforms. Indeed, as O'Donnell states, "social demands and media coverage, especially if they are abundant and refer to issues that are considered important by public opinion, tend to create a climate of public disaffection with the government (and sometimes with the regime itself) that may obstruct its policies and lead to its defeat in the next round of elections" (p. 30).

The concept of equality among citizens comes in for an equally restrictive rendering in this tradition of political thought, partaking more of the procedural than the substantive. This redefinition has major consequences for the design and legitimation of poverty reduction strategies. Here, "equality" does not include equal access to socio-economic resources such as education, health care, and basic nutrition, which serve as a precondition for democratic citizenship. On the contrary, economic and political democracies are kept separate. To quote a standard work in this tradition: "The term *democracy* is used in this book to signify a political system, separate and apart from the economic and social system to which it is joined. Indeed, a distinctive aspect of our approach is to insist that issues of so-called 'economic and social democracy' be separated from the question of governmental structure" (Diamond, Ling, and Lipset, 1990: 6). This conceptual distinction underlies the thinking on reform of political systems that we have discussed so far. It goes far in explaining the "repoliticization" of the most recent generation of poverty reduction strategies. Indeed, it could serve to subordinate—and potentially to delegitimize—any attempt to tie the redistributive functions of the state to its responsibilities and duties toward citizens in a democratic system.

The risk of such an eventuality was already evident in the background work to the *World Development Report 1997*, which advocated a reconceptualization of the role of the state (World Bank, 1997). This is particularly evident in the writings of the report's architect, Joseph Stiglitz, who proposed that the concept of social justice was "in evolution." Stiglitz writes that "while economists traditionally approached these questions using a social welfare function, development economists have often taken a different tack, emphasizing 'basic needs.' But more recently, the focus has turned to opportunities." He concludes that "social justice should not be evaluated in terms of equality of outcomes but in terms of equality of opportunities" (Stiglitz, 1997: 79).[5]

The same functionalist tradition in political science not only provides the basis for an instrumentalized, teleological view of the state, but also inspires the "repoliticization" of the concept of governance, now referred to as "effective governance." This concept is in academic writings (see, for example, Lowenthal and Dominguez, 1996), as well as in the documents of the World Bank itself, and it is illustrated by its strategy of "decentralized governance." In this latter concept, to the extent that political stability is seen as dependent upon the equilibrium to be established between local and central interests, by inference, interest groups with no access to these power dynamics, or to the levels of government foreseen by the rules of decentralized governance, risk being classified as destabilizing forces (Campbell, 2000b). Under such circumstances, interest groups whose actions have previously been considered at the heart of liberal pluralism could well be excluded from what is now presented as "effective governance," which requires "stable coalitions and an executive with reasonably strong and clear powers" (World Bank, 1999c: 121).

It is clear that the concepts employed by the World Bank offer a singular conception of the workings of political processes. The perspective supports institutional arrangements designed *a priori* to maintain a situation of equilibrium, with the predefined ends of stability and system persistence. This view contrasts with other, more dynamic and open ones, in which social movements and political forces are seen as political actors who seek to construct their own history and shape the objectives of their particular societies. The latter view implies a fundamental element of contingency that precludes such *a priori* constraints. The prevailing functionalist approach thus provides a good fit with a development model whose purpose—growth and the means to achieve it—is also determined in advance. However, this conceptualization of political processes, which emphasizes top-down strategies, minimizes the role of elected officials, political parties, and parliaments in the definition and introduction of a collective project for society. Bodies other than the executive branch are basically relegated to the role of watchdogs; they are not allowed to be initiators of public policy on an equal footing with the executive. One can hardly demur from the need for checks on the executive to ensure that it remains accountable, but it is problematic that this concern goes along with a model of political processes in which parliaments play a role that can only be termed marginal. In such a context, the necessary debates to which we refer above—concerning the finality of poverty reduction strategies, as well as the tensions between technification and political processes—are in serious danger of being ignored or even suppressed. Under these circumstances, it is not inappropriate to ask whether, with the publication of the World Bank's *World Development Report 1999/2000: Entering the 21st Century* (World Bank, 1999c), and the attempt to use institutional reform to institute "effective governance," we are witnessing the distancing from a liberal and pluralist model, based on a participatory ideal, in favour of a more neo-conservative authoritarian model, based on a technocratic ideal.

V. Debt relief and institutional reform: a "locking in" of Africa?

Specific institutional reforms, considered as the central feature of poverty reduction strategies, have potential consequences for political processes and democratic space in the countries concerned. We shall now tie this analysis to several African countries' recent experience with debt relief under the Enhanced HIPC Initiative. The issue that we wish to raise in this last section is the possibility that the manner in which existing mechanisms link debt relief to institutional reform in this area may in fact represent a new form of restriction on the notion of sovereignty of the states concerned. In order to do this, it is important to briefly illustrate the scope and nature of the institutional reforms which are required of highly indebted poor countries. Three examples will be used: Mozambique, Rwanda and Senegal.

Mozambique is one of the African countries that has benefited from the HIPC Initiative and in June 1999 the World Bank and the IMF agreed that Mozambique had reached 'completion point' and could apply for funds provided by the Initiative.[6] As a condition for aid and debt relief, however, former conditionalities were reinforced and broadened: while the macroeconomic, structural and institutional reforms introduced under previous structural adjustment programmes remained on the agenda, new and quite rigorous measures related to governance, the expansion of the private sector and budgetary monitoring were added. These measures were incorporated into the government's PRSP on the "advice" of the World Bank and the IMF. The scope of the areas to which the new conditonalities apply is illustrated by the fact that the PRSP identifies six priority areas: education, health, agriculture and rural development, basic infrastructure, good governance and improved macroeconomic and financial management (World Bank, 2000b).

In the case of Rwanda,[7] the *Rwanda: Country Assistance Strategy (CAS)-Progress Report* developed by the International Development Association (IDA) of the World Bank Group sets out a range of structural reforms under the rubric of a 'Strategy Matrix' (IDA, 1999) that sought to revitalize the rural economy and the private sector (Ngirumpatse, 2004). Thus, while the Matrix suggests the decentralization of decision making and of policy implementation, as well as the reinforcement of community based participation, it simultaneously calls for the revision of the Internal Trade Act so that price, profit and inventory controls are abolished, the abolition of the government controlled Chamber of Commerce, and the elimination of the coffee export tax. These centrally directed measures seem to stand at odds with the call for participative decentralization. So too does the recommendation that the country identify state-owned enterprises for privatization. In this light, it is revealing that the subsequent Decision Point Document prepared in 2000 under the Enhanced HIPC Initiative specified that the structural reforms and privatizations to be carried out reinforced measures introduced under the country's pre-existing Poverty Reduction and Growth Facility (PRGF). While the PRGF had specified, as a conditionality, the sale of 51 per cent of the shares of the state-owned telecommunications company and the placing under private management prior to privatization of the state-owned water and electricity distribution company, the PRSP (République rwandaise, 2001) went on to call for a range of further privatizations: at least two of the nine tea factories, a textile firm, a brewery, maize and rice processors, the parastatal agricultural marketing board, a coffee exporter and several hotels. The fact that the reform measures identified in the CAS or the PRGF-supported programmes are to be found as well in the country's poverty reduction strategy is illustrative of the "convergence" between the recommendations of the Bretton Woods Institutions and the "national" policy process, suggesting that debt relief is indeed linked to a set of reforms that are predicated upon restricting the autonomy of the government.

The institutional reforms required of Senegal under its PRSP programme similarly illustrate the way in which debt relief can be used to promote the intrusion of the international financial institutions in national decision making processes. In its "Country Partnership Strategy Matrix" (World Bank, 2003) Senegal is, in essence, required to restructure the state. The Matrix calls on Senegal to improve the legal and regulatory framework in order to foster anti-corruption efforts, strengthen the judiciary, as well as reform, modernize and decentralize the civil service. The benchmarks established to measure the government's progress for this area of reform and to which funding will be conditional include continuing judicial reform, decentralizing the delivery of public services and executing a greater share of budget at the decentralized level. Although put forward as administrative reforms to foster good governance, it would be difficult to ignore the political implications of such measures which involve clear shifts the locus of power and a redefinition of political processes.

The experiences of these three countries are not unique. They serve to illustrate a pattern in which the degree of external influence in the determination of each country's institutional reforms clearly represents a severe restriction on the forms of local participation, on the nature of "ownership" of the reform process and more fundamentally, on the notion of sovereignty itself. However, the process through which funds are made available may also be seen as an additional form of constraint. In this regard, there is no disputing that the Enhanced Initiative does offer eligible countries a substantial opportunity for debt reduction. According to the Debt Sustainability Analyses considered in a study undertaken by the North-South Institute (Serieux, 2001), in late 2000 of the 41 countries with HIPC status, 22 had reached the decision point for adopting a poverty reduction strategy. In so doing, they had become eligible for a 50 per cent reduction in the nominal value of their present debt (Serieux, 2001: 527). Of the 19 HIPC countries that had reached the decision point on implementation of a PRSP for which recent information exists, 15 are in Africa.[8]

The Enhanced Initiative assumes that the funds released for poverty reduction will be close to the amounts necessary to achieve the objectives set at international conferences. However, Serieux notes that

> there is no necessary correlation between the resources needed to generate the rate of poverty reduction that is required for meeting internationally agreed targets (such as that of halving world poverty by 2015) and the poverty reduction engendered by debt relief. It is the level and depth of poverty existing in each country that will determine the rate of improvement in material circumstances necessary to pull half of the disadvantaged out of poverty, whereas debt-relief levels are related to debt ratios that have little direct relation to poverty (Serieux, 2001: 534).

Indeed, several in-depth empirical studies reviewed by Serieux suggest that the amounts needed to achieve poverty reduction levels in line with international targets imposed on the HIPC countries far outstrip what would be made available by the proposed debt relief mechanisms: there is a blatant mismatch between these two parameters. Specifically, studies of Uganda, Mali and Ethiopia show that

> ...the experience of a sample of these countries suggests that HIPC debt relief will only release a fraction of the resources necessary for the poverty reduction envisaged by these countries' poverty reduction strategies. Yet, these programs have poverty reduction targets that are at or below the internationally agreed target (of halving world poverty by 2015). Also, since the dividend from debt relief will become smaller over time, that funding gap will widen (Serieux, 2001: 536-7).

Thus, although the Enhanced Initiative specifically identifies poverty reduction as one of its objectives, the adequacy of the resources available for this purpose represents simply a hypothesis whose validity must be assessed. Moreover, it is even less clear whether the Enhanced Initiative offers an adequate framework and sufficient levels of relief to guarantee a long-term solution, as opposed to a short-term fix, to insupportable debt. At the same time, recall that a central component of the policy framework to which Enhanced

HIPC Initiative countries must subscribe is institutional reform. It is in this light that the issue of the need to reconceptualize intervention strategies designed around a CDF and its attendant PRSP if they are to be adjusted to deal with new realities can be raised.

Serieux, for example, suggests that while the export volume and profile of the countries concerned were key factors in explaining the high debt ratios in the mid-1980s, they were less relevant in 1998 (Serieux, 2001: 540). Moreover, in reviewing several studies he found that weak domestic institutions did contribute to indebtedness, but only as one factor among others. Yet this factor is always singled out in order to justify the introduction of specific reforms within the PRSP process. What Serieux's analysis does indicate is that small countries with high illiteracy rates and which are heavily dependent upon raw material exports are particularly susceptible to indebtedness. He suggests that statistically, indebtedness in 1998 is best explained by "development" when it is measured by variables such as literacy. Indeed, he uses World Bank data to show that "countries classified by the World Bank as severely indebted in 1998 are disproportionately least developed. This would tend to support the contention...that while a wide range of economies (in terms of development level) were heavily indebted in the mid 1980s, it was the weaker economies, dependent almost exclusively on public credit, that remained heavily indebted in the late 1990s" (Serieux, 2001: 542). Serieux concludes that if these countries are to avoid insupportable debt in the future, it is necessary to reconsider the nature and pattern of resource flows for poverty reduction, as well as the provisions for mitigating external shocks. In the absence of such a reconsideration, one seems justified in concluding that the very strategies intended to reduce poverty—such as debt relief mechanisms—might actually contribute to the perpetuation of extreme poverty by reinforcing the asymmetrical integration of these economies into world markets. In so doing, current poverty reduction strategies might contribute to reinforcing, rather than attenuating, the existing hierarchy of poor countries.

With the criteria for access to these resources becoming increasingly stringent, since they are conditional on the introduction of specific institutional reforms, HIPC countries attempting to take advantage of the new debt relief mechanisms are finding their room to manoeuvre ever more limited. Significantly, Larry Diamond, in *Prospects for Democratic Development in Africa*, published by the Hoover Institution on War, Revolution and Peace, had, in 1997, recommended that political conditionalities be required of African countries. These political conditionalities are strikingly consistent with both the academic discourse that underpins World Bank concepts of institutional reform, and with the actual conditionalities required as a result of the PRSP process. Thus, Diamond argues that

> the Western side of the bargain would be a new partnership for democracy and development in Africa. For those countries that meet the above conditions, debt servicing should be suspended, official assistance (of particular kinds, as discussed below) should be increased, and the stock of debt should be retired at a fixed rate (say, 10 percent a year) for each year that they maintain a broad commitment to economic reform, political pluralism and freedom, accountability, and good governance (Diamond, 1997: 39).

However, Diamond also prescribes some more specific arrangements: "if this commitment could be locked into place for a decade, time would be purchased for democratic institutions and practices to take root and for economic reforms to show results. If the democratic commitment is abandoned...all official assistance and debt relief should automatically be suspended" (p. 39). Diamond's use of the term "locking in" is an increasingly germane description of what is actually happening as a result of the PRSP process, as is Paul Collier's use of the same term to denote the application of increasingly restrictive conditions for stability to promote private investment (Collier, 1999: 315). The institutional reforms propounded by the World Bank offer a conceptualization of the working of political processes predicated upon stability and system persistence. Despite the official rhetoric, this view emphasizes top-down strategies laid out by the executive, and minimizes the role of elected officials, political parties, and parliaments. It is a particularly technocratic approach to democracy, based upon seeking to depoliticize the political, and, in so doing, could be argued to be creating a substantial distance from the liberal and pluralist model of democracy that many in Africa would seek. Finally, there is serious reason to believe that the nature of debt reduction mechanisms, conditional as they are on the introduction of specific institutional reforms, and which are considered as the central feature of poverty reduction strategies, by contributing to the "locking in" of African states may well represent a new restriction on the notion of their sovereignty.

VI. Conclusion

Over the last five years the World Bank's commitment to poverty reduction has become increasingly tied to the introduction of specific institutional reforms that have, under the CDF and the PRSP process, become a condition of access to multilateral funds in this crucial area. In this chapter we have tried to critically interrogate these recent developments. To that end, we have analyzed the documents of the multilateral agencies in order to discern the relationships that are asserted to exist between institutional reform, good governance and poverty reduction. We have taken particular care to examine the conception of the political process underlying recent attempts at institutional reform, which are characterized by such concepts as the "self-restraining state," "horizontal accountability," and "effective governance." In this light, we have sought to demonstrate certain potential consequences of these recommendations for political space and democracy in the societies in which such reforms are proposed for implementation. We have lastly, briefly, tied these theoretical ideas into recent research on poverty reduction in Africa, with reference to the new debt relief mechanisms prescribed by the Enhanced HIPC Initiative and considered the potentially restrictive implications of these mechanisms for the notion of sovereignty in the countries concerned.

The criteria for access to debt relief is becoming increasingly stringent, since it is becoming conditional on the introduction of specific institutional reforms. As a consequence, countries that qualify for the Enhanced HIPC Initiative, and particularly those in Africa that are attempting to take advantage of the new debt relief mechanisms, are finding their room to manoeuvre ever more limited. Perhaps even more troubling, however, are the political implications of the institutional reforms introduced as conditions for access to poverty reduction funds. Domestic political processes, it is clear, are now being subjected to forces that may very well result in a narrowing of political space, without any guarantees that the debt reduction mechanisms or poverty reduction strategies will give rise to equitable and lasting solutions.

Footnotes

1 We wish to thank Peter Feldstein for his excellent assistance in translating this text from French to English.

2 This paper builds on previous work, which includes Campbell, 2000a, 1997a, and 1997b.

3 Reference to these background papers is helpful in tracing the logic leading from governance to poverty reduction in the final version of the Report, due to its somewhat hermetic style. Moreover, the argument is explicit, for example, in the reworking of the concept of the rule of law that appears in the section entitled "Poor People and the Rule of Law." The use of the concept of the rule of law also illustrates the functionalist approach of the analysis contained in the final version of the report: "the rule of law is associated with better overall economic performance (figure 6.3), and in this sense it also promotes poverty reduction. It does this by creating a predictable and secure environment for economic agents to engage in production, trade, and investment, thereby expanding poor people's employment opportunities and incomes" (World Bank, 2001: 103).

4 We wish to thank to Angel Saldomando for drawing our attention to the existence of this Internet resource: World Bank, "Toolkit: Commitment to Reform Diagnostic — *Institutional Analysis and Assesment*," http://www.worldbank.org/.

5 The example of equal opportunity given by Stiglitz in this passage — that of education — seems paradoxical when it is considered that an increasing number of children must work rather than go to school, and that free education has been seriously jeopardized by structural adjustment programmes. "If society provides educational opportunities to all children, it has fulfilled its responsibility, even if some individuals fail to avail themselves of those opportunities" (Stiglitz, 1997: 79).

6 We wish to acknowledge the helpful collaboration of Fancine Godin concerning the experience of Mozambique.

7 We are grateful to Pauline Ngirumpatse for the information on Rwanda, which is drawn from her research for her Master's thesis "L'initiative d'allègement de la dette des pays pauvres très endettés: adéquation entre allègement de la dette et réduction de la pauvreté — le cas du Rwanda," Université du Québec à Montréal, 2004.

8 An additional three — Guinea, Guinea-Bissau and Rwanda, again African countries — are also eligible, but relevant data were not provided in their Debt Sustainability Analyses and therefore they are not considered in the study undertaken by the North-South Institute.

Chapter 14

DECENTRALIZING NATURAL RESOURCE MANAGEMENT: A RECIPE FOR SUSTAINABILITY AND EQUITY?

Wicky Meynen and Martin Doornbos

I. Introduction

IN recent years there has been a considerable restructuring of the institutional arrangements governing natural resource management (NRM).[1] This restructuring has taken place in the context of ongoing efforts at economic reform and decentralization in various countries, which a number of contributions in this volume explore. Deliberate policy interventions by the state and donor agencies, initiatives by voluntary agencies and local groups, and the impact of market forces on local economic structures have all contributed to this restructuring. In these interventions various non-state solutions have been favoured in response to a variety of factors, including perceived shortcomings and rigidities in earlier institutional forms as well as global and fiscal pressures to reduce the role of the central state. Initially, market deregulation and privatization were the guiding principles in these endeavours, and more recently decentralization of governance and local participation have received emphasis. These institutional changes amount to a redefinition of the role of the state and have stimulated further exploration and experimentation that examine a variety of non-state forms of management and co-management. Restructuring efforts of this kind often involve local communities and user groups, joint environmental management schemes, non-governmental organization (NGO)-based initiatives, cooperative bodies, and other actors at the micro and meso level. Such altered institutional arrangements have been done, it is often argued, so as to bring about more sustainable and equitable forms of NRM through the enhancement of grassroots participation.

However, it remains to be seen whether these institutional changes, and particularly decentralization, can promote more sustainable NRM practices. In order to achieve this outcome, new practices must be capable of transcending past institutional rigidities. They must be capable of containing environmental degradation, promoting sustainable and equitable natural resource use, allowing more effective handling of resource conflicts, and facilitating joint environmental resource development, all of which indicate the need to identify and rectify pre-existing problems in the field of policy. At the same time, though, there may be potential policy tension between the equity of access that sustainable NRM practices demand and the process of decentralization that facilitates more sustainable NRM practices. Moreover, many of the arrangements concerned seem to have made an already competitive situation regarding scarce natural resource utilization all the more complex. Thus, despite the potentially positive effects of decentralization and participation in opening up or enlarging space for peoples' movements and other forms of collective action from below, it nonetheless appears appropriate to take a critical look at current modes of thinking and practices regarding decentralization and participation in NRM.

II. Theoretical and policy debates

The changes in institutional arrangements we are concerned with have given rise to several theoretical and policy debates. Within the realm of theory, Hardin's (1968) thesis of "the tragedy of the commons" had, at an early stage, set in motion an intense discussion among social scientists on the role of property rights regimes and related institutional arrangements in the management of natural resources. In particular, the merits and demerits of private, state, and community-based resource management systems became a hotly debated issue. Among economists this debate initially focussed on the question of whether decentralized collective action could be effective (White and Runge, 1995: 1683). In sharp contrast to this, anthropological perspectives tended to highlight the historically well-adapted, flexible, and potentially renewable roles of traditional local communities and institutions in NRM (Klooster, 2000: 2). The correlates of the relative success of such resource management systems in terms of ecological and social sustainability similarly came under debate (see, for example, Bromley et al., 1992; McCay and Acheson, 1987; Ostrom, 1990;

Runge, 1986; Wade, 1988). These debates have centred on the conditions that facilitate or hamper the emergence, maintenance, and sustainability of such institutional arrangements (Klooster, 2000; White and Runge, 1995).

Despite these different perspectives, there is broad consensus among researchers and policy-makers on the pivotal role of institutional arrangements in shaping peoples' interactions with their natural environments and negotiation processes in NRM. These arrangements determine who has what kind of access to which kind of natural resources and what use they can make of such resources. While institutional choice theorists like Ostrom (1990, 1992) are particularly interested in grasping processes of institutional crafting and consolidation, reflexive, explanatory approaches have highlighted serious limitations of many design-oriented approaches. In the adherence of design-oriented approaches to rational choice-based models, it has been argued, design-oriented perspectives negate the complex nature of institutions and run the danger of imposing formal institutional forms on previously existent, informal, but often invisible, ones (Cleaver, 2000; Klooster, 2000; Leach, Mearns, and Scoones, 1997, 1999). According to these critics, the inherent tendencies of functionalism in design-oriented approaches and the view of institutions as simply "rules-in-use" progressing from weak to robust forms and to steady states given adequate support, are oversimplified, static, and evolutionistic.

In these critical perspectives, institutions encompass not only sets of formal and informal rules, regulations, and norms, but also social meaning, namely shared values, understandings, and perceptions of "the right way of doing things" (Cleaver, 2000: 368). Thus, institutions are intrinsically permeated and shaped by notions and ideologies of gender, class, and other social divisions. Related "deeply-sedimented social practices" may also be considered as institutions, or as part of institutions (Giddens, 1979: 80). In much of the literature, an even broader concept of institutions that encompasses organizations is used. However, such a conception has to be handled with caution, even though the idea of viewing institutions simply as rules, and, thus, sharply distinguishing rule from practice, has been dismissed. As noted by Leach et al. (1999: 237), only some institutions that are of critical importance to resource access and control have organizational forms. Many have "no single or direct organizational manifestations, including money, markets, marriage, and the law."

These critical views emphasize the diversity, multiplicity, and interrelatedness of the institutions involved in NRM, among which are many informal ones, as well as their dynamic and often conflict-ridden nature. Institutions are "subject to multiple interpretations and frequent redefinition in the course of daily practice" and "often operate as arenas of negotiation and struggle," as Berry (1993: 4, 20) states. In other words, they constitute contested terrain in which different interests are played out, subject to power dynamics of human agency. Institutions thus have to be analyzed not only in relation to material resources, but also in relation to culture and to power and authority relations, including gender relations. Due attention should be given to the contested dimensions of institutions, and to their potential for change under the influence of human agency (Berry, 1993, 1997; Cleaver, 2000; Klooster, 2000; Leach et al., 1997, 1999; Mosse, 1995, 1997).

The embracing of decentralized and participatory NRM approaches in many countries since the 1980s has entailed extensive discussions and debates concerning the merits of such organizational and institutional interventions. Among policy-makers as well as academics there appears a widespread consensus at one level about the desirability of decentralization, derived from the commonly held idea that devolving powers from the centre to lower political and administrative levels may facilitate people's participation in development and resource management. Beyond this, however, there is profuse divergence in the meanings attached to the term "decentralization," the views about the extent and forms of participation to be realized, the institutional changes needed in the role and apparatus of the state, and the way in which the restructuring process would be achieved. Not surprisingly, these differences and the respective debates about them reflect the theoretical, ideological, and political interests of the advocates (Carney and Farrington, 1998; Mohan and Stokke, 2000; Webster, 1995).

The most influential actors in the decentralization arena are, first, neo-liberal public-choice advocates, who start from a market-focussed agenda designed to "role back the state" and achieve delivery efficiency through privatization or through delegation, with a preference for such delegation being outside the public sector. Within this perspective, "participation" implies market transactions, with "the people" in the role of consumers and possibly providers. Accordingly, in the field of NRM, the idea to contract out services for local natural resource management to NGOs, or to develop joint delivery systems that bring together NGOs and private sector actors, is increasingly articulated. For example, since the late 1980s, a range of Indian policy documents concerning forest and watershed development have been making recommendations in this vein (Baumann, 2000: 16-17). The state is basically considered a constraint on efficient management, although, using the discourse of "the enabling state," neo-liberals lately have argued it should provide the kind of administrative and political institutional context necessary to facilitate efficient and effective service delivery (Mohan and Stokke, 2000: 248). In operational respects, the latter perspective has strengthened the overlap of the public-choice agenda with a second stream of thought that moulds the ideas and practices of decentralization: the "good governance" agenda. The good governance approach has clear neo-liberal overtones even as it advocates institutional reforms that should "bring the state closer to the people" and increase its accountability and transparency (Baumann, 2000: 17; see also Campbell et al. and Van Arkadie, this volume). This is to be achieved by administrative and political decentralization, in combination with a strengthening of local government capacities and efforts to involve the participation of local communities and other local stakeholders in development and NRM activities.

Both the public-choice and the good governance approaches start from a top-down institutional restructuring process in which the state is expected to play a central role, with NGOs as key allies. However, the possibility of resistance to such restructuring within the state apparatus, as opportunities for clientelism get lost and power and resources are relinquished to local actors in the periphery, tends to be overlooked in these perspectives. At the same time, the importance of structural inequalities at the local level, and related external and internal patronage and power relations, also tends to be neglected. However, this omission may not necessarily be due to the technocratic perspectives of neo-liberals and donor bureaucracies. It may also result from populist influence over the shaping of decentralization policies, particularly in the field of NRM. Populist advocates of community-based NRM approaches tend to turn a blind eye to local social inequalities and related intra- and intercommunity resource interest controversies and struggles. This allows them to uphold a highly romanticized vision of so-called traditional communities as homogeneous and harmonious entities, inherently capable and inclined to maintain socially and ecologically sustainable NRM systems (Agrawal and Gibson, 1999; Li, 1996: 502, 509). The use of such idealized representations of community in the policy arena can produce strategic gains "in ongoing processes of negotiation," according to Li (1996: 502, 509). However, she cautions against the translation of these images at the operational level because of their misleading generalizing and exclusionary tendencies.

At the operational level, the adoption of decentralized and participatory NRM approaches frequently has taken place within the context of particular programmes or projects for sustainable development that utilize sectoral approaches (Leach et al., 1997). As a consequence, the different forms of institutional arrangements available in given sectoral contexts such as forestry, watershed management, fisheries, and the like, and their appropriateness for the management of the types of local resources concerned, have now become frequently debated issues. One stream of this literature focusses on apparently successful NRM undertakings to contemplate the lessons they provide (for example, Bromley et al., 1992; White and Runge, 1995; Veit, Mascarenhas, and Ampadu-Agyei, 1995). A more critical discussion questions the appropriateness of present community-based and joint NRM efforts on various grounds often related to their technocratic, ahistorical, and apolitical features (see, for example, Mosse, 1997; Steins, Edwards, and Röling, 2000). In particular, the conceptual and operational approaches commonly adopted in respect of "community," "participation," and "jointness" have been repeatedly criticized (Agrawal and Gibson, 1999; Mosse, 1997; Nelson and Wright, 1995; Sundar, 2000; Utting, 2001). Also, it has been advanced that the uncertainty of the socio-political, economic, and ecological conditions that shape people's use of natural resources and livelihoods should be seriously considered in decentralized, community-based, and joint NRM efforts (Mehta et al, 2001).

A related discussion concerning forms of NRM decentralization has narrowly focussed on the extent to which the state should devolve management authority and property rights to local communities and groups (Agrawal and Ribot, 2000; Poffenberger and McGean, 1996). The perspective on decentralization has been narrowed further by the prevalence of the sectoral approach in project operations and in many discussions concerning NRM. These factors may help explain why a common opinion about devolution favours the maximum devolution of governance to local user groups. However, in embracing this position it appears that the limitations and pitfalls of "going local," as Mohan and Stokke (2000: 254) call it, have been receiving insufficient attention.

III. Decentralizing NRM: mixed objectives, mixed results

Clearly, strategies for decentralization and participation at an operational level tend to be informed by a mix of policy objectives, which may be inconsistent or even contradictory. As noted, their sources of inspiration are often markedly heterogeneous. On the one hand, national and international agencies promote market mechanisms, designed to mobilize capital internally and facilitate economic globalization by opening up local economies to international capital. This requires attuning of institutional and organizational arrangements. As a result, promotion of local participation is often focussed on supporting local private enterprise in the commercial exploitation of natural resources. On the other hand, decentralization strategies are expected to promote local participation in NRM from below, with the objective of defending the subsistence and resource interests of poor communities and user groups dependent on a particular natural resource base. These opposite demands give rise to various political, economic, and administrative contradictions in the moves towards decentralization.

A lack of matching objectives, arising from different conceptual and policy approaches to decentralization, may be reflected in inconsistencies in legislative and policy frameworks. Conceivably, contrasted and opposed policy goals from different state agencies may result in or fuel resource conflicts and power struggles at various levels. These may occur within the state and local government apparatus, between various state agencies and local communities, and within local communities. For example, in Bangladesh the ministry in charge of the development of fisheries resources has been hampered in developing and implementing an ecologically adequate fisheries policy due to the overlapping involvement of competing ministries in the floodplains concerned (Rashed, 1998). The priorities of the latter are in commercial or revenue-raising resource management activities rather than resource conservation activities. This situation has not only led to power struggles among different ministries and departments, but also to local level resource conflicts between farming and fisheries communities, and within fisheries communities between

273

fish traders and artisanal fishermen (Rashed, 1998). The tendency for different interests to find support in different branches of the state, such as the conflicting claims of natural resource conservation versus the intensification of agriculture, has also been reinforced by global institutional factors. Different international donor agencies have often advocated different and conflicting strategies for rural and environmental resource management and development (Lélé, 1991; Utting, 1993: ch. 12). The implications of such policy inconsistencies and institutional fragmentation for resource conservation efforts at the local level can be considerable.

The question of conceptual and policy inconsistencies can also be looked at from yet another angle. In constitutional terms, decentralization has often been based on a principle of "subsidiarity," the premise that higher state bodies should not be doing what lower organs can do better (Martinussen, 1997: 215). In theory, this remains a useful point of departure to determine what decision-making powers may best be placed at what level. The test for meaningful decentralization then becomes the extent to which lower organs are in a position to set their own priorities within the parameters for their jurisdiction. Further preconditions for decentralization to become successful are that the lower level organs should enjoy legitimate authority and adequate capacity, and also have sufficient autonomous financial capability to execute what they have been authorized to do, from taxes and revenues and/or from central grants. Nor should such arrangements absolve higher level bodies from their informational, supervisory, coordinating, and possible conflict-resolving roles with respect to the execution of decentralized NRM functions, or from ultimate authority over the field of activities concerned.

However, a number of recent examples indicate that decentralization policies may mainly amount to a selective deconcentration of state functions under the control of the central government. In respect to west Africa, for example, "the reality of decentralization so far is that local decision-makers have very little discretion in decision-making, and few skills for effective implementation and monitoring of decisions taken" (Moore et al., 2000: 1). Such policies have often been adopted, it appears, as a way of freeing governments or higher level organs from financial and administrative responsibility for the activities concerned. Such cost-saving devices have been part of the general drive to push back the role of central government under the aegis of structural adjustment programmes. With reference to certain Sahel country governments, for example, Toulmin (1991: 35) suggests that

> the only 'responsibilization' that will take place…is likely to concern cases where the state can divest itself from certain costly obligations, for example by transferring responsibility for maintenance of bore-holes to pastoral associations, and by handing over the role of maintaining irrigation schemes to water user groups.

Decentralization, which in this and other instances may be closely linked to privatization, may thus be introduced as a device to generate fiscal savings. In such circumstances the decentralized entities concerned, which may be districts or lower levels of government, are actively encouraged to find their own resources for the activities they wish to undertake. However, different regions and localities will start out with unequal endowments, and are unlikely to find that their respective governments are prepared to come forward with significant redistributive measures (De Bruijne, 2001: 24, 29). This implies that poor districts and local communities will be less capable than better endowed ones to make use of the new opportunities. Moreover, environmental protection and equitable participation in NRM may not rank very high on the list of priorities to which modest resources are allocated. What then remains is, at best, the possibility of a foreign donor being prepared to step in and fund the initiation of environmental projects thought to be of longer run relevance, even though such an intervention is, in principle, temporary and will generate the need for sustainable follow-up.

Closely related to the subsidiarity rationale for decentralization is the argument that decentralization can build on the efforts of local groups and communities, engaging local knowledge to resolve local problems. However, within the local context broader, more comprehensive perspectives on the interlocking problems of a particular natural resource base may not always be articulated. Indeed, different stakeholders may be inclined to act on matters in line with their own specific interests and horizons. In many situations there are no mechanisms to juxtapose these different interests. Where such institutional gaps occur, it would be important to at least try to overcome them through the creation of channels for informed dialogue among stakeholders. This may raise awareness of the implications of their respective actions on the interests and welfare of others, and of the legitimate claims of other users to be able to access the resource base concerned. Attempts to do this have been advocated, and tentatively pursued, with reference to resource conflicts involving various pastoralist groups and cultivating communities in the Horn of Africa (Doornbos, 2001). However, whether they will be sufficient to meet the demands of equity still remains to be seen.

An important, related, question concerns the determination of the stakeholders that are involved. If decision-making on such issues is based on prevailing institutional patterns in respect of property rights or images of identities, women will not be defined as stakeholders in most instances. The likelihood of such a course of affairs is particularly great if existing networks of local leaders and "knowledgeable" state and NGO representatives play a key role in establishing contacts and gathering information, as is frequently the case. Local leadership institutions, as well as state and NGO agencies working in the fields of agriculture, forestry, and water resource management, are in general "male spaces" that lack gender sensitivity. In short, "stakeholder consultations, if not handled properly, may serve the ends of (continued) social exclusion—most especially that of edging women out of the process" (Pantana, Real, and Resurreccion, n.d: 17).

The Indian experience further illustrates the extent of unfulfilled expectations connected with decentralization policies. In India there has been considerable pressure from below, exerted by various people's movements and NGOs, for both the decentralized management of natural resources and increased people's participation in such management (Dwivedi, 2001; Poffenberger and McGean, 1996; Sinha, Gururani, and Greenberg, 1997). At the same time, consistent with worldwide trends stimulated by the international financial institutions, the central Indian government has, in recent years, initiated decentralization of NRM along sectoral lines by establishing guidelines for devolving decision-making powers and central government funds to lower levels of administration. Decentralization further down to community level is also encouraged, facilitating participatory resource management that focusses on local community-based user groups. However, as economic globalization has increasingly demanded the opening-up of local economies, local NRM in many parts of the country has become geared towards commercialization rather than the subsistence interests of the poor, or, indeed, the protection of natural resources.

These contradictory decentralization dynamics have been compounded by a complex set of political, economic, and administrative problems. First, the central government of India has issued not only specific guidelines for the sectoral decentralization of NRM, but also legislation and guidelines that stipulate decentralization of government itself, with the latter, not surprisingly, having implications for NRM. The ways in which these two forms of decentralization should interface in practice has remained an unresolved question, however. This is partly due to the fact that it has been largely up to the state governments, and, in the case of specific natural resources, to the line departments within states, to implement the various sets of decentralization guidelines in ways they see fit. Thus, the forms and political and legal contents of decentralization depend largely on the particular constellations of political forces within the various state polities and administrations. It appears that in many states devolving adequate resources, powers and authority to elected local government or *panchayati raj* institutions and to user-group formations has been thwarted by politicians, bureaucrats, or members of legislative bodies. Often, decentralization of NRM initiatives have been hijacked by local politicians and power-holders for electoral and related purposes. Serious attempts have been made to carry through democratic decentralization in only five or six states (Manor, n.d.; Webster, 1995). When noting this, though, we should also remind ourselves that this record still contrasts favourably to that of many other countries.

Aside from intra-state obstacles, constructive implementation of both the *panchayati raj* and NRM forms of decentralization has been frustrated by political strife between the central and state governments. Their fight is over functions, powers, and authority within the policy field of development planning and implementation, which happens to be the core area for both the *panchayati raj* and NRM decentralization activities (Baumann, 1998). The multi-layered administrative and political competition and conflicts accompanying decentralization in India are also fuelled by problems in the relationship between the system of *panchayati raj* and newly evolved sectoral NRM institutions at the local level. The same is true for the relationship between different sectoral NRM institutions established within the same geographical area. Concerns noted in this respect include a lack of complementarity in the functioning of the different institutions and a lack of constructive interlinking between different institutions (Kant and Cooke, 1998). Instead, there is often a tendency to sub-sume local user groups into local government bodies, which may erode their effectiveness (Poffenberger and Singh, 1996). The reverse — sectoral NRM in-stitutions taking on the functions assigned to *panchayati raj* institutions — may also take place (Baumann, 1998). Evidently, therefore, where the democratic functioning of local bodies is impaired and internal political deadlocks occur, weaker user groups are disadvantaged in conflicts regarding resource alloca-tion. In such circumstances, decentralization may mean further empowerment of the powerful and the progressive weakening of the poor. At a range of dif-ferent institutional levels, new NRM policies and arrangements may thus con-stitute fresh targets for political gain and competition. Such anomalies may oc-cur particularly during transitions towards decentralization, though there is a danger they may turn into more permanent features.

In its attempts to create a more market-friendly economic framework, the Indian government has also been encouraging an increased role for the private sector, thus allowing resource-management regimes in various areas to be-come oriented towards, if not governed by, specific user categories of particu-lar environmental resources. For example, in several parts of India, poor owners of small ruminants and other resource users have been losing their customary access to village commons, as these areas have been given over to grass culti-vation by cooperatives of commercial dairy farmers (Doornbos and Gertsch, 1994). Similar selective group privatization has been noted in other commer-cial farming activities, and commercial woodland exploitation (Agarwal, 1992; Blair, 1996). Resource use clashes pertain not only to land-based resources, but also increasingly to maritime resources, over which artisanal fishermen have been competing with the mechanized sector for their livelihood (Kurien, 1992; Meynen, 1989). Similar to what has happened in the case of forests, this process has resulted in the formation of various social and political movements for the protection of the rights of the artisanal sector and the conservation of the resource base.

Clearly, conflicting pressures arise from the opening-up of local markets under the impact of globalization and liberalization on the one hand, and the demand to ensure equitable access to environmental resources to the weaker sections of local populations on the other. First, market forces may influence the incentives for collective action positively as well as negatively. Hobley and

Shah (1996: 5), for example, note the potentially positive role of market incentives in inducing local group-based NRM efforts. However, they also warn
that "markets are difficult to predict and products that have a high value today may equally have a low value tomorrow, possibly endangering the viability of resource management organizations." Moreover, differences in market
access among users of a particular resource are a crucial source of conflicting demands, and this may also constrain or jeopardize cooperation in NRM
(Kurian, 2001; Meynen, 1989). The more heterogeneous the resource-use interests and household endowments of a community, the more susceptible they
may be to such conflicting pressures. Out of fear of the squabbles that might
ensue, some Indian *panchayats* even appeared to be reluctant to engage in community-based forest management endeavours (Blair, 1996: 489). The influence
of community heterogeneity on the scope for community-based or collective
NRM may not always be negative, however. According to Hobley and Shah
(1996), it will depend largely on the representativeness and effectiveness of
management and decision-making structures.

Several authors stress that technocratic paradigms in and of themselves may
leave a strong imprint on current approaches towards decentralized and participatory NRM (Cleaver, 2000; Gauld, 2000; Gronow, 1995; Utting, 2001).
One of its implications is a selective targeting and mode of implementation of
environmental and sustainable development concerns. This can have far-reaching consequences, including the adoption of a divisible and fragmented perspective on "nature." Decentralized interventions in NRM tend to focus on
specific natural resources, like forests, wildlife, or water. The choice of specific
resources is strongly influenced by environmental and economic fads and fashions. Such a perspective treats specific natural resources as isolated systems. It
negates the nested and interdependent nature of ecosystems, and thus the need
for an integrated and holistic approach to ecosystem regeneration (Agarwal
and Narain, 2000; Uphoff, 1998).

Representing a further area of bureaucratic reification, communities and
user groups, which are conceptualized as spatially and socially bounded entities, are frequently put centre stage in conservation and resource management,
to the neglect of broader identities and wider relationships and their fluid and
ambiguous institutional boundaries. This tendency obscures how newly established or reconstituted and formalized institutional spaces are being used

politically for the sake of reshaping social, economic, and political relationships between genders, ethnic groups and the like in the interest of dominant parties (Mosse, 1997; Rashed, 1998). In addition, it negates the possibility that decentralizing resource management and use rights to relatively small,
spatially bounded, permanent units, if considered from a wider perspective,
may be counter-effective in terms of sustainability (Agrawal and Gibson, 1999;
Uphoff, 1998). The ways in which the above problems are a real threat to sustainability, not only in ecological but also in social terms, can be seen from
various case studies of newly established community forest- and watershed-
management systems in India. They reveal inter-village as well as intra-village
conflicts over boundaries, the barring of access to enclosed commons, and the
overriding of the rights of weaker communities or subgroups, such as tribals,
landless, herdsmen, women, and migrants, by more powerful ones (Ahluwalia,
1997; Poffenberger, 1996; Sarin, 1996). For example, in a study of a forest regeneration programme by Shah and Shah (1995), a decentralized village-based
approach to NRM is reported to have given rise to fierce confrontations between the different villages involved in the programme. This was due to the
fact that the most forest-dependent members of such villages came to raid the
forest areas of adjoining villages to allow for the regeneration of their own forest. The extent to which this situation threatened to disrupt the widespread
network of social relationships on which the sustainability of the village communities depended is very well portrayed by the following lament by one of
the village leaders concerned:

> I am wondering what we [Pingot people] are gaining from protecting our forests so reli-
> giously?… If it continues like this, every village around Pingot will be our enemy. Then
> their relatives in other villages will become our enemies as well. At this rate our daugh-
> ters in Pingot will never be able to get married. Who will want to marry an enemy's
> daughter? (Shah and Shah, 1995: 81)

It is not only in respect of community groups that sensitivity to the possible negative consequences of place-based boundary setting for sustainable
and equitable natural resource use and development has been frequently lacking. The same is true in respect of districts and local government units. As Veit
(1996: 1) notes with respect to the African context, "too often, local administrative boundaries are not conducive to or supportive of local-level socio-eco-

nomic development or environmental management." Instead, he recommends boundary setting, or "redistricting," as he calls it, "more sensitive to ecosystems and natural resource endowments" (p. 2). Elsewhere, the same discrepancy has been observed between the boundaries of specific ecosystems and those of respective local government units that should manage them. In the Indian context, a lack of dovetailing of the roles of different institutions with a formal or customary mandate to manage natural resources in a certain region adds to the complexity of boundary questions. Thus, in some areas competition and conflicts arising from the overlap of roles and/or jurisdictions appear to exist between *panchayats* and newly established watershed committees, and between the latter committees and the new forest protection committees. Competition and conflicts are also evident between these formal institutions and informal institutions operative in the same area (Baumann, 1998; Kant and Cooke, 1998). Evidently, decentralized sectoral approaches to "nature" and to "people" present a danger of producing a fragmented and disjointed approach to policy and governance. It is possible to end up with situations in which no institution has sufficient authority and scope for coordination and accommodation of the diversity of resource interests and/or the aggregate of formal and informal institutions with a resource management role.

Cumulatively, these factors would accentuate rather than diminish resource conflicts, the unsustainable use of certain natural resources, and social inequality. This danger is aggravated by the partial or complete exclusion from access to NRM endeavours of insufficiently represented or, indeed, non-represented interests and their likely reaction. These interests are likely to include female community members, mobile and/or transitory user groups, non-residential stakeholders, or villages located elsewhere within the geographical spread of the resource concerned. Women in particular are frequently excluded through representative systems of community institutions and organizations. Such institutions often accept only one member per household, and this is usually the formal head, the formal titleholder, or the "owner" of certain resources such as land, trees, or forest resources. These positions are largely occupied by men. Moreover, even without formal exclusion, women are often unable or unwilling to participate in formal mixed-gender meetings. Indeed, even if they do participate, they may be unable or unwilling to voice their views and concerns. This can be due to numerous factors, such as restrictions on women's mobility, skills, time, access and control of resources, and authority and constraints in the discursive interactions between men and women (Jackson, 1997; Mayoux, 1995: 246–47; Zwarteveen, 2001: 3–5). With such problems in mind, Meinzen-Dick and Zwarteveen (1997: 4), writing on south Asia but with wider relevance, conclude that attempts at improvement "cannot be left to local communities" but will need "external pressure, guidance and intervention." It can be added that it is not only local communities that need this kind of external pressure and support to improve their gender equity. The same is true for many state and NGO agencies engaged in NRM in the fields of agriculture, forestry, and water resources. Preferably, local women's movements and organizations with sufficient gender expertise in the areas concerned should take the lead in this, as they already do in various instances.

Another related, frequently reported, source of exclusion, with harmful implications extending beyond gender relations, is systems of representation in NRM that rely on constructs of property or usufruct that neglect the multidimensional nature of overlapping and nested rights to, and uses of, natural resources (Rocheleau and Edmunds, 1997). This problem has been long-standing. For example, Sundar (2000: 253) observes that in northern India in the early and mid-nineteenth century, village commons were established by enclosures, which annihilated existing communal relationships between highland and lowland cultivators. The same practice occurred during the Peruvian agrarian reform of the 1970s, when collectives were created in valleys of the Sierra with boundaries that negated the user rights of, and exchange relationships with, agro-pastoralists of the Alteplano. Again, recent community-based NRM approaches exhibit similar tendencies of exclusion, which impinge especially on mobile and non-residential user groups like pastoralists, shifting cultivators, seasonal gatherers and migrants. An important reason for the latter phenomenon is, as earlier suggested, that the enclosure of commons is frequently linked conceptually to a notion of local community, which is conceived in terms of "permanent, year-round residency" (McLain and Jones, 1998: 1). This community is thought to have a clear-cut, "identifiable relationship to an identifiable resource," to use the words of Sundar (2000: 254). Other characteristics commonly attributed to the community are that it "consists of stable married households" and "privileges the male links of property as against the multiple other links that individual households share with their affines"

(Sundar, 2000: 254). Clearly, these assumptions tend to particularly harm the resource-use interests of women.

Thus, the analytical, empirical, and policy prioritization of going local through decentralization and participation may fail to place the institutional issues concerned within a wider complex and network of interactions, making it difficult to capture the combined effects of various kinds of institutional interventions. Questions about the interrelations, interactions, and possible contradictions among different institutional arrangements for resource management certainly appear to have received less attention than they deserve. The same is true as to whether there are sufficiently meaningful mechanisms in place for overall resource use coordination, including the handling of changing resource claims, resource conflicts, and instances of unwarranted exclusion.

IV. Conclusion

One of the basic problems encountered in NRM decentralization efforts concerns the contradictory dynamics arising from policy inconsistencies. The pressures exerted by global economic forces and processes, and the policy prescriptions of the international financial agencies, often do not leave states much choice except to adopt liberalization, privatization, and market deregulation. The weaker the resource base of national economies and the more they suffer from debt burdens and political instability, the less room to manoeuvre they will have vis-à-vis these international pressures and demands. Moreover, sometimes the same international agencies that prescribe economic policies favouring opportunities for private capital to lay claims on and exploit valuable natural resources also advocate community-based NRM approaches presumed to strengthen the resource base and livelihood options of poor people. Thus, policy inconsistencies at national levels, and the kind of economic reforms and institutional restructuring processes they have given rise to, reflect and are strongly conditioned by interactions with international actors and factors. Only strong states, which have over time maintained a relative autonomy and capacity to govern, would be able to manoeuvre in international and national arenas in ways that will allow national policy reforms to be consistent with the requirements of truly democratic decentralization. This, of course, is under the assumption that they have the political will and determination to do so.

An equally basic problem standing in the way of meaningful NRM decentralization concerns structural inequalities, which prevent politically and economically marginalized classes and categories from effectively voicing and defending their resource interests and claims vis-à-vis powerful competitors and in decision-making processes at large. In many countries, redressing such inequalities would require interventions in production and property systems in ways counter to the dominant forces and processes at work. With respect to presently favoured property systems, it should be noted, for example, that even those rural people who are involved in NRM activities under community-based or co-management programs often do not have secure, long-term property or usufruct rights to the natural resources they are expected to manage.

Yet another point about NRM decentralization is that decentralizing state organs should not be allowed to abandon their final responsibility for natural resource policy, if the gains from decentralization of decision-making and community participation are to materialize. Instead, they should ensure that the decentralized organs command sufficient powers, including financial and judicial powers, to execute their responsibilities adequately. Moreover, with many different institutional initiatives for resource management at the local or micro levels, there is a need for adequate mechanisms at a common or central level that can handle potentially conflicting or even exclusionary NRM initiatives. For such mechanisms to be meaningful, however, requires taking account of the kinds of interests that dominate policy processes. Interest in the promotion of grassroots involvement in NRM should not be allowed to degenerate into a cover for participation by powerful local interests to capture and exploit a particular resource base.

To add to the complexity, it is important to anticipate that beyond broad structural similarities different situations may also present different kinds of contradictions. There is a need for solutions sensitive to the situation rather than those that apply uniform NRM models. For example, in some resource conflict situations, state agencies representing a particular interest may themselves figure as one of the key parties in conflict over access to environmental resources. Thus, forest departments have been known to try to prevent forest dwellers from encroaching upon the forest so that they can harvest its products (Matose, 1997; Pathak, 1994). In other situations, the state may find itself called upon to protect the weaker interests of resource-dependent communities vis-à-vis more powerful private agents capturing the resource benefits. While the shaping or reshaping of political arenas, through decentralization or otherwise, will give rise to changing opportunity structures to different interests, the precise alignment of weak and strong may vary from case to case, which calls for differentiated responses.

In short, if decentralization of NRM were to stand any chance of success, a variety of demands must be made on the process of decentralization. However, these can hardly be realized without well-organized local bodies and civil society groups capable of articulating and effectively pursuing the diversity of local interests, particularly those of politically marginalized categories. By itself this is difficult enough, yet the other condition for meaningful decentralization is even more problematic. This is the building of powerful countervailing forces at the global level to achieve a more enabling global environment that can sustain, if not promote, effective NRM strategies at different levels. The latter would require a fundamental reversal of the way policy priorities are presently established, which, however, will take time and perseverance. In the interim, the most one may expect is no more than piecemeal gains within a framework of continuing contradictions and contestations between and among global, local, and intermediate interests.

Footnotes

1   The authors thank Dr. K.N. Nair of the Center for Development Studies, Trivandrum, India, for his contributions to a provisional collaborative project outline, which served as a point of departure for the present chapter. Thanks for the constructive criticisms are also due to colleagues at the Centre for Development Research, Copenhagen, where Wicky Meynen worked on a preliminary draft of the paper.

Chapter 15

THE IMPORTANCE OF CONTEXT FOR ECONOMIC POLICY: THE CASE OF SCOTLAND

Alexander C Dow and Sheila C Dow

I. Introduction

WITHIN the social and economic development literature modernism can be thought of as the general application of a process of market-driven modernization through expanding commodification, enhanced specialization, coercive competition, and the binding constraint of profitability. It is based upon the experience of developed countries, and is expected to bring economic development to those countries that are not yet developed. This approach can be closely associated with the structural adjustment programmes of the International Monetary Fund (IMF) and the World Bank. However, as the modernization process that these two institutions confidently promoted was being implemented in developing countries there was an increasing loss of confidence in government intervention in the developed world. The rise of free market politics and the emergence of a neo-conservative consensus in the 1980s and 1990s in the developed market economies provided an impetus for significant shifts in the ways in which governments intervened in economies.

Loss of confidence in the ways government managed the economy mirrored a cultural trend: postmodernism. Although postmodernism was manifest across a wide range of areas, such as architecture and literature, it also found its way into the social sciences (Doherty et al., 1992). In economic theory, for example, the shift of focus to a reductionist form of macroeconomics could be taken to be a sign of postmodernism (Dow, 1991). In development theory, postmodernism took the form of privileging the knowledge and experience of those in the local situation to which policy was directed over the knowledge and experience of outsiders such as those from the IMF (Lee, 1994). There were, indeed, also specific critiques of the whole notion of the development expert (Parpart, 1995).

Across a range of disciplines, including economics and development studies, modernism and postmodernism have struggled and continue to struggle for dominance. A central contention of this chapter is that a middle way is required. This is because a pure modernist approach or a pure postmodernist approach has been unable to provide adequate grounds for policy action and, ultimately, the role of theory is to inform policy action (Dow, 2001). Postmodernism has not been a development panacea because the local context is constrained by external forces, and policy advice and action therefore require something beyond the local context so beloved of postmodernists. At the same time however it is clear that lessons that are learnt from one context will impinge on another context, albeit in ways that require case-by-case justification, and which thus demonstrate the fallacy of a purely modernist approach to policy advice and action. More generally, then, while there is a role for theory in informing economic policy advice and action, and while this theory cannot be universal, it must nonetheless abstract from the local situation in order to shed light on it.

In this light, we start this chapter by considering the philosophical and methodological basis for a middle ground approach to theory and policy advice which is neither modernist nor postmodernist but which is rooted in critical realism. This approach steers between looking for general analytical principles on the one hand and ways of adapting these general principles in order to enhance the understanding of specific contexts, within the overarching aim of designing more effective policy action. We call this approach structured pluralism. We then make the discussion more concrete by considering the case of Scotland, which is a small open economy within which there are development disparities. The discussion focusses upon how general economic forces shape the policy possibilities of the specific context. The new opportunities offered by the reinstitution of the Scottish Parliament in 1999, albeit with limited powers, provides a particular edge to questions raised in the discussion, not only of economic development, but also of social transformation.

II. Critical realism and the methodology of economic policy

In analysing the planning approach of the Schreyer government in the Canadian province of Manitoba in the 1970s, Loxley (1990) articulated a position within the middle ground between centralized planning and the free market. He introduces the analysis as follows:

> There is a growing consensus that centralized material planning, while perhaps imperative in the earlier years of structural transformation, is cumbersome, unwieldy and far too autocratic as a method of planning a sophisticated economy en route to socialism. Thus observers are giving sympathetic consideration to blends of direct controls, and the use of market forces (Loxley, 1990: 318).

and concludes:

> The state must be prepared to reject the *primacy* of private enterprise and the free rein of the market and it must be able to create supportive, nonhierarchical, nonelitist central planning agencies, while at the same time being prepared to devolve decision taking and funding to both regional and community levels (Loxley, 1990: 332, emphasis added).

This middle ground between central planning and the market, between the macroeconomic and the microeconomic, and, in effect, between modernism and postmodernism, appears to be consistent with one approach to economic methodology that has its origins in Marxism: critical realism. The fullest statement of critical realism can be found in Lawson (1997; see also Fleetwood, 1999). Critical realism is derived from the philosophy of transcendental realism as stated by Bhaskar (1975), which emphasizes the importance of distinguishing between the levels of existence (ontology) and knowledge (epistemology), and in so doing separating the nature of the real world from our knowledge of it. A starting point of the approach is the proposition, in line with postmodernism, that our knowledge is socially constructed. Thus, however much we aim to identify true knowledge about the real world we cannot be sure of having done so, or that others have not found equally valid accounts of reality.

Nonetheless, it is the nature of the real world that determines whether or not there is scope for identifying economic laws. In particular, the law-like behaviour depicted by modernist orthodox economic theory is only possible if the economic system is closed. More specifically, it must satisfy the conditions of extrinsic closure, in which there are no unaccounted outside influences, because randomness of relationships implies knowledge of randomness. It must also satisfy the conditions of intrinsic closure, in which the components of the theory, that is to say individual human beings, are independent with given interrelations.

Transcendental realism involves a philosophical argument that the real world is not closed in this way—rather it is open and organic. Neither of the conditions of closure necessary for modernist economics is met: the economic system is understood to evolve, so that not all relevant variables can be identified in advance. That evolution is primarily the outcome of changes in behaviour and institutions, where individuals are understood as socially interdependent as well as creative. It is, it should be stated, not necessary to arrive at this ontology in the same way as transcendental realism. Rather, the particular importance of critical realism for economics is the implications that arise when starting from an ontology of the real world that is open and organic.

Critical realists seek to identify the underlying causal forces that generate the actual events we experience, and in turn the empirical data which are the primary focus of modernist closed-system analysis. These forces are understood as powers or tendencies, not necessarily in operation in any one period, and potentially operating in different directions. Specific prediction of data series is therefore not seen as feasible, useful or even relevant, based as it is on a necessarily closed structure. Rather, policy advice involves identifying and understanding the range of causal forces that might operate in a particular context. Since the ultimate goal is to effect social transformation, an understanding of the mechanisms currently in operation, or potentially in operation, is essential in the formulation of policy advice.

In seeking to identify and understand the range of causal forces that might operate in a particular context, critical realism stresses the need for a pluralist methodology (Salanti and Screpanti, 1997). The pluralism can involve classical logic and formal mathematics, but can also involve institutional analysis, historical analysis, textual analysis, questionnaire surveys, and so on. This methodological pluralism allows it to steer a course between looking for general analytical principles on the one hand and adapting these general principles to enhance understanding of particular contexts on the other, with the aim of designing effective policy. We call this approach structured pluralism.

This approach was made specific in Clive Thomas's (1974) volume, focussed on Tanzania, but drawing on experience and analysis developed elsewhere, and designed to be adapted to other circumstances. Thomas focussed on the context of the small open economy, which he defined in terms of power relations rather than trade exposure. He thus immediately puts the focus on underlying causal mechanisms, enveloping the economic in the social, in a manner also characteristic of critical realist analyses. Further, in concluding, he refers to Sweezy's assumptions concerning the transition to socialism. In doing so, he spells out the same kind of middle ground between particularity and generality that we have been discussing in relation to structured pluralism:

(1) There is no such thing as a general theory of the transition between social systems. This is not because relatively little attention has been paid to the subject—though this is undoubtedly true—but because each transition is a unique historical process which must be analysed and explained as such.

(2) Nevertheless, a comparative study of transition can be extremely valuable. In particular, the study of past transitions can help us to ask fruitful questions about present and possible future transitions, to recognise similarities and differences, and to appreciate the historicity and totality of the process under examination (Thomas, 1974: 308).

In what follows, we consider how a structured pluralist analysis of the sort espoused by Thomas, Loxley, and critical realists more generally, might be extended to understanding the particularities of the case of Scotland.

III. The case of Scotland

In considering the specific context of Scotland, we start by describing key features of this context, and then offer a brief analysis. The emphasis of the analysis is on the complex interdependence between, on the one hand, generality and, on the other, particularity, in order to stress both the complex set of causal forces that structure Scotland's economic development and the constraints and opportunities for policy makers seeking to intervene in order to reshape the pattern of Scottish economic development. This analysis, drawing on an approach informed by the experience of small open economies in the developing world, as well as in Canada, will also be contrasted with a mode of economic analysis that is rooted in the principles of neo-conservativism.

i. Scotland's political economy

The key sectors in the Scottish economy are evident from an inspection of the national accounts (Caledonian Blue Book, 1997). For a quarter of a century the Scottish economy has been driven by oil, electronics, whisky and financial services. As elsewhere, services have grown in importance, and now the value of business and financial services exceed the value of manufacturing in the Scottish national accounts. All of these sectors are focussed on markets outside Scotland, so the Scottish economy is much more dependent on external demand than the UK economy as a whole. The public sector—education, health and social services—is quantitatively of less importance than either of the above measured by gross domestic product (GDP), but is the most important sector for providing employment and is relatively large compared with the rest of the UK. It is generally but not universally the case that per capita income is lower than the UK average, and unemployment higher, and that there is greater volatility in both variables.

After a century of administrative devolution, in a major constitutional innovation Scotland achieved political devolution in 1999 with the establishment of the Scottish Parliament in Edinburgh and the formation of the Scottish Executive, the term "government" being reserved for the Westminster Parliament in London. The architects of the new devolved settlement hoped for an improvement in Scottish economic performance as a result of more finely tuned economic policies and better, regular scrutiny of them (Hassan and Warhurst, 1999). This in turn, it was hoped, would create a positive dynamic in the Scottish economy, which would act as a spur to economic growth. For some, though, the broader political goal was for policy to accord more closely with what were perceived to be particularly Scottish culture and values. In other words, some form of social transformation was envisaged.

Only some of the powers residing in Westminster were devolved to Scotland, with macroeconomic and monetary policy continuing to reside with the Treasury in London and with the Bank of England, although there may be an increased regional awareness associated with the new arrangements. The powers of the former Scottish Office, which administered Scotland, were inherited by the Scottish Executive. The devolved powers include running the National Health Service in Scotland, education and training, local government, housing, economic development, environmental matters, agriculture, forestry and fishing, statistics and buried treasure. In addition to macroeconomic concerns, other important economic omissions are social security, including pensions, unemployment benefit and safety net programmes, employment legislation, immigration and UK strategic transport developments. Scottish "quangos," such as Scottish Enterprise, the leading development institution, also came under devolved Executive control.

The Scottish budget arrives as a block grant from Westminster, largely determined from the historical allocation to the Scottish Office, with ongoing adjustments. Tax powers are limited to the possibility of raising or lowering the UK rate of income tax by up to three percentage points, although so far politicians in Edinburgh have shied away from utilising this new policy tool. Thus, with the exception of its unused income tax powers, the Scottish Executive can in theory affect the composition of public expenditure, not its size. In fact, by squeezing local authorities and forcing them to augment their incomes from their tax base and charges, some leeway does exist for the Executive to switch expenditures, which are financed ultimately by higher taxes and charges. No long-term borrowing is permitted.

All told, it appears that this constitutional arrangement institutes a level of government in Scotland with rather less economic power than the provinces of Canada or the states of the USA. Elsewhere in the UK the Welsh Assembly has less power than the Scottish Parliament, and in Northern Ireland the Assembly has more. At the same time, the experience of devolution has, of course, been coloured by a particular political configuration, namely that the Labour Party has the largest representation in the Scottish Parliament as well as a majority in Westminster. The scope for the Scottish Executive to pursue different policies has thus been heavily circumscribed by this configuration of political power.

ii.   *Evaluating the capacity for social and economic transformation*

Given the short length of experience with devolution, it is too early to comprehensively assess how it has affected the Scottish economy. What can however be evaluated, in a highly preliminary fashion, is whether the Scottish Executive can effect social and economic transformation. It would be hoped that the Executive would, on some set of criteria, have improved Scottish economic performance. However, there may be larger economic forces at work, that Scotland cannot influence, that determine whether the country prospers or languishes.

In undertaking such an evaluation, much depends on how the Scottish economy is analyzed. The predominant form of analysis, both at the UK level and the Scottish level, is based on the neo-conservative consensus. Thus, the Treasury (2001) paper on regional economies within the UK focusses on productivity differentials and supply-side solutions, while the Scottish Executive (2000) strategy also focusses on the supply side. The Executive portfolio dealing with the economy is the Ministry for Enterprise and Lifelong Learning, while the bodies charged with promoting economic development are called Scottish Enterprise, and Highlands and Islands Enterprise. Again, supply-side factors are emphasized. This approach thus presumes uniformity in underlying forces that allow a common approach regardless of context. What promotes enterprise and increased productivity may vary in the detail from region to region, but the underlying theory offered at both the UK level and the Scottish level is a modernist, universal one.

Here, instead of adopting the modernist analytical perspective used by the Treasury and the Executive, we want to consider the underlying causal forces which generate the actual events that we identified above as the object of critical realism and analysis. This is an attempt to use structured pluralism to draw on the identification of causal mechanisms from other, similar, economies' experiences as a starting point in the identification of the particular mechanisms that are the driving forces in the Scottish economy. We therefore consider in turn the following four forces as a basis for analysis: globalization, peripherality, depopulation, and the tradition of civic society.

a. Globalization

The identification of globalization as a significant causal force in a wide range of contexts has been the intellectual fashion of the 1990s, although there are some signs that a revision of the consensus regarding its importance has begun. Without doubt multinational corporations have attained unprecedented power over world change in the economic and political sphere. Yet it is not boundless. Major international firms such as Enron, WorldCom and Arthur Andersen fail, while others, such as Marconi, are very much diminished. Authors question the inevitable nature of global corporate power (Hirst and Thompson, 1999), or argue that the phenomenon is regional rather than global (Rugman, 2000).

In pre-devolution Scotland, neo-conservative policies had been pursued, focussed on embracing multinational capital, offering a range of incentives and dedicating a tax-funded institution, Locate in Scotland, to its attraction. The inflow of US, Japanese, and Korean electronics firms led to the wryly named "silicon glen" phenomenon, which has created jobs and exports for Scotland over the last two decades (Peat and Boyle, 1999). Undoubtedly a success at one level, the major disappointment has been the almost total lack of techno-logical spin-offs from these firms to indigenous industry (Scottish Executive, 2000). There has been, in short, a lack of demand for new skills by indigenous industry. This has happened despite the best efforts of Scottish Enterprise to encourage networking. The dynamic of self-sustaining economic development has been furthered less than the immediate goal of job creation.

The devolved Executive has recognised this problem, and has launched a new policy called "A Smart Successful Scotland." Still leaning towards neo-conservativism, the policy's vision is one of more selective recruitment of mul-tinational firms, with a view to forcing as far as possible technological spin-offs to domestic firms. In this spirit the agency responsible for attracting foreign capital has been renamed Scottish Development International.

Useful as this reorientation may be, it must be asked whether the new policy framework is grounded in the reality facing Scotland at this time. Globalization is still seen as the basis of a solution to Scotland's economic problems, rather than, at least in part, a cause. Further, it is really very curious that, after twenty years of continuous cuts in funding for higher education (measured in re-sources per student), a trend halted only in the last year, the major thrust of development policy in Scotland has been directed towards a transformation which requires technological and business skills of a high order to absorb new technologies and organizational modes (Zanfei, 2000). Indeed, the reduced funding for higher education itself reflects the neo-conservative agenda, with universities increasingly being encouraged to earn resources by undertaking market-based activities, a strategy expressed in terms of improving the pro-ductivity of teaching and research. The thinking is clear in the combining of Enterprise with Lifelong Learning in one portfolio. However, a lack of clarity in the understanding of how knowledge is created through education, and the mechanisms through which knowledge feeds into the economic process, may mean that the new policy will fare no better than the old. Indeed, there is the downside risk that, footloose as global capital now is, the new policy may do worse. Recent closures of multinational plants in Scotland demonstrate clearly the sensitivity of silicon glen to decisions made elsewhere for reasons not always related to productive efficiency.

How well-founded is a policy based on the linkage of skilled graduates to technological innovation and so to improved economic growth? In the most authoritative recent review of the literature, Krueger and Lindahl made this assessment:

> A large body of research using individual-level data on education and income provides robust evidence of a substantial payoff to investment in education, especially for those who traditionally complete low levels of schooling… The macro-economic evidence of externalities in terms of technological progress from investments in higher education seems to us more fragile (Krueger and Lindahl, 2001: 1130).

b. Peripherality

According to the neo-conservative agenda, international capital flows and technology transfers in free markets are the vehicles for economic convergence, whatever the context. Remote economies are the beneficiaries of capital and technology imported from the centre. Physical remoteness is, however, a slippery concept in a context of globalization and advanced telecommunications technology, when sub-editors based in India can directly work for London publishers using online technology. Nonetheless, for Scotland, with the continuing importance of the manufacturing and natural resource sectors, physical transport links—to England, to mainland Europe and to North America—are of major importance. If the new devolved arrangements lead to an improved infrastructure, economic activity may improve as real and travel time costs of operating businesses in Scotland decline. Of course, these cost reductions work both ways, and Scottish businesses may face increased competition from elsewhere if effective improvement occurs, just as efficient capital markets can ease capital outflows as effectively as inflows. The least encouraging aspect of the situation is an absence of debate, an absence of the consideration of context and its effects, as to whether Scotland will be a net beneficiary of expenditure on externally focussed transport infrastructure.

Peripherality is perhaps a clearer concept than remoteness, focussing as it does on power relationships in their spatial dimension. It has been analysed, particularly in the Latin American literature, in terms of dependency relations regarding trade and investment (Frank, 1967). In the case of Scotland, pricing of raw materials in particular reflects power in markets. More specifically, in the case of oil, unusually, much of the power is held by the multinational producers but is exercised by them outside the economy, despite the major implications for the Scottish economy. Inward investment too is a matter of power relations. It is a commonplace argument that branch plant closures cannot fully be explained by productivity differentials, and that the ability to use power may be a factor in its use by international corporations.

Knowledge is a central feature of power relations. Knowledge of the future is inevitably held with uncertainty, and different knowledge is held by different parties. It is an important issue in globalization, in that decision-making occurs increasingly remotely from the location of production, so that knowledge of local conditions is inevitably more limited. This is a particular issue for the provision of finance, in that, in many instances, limited local knowledge by firms and banks may lead to enhanced volatility of capital flows when international firms are confronted with sharp reversals in expectations. Whether this may be the case in Scotland is an open question. There has been, as mentioned above, an expansion of financial sector activity located mainly, though not exclusively, in Edinburgh and Glasgow. However, despite the huge sums intermediated through the banks, insurance companies and trust companies, very little of this investment, as much of it ultimately becomes, enters the Scottish economy. Scotland benefits substantially, of course, from the intermediary function, in terms of jobs and added income, but the likely benefits from, let us say, an investment boost to economic growth are much less apparent. Perhaps the reality of footloose capital precludes overt taxes on these activities, other than those that already apply in the UK's level playing field. However, the devolved settlement means that no such power resides in the Edinburgh Parliament in any event. More surprising, given the cohesiveness of the Scottish financial sector within a cohesive Scottish society, is the absence of informal mechanisms to leach more of the funds managed in Scotland into Scottish enterprise. Here, peripherality may be an issue: Scotland's volatile economic growth over the last century may have led it, in common with many other peripheral economies, to have a relatively high liquidity preference as a general rule. The term liquidity preference is being used, in this instance, in its broadest sense, meaning the extent of the willingness to go illiquid by increasing physical investment, and by taking on debt, as well as the disposition of savings. In other words, a peripheral and volatile economy can be characterised by lower investment, lower domestic demand and lower borrowing to finance these activities, as well as the more conventional expression of liquidity preference in holding assets that are more liquid. Taken together these factors can lead to lower economic growth (Dow, 1990).

The neo-conservative view is that capital flows promote economic convergence. If productivity is relatively low in Scotland, then net capital outflows will reduce the level of investment, and thereby increase the marginal productivity of capital to levels experienced elsewhere. Lower rates of growth are thus to be expected in the transition. However, over most of the postwar period, with the exception of the early 1990s, Scottish rates of economic growth seriously lagged behind the UK average, buoyed as that is by the prosperous southeast of England. This has continued to be the case after devolution, although within Scotland the experience is uneven, with hot spots around Edinburgh contrasting with the duller economic performance of the west of Scotland.

c. Depopulation

Economic growth is the outcome not only of capital growth but also of population growth, although outmigration is another aspect of the neo-conservative adjustment mechanism for lagging regions (see Courchene, 1981). After a brief reversal in the early 1990s the century-long experience of net out-migration of population from Scotland has resumed (Webster, 2000). Population has been the subject of a recent report by the Government Actuary in consultation with the Registrar General for Scotland (Government Actuary, 2001). Their forecast is for a gradually declining Scottish population over the next forty years, dropping below five million by 2021 and trending through 4.6 million by 2040. Declining fertility and a death rate, which, though declining, will be higher than that forecast for England and Wales, drives these predictions. Despite the overall tendency of falling mortality, a social clue as to the nature of life in Scotland now is that for males in the 25–34 age range mortality is predicted to increase slightly in the early years of the projection, reflecting current trends. The poor health, relative to developed country standards, of much of the Scottish population is a matter of national concern. Put together with out-migration, we have a force for worsening economic growth in the future. Certainly, productivity growth can offset the effects of declining fertility rates, as Clarence Barber (1979) argued with reference to Canada. But net out-migration and increasing mortality rates for certain groups are symptoms of underlying forces which themselves are likely to undermine attempts to raise productivity.

d. Civic Society

The three forces considered so far are curious, in that according to the neo-conservative perspective each can be discussed in connection with market forces as a mechanism for economic convergence. However, rather than emphasizing the generality of the processes at work, we have referred to arguments in terms of economic divergence, depending on the particularities of specific circumstances. The fourth causal mechanism is not something which features in neo-conservative discussion in economics: the tradition of a civic society, which has been identified in Scotland, and incorporated within the conceptual framework of the Scottish political economy tradition (Dow, Dow and Hutton, 1997; 2000). This ethos sees a legitimate role for various groups to participate in and shape the changes of an evolving society. It is based on a theory of human nature in which man is fundamentally a social being. The churches, the trade unions, business, the universities and the civil service are all seen as entitled to a voice in shaping outcomes. Indeed, in the form of a Constitutional Convention, such participation was instrumental in shaping the devolved constitutional arrangements.

Neo-conservatism has not affected public attitudes toward this tradition in Scotland as it has in many other English-speaking nations. In this respect Scotland remains somewhat closer to France or Germany than to the south of England, the USA or Canada. Transformation can be discussed in terms wider than individual prosperity without reducing the audience to a minority. Aspirations in Executive publications are often community-oriented. Criteria for success devised for the development quangos, Scottish Enterprise and

Highlands and Islands Enterprise, are multi-faceted. Indeed, there are successes in those dimensions. For example, unemployment has been falling in the late 1990s: the Scottish rate of employment stands at 72 per cent, compared with an Organization for Economic Cooperation and Development average of 68 per cent. Nursery education has expanded rapidly recently: 97 per cent of 4 year olds were in grant-funded places by 2000 (Scottish Council Foundation, 2001). Yet, that being so, it must be admitted that the position of the Scottish economy is precarious. North Sea oil and gas has provided a regular stimulus to the economy for a quarter of a century, but at last a steady decline seems inevitable. Silicon glen is a genuine achievement, but technological drift into indigenous Scottish enterprise has, as has already been noted, been limited. The key policy of Scottish Enterprise, the development agency, to promote small business start-ups, has not succeeded, and has now been modified (Dow and Kirk, 2000).

There is in fact a contradiction between the continued importance of civic society for Scotland and the hope that devolution would effect a social transformation. It was hoped that devolution would empower society, even though the prevailing analysis of the Scottish economy is based on an individualistic understanding of the rational economic men who make up that society. Indeed, that the latter analysis generates solutions from a universal theoretical framework is widely accepted without question. Such acceptance is deeply problematic. Where economic policy analysis in Scotland does focus on the local context, other than as providing detail for the universal framework, therefore, it does so without drawing on theory. For example, the entry on economic development in a collection assessing the first year of the Scottish Parliament (Hassan and Warhurst, 2000) was solely addressed to administrative arrangements. The globalization of ideas in the form of the neo-conservative agenda has created the impression that there is no other basis for economic analysis.

Crucially, it is in the general unwillingness to engage in serious debate about the analysis of the Scottish economy that the threat to the future of this process lies. The "chattering classes" operate in fractured networks interacting more with the south of the UK and the world than within Scotland. In universities a bureaucratic research assessment exercise used to allocate central funding tends to give less reward to work of local significance than to the international; globalization is at work through the academy. Thus, what should be an evolutionary mechanism with respect to ideas on the Scottish economy is missing. It is in debate and interaction that the theory illuminating a Scottish transformation can be devised to suit the particulars of the present time. That there is only a limited will, and a set of institutional mechanisms, to encourage this evolution is perhaps a mechanism of globalization as well as a cause for concern for the future direction of the Scottish civic society.

V. Conclusion

In this brief account of the reality of Scotland today certain points emerge. The picture drawn is selective and partial, reflecting a particular view of the reality of the current situation. This groundedness does not in our opinion preclude insights from theoretical perspectives, though these will also be selective and partial. Indeed, without such reference there is no way to address the fundamental issues and to achieve an informed understanding on which suitable policy can be built. What we see in this case study is a modernist application of economic theory that gives primacy to supply-side productivity considerations, alongside a postmodern focus on local detail without the benefit of any theory. The local focus derives from an understanding of reality that is often at odds with prevailing economic analysis. Unless the resulting contradictions are addressed, little progress can be made.

What we have attempted to highlight here is the importance of challenging the modernist approach to economic theory as a basis for development strategy in particular contexts. We have also, however, demonstrated that the postmodern focus on the local offers little by way of explanation. There is instead a need to outline a complex reality in which particularity and generality intersect. We have attempted to do this, being guided in our efforts by a structured pluralism rooted in critical realism. Thus, in examining the Scottish economy, rather than emphasizing solely the supply-side factors of the neo-conservative consensus, we have examined them within the context of four underlying causal mechanisms partially derived from development economics that, in our view, shape the current prospects for the Scottish economy. Those factors were globalization, peripherality, depopulation and civic society. In our view, and as we hope we have demonstrated, the analysis that can be undertaken using these factors is both rich and provocative for policy makers. However, we accept that the approach we have used is a decidedly minority viewpoint. The economics profession has been successful in promoting the view that there is no alternative, so that there is widespread public perception that there is no solution to any of the contradictions between theory and local reality. However, as Loxley (1990), in his theoretical, policy and practical work has demonstrated, the solution lies in understanding that local reality, drawing on knowledge built up from experience of other contexts, and developing an analysis specific to that context.

PART 4

Alternative Budgets and the Democratization of Economic Policy-Making

Chapter 16

FISCAL POLICY: THE DEMOCRATIC CASE FOR GENDER BUDGETS

A Haroon Akram-Lodhi

I. Introduction

OVER the course of the last 25 years there has been a paradigm shift in mainstream economic policy in the north and in the south. The concern with living standards that characterized the "golden age" of capitalism between 1945 and 1973 came under sustained attack in the mid- to late 1970s. In an effort to reduce inflation, northern governments, led by the United Kingdom and the United States, imposed austere monetary policies that ratcheted up interest rates, crowded out investment, and increased unemployment (Armstrong, Glyn, and Harrison, 1991). At the same time, governments actively sought to squeeze the state by reducing its spending, privatizing state-owned enterprises, and allowing public goods to be provided by the private sector. The transformation in the parameters of economic policy in the north was followed by a similar transformation in the south. The debt crisis initiated by Mexico's default in August 1982 and the introduction of the first formal structural adjustment programme in Ghana in 1983 heralded a transformation that, by the late 1980s, had affected, to greater and lesser degrees, Africa, Latin America, Asia and the newly emerging transition economies (Loxley, 1998). The quest to fulfil basic needs, which had been a central policy objective in the south since the late 1960s, was abandoned in all but name. In the effort to cut budgetary and balance-of-payments deficits, currencies were devalued, government spending was slashed, and parastatals privatized (George and Sabelli, 1994). Thus, there was a worldwide shift towards the adoption of neo-conservative market-friendly policies predicated upon external trade liberalization, internal deregulation, the globalization of economic activity, and the creation of a smaller, private-sector supportive state (World Bank, 1993).

The impact of adjustment on the social sector, in both north and south, was severe. Governments first cut social sector spending and then sought to entice the private sector into social sector provision by fostering an environment conducive to the generation of profits (Caufield, 1996; Lipietz, 1992). Increasingly, social policy came to be seen as a residual. The fiscal envelope available to a government determined the depth and breadth of the commitment governments were willing to make to the social sector, and the private sector was allowed to provide those areas of social policy that fell outside the envelope. In this way, social policy became an outcome of the macroeconomic policy stance formulated by finance ministries.

At the same time, finance ministries became increasingly technocratic. Rules were established to limit their freedom of action, under the rubric of the overarching need for a stable economic framework for business. This was most clearly witnessed in Europe, where the European Union's Growth and Stability Pact placed major constraints on the formulation and implementation of fiscal policy (McGiffen, 2001). It was also witnessed, to a lesser extent, in the United States, where rules capping discretionary spending were introduced in 1990. More widely, there were proposals, particularly from neo-conservative think-tanks, in a number of countries, for the creation of independent financial agencies that would manage fiscal policy according to predetermined guidelines, mirroring the creation of independent central banks that controlled monetary policy. Similarly, it was witnessed in the creation of authorities in a number of countries in the north and the south that implemented key aspects of fiscal policy, such as the collection of revenues (World Bank, 2002c). In the south, these authorities were, in part, promoted by the rising number of elite local policy-makers who had been educated in orthodox economics in universities in the United States, and who had, as a consequence, adopted a neo-conservative outlook. The authorities were also, however, promoted by neo-conservative international financial institutions.

The shift towards technocratic policy formulation and implementation was deeply depoliticizing, as it was meant to be. The key strategic economic issues facing countries became submerged in a sea of seemingly drab economic details regarding the approval of particular actions, the resolution of faceless disputes, and the issuing of complex directives. In the world of the technocrats, "[W]e decide on something, leave it lying around and wait and see what happens. If no one kicks up a fuss, because most people don't understand what has been decided, we continue step by step until there is no turning back (*The Economist*, 14 September 2002).

Technocrats generally believe their analysis and policy proposals are, at the macroeconomic level, gender-neutral (Sen, 2000). They are not. Policy has the potential to broaden or narrow gender-based differences in incomes, assets, health, education, and living standards. In so doing, policy can make some groups of men and/or women relatively better off, while other groups of men and/or women become relatively worse off. It is not so much that increasingly technocratic macroeconomic policy is gender-neutral, but rather, that it is gender-blind. Technocratic policy-makers fail to realize that "(state) funds are allocated by individuals whose social identities shape their perception of priorities" (Folbre, 1997: 271). Technocratic policy makers also fail to realize that men and women are the basis upon which their interventions are played out. They fail to appreciate how asymmetries between men and women can be reduced or can be reinforced as a result of their interventions (Hanmer and Akram-Lodhi, 1998).

II. Gender blind macroeconomics

According to a standard undergraduate economics textbook, macroeconomic policy seeks "to affect the performance of the economy as a whole....[The government] levies taxes, commissions spending, and influences the money supply, interest rates, and the exchange rate" (Begg, Fischer, and Dornbusch, 1994: 341). The purpose of this is to promote sustainable increases in national output, and in so doing foster full employment, income increases, and price stability. Sustainability requires that, over the course of the business cycle, government expenditure does not exceed government income. It also requires that the trend in the balance of payments produces no structural trade deficit. The focus of macroeconomic policy becomes the employment level, the price level, the rate of growth of income, the magnitude of the government budgetary deficit or surplus, and the magnitude of the balance-of-payments deficit or surplus.

That gender should be examined within the context of macroeconomic policy might seem obvious. There is now some acceptance of the proposition that "the macroeconomic context within which expenditure, taxation, and budgetary decisions are made can have gender dimensions" (Cagatay, Elson, and Grown, 1995; World Bank, 2001a: 270). Indeed, the two key reasons that are usually cited to justify the economic case for public intervention — market failure and redistribution — can both be the outcome of the structure of gender inequalities (Akram-Lodhi, 2000). For example, factor markets — and not just labour markets — are commonly segmented on the basis of gender (Blau, Ferber, and Winkler, 1998). Such segmentation can affect production, productivity, and incomes, and thus growth. At the same time the distribution of income and the distribution of wealth is often gender-differentiated within and between households, which can affect consumption and investment choices, productivity, and growth (Agarwal, 1994; Haddad, Hoddinott, and Alderman, 1997). Gender inequalities can affect aggregate investment, aggregate production, and economic growth, and can lead to sub-optimal outcomes (Hanmer, Pyatt, and White 1997). The response of the government to such sub-optimal outcomes can affect the government's budgetary position, as well as its balance-of-payments position. Therefore, it might appear that macroeconomic policy should, as a matter of course, take into account the effects of gender inequalities on the efficiency and equity of public spending.

However, it does not. A cursory glance at the macroeconomics sections of any major economics textbook will reveal no references to gender relations, demonstrating that for many economists, macroeconomics, the theory of public finance, and monetary theory are implicitly gender-neutral. This lack of attention has clear implications for the overall effectiveness of macroeconomic policy. Simply put, gender inequality renders an economy less efficient (Cagatay et al., 1995; Hanmer et al., 1997). There is evidence that gender biases against females in primary and secondary education reduce the rate of growth of gross national product (Hill and King, 1995). Gender relations also affect supply responses to incentive structures. Women may not be able to respond to price incentives in product markets or wage incentives in labour markets because of their double burden of productive and reproductive labour (Hanmer, 1994; Palmer, 1995; Tibaijuka, 1994). The gender division of labour constrains the capacity of women to respond to changes in market-based incentive structures because of the time burden imposed by the socially necessary household activities they perform prior to undertaking market-based activities. In this way, the operation of the commodity economy can be fundamentally affected by the socially necessary allocation of labour into the unpaid care economy. The operation of the commodity economy is constrained by the operation of the care economy (Elson, Evers, and Gideon, 1996; Folbre, 2001; Wheelock, 1996). The impact of this constraint can be accentuated by discrimination in labour markets, which reduces the relative rewards to productive labour between males and females, limits supply responsiveness, and at the same time constrains incomes. Easing this constraint may indeed be a precondition of increased incomes for many households.

In addition to its effects on growth, there may be gender differences affecting productivity (Elson and Pearson, 1981). At the same time, research in Africa indicates that the provision of agricultural inputs and education to women on a level that is on a par with men increases farm yields and thus boosts current productivity (Saito and Spurling, 1992). Both labour productivity and capital productivity can improve because of increased gender equity. Moreover, improving women's living standards in terms of education and income increases child school enrollments and nutritional levels, and thereby boosts children's health and education (Hill and King, 1995). This in turn boosts intertemporal productivity (World Bank, 1995b).

Clearly, gender relations affect the way in which economies operate. If women are given greater control over resources, and incentive structures appropriately reward effort in both the commodity and care economies, there can be efficiency gains in an economy predicated upon improvements in gender equity (Budlender, Elson, Hewitt, and Mukhopadhyay, 2002). In this sense, then, although the gender analysis of macroeconomics is an issue for only a limited audience, there are clear ramifications of gender blindness on the efficacy of macroeconomic policy.

III. The gender budgets approach and the analysis of public expenditure

In this light, over the course of the last decade a new approach to the analysis of macroeconomics has emerged. This approach explicitly addresses the gendered impact of macroeconomic policy in general, and fiscal policy in particular (Cagatay et al., 1995; Grown, Elson, and Cagatay, 2000). Such work has attempted to consider gender in the appraisal of government spending and taxation, the effectiveness of public expenditure policies, and the gender-awareness of budgetary strategy (Elson, 1998). As a result of its emphasis on budgetary processes, this approach is commonly called the "gender budgets" approach (Budlender, 2000). The gender budgets approach magnifies the gender sensitivity of budget processes and allocations so that women's access to resources and government services can be enhanced (Budlender and Sharp with Allen, 1998; World Bank, 2001a). Most of the work done on the gender budgets approach has focussed on gender inequalities at the microeconomic and sectoral levels, probably because changing policies and priorities at these levels can significantly reduce gender inequity and because gender inequity is easier to distinguish (United Nations Development Programme, 2000). Nonetheless, researchers have also undertaken conceptual and empirical work to integrate gender analysis into the macrodynamics of the budgetary process.

Gender budgets proceed from principles that differ from those in orthodox neo-classical economics. Three propositions guide gender budget exercises (Elson and Cagatay, 1999). The first proposition is that economic institutions—states, markets, and households—"bear and transmit gender biases" (Elson and Cagatay, 1999: 3). The second is that the macroeconomy must be redefined so as to include the unpaid caring work that goes into household maintenance activities (Wheelock, 1996). The third is that gender relations affect the division of labour, the distribution of productive inputs, the distribution of employment, the distribution of income, and the distribution of wealth. In so doing, gender relations affect aggregate production, aggregate savings, aggregate investment, and aggregate net exports. Gender relations are thus closely interconnected with macroeconomic processes.

These insights have been crystallized into five key issues that require investigation if a systematic evaluation of the gender sensitivity of the state budgeting and spending process is to be undertaken (Commonwealth Secretariat, 1999; UNIFEM, 2000a).

i. Public expenditure incidence analysis
The first key issue deals with the recipients of public spending. Gender-specific or equal-opportunities public expenditure constitutes a small fraction of to-

tal public spending in most countries (Budlender and Sharp with Allen, 1998). Sharp (1995) has argued that public spending can, in general, be divided into three categories: specific items targeted at men or women; spending on equal-opportunity measures, particularly in employment; and the residual expenditures for both men and women in general. However, it is obvious that typical public-spending policies—that is to say those that are not gender-specific and do not promote equal opportunities—constitute most public spending and yet do not necessarily benefit men and women equally. This severely complicates the analytical issues raised in a gender analysis of public expenditure. For example, women in public sector employment may experience different terms and conditions from those in the private sector. If no such difference exists for men, or if the parameters of the difference for men are not the same as those for women, public spending would have a differential impact upon women and men. Analytically, this should be taken into account when examining, for example, the reform of state-owned enterprises, because such a differential impact can affect intra-household relations and other aspects of gender relations. Similarly, men more commonly participate in relatively more capital-intensive activities than women do; thus, policies that promote the substitution of capital for labour may be implicitly gender-biased. Again, subsidies can have differential effects on men and women, depending on which prices and which goods and services are affected, and these effects must be evaluated from a gender perspective before advocating, say, the elimination of a particular subsidy. It is well established that public service delivery can affect the unpaid economy and thereby affect gender relations within the household. For example, the widespread introduction of user fees in the delivery of health care has resulted in a marked increase in home care, tasks that are predominantly done within the household by women (Folbre, 2001; Hanmer, 1994). Finally, transfer payments from the government to individuals affect the unpaid economy and, in so doing, gender relations. For example, the payment of a pension to a man or a woman may have gender-differentiated effects, in that men and women may use their pensions differently. Therefore, transfers should be distinguished along gender lines.

Gender budget analysis seeks to undertake an incidence analysis that focusses upon non-gender-specific, non-equal-opportunities public spending, using gender as the key variable (Demery, 1997; Elson, 1998). Linking public-spending data with household survey data can help create this incidence analysis, making it possible to assess the distribution of the benefits of public expenditure by gender. Public-expenditure incidence analysis is now a reasonably well-established domain of investigation in public economics. While the costs of such analyses and the data problems that can arise in undertaking them should not be minimized, it is technically feasible to conduct public-expenditure incidence analysis that is gender-aware, especially when a measurement survey of living standards is available, as is the case in many developed market economies and many middle-income developing countries.

ii.   Public revenue incidence analysis

The second area analysts should investigate for gender differentials is the financing of public spending. Direct taxes can have a greater impact upon men because of their wider access to paid employment (Bakker, 1994: 27; Elson, 1998). In contrast, indirect taxes have a greater impact on women because of their ongoing role as managers of household maintenance activities and the household consumption budget. Finally, wealth taxes often derive from unstated assumptions about family structures and property relations within households, and, in particular, that resources are equitably distributed between males and females (Agarwal, 1994). There is, therefore, a need, when evaluating public expenditure, to decide on whom the burden of taxation lies, and, in so doing, to evaluate the gender equity of taxation structures. The procedure is analogous to that used for public-expenditure incidence analysis, in that public revenue data should be linked to household survey data. However, this is more complex, given the difficulty of dividing collective tax payments made by the household among the individuals within it. Nonetheless, such an area of investigation is important. The limited evidence available suggests that revenue acquisition mechanisms can have gender-differentiated impacts, with men and women facing different types or different levels of tax payments (van Staveren and Akram-Lodhi, 2002).

iii.   Gender disaggregated beneficiary assessment

The third area of investigation should be to evaluate budget priorities and public service delivery from the standpoint of the intended beneficiaries (Elson, 1998). Given that men and women may not have the same views on budget priorities and public service delivery, such assessments should be disaggregated on the basis of gender. Impressionistic evidence suggests that the evaluation of public goods in general, and public services in particular, may not be gender-neutral. This is not just because of the distributional impact of revenue acquisition but also because the behavioural impact of revenue acquisition mechanisms may be gender-differentiated, resulting in such services being received unequally. If these methods of raising revenue are not gender-equitable, either in how the revenues are collected or in how recipients perceive they are awarded, it is unlikely that men and women would, as intended beneficiaries, assess public revenue acquisition and expenditure uniformly. At the very least, this would have implications for the analysis of the equity of public expenditure.

iv.   The impact of public spending on time use
The fourth area of investigation should assess the impact of public expenditure on the gender division of labour (Elson, 1998). Available evidence overwhelmingly suggests that women work consistently more than men at each point in the life cycle (UNIFEM, 2000b), in particular by spending substantially more time than men do in household maintenance activities (United Nations Development Programme, 1995). The gender division of labour thus constrains women from taking advantage of economic opportunities beyond the household. This has been termed the "reproduction labor tax" (Palmer, 1995): women supply their labour to household maintenance activities at no cost, which affects the allocation of resources by imposing a constraint upon the participation of women in other activities beyond the household. The revenue and expenditure activities of the state can alter this constraint by tightening or loosening it (Hanmer and Akram-Lodhi, 1998). This suggests, in turn, that public expenditure affects time use, and such effects require investigation.

v.   Articulating gender concerns
Undertaking a successful gender-aware analysis of the budgeting process requires conducting gender-aware policy analysis and appraisal. This is the fifth issue that needs to be addressed in the gender budgets approach (Budlender and Sharp with Allen, 1998; Elson, 1998). Budgetary decision making is inherently political in nature. As such, it is fanciful to believe that the deci-

sion-making process is gender-neutral. Rather, the role of the state in the budgetary decision-making process can have a profound effect upon material and behavioural gender inequity (Hanmer and Akram-Lodhi, 1998; Sharp and Broomhill, 1990). Therefore, researchers must first assess the extent to which gender concerns have a voice in the policy process. A focus on the gendered outcomes of spending, while very important, is, at best, a limited means to evaluate policy from a gender perspective. There is a more fundamental need to create a gender-aware policy analysis that examines both the inputs and the outputs of public expenditure and revenue-acquisition policies.

vi.   Gender, the fiscal envelope and macromodeling
Addressing these five issues adequately requires integrating gender analysis into the budgetary process. This can be done formally in either of two ways. First, the government can seek to produce a gender-aware budgetary statement. Such a statement is, in effect, a gender audit of its policies, programmes, and resource allocation decisions. The gender audit uses the tools of gender-aware policy appraisal, gender-disaggregated beneficiary assessments, gender-disaggregated public-expenditure incidence analysis, gender-disaggregated tax incidence analysis, and gender-disaggregated analysis of the impact of government spending on time use. The gender audit is, in effect, a statement of accountability. The gender-aware budgetary statement can be presented alongside the budget by the government, can be presented by the legislature in its debate over the budget, or can be presented by non-governmental organizations that seek to intervene in debates about the budget, both before and after its presentation.

The gender-aware budgetary statement should also be considered in light of the second mechanism, a gender-aware, medium-term economic policy framework. Governments in the north and the south seek to develop medium-term policy objectives, and determine the cost of meeting those objectives. To do this, policy objectives are turned into quantifiable indicators of outcomes, which are then translated into financial equivalents by estimating the cost of attaining the quantifiable outcome. The determination of medium-term policy objectives should be subject to a gender audit that assesses the impact of policy objectives on gender relations. The determination of the financial resources needed to meet the agreed quantifiable outcomes that represent policy objectives can be adjusted to meet any questions raised by the gender audit. Presumably, one pivotal question raised by the gender audit would be the impact of policy objectives on gender equity. As a consequence, policy adjustments would involve some kind of gender-equity parameter, even if the definition of such a parameter may be conceptually difficult (van Staveren, 2002).

Gender-sensitive financial allocations can then be built into the economic models used by finance ministries. Budgetary allocations made by governments are based upon economic models that seek to forecast the revenue and spending position of the government, the fiscal envelope available to it, over the medium term. In this way, spending and revenue decisions can be both intra- and intertemporally consistent. However, gender is very rarely explicitly incorporated into the macromodels used by finance ministries to estimate streams of revenue and spending, so the medium-term fiscal envelope may be gender-blind. To overcome this blindness, it is necessary to refine modelling to incorporate the implicit assumptions regarding the operation of households and markets in societies, and, in particular, the gendered character of households and markets, and how such institutional characteristics structure the operation of the economy. In addition, it is necessary to greatly expand the data used in modelling, so that it disaggregates variables by gender and incorporates, in addition to the data contained in the national income accounts, the allocation of time devoted to caring activity. In this way, the fiscal envelope factors in the role of unpaid household maintenance activities and the labour reproduction tax. Having done this, it becomes not only possible to develop medium-term policy objectives that are gender-aware, but also translate gender-aware, medium-term policy objectives into a set of indicators that can be financially assessed (van Staveren, 2002).

Gender budget analysis has been promoted in a number of countries, at the sub-sectoral, sectoral, and national levels. The most famous examples of gender budget analysis come from South Africa and Australia, where the techniques were pioneered (Budlender, 1996, 2000; Sharp and Broomhill, 1990). However, a recent compendium of gender budget initiatives indicates the extent to which gender budget analysis has become part of the discourse of the budgetary process (Budlender et al., 2002). As of 2000, 12 countries had gender budget initiatives in Africa, seven in South and Central America, two in North America, eight in Asia and the Middle East, 11 in Europe, and two in Australasia (Budlender et al., 2002). Some countries had more than one organization undertaking gender budget initiatives. In addition to resources from the countries themselves, the funding for gender budget initiatives in developing countries had come from UNIFEM, from the Commonwealth Secretariat, from the Canadian International Development Agency, and from the Netherlands Ministry of Development Cooperation.

IV. Gender budgets and democracy

Women are an increasingly important part of the global economy, and yet women's labour time in the care economy remains largely unvalued and, by implication, devalued (Folbre, 2001). Despite some progress in the last few decades, gender inequalities remain a basic structural feature of the political economy. There remain basic inequalities in access to assets, in access to education and health, in the distribution of income, and in the distribution of poverty (World Bank, 2001a). These inequalities are mirrored in formal decision-making structures. In government, women's representation marginally increased during the 1990s (UNIFEM, 2000b). In the private sector, likewise, the share of women in senior positions increased marginally during the 1990s.

In a widely cited formulation, Dahl (1971) argued there are three basic characteristics of democracy. The first is widespread and substantive competition among individuals and organizations for major positions in government. The second is inclusive participation in the selection of leaders and the development of policies, so that no major group is excluded. The third is a degree of civil and political liberties sufficiently adequate to render effective political competition and participation possible. This includes freedom of expression, freedom of the press, and freedom of association. Such civil liberties help ensure that decision-making processes are accountable and transparent, in part by allowing citizens to organize themselves into autonomous civil society organizations. Civil liberties help ensure that the potential for the bureaucracy to act unilaterally is limited because of clear rules that can be easily examined and, if necessary, enforced through the legal system, and because individuals have multiple channels of access to the state bureaucracy.

This orthodox conceptualization has flaws. In particular, its emphasis on the formalities of the electoral process, civil liberties, and human rights ignores the extent to which historically formed structural inequalities in the distribution and control of wealth can shape the procedures, processes, and outcomes of a formally democratic framework in profoundly anti-democratic ways (Cohen, 1988; Lukes, 1985). Notwithstanding this point, however, it is obvious that in many countries Dahl's three characteristics are not found. Moreover, even in many countries formally defined as democracies, the capacity to fulfill these criteria is limited. Poverty undermines the capacity to demonstrate freedom of expression and freedom of association, and reduces political participation, political competition, and the extent of civil and political liberties that can effectively be used (Sen, 1999). It encourages a lack of accountability and transparency, and bureaucratic domination of an emasculated civil society. Poverty, as a global phenomenon, is gendered (World Bank, 2001a). For these reasons, democratic economic development requires, at a minimum, a degree of gender-equitable income equality (Vilias, 1997). Similarly, the effective exclusion of women from formal decision-making bodies suggests that the selection of leaders and the development of policies may also be gendered, further restricting civil liberties and serving to delegitimize political authority. Furthermore, the fact that there is effective exclusion of women means that competition for positions in government by individuals and organizations is by definition restricted and political authority delegitimized. In other words, from a gender perspective, no country is really democratic, although some may be relatively more democratic than others because of what is effectively gender-segmented participation in social, political, and economic decision-making.

Gender-segmented participation in social, political, and economic decision making is reinforced by state structures. The budgetary process provides an appropriate example of the structural constraints as well as a possible means of overcoming these constraints. Government capacity to undertake a gender analysis of public-expenditure policies is usually limited by weaknesses in the formal policy-review process. Within central government ministries and lower tier departments that formulate public revenue and expenditure priorities, there may be no sections that are supposed to monitor and evaluate policies for their impact on gender relations. There may, occasionally, be parts of the state that are supposed to monitor and appraise policy for its impact on women, such as a ministry for women. In practice, however, such organizations, when they are actually consulted in a substantive sense, often do not review existing policy for its impact on women. Rather, they promote new policy initiatives.

Moreover, these organizations often have minimal capacity—they may be underfunded and understaffed, commonly as a result of economic adjustment. In some instances, and in particular in some transition economies, they may not even have women in senior positions. As a consequence, the potential roles of such organizations to act as advisory centres on the impact of the state on women are compromised. Indeed, at times, and particularly in the south, they are often not even able to properly monitor programmes targeted at women.

Similarly, within the bodies of elected representatives that ultimately offer formal approval of public revenue and expenditure priorities, there may be, at various levels, women's committees. However, these committees usually have little voice in economic affairs. Rather, they may share responsibility for softer social sector and cultural issues, such as health and the media. Moreover, the focus of this responsibility is almost always on women, and not on gender relations. The same is often true of political parties. Their women's committees often do not review and evaluate the impact of economic policy proposals on women, let alone on gender relations. This means that members of parties, like those within the state, who seek to articulate gender concerns in economic policy-making can do so only through personal networks. Finally, the mass organizations of civil society, such as the trade union movement or religious organizations, may not have the institutional means or the technical expertise to comment upon, let alone review or revise, state revenue and expenditure policies in terms of gender. If they can influence policy, it is only through their connections to government or to the ruling party, connections that are based upon personal relationships and are, therefore, at best, a very indirect means of influencing budgetary processes.

It is, therefore, common to find a lack of institutional structures within ministries, within bodies of elected representatives, and within mass organizations that can monitor, evaluate, and, if necessary, compel revisions of budgetary decisions because of their impact on the structure of gender relations. Governance in many developed market and developing countries is, despite the façade of democracy, very hierarchical, and this hierarchy limits the extent to which the impact of policy on gender relations is evaluated. Where there are formal institutional structures to monitor and evaluate the impact of budgetary decisions on gender relations, these are the result of extensive interventions by civil society (Commonwealth Secretariat, 1999).

Democratic economic development requires that this gender-segmented participation in social, political, and economic decision making be transformed (MacEwan, 1999). In essence, governance must be engendered (UNIFEM, 2000b). There is an overarching need to increase women's voice in both the institutions of politics and the institutions of the policy-making process. This is not only good for gender equity, but also for democracy. Increased participation is a prerequisite of enhanced accountability, which promotes the transparency that is central to the capacity of a democracy to sustain the civil rights of its citizens. Moreover, in so doing, increased gender equity in politics and policy-making reduces the scope for bureaucratic inertia and corruption. Engendering democracy would also, by definition, affect the design, implementation, and evaluation of policies, programmes, and projects (World Bank, 2001a). This should lead to a different emphasis in the policy process, one that places greater attention upon the basic skills and social needs required by societies and which also contribute to a more equitable growth process.

Engendering democracy by engendering the institutions of society is unlikely to come "from above." Where efforts have been made to engender democracy, pressure has come from below, and here gender budgets have had a salutary impact by demonstrating the gendered nature of the economic policy process. In order to sustain such pressure from below, women's civil society organizations need to build alliances to strengthen their position in negotiating with the state and with developmental agencies. This is necessary to improve access to information, to enhance accountability and participation at the local level through decentralization, and to press for national mechanisms to promote gender equity and empower women in policy analysis. It is also extremely important to strengthen "the mechanisms for inputs of and reactions by communities and associations of local beneficiaries and users" (Budlender et al., 2002: 58). It is no coincidence that access to information, accountability, and the participation and empowerment of women in the policy process is central to gender budgeting. Gender budgets are about opening up the black box of economic policy-making and revealing the inherent gender biases in the processes at work. Once open, the demystification serves as a foundation upon which a more gender-aware democratic process can be constructed. Such a process requires the construction of a gender-"enabling legal and institutional framework, and empowerment of citizens and civil society organizations so that they become capable of reaching up to the authorities" (Martinussen, 1997: 304) and work to fundamentally affect the actions of the state. In this way, gender budgets help to foster gender-aware participatory planning and implementation that can, not coincidentally, foster more effective and more equitable interventions (Isham, Narayan, and Pritchett, 1995).

V. Conclusion

Since the late 1970s macroeconomic policy-making has become increasingly technocratic. However, technocrats within the state have failed to recognize that the approaches they have adopted tend to be gender-blind. In part, this is a failing of the theoretical perspective that informs their approach. Macroeconomic theory is gender-blind, and this has an impact on the efficacy of the outcomes generated by policy interventions. Gender budgets have emerged in response to the gender inequities that macroeconomic policy can serve to sustain. Gender budgets are a gender-aware approach to macroeconomics in the sphere of fiscal policy. Gender budgets unpack the biases of the policy-making process, and, in so doing, demystify fiscal policy. For these reasons gender budget initiatives have spread rapidly. By allowing people to enter into concrete debates about the gendered impact of fiscal policy, gender budget initiatives have enhanced democracy in societies that, while formally democratic, may be in reality less democratic than is commonly supposed. Gender budget initiatives thus not only promote the democratization of fiscal policy but also, and more meaningfully, promote the engendering of democracy.

Chapter 17

DEMOCRATIZING ECONOMIC POLICY-MAKING IN AN AGE OF GLOBALIZATION

Roy Culpeper

I. The argument

AT the end of the 20th century, it seemed that development economists were a dying breed. Much of the work generated in the heady post-war years, with its plethora of new institutions and programmes of international cooperation, its optimism over the prospects of countries newly liberated from colonialism, and its faith in government planning, was in disarray, a victim of the crisis-ridden 1970s and 1980s.[1] The ensuing resurgence of market-oriented neo-classical economics was bolstered politically in the industrial countries by the neo-conservatism of Margaret Thatcher and Ronald Reagan, which persisted into the 1990s, despite the electoral victories of "liberals" such as Bill Clinton, Jean Chrétien, and Tony Blair.

Accordingly, academic scholars wishing to pursue a career in development economics have had to earn their stripes largely within the neo-classical paradigm, with its penchant for abstract model building based on the axioms of market rationality and equilibrium. How far these economists have drifted away from the common sense of Dudley Seers in 1963, when he warned about the dangers of uncritical application to developing countries of models fashioned on the industrial world, with their profoundly different social and economic structures!

At the same time, the application of market-oriented economic reforms could hardly be declared a success in large portions of the developing world, such as sub-Saharan Africa or the post-Soviet transition countries. Economic growth was anaemic if not negative; poverty remained at persistently high levels or deepened; and structural change was conspicuous by its absence. Neither could the east Asian success stories of Japan, South Korea, and Taiwan be attributed to free-market policies; instead, they practised, in various combinations, export promotion, domestic market protection, and the subsidization of selected industries. Fortunately for the credibility of the economics profession, awareness of the critical importance of institutions and institutional change was reignited, thanks in part to Douglass North (1990) — although the change in emphasis was still clearly rooted in the market-oriented models of the time rather than in Seers's more holistic approach.

Indeed, the calamitous economic performance of much of the Third World in the last two decades demands new approaches by those who are intrepid enough to work on development issues. But it is argued here that the primary challenge is not that of creating a new Grand Theory, like that of the post-war pioneers such as Rosenstein-Rodan, with which to understand, and respond to, the economic problems and opportunities facing the world community. Rather, the challenge is to deepen and deploy the skills of applied economists, heeding the circumstances unique to each country, in order to help eradicate poverty, reduce inequities, and advance sustainable development. In other words, economists should address the policy agenda of the real world, in all its untidiness and diversity. Dudley Seers, who shunned grand theories, believed that economics is about how economies work. It is Seers's spirit of radical economic pragmatism, rather than the abstractions and ideology-laden approach of the neo-conservative model builders, that holds most promise in the 21st century

For economic pragmatists, democratization has opened up a political space in which this challenge must be met, but democracy is itself a work in progress. The frontier economists must explore and help to settle is the democratization of economic policy-making, both in industrial and developing countries. With greater calls for inclusion and popular participation in economic policy-making, economists will be needed to work with their fellow-citizens, partly as experts, partly as educators and facilitators. Their tasks will include identifying what used to be called the social welfare function, translating it into a series of social choices or possibilities constrained by available resources, and determining the set of fiscal, monetary, exchange-rate, trade, and other policies that are both consistent and politically viable—although what is "politically viable" is not a given, but a subject of debate and contestation.

In other words, economic planning is on its way back, but this time it is planning from below, unlike the top-down, state-dominated exercises that characterized post-war planning. Poverty Reduction Strategy Papers (PRSPs) are a manifestation of the shape of things to come in the poorest countries. An important question considered here is what difference PRSPs will make to policies actually adopted and to real outcomes. An increasingly globalized economy limits and, to some extent, also enhances the choices and possibilities open to each society by providing new opportunities for investment, production, and trade at the same time as it creates competition for jobs and markets. Planners must take into account the mobility of factors of production, particularly that of capital (which is increasingly welcomed) and labour (which is constrained, particularly unskilled labour), in determining what policies are consistent and politically viable.

II. Democracy for the people, economic policy-making by the experts

Amid the bloodshed and strife of the last two decades of the 20th century, authoritarian regimes in Europe, Latin America, and to a lesser extent, Asia and Africa have gradually given way to democracies, with freer elections, more accountable government, and the observance of basic human rights. To be sure, many of these political gains have been in form rather than substance, while basic rights have often been observed in the breach. Nonetheless, the world today is arguably more "democratic" than, say, in 1975.

At the same time, a vigorous expansion of global markets has been stimulated by liberalized trade and investment policies, and by increasing capital mobility across borders. As a result, governments everywhere, democratic or otherwise, have been forced to rethink the nature, and inclined to reduce the scope, of their activities in light of what international markets find desirable or deem appropriate. The voice of the people, in a globalized environment, has to reckon with the will of the markets.

Even in the most established political democracies, however, there have always been limits to transparency and accountability, particularly in the realm of economic policy-making. Fiscal and monetary policy, along with foreign trade, have long been the preserve of experts, and protected by commercial confidentiality or national security constraints. Indeed, the trend over the last two decades has been to increase the autonomy of the policy-making experts, particularly in monetary policy. The notion that central banks should be independent from political authority, so they can go about their business of maintaining price stability, belies a fundamental distrust of government, democratic or otherwise.

The detachment of economic policy-makers from their domestic constituencies has widened with global integration and the increasing power and influence of the multilateral organizations. For many developing countries, the International Monetary Fund (IMF) and the World Bank have a determining voice in macroeconomic and structural policies, including trade and exchange rate policies, and policies of privatization and deregulation. Moreover, in all countries, industrial and developing, global and regional trade agreements impose disciplines on national governments and constrain their policy latitude. Under the rules of the North American Free Trade Agreement (NAFTA), for example, foreign corporations have the ability to sue national governments if they believe their commercial rights are infringed by the host government.[2]

Granted, in most democratic regimes, there is an established process of economic governance, featuring parliamentary oversight and debate, which ensures a measure of legitimacy, transparency, and accountability. This would include, for example, the annual budget. But there are limits to this process—well-funded lobby or special interest groups tend to be far more effective in shaping the budget process than are civil society organizations or ordinary citizens. Moreover, the ultimate recourse of an electorate disaffected with the government's economic policies is to "throw out the rascals" at the next poll. However, it is increasingly the case that no matter what its candidates say in the election campaign, once in power, the party in opposition is likely to pursue more or less the same economic policies as its predecessors.

The excuse of democratically elected governments for offering less and less choice is that "there is no alternative," to use Margaret Thatcher's pungent phrase, to the kinds of economic policies compatible with more integrated global markets. If a government fails to deliver such policies, it is argued, the country could be faced with a loss of business confidence, capital flight, a depreciating currency, and associated economic hardships. A stark illustration is provided by the Asian financial crisis, for example, when exchange rates fell from 30 to 80 per cent below their pre-crisis levels, net private capital flows swung from an inflow of US$62.9 billion in 1996 to an outflow of US$29.6 billion in 1998, and real gross domestic product fell by 10 to 15 per cent at the depth of the crisis in Indonesia, Malaysia, and Thailand, the worst-affected countries (IMF, 1999: Ch II).

All this is not to say that democracy is becoming irrelevant or unimportant. Rather, it suggests the scope for alternative economic policies may be narrowing significantly. In other words, there is a diminishing possibility of using the state to redistribute income or wealth, to invest in priority sectors, or to maintain full employment, even if electorates want their governments to pursue such objectives. Instead, the instruments of economic policy must be skewed toward encouraging the private sector, whether it be domestic or foreign, to do those sorts of things, whether through altruism, in the case of redistribution, or through monetary policy, tax incentives, and subsidies, in the case of investment and aggregate demand.

In general, however, the scope to achieve public objectives via fiscal policy is increasingly constrained by the need to maintain balanced budgets or surpluses while reducing taxes to internationally competitive levels, and thereby maintain an acceptable climate for business. In Europe, the Growth and Stability Pact codifies the bias against using fiscal policy. In developing countries facing external economic shocks such as the financial crises of the 1990s, adjustment policies prescribed by the IMF typically point fiscal policy in the wrong direction by cutting expenditures and raising taxes exactly when they should be doing the opposite. To cite Ocampo (2001), for developing countries managing counter-cyclical macroeconomic policy is no easy task in the context of global financial markets, which generate strong incentives to overspend during periods of financial euphoria and to overadjust during crises.

It would be only partially correct to associate these policy shifts with the demise of Keynesianism dating from the Thatcher-Reagan years. The last refuge, perhaps, of counter-cyclical Keynesianism is monetary policy; and none other than Alan Greenspan, chairman of the US Federal Reserve, has, since 1987, been one of its most astute practitioners. However, the scope of monetary policy is also constrained to the extent it is aimed largely at price stability, and is in the hands of a central bank independent of the elected government. Moreover, as Krugman (1998) has argued, the more successful are central banks in achieving price stability and the lower are interest rates, the less room there is to manoeuvre on the downside through interest rate reductions. Japan, where interest rates have been close to zero throughout its decade-long depression, illustrates once again that monetary policy is better at slowing the economy down in the upswing, than stimulating it in the downswing.

III. Can economic policy-making be democratized?
The PRSP model

Non-governmental and civil society groups have recently challenged both the process and the product of economic policy-making. The most vocal protests have been aimed mainly at the international level and at intergovernmental organizations such as the World Trade Organization, the World Bank, and IMF, as they bring into being an increasingly liberalized global economic order. While the aims of such groups vary considerably, and are sometimes at odds, common themes among the non-governmental organizations (NGOs) include respect for national sovereignty, the environment, and workers' rights.

Increasingly, NGOs are also mounting challenges to the process or product of economic policy-making at the *national* level. Typically, these challenges tend to be less vocal or prominent than the movements against the international organizations, since they take place within the more orderly, workaday contexts of national decision making (see Cagatay, Keklik, Lal, and Lang, 2000, for a recent survey). Yet, these movements organized at the national level are likely to have far greater impact than those at the international level, since it is national governments, not intergovernmental organizations, that must negotiate and implement the terms on which countries are integrated into the global system. For the most part, the initiatives launched by NGOs audit or monitor the impact of the official budget on the poor, on women, etc.; or articulate how the official budget might be constructed to be more gender-sensitive, or have a greater pro-poor impact.

Oddly enough, it is in the world's poorest countries, including some of the *least* democratic, that participatory policy-making is now being espoused by the international financial institutions and the leading industrial powers themselves. This turn of events emerged from the debt relief initiative for the Heavily-Indebted Poor Countries (HIPC) launched by the G7 industrial countries in 1996 after years of sustained lobbying by NGOs and church groups. The HIPC Initiative was subsequently enhanced in December 1999, under continuing NGO pressure, in order to deliver faster, deeper and broader debt relief. To help ensure that the ultimate beneficiaries are the poor rather than the privileged, the HIPC required that the proceeds of debt relief be allocated to poverty reduction, rather than to arms purchases or to the bank accounts of elites.

By articulating how those resources are to be allocated, the PRSP, also launched in 1999, is the chosen vehicle for the process. The poverty reduction strategy is to emerge in each country from a participatory process involving civil society, including representatives of the poor. The idea is that if the formulation of such strategies involves civil society, rather than being entrusted solely to government officials or politicians, there would be genuine local ownership over the allocation of resources and the economic policy framework governing it.

The importance of national ownership of economic policies emerged during the 1990s, after two decades of failed structural adjustment policies imposed on developing countries by the IMF and World Bank. These policies, according to some critics, rewarded a few while contributing further to the marginalization and impoverishment of local populations (Structural Adjustment Participatory Review Initiative Network, 2002). It was increasingly accepted, by the official donors themselves, that recipient countries must "own" their development projects, policies and strategies, if they are to achieve their fundamental economic and social objectives (see, for example, Organization for Economic Cooperation and Development [OECD] 1996). Thus, referring to the fundamental goals of development (which subsequently became enshrined in the Millennium Development Goals) the OECD (1966: 2) states "these goals must be pursued country by country through individual approaches that reflect local conditions and locally-owned development strategies." In practice, however, the very concept and implications of "ownership" raise a host of contentious issues.

Although developed for the heavily indebted poor countries, the PRSP has since become the principal vehicle for policy formulation in all the poorer borrowing member-countries of the World Bank, whether eligible for HIPC debt relief or not. In practice, this means all those countries eligible to borrow only from the Bank's soft-loan window, the International Development Association. Again, the principal motivation has been to ensure local ownership over the policies and strategies that result from World Bank borrowing, and, hence, greater political acceptance for the economic policy framework.

Paradoxically, then, the PRSP may confer the world's most democratic system of economic policy-making on some of the world's least democratic societies. However, could it result in such countries' adopting economic policies that, in the eyes of the international financial institutions and their major industrial-country shareholders, are inappropriate? If a participatory dialogue produces "locally owned" policies opting for greater state control and higher taxation, and more restrictions on foreign investment, will such heterodox policies nonetheless be acceptable to the international financial institutions (IFIs) and their major industrial-country shareholders (Dante, 2002)? The answer of the sceptics, who see the PRSP as the latest colours on the same old chameleon of structural adjustment, is "not likely." More generally, there is a critical tension—if not a contradiction—between the PRSP instrument, which is mandated on the one hand by the World Bank and IMF to implement international poverty objectives, but on the other hand is supposed to be embodied in a nationally owned plan (Nelson, 2002). As a result, there may be an inclination for government authorities, particularly those from finance ministries and central banks, to anticipate what the IFIs would find acceptable and not to challenge the prevailing neo-conservative orthodoxy on, for example, trade liberalization or privatization.

Reasons for scepticism deepened after the first formal review of the PRSP by the World Bank and the IMF, two years after its launch. While reaffirming the objectives of the PRSP approach, the review acknowledged the formidable challenges posed to low-income countries required to put together "an integrated medium-term economic and poverty reduction strategy, complete with short- and long-term goals and monitoring systems; these are a set of tasks that few industrial countries could systematically do well" (International Development Association [IDA] and IMF, 2002: para 6). Unsurprisingly, therefore, only nine countries[3] had managed to complete a PRSP, while 42 other countries resorted to preparing an "Interim" PRSP, which was meant to provide a road map or plan of how they proposed to go about preparing a "real" PRSP.

The review pointed to shortcomings in both the process and content of PRSPs. For example, with respect to *process*, despite the emphasis on participatory dialogue, it indicated that the role of parliaments in the preparation, approval, and monitoring of PRSPs was generally limited. It also reflected concerns that, in various countries, specific groups had been excluded from the participatory process: civil society organizations out of favour with the government; local government officials; private sector representatives; trade unions; women's groups; and, ironically, "direct representatives of the poor" (Nelson, 2002, also points to the absence of the poor from the PRSP dialogue). Furthermore, some civil society groups expressed the view that governments limited participation to information sharing and consultation rather than decision making, while limiting the discussion to targeted poverty reduction programmes, to the exclusion of macroeconomic policy and structural reforms such as trade liberalization and privatization (IDA and IMF, 2002: paras. 21-22; Nelson, 2002).

The last concern touches on a major shortcoming in the *content* of PRSPs. To the extent that they deal principally with poverty reduction programmes without addressing the more general macroeconomic and structural policy framework within which they operate, PRSPs could be regarded as little more than the programmes of the 1980s and 1990s designed to mitigate the impact of structural adjustment. Despite the concerns articulated by civil society participants, the joint IMF-World Bank review suggests a degree of consensus regarding the macroeconomic policy framework: "countries recognized the paramount importance of macroeconomic stability to growth and poverty reduction and put forward macroeconomic frameworks that were consistent with these twin objectives." However, the review acknowledged that in the first group of PRSPs, the discussion of the macroeconomic framework, particularly with respect to its linkages to poverty reduction, was limited (IDA and IMF, 2002: para. 37).

A review of PRSP implementation undertaken later in the year for the IMF-World Bank Development Committee (2002) noted that nine more countries had prepared full PRSPs by mid-August,[4] but reiterated many of the concerns raised earlier. Capacity needs to be built for better poverty reduction policy design, implementation, and monitoring; poverty reduction strategies need to be better integrated into budgetary and core decision-making processes; external assistance needs to be aligned behind national strategies; and, perhaps most significantly, the policy dialogue needs to be deepened on several levels, including the design of the macroeconomic policy framework, the development of alternative scenarios and policy options, and improvement of the participatory process (Development Committee, 2002: para. 3).

On the basis of the criticisms and shortcomings of the PRSP process to date, including those of its leading proponents, it would be easy to dismiss the whole endeavour as deeply flawed, a disingenuous attempt to legitimize failed orthodox policies under a new banner of participatory dialogue. However, PRSPs nonetheless present an opportunity to achieve genuine democratization and local ownership of economic policy-making. Are there other models that could help PRSPs fulfill this mission?

As Nelson (2002) points out, the PRSP suffers from inherent tensions in that it is imposed by the donor community and yet is supposed to be owned by developing country recipients. Spontaneous, grassroots initiatives to democratize economic policy, on the other hand, are the creation of the civil society organizations that gave birth to them, and, as such, are almost by definition "locally owned." It happens that there are a number of such spontaneous grassroots initiatives around the world, focussed on the national budget (Cagatay et al., 2000).

Most prominently, since 1995, the Canadian Alternative Federal Budget (AFB) has brought together various civil society organizations—farmers' associations, women's groups, small businesses, labour unions, academics, and NGOs throughout Canada—to put together a federal budget that advocates monetary and other national economic policies based on the concerns and needs of Canadian society, as articulated by these groups (Canadian Centre for Policy Alternatives and CHO!CES, 1998). The AFB evolved from a similar exercise developed over several years in the Province of Manitoba (Stanford, this volume). Among the various initiatives launched by civil society to democratize economic policy-making, the AFB is unique in that it presents a complete budget within a coherent macroeconomic framework, including monetary policy, debt management, and targeted social policies (Cagatay et al., 2000: 28-31). The AFB, from the beginning, has had no official status or role in the formal budgetary process. Rather, it has been a spontaneous expression of some citizens and civil society organizations seeking a coherent alternative to the economic policy framework put forward by the federal government. To date, it has had little verifiable impact on the official budget other than the fact that the organizers of the AFB regularly met with the former Minister of Finance, Paul Martin, in the course of annual pre-budget consultations.

What is particularly relevant for the PRSP in the AFB model, as well as many of the other spontaneous initiatives highlighted by Cagatay et al. (2000), is the centrality of the macroeconomic policy framework to the exercise: not merely the fiscal policy issues of expenditure, taxation, and budget balance, but also monetary, exchange rate, and trade policies. The PRSP process, by contrast, on the admission of the World Bank and IMF (2002), is disconnected from the national budget and core economic decision-making processes, and does not adequately consider alternative macroeconomic policy options. It is essential, in the words of a recent United Nations Conference on Trade and Development (2002) report on Africa, that the new emphasis on poverty embodied in the PRSP be founded on a careful and frank, independent assessment of alternative core macroeconomic and structural policies on growth, distribution, and poverty. The ideal would be to assess holistically the impact of macroeconomic policy, considered as an entire package of policies, rather than, as under the present system, to assess the negative or positive impact on poverty policy components piecemeal (see Schmidt, 2002).

On the other hand, as long as grassroots exercises in economic policy-making like the AFB have no part in affecting the official process, they may also be regarded as marginal. Yet, they are all potentially important models; indeed, there are synergies between these initiatives and the PRSP that urgently need to be explored and exploited. For example, if partnerships could be established between the coalition behind the Canadian AFB and counterparts in countries undertaking PRSPs, the latter could adapt the AFB model to their own circumstances. The crucially important product of these partnerships would be to move the core fiscal, monetary, and structural economic policies to centre stage of the PRSP process. Such partnerships could be supported financially by donors as a form of technical assistance—considerable capacity building would be needed to enable NGOs, unions, and the poor to be able to engage in the manner of their Canadian counterparts—as long as the key civil society players remain in charge of the process and the agenda. Moreover, to return to a main theme of this chapter, the active participation of economists in such initiatives will be crucial, to ensure the technical consistency and credibility of the outputs. Such economists will need to work in concert with members of civil society and other professionals, including sociologists and political scientists.

If democratic planning and economic policy-making are the way of the future, leadership and local ownership should come from within each country. It is not surprising that consultants from northern universities and think tanks were invited by the Bretton Woods organizations to help draft some of the first generation of PRSPs. The predictable excuse was that there is a dearth of local expertise, which is often the case. The corollary may be that PRSPs, particularly in the smaller and poorest countries, cannot be conjured up overnight. Moreover, if local ownership is to be more than a token objective, there may be no alternative but to ensure that local skilled economists and other professionals are available to exercise the necessary leadership, something that can only take a considerable amount of time to achieve.

IV. Democratizing the governance of the global economy

Democratization of the economic policy-making process will not, by itself, go very far toward making possible differentiated national strategies that are truly owned locally. In that sense, the sceptics are right to say that the process may indeed be more inclusive, but if all national economic policies are constrained by global market forces, what difference will it really make?

As Rodrik (1999) has argued, the lesson of history is that ultimately all successful countries develop their own brands of national capitalism; accordingly, the rules of the international economy must be flexible enough to allow individual developing countries to develop their own styles of capitalism, in the same way that Japan, Germany, and the United States have evolved their own models. Thus, while development economists help each country evolve its own brand of capitalism at the national level, at the international level, they must help bring about a rule-based system flexible enough to allow, indeed, to nurture, such economic diversity among countries. Without complementary actions at the global level, the range of choices open to national policy-makers is likely to be limited; in that sense, perhaps, Margaret Thatcher was right. As Helleiner (2000) recently put it, globalized markets operate within politically defined rules and governance institutions, which are currently dominated by the most powerful countries and private market actors. The current global rules and economic governance institutions are in need of repair, updating, and relegitimization.

However, it would not be fruitful to convene a new Bretton Woods in order to craft a kinder and more democratic international architecture, just as a new grand theory of economic development would not be the best way of achieving progress where it counts most—on the ground. Instead, even though the potential reform agenda at the global level is formidable, improvements to the rules and institutions are much more likely to come about through sustained and incremental efforts, organization by organization. To quote Helleiner again, reforming global governance should be thought of as a communicative and consultative process, through which genuine consensus is gradually built, rules and customs mutually understood and agreed upon, and performance is continually reviewed. Universal rules and completely level playing fields—constant refrains in the lexicon of those who promote market liberalization—are inconsistent with the need for local ownership of development policies.

Therefore, in conclusion, economists must engage in two fronts: at the national level, by working to democratize economic policy to promote economic and social equity; and at the international level, by working to democratize the international rules and institutions. In both cases they will engage, allied with governments and civil society, primarily as economic practitioners and policy-makers, albeit armed with the insights of many eminent development theorists, past and present.

Footnotes

1 I am grateful for comments on an earlier draft to my colleagues Rudyard Robinson and Ann Weston; to participants in a conference on 'The Need to Rethink Development Economics' organized by the United Nations Research Institute on Social Development in Cape Town, South Africa, in September 2001; and last, but not least, to Haroon Akram-Lodhi.

2 For example, Chapter Eleven of NAFTA contains provisions designed to protect cross-border investors and facilitate the settlement of investment disputes. For example, each NAFTA Party must accord investors from the other NAFTA Parties national, that is to say non-discriminatory, treatment and may not expropriate investments of those investors except in accordance with international law. Chapter Eleven permits an investor of one

NAFTA Party to seek money damages for measures of one of the other NAFTA Parties that allegedly violate those and other provisions of Chapter Eleven.

3 Bolivia, Burkina Faso, Honduras, Madagascar, Mauritania, Mozambique, Nicaragua, Tanzania, and Uganda.

4 Albania, Gambia, Guinea, Guyana, Malawi, Rwanda, Vietnam, Yemen, and Zambia.

Chapter 18

REFORM, REVOLUTION, AND A BOTTOM LINE THAT HAS TO ADD UP: BALANCING VISION AND RELEVANCE IN THE ALTERNATIVE BUDGETING MOVEMENT

Jim Stanford

I. Introduction

IN 1987, I visited revolutionary Nicaragua as part of an international solidarity project.[1] One day, approached by some poor children begging for gum, pens, or food, we asked one of our guides about Sandinista policy on begging. We wondered if we should give the kids some handouts, or was it more politically correct to hold back? The guide shrugged and said "the revolution may be tomorrow, but the hunger is today."

For me, this response memorably summarized a central and long-standing tension in left politics between the need to advocate and prepare for deep structural changes in society, on one hand, and, on the other, the simultaneous need to help people survive the hardships and traumas of an oppressive society. Should we focus on aiding and protecting the victims of exploitation and exclusion, through concrete and incremental reforms, or should we challenge the causes of exploitation and exclusion by working towards some far-off revolution? Rosa Luxemburg argued famously, and convincingly, that both are needed. However, it hasn't become any less difficult for progressives in the intervening decades to strike an effective balance between the two sides of our work.

One example of the ability to bridge this dichotomy and to address the lofty and utopian as well as the concrete and the here and now is the work of John Loxley. In the course of a single multidestination international journey, for example, John might be consulting on global development policies with African banking officials, stopping over in London to debate conceptual aspects of regulating international capital flows, then spending a night or two in

Ottawa to help community activists frame an approach to the federal government, before flying home to Winnipeg. Within the week he could be back on a plane, this time to northern Manitoba to work with a First Nations community on the nitty-gritty details of a community economic development budget. John's attempts simultaneously to pursue big-picture social change, while actively supporting the incrementalism of reform and community development neatly personify the left's perpetual balancing act between the visionary and the immediate.

One particular project, which John Loxley was instrumental in initiating and supporting, has faced an interesting ongoing challenge to balance these two faces of progressive endeavour. The Alternative Federal Budget (AFB) has been produced annually since 1995 by a coalition of labour and social advocacy organizations. It aims to produce a complete and internally consistent alternative budget document for Canada's federal government, complete with line-by-line revenue and expenditure estimates. The goal is to demonstrate that a more progressive and humane set of fiscal and social policies is economically and fiscally feasible. The unique constraints of this particular project, which has as its central feature a complete budget that convincingly "adds up" at the bottom, highlights the challenges facing a progressive community that wants to keep its eyes on the sky, but its feet on the ground.

II. The economic and fiscal context for the alternative budgets

Canadian politics were dominated in the mid-1990s by a fiscal retrenchment on the part of federal and provincial governments that was extraordinary, in the context of both Canadian history and the experience of other leading developed economies. During the early 1990s the Canadian macroeconomy was hammered by a conjuncture of factors: a massive one-time restructuring of industry in the wake of the 1989 Canada-US Free Trade Agreement; the spillover impact of the US economic slowdown that followed the 1991 Gulf War; and the negative domestic repercussions of a monetary policy stance that was unusually harsh. The Bank of Canada, led at the time by Governor John Crow, was possessed by an anti-inflationary zeal significantly more extreme than most other central banks, including the US Federal Reserve. At times, senior Bank of Canada officials even indicated their preference for a regime of full price stability — that is, a zero inflation target. Many Canadian economists have since concluded that this unilaterally tight monetary policy stance was the major factor explaining Canada's relatively poor macroeconomic performance, compared to other Organization for Economic Cooperation and Development economies, during the early 1990s (Fortin, 2001; Osberg and Fortin, 1995).

Figure 1 below indicates that Canadian real short-term interest rates during the early 1990s were extremely high, and this contributed to a recession that was significantly deeper in Canada than in the US. Even after that recession officially ended, growth remained sluggish and uncertain: annual real gross domestic product (GDP) growth rates averaged just over two per cent from 1992 through 1996, which were barely enough to keep up with Canada's relatively rapid population growth. It took six years for real per capita GDP to regain its pre-recession peak. The vitality of the mid-decade recovery was also undermined by repeated episodes of international economic instability, including, most notably, the Mexican foreign exchange crisis of 1995.

The response of monetary policy to the Canadian recession and subsequent shaky recovery was less than helpful. Real interest rates remained high, averaging over four per cent on short-term assets, throughout the recession and the initial recovery, with the Bank of Canada remaining committed to a uniquely severe anti-inflation stance. John Crow was replaced as governor in 1994 under a newly elected Liberal federal government; his replacement, Gordon Thiessen, followed a rather more balanced approach, but his ability to engineer rate reductions was initially hampered by the 1995 Mexican foreign exchange crisis, which put significant downward pressure on the Canadian dollar. Only in 1996 did interest rates finally move lower on a sustained basis, partly in response to the macroeconomic side effects of fiscal restraint; short-run real rates have averaged about three per cent since that time, and growth rates have responded accordingly. Beginning in 1997, Canada's economic expansion finally took hold in earnest, and real growth exceeded four per cent every year until 2001. Canadian economic performance lagged notably behind US growth until 1996, but since then Canadian growth has matched or exceeded US growth every year.

In the wake of a painful recession, a slow and uncertain recovery, and continuing high interest rates, it is no surprise that the fiscal position of Canadian governments deteriorated dramatically during the early 1990s. Tax revenues were undermined by a weak economy, which simultaneously pushed up the cost of income security programmes. As a result, debt service costs ballooned, as real interest rates exceeded the real rate of growth and generated a rapid rise in the debt burden (Courchene, 1994; Stanford, 1997). Federal deficits averaged five per cent of GDP from 1990 through 1994, as demonstrated in Figure 2. Including large deficits held at the provincial level, the total government sector deficit averaged nearly eight per cent of GDP during this period, which was twice as large as average total government deficits in other G7 economies. The net public debt burden grew by 25 percentage points of GDP between 1990 and its peak in 1995, when total government sector net debt reached almost 100 per cent of GDP. This figure was the second highest in the G7, behind only Italy. About half this debt growth occurred at the federal level, and half at the provincial level. Deficits in some provinces during this time, including Ontario, the largest Canadian province, reached over 5 per cent of provincial GDP. Given the limited capacity and higher costs of provincial debt financing operations, in that they must pay an interest rate premium on their bond issues compared to sovereign rates, this was an especially serious development. Several provincial governments faced downgrades in their credit ratings, and indeed even the federal government was downgraded by Moody's in 1995.

None of this is to imply that Canadian governments had no choice but to embark on the socially harmful course of action that followed. However, it is certainly the case that Canadian governments faced a serious and unsustainable fiscal challenge. Pressed by politically powerful constituencies, including the financial sector, business lobbyists, and high-income households, governments prepared for a fundamental restructuring of their finances. Addressing the emerging debt crisis was not the sole, nor even the primary, motivation for this restructuring. Some of the programmes that were scaled back or eliminated entirely had been the target of long-standing neo-conservative ire. For example, Canada's modern unemployment insurance system had been opposed by conservative critics since its implementation in 1971. The apparent fiscal emergency of the 1990s provided an opportunity to finally overcome political resistance to cutbacks in this programme. Governments faced an historic and immediate challenge of balancing their books. Moreover, they would take the opportunity provided by the moment to more fundamentally redefine their overall presence in Canadian economic and social life.

Canada's historic fiscal retrenchment was announced with a cannon shot in the form of the 1995 federal budget, the second brought down by Liberal Finance Minister Paul Martin. He set a cautious but strict deficit reduction timetable, and vowed famously to honour that timetable "come hell or high water." The financial community was thrilled with Martin's approach, recognizing immediately that the measures contained in his budget were consistent with a far more aggressive deficit reduction schedule than was implied by his official timetable. The largest share of federal deficit reduction progress was attained through cutbacks in programme spending, rather than through increases in taxation. Indeed, throughout the 1990s, federal revenue flows stayed remarkably stable, at 16 to 17 per cent of Canadian GDP, as illustrated in Figure 3, declining slightly after 2000 in the wake of significant federal income tax reductions. In aggregate, therefore, taxes were not increased to reduce the deficit. Federal programme spending, on the other hand, declined sharply, from a peak of 18 per cent of GDP in 1992 to just over 12 per cent by 1997, a one-third reduction in relative economic importance, and the lowest level of federal programme spending in Canadian post-war history.

Governments in most provinces, including a newly elected neo-conservative regime in Ontario, followed suit. For the government sector in total, including the important programmes operated by provincial and municipal governments, programme spending declined from 42 per cent of GDP in 1992 to 35 per cent in 1997. At the federal level, the bulk of spending reductions was attained through cutbacks in transfer payments. In particular, fiscal transfers to provincial governments were sharply scaled back with the introduction of a new unified funding envelope called the Canada Health and Social Transfer (CHST) in the 1995 budget, while transfers to persons were reduced primarily through dramatic cutbacks in unemployment benefits. The effective benefit level of the unemployment insurance system, measured by average benefits per unemployed person, was cut roughly in half between 1990 and 1997. The social consequences of this deep and rapid reduction in public programmes were predictable, painful, and well documented (Stanford, 2001). Even mainstream analysts such as Rubin and Lester (1996) acknowledged the severe contractionary macroeconomic impact of the spending cuts.

On the strength of these spending cutbacks, together with a gradual recovery in economic growth and a gradual reduction in interest rates, the fiscal balances of Canadian governments improved dramatically. By fiscal 1997, just two years after Paul Martin's landmark budget, the historic battle had already been won, two full years ahead of Martin's own timetable. The total government sector in Canada balanced its budget for the first time in a generation, making Canada the first of the major industrialized countries to achieve that goal, even though Canada's fiscal situation in the early 1990s was much worse than that of most other countries. The public debt burden plateaued, and then began to decline rapidly in 1998, driven partly by debt repayment out of growing budget surpluses but mostly by the helpful effect of a rapidly growing economy on the debt-to-GDP ratio. By 2001 the federal debt ratio fell below 50 per cent of GDP, its lowest level since 1985, and well within a range that could be considered sustainable.

Did this dramatic and historic fiscal reversal by Canadian governments work? In a narrow sense, the governments' strategies were obviously successful in engineering a dramatic improvement in fiscal balances and indebtedness. In a political sense, these strategies were also successful. Thanks to some careful and sophisticated political preparation and "messaging," most of the governments that engineered deep spending cutbacks, including the federal government, did not suffer politically for their actions, despite the resulting social hardship. Indeed, in many cases, the budget-cutting politicians were rewarded for their efforts, successfully portraying themselves as leading Canadians to overcome an historic, collective challenge to slay the deficit monster. Nevertheless, Canadians paid—and continue to pay—a steep social and economic price for this one-sided and needlessly aggressive strategy to restore fiscal sustainability, in the form of a broad-based retreat by government and the public sector from many spheres of the economy, and a resulting heightening of the vulnerability of Canadians to the instabilities and inequalities of the private market system.

III. The alternative budgeting movement
The alternative budgeting movement in Canada was born in Manitoba as a result of a collaboration between progressive academics, including John Loxley, and community activists (Loxley, 1993, 2003). Their goal was to refute the arguments of neo-conservative budget-cutters that spending cuts were fiscally and economically unavoidable. To do this, the alternative budget committees generated and publicized complete, internally consistent budget frameworks that

provided additional funding for important public services, programmes, and facilities. The civic and provincial alternative budgets pioneered in Manitoba met with encouraging public reaction, and the technique soon caught the eye of hard-pressed social activists elsewhere in Canada.

As we have seen, by 1994 the writing was on the wall regarding the likely direction of future fiscal policy at the federal level. Following an initial conference in Winnipeg, a coalition of participants came together to prepare the first-ever AFB, which was released in 1995 as a counterpoint to Paul Martin's watershed official budget of the same year. The federal project was cosponsored by the Canadian Centre for Policy Alternatives (CCPA), an Ottawa-based progressive think-tank, and by CHO!CES, the Winnipeg-based social action coalition that had sponsored the initial civic and provincial alternative budgets in Manitoba. The rough division of labour that eventually emerged between the two cosponsors would see the CCPA coordinate the writing, production, and national-level dissemination of the actual budget documents, while CHO!CES focussed on gathering regional input, sponsoring regional budget workshops, developing more popularized versions of the AFB documents, and regional dissemination of budget materials. This division of labour was, at times, contested. Funding was provided by a range of groups, but most was donated by the Canadian Labour Congress (CLC) in the form of special levies collected from its affiliated member unions. For this reason, the AFB was pegged by some media commentators as representing the fiscal priorities of "big labour" even though the sponsoring coalition was significantly more diverse.

The CCPA and CHO!CES produced AFBs annually from 1995 through 2000. The first few versions of the AFB featured both a budget document outlining the crucial fiscal parameters of the budget and a summary of key policy measures, as well as a longer framework document which included lengthier discussions of policy issues in a number of key areas. The framework document was abandoned after 1998, partly due to funding shortfalls, and partly because it became largely repetitive from year to year; latter versions of the AFB thus contained only the budget document. The 2001 budget did not appear, for a variety of reasons: the normal February federal budget was cancelled that year, having been pre-empted by the December 2000 federal election; meanwhile, the normal AFB funding process was disrupted by financial difficulties at the

CLC. In the wake of those difficulties, financial support from the national level to allow for the continuing cosponsorship of the project by CHO!CES was no longer forthcoming, and the project became a sole undertaking of the CCPA. The AFB released a short fiscal statement in December 2001 to coincide with a hurried and unconventional federal budget released in that month (CCPA, 2001). This statement merely outlined the broad fiscal alternatives facing the government, and did not constitute a full alternative budget. The CCPA then released a more complete alternative budget again in February 2003.

IV. The shifting balancing act of the AFB

The content of the AFBs evolved over time to reflect the broader political debates with which they engaged. Of course, the core message of every AFB stressed that if Canadians decided to allocate resources to desired public programmes, those fiscal and economic resources could be located and mobilized. A real or purported shortage of funds was not an adequate excuse for cancelling or cutting back those programmes. Canadians could feasibly continue to enjoy those programmes, despite the air of fiscal crisis that dominated political debates during those years, if they insisted that these programmes were their political and fiscal priority. As emphasized in the opening text of the very first AFB, budgets are inherently political documents, not financial or economic ones; budgets, in other words, are about choices: "The fundamental premise underlying the Alternative Budget is that a budget embodies choices, and that the choices that are made reflect the political values and priorities of the government" (CCPA and CHO!CES, 1995: 1). The central goal of the AFBs, therefore, has been to show that citizens indeed possess the power to choose. Adequate resources can be found to support public programmes, opening more latitude in budget-making choices than is acknowledged by those who argue there is no alternative to fiscal restraint.

This central message seems in some ways to define the AFB as an inherently incremental exercise: its goal is to show that incremental resources can be mobilized to finance more humane public programmes by incrementally expanding a budget that still "adds up." The political message of the AFB is precisely that it is possible to pay for public programmes, whether they are existing programmes that are threatened by cutbacks, as was the case in earlier AFBs, or new programmes that require incremental new resources, as was argued by the latter AFBs. Hence, the very nature of the project would seem to downplay more far-reaching, "out of the box" policy thinking. To fit within the AFB's purview, a programme or initiative needed to be describable within a budget line item and matched with a corresponding revenue flow. Moreover, since the AFBs typically contained only a two-year expenditure and revenue forecast, new initiatives also generally had to be describable within a relatively short time frame. The scope of the AFB's incrementalism, in this understanding, could be measured by the amount of additional programme spending its budgets were able to mobilize and allocate.

There is no doubt, however, that the activists and researchers who came together to formulate the AFBs had more in mind than simply proving that governments retain the capacity to spend money, should they choose to. In addition to defending the resource allocations for existing programmes, many AFB participants also hoped to show how those programmes could be improved and, in some cases, completely restructured. Indeed, many AFB participants also wanted to develop, over time, a deeper and more effective critique of those structural features of Canadian society that cause the fiscal and social problems the resources mobilized in the AFBs are intended to mitigate. In other words, the mandate of the AFB project was broader than simply showing that resources can be found to help those who are exploited or excluded by the current neo-conservative socio-economic regime. The AFB was also imagined as a vehicle for developing and enunciating more far-reaching and fundamental changes in that regime. This goal would be difficult to accomplish within the relatively short time constraints of a single budget, of course; no deeper change in society could ever occur within that time frame, let alone within those fiscal constraints. However, since the AFB was envisaged from the beginning as an annual exercise, perhaps a more critical and fundamental discourse could be constructed over a longer period of collaborative work, to supplement the incrementalism of the AFB's more pragmatic budget forecasts.

For several years the AFB ranked as one of the highest-profile, best-funded, and most successful projects undertaken by the Canadian extra-parliamentary left. It assembled a unique collection of progressive policy experts and researchers, together with grassroots organizers and campaigners. During its first years it sponsored a relatively intense process of regional consultation and participation. In terms of its immediate "deliverables" the AFBs exceeded most expectations: the actual documents were credible and professional, and they generated favourable attention and responses among both national-level media and political constituencies, and local and regional social advocates. However, in terms of the bigger, more complex task of developing a cumulative and sustained progressive social and economic vision, the AFB project was less successful. In the annual rush to get the budget done on time, and amid the inevitable bargaining sessions between AFB cosponsors about the direction and content of those budgets, the opportunity to use the AFB platform to explore and advance more fundamental political and economic arguments was usually passed over. In short, the tension between the immediate issue of producing a budget that adds up for next year, and the visionary thinking that is essential to progressive politics and that involves imagining a much better society, sometime, was not resolved.

i.   Budget balance

One important way in which the AFBs deliberately chose not to break from orthodox practice was its acceptance of the same overall budget balance targets as were adopted by the federal government. The AFB acknowledged that large ongoing budget deficits are not sustainable, and accepted Paul Martin's official timeline for their elimination, as summarized in Table 1. Of course, federal budget actions were consistent with an unstated deficit-reduction timetable that was, in fact, much more aggressive than Martin's official timeline. Clearly, the AFBs were not as tough on the deficit as Paul Martin, though Martin's more gradual official timetable allowed the AFB to position itself that way.

Once the federal budget was balanced in 1997, the AFB then accepted the preservation of that balance as its global fiscal target. This was nominally consistent with the government's official policy of planning for a balanced budget each year after 1997. In practice, however, through the use of contingency funds and other artificial budgeting practices, federal budgets since 1998 have actually been designed to generate large surpluses. Notwithstanding these practices, however, the AFB's acceptance of the same official budget targets as Paul Martin represented an effort to shift public debate away from whether the budget should be balanced, to what AFB proponents thought was a more fruitful and credible line of argument: how would the budget be balanced, and who would bear the cost of that balancing.

The Alternative Federal Budget fundamentally opposes the slash-and-burn approach to reducing budget deficits that has resulted in so much unacceptable and unnecessary hardship in our society, and poses such a tremendous danger to Canada's long-run social and economic prospects. Nevertheless, we do accept the basic premise that large budget deficits are unsustainable, and that government deficits and debts must be reduced...The current debate, therefore, is not whether Canada's budgets should and will be balanced. The real issue, rather, is how they should be balanced, and how quickly; in short, the real debate is over what type of Canada will emerge when that balancing act is completed. (CCPA and CHO!CES, 1997: 7)

This general approach represented a significant departure (Robinson, 1995; Stanford, 1995) from some less credible, previous left arguments regarding the deficit, which had typically suggested that the deficit was an invented or exaggerated problem, and that the progressive response to deficit-mania should be to simply ignore the problem. But the AFB's adoption of mainstream budget targets was nuanced. The AFBs emphasized that budgetary balance was not an end in itself, but rather a condition for a more important underlying goal: maintaining public debts at a sustainable level. Beginning in 1996, the AFB explicitly adopted a debt-ratio target, borrowing the Maastricht treaty's target of limiting net debt to 60 per cent of GDP, and pledging to do it by 2000. The depth of Canada's fiscal problems, however, implied that Paul Martin's deficit reduction timetable had to be followed anyway, in order to meet this paramount debt target. AFB documents rejected balanced budget laws and other fiscal gimmicks that many governments implemented later in the 1990s. The AFB also experimented with espousing firm targets for other key socio-economic variables, in addition to fiscal ones. Explicit targets for job creation were established in the 1995 and 1997 AFBs, for the unemployment rate in the 1998 AFB, and for the poverty rate in the 1998 and subsequent AFBs. Thus, the AFB's acceptance of the official timetable for deficit reduction featured a broader and more critical analysis of the context and politics of balanced budgets than was true of budget-cutting politicians. Nevertheless, there was nothing unorthodox about the AFB's overall budgetary balances.

ii. Monetary stimulus
Progressive critics widely agreed that much of the fiscal imbalance of the early 1990s was the consequence of the uniquely tight monetary policy pursued in

Canada during that time. Naturally, then, proposing a relaxation of monetary policy would play an important role in any overall alternative deficit reduction scenario. The first several AFBs, operating in the context of lingering high real interest rates and the interest rate spikes that occurred in 1995 and 1998 amidst international financial instability, placed a significant emphasis on the importance of monetary easing. By stimulating more growth, job creation, and federal revenue, simultaneously easing the government's own debt service costs, lower interest rates drove a two-pronged improvement in federal finances.[2] This allowed AFB proponents to argue that neither higher taxes, nor spending cutbacks, were the crucial ingredient in deficit reduction; instead, putting more Canadians back to work could be the main engine of fiscal repair.

Table 2 summarizes the evolving monetary policy pronouncements of the AFB. These pronouncements were relatively modest, calling for reductions in real interest rates of two percentage points or less and, beginning in 1996, a limited refinancing of existing government debt by the Bank of Canada. By late in the 1990s, under the leadership of a kinder, gentler Bank of Canada, a new era of lower interest rates was well established. Hence the last two AFBs, and the 2001 statement, downplayed the general issue of monetary policy.

iii. Programme spending

"Show us the money!" was a slogan that was aptly featured on several AFB materials. Indeed, since the project's core goal was to show that government could indeed pay for quality public programmes, if it chose to do so, one obvious axis along which to measure the AFB's evolving policy stance is by the amount of new programme spending that was allocated in its respective budgets. This record is summarized in Table 2; two measures of the relative spending power of each AFB are provided. Most straightforward is the total new funds allocated to programme spending in each of the first two years of the AFB. Table 2 also reports the net fiscal stimulus injected by each budget, measured as the change in the difference between programme spending and taxes as shares of GDP over the first two years.[3]

This evidence indicates that the early AFBs would not have been very stimulative at all, in terms of their immediate fiscal impact; in fact, since discretionary new spending, measured as a change in the ratio of programme spending to GDP, was more than offset by discretionary new taxation, these budgets were actually contractionary, in the narrow sense. Since the early AFBs were released during an era of fiscal imbalance, and since the AFB had accepted the need to reduce deficits, this result was preordained to some extent. The AFB's use of lower interest rates to stimulate job creation and new revenues could do some of the work of deficit reduction, but not all; further budgetary progress required tax increases that more than offset programme spending increases. In subsequent years, as the federal budgetary balance improved, the AFBs could afford to be more expansionary, while still living within their defined budget targets. As a result, these later AFBs could increase programme spending by C\$20 billion or more in a single year, some two per cent of GDP, while holding taxes constant in relation to GDP.

One ironic result of this approach is that the AFBs were not countercyclical in their fiscal effects. They were the least stimulative in the mid-1990s, when the Canadian economy was the weakest, and much more stimulative in the late 1990s when the Canadian economy was growing strongly. This outcome reflects the fact that the AFB's main focus was not to emphasize fiscal policy as a source of short-run macroeconomic stabilization. Rather, fiscal policy was seen to reflect a longer term social policy choice: how much government revenue should be collected, in order to finance a desired level of public programme delivery.

iv. Other labour market programming

Expansionary macroeconomic policies carried the main responsibility for revitalizing labour markets in the first several AFBs. Given the relatively depressed labour market conditions of those years, however, these AFBs also proposed additional direct job-creation measures, including infrastructure spending, youth job creation programmes, and measures to reduce working hours in the federal jurisdiction. These initiatives are summarized in Table 2. Since labour market conditions improved dramatically by the end of the decade, these initiatives also became less prominent in the latter AFBs.

v. Aggregate taxation level

Another common left-populist response to the large deficits of the early 1990s was that the deficits could be erased by raising new taxes from corporations and high-income individuals. Although Canada's overall business sector could

347

hardly be described as prosperous during this period, with business profits reaching post-war lows in 1992 as a share of GDP, segments within the business sector nevertheless remained profitable. The overdeveloped Canadian financial industry in particular remained buoyant. At the same time, high-income households enjoyed continued wealth. However, upon examination of the hard evidence regarding the sheer size of the deficit, and the difficulty of raising sufficient funds from a well-off but narrow tax base, this line of argument never played a prominent role in the AFBs. Indeed, the AFBs generally avoided relying on higher taxes to reduce deficits, preferring instead to emphasize the fiscal benefits of economic growth and job creation. Early AFBs contained relatively modest discretionary increases in overall federal tax collections, never exceeding a single point of GDP, as shown in Table 3. The first AFB in 1995 was the most ambitious in this regard, relying on discretionary tax increases to fund one-third of the deficit reduction projected over two years. Modest tax increases in these early AFBs were justified on grounds that the up front costs of deficit reduction should be widely shared, rather than concentrated on the shoulders of those who depend on public programmes. In later years, when fiscal conditions were more expansionary and political sentiment against taxes was stronger, the AFB simply froze aggregate tax rates at existing levels. Thus, where early AFBs argued that public programmes could be protected while still reducing the deficit, which was the bogeyman of the mid-1990s, later versions argued that public programmes could be expanded without increasing taxes, which became the bogeyman of the late 1990s.

vi.   Tax redistribution

A distinct issue from the overall level of taxation is the question of how the tax burden is distributed, and on this point the AFBs adopted a consistent and relatively ambitious position. Each AFB featured a range of measures that would significantly redistribute the burden of taxation from lower and middle income households, onto high-income households and the business sector. These measures are summarized in Table 3. Common features of this approach included the addition of extra personal income tax brackets for high-income taxpayers, the closing of loopholes in the corporate and personal tax systems, the imposition of a wealth transfer tax, and the use of carbon or gasoline taxes. The overall package of tax redistribution measures became somewhat simpler and less aggressive in latter versions of the AFB, which focussed on opposing the aggressive push for broad across-the-board tax cuts that conservatives had launched in the wake of balanced budgets. The primary AFB response to this new climate was to argue that paying taxes in return for quality public services and enhanced social security was a desirable trade-off. In this context, devoting a lot of attention to correcting perceived injustices in the tax system seemed counterproductive.

vii. Policy innovation

The political context of the early AFBs, and their overarching priority to support popular resistance against deep government spending cuts, contributed to a certain inherently defensive tone in much of the argumentation. Yet the architects of the AFB never intended to call simply for the restoration of fiscal and social policies to some pre-cutback status quo. There was also an explicit recognition that progressive changes should be implemented in the design and delivery of many public policies and programmes. So, in addition to showing that resources were available to fund the continued provision of key programmes and services, to a lesser extent all the AFBs also argued for some innovation in the structure and delivery of those programmes.

The major policy innovations proposed in each of the AFBs are summarized in Table 4. The first AFB in 1995 was a short, dense document that focussed on showing that funds could be found to support public programmes. Subsequent AFBs became more elaborate, with comprehensive arguments summarized in the budget document itself, and explored in more detail in the accompanying framework document and technical papers, for the redesign of key components of Canada's social and fiscal policy framework. One major innovation in the 1996 AFB, preserved in every subsequent edition, was the establishment of issue-specific transfer payment envelopes to govern federal transfer payments to the provinces or to individuals. A total of seven different social investment funds was proposed, for child care and early childhood education, health care, income security, unemployment insurance, seniors' benefits, housing, and post-secondary education. Each fund had its own rules and its own funding formula; this approach was an effort to reverse the "basket approach" to provincial transfer payments that the federal government implemented in 1995, with the advent of the CHST. The extent of the AFBs' policy innovativeness probably reached a peak with the budgets of 1997 and 1998. Additional policy innovations included proposed legislative initiatives to set national standards for public service delivery, phased-in federally supported pharmacare and home care benefits, the establishment of an Atmospheric Fund to address climate change issues, and a proposed Equity Participation Foundation to fund enhanced democratic participation in society. The 1998 AFB featured two especially unique initiatives that challenged the ideological nature of conventional budgets and economic statements. It commissioned a detailed report on the gender content of budgets and macroeconomic policy-making, with a corresponding recommendation to subject subsequent budgets to a thorough gender review (Bakker and Elson, 1998). It also contained the most detailed statement yet on how the AFB could be "greened," so as to become a more forceful vehicle for promoting environmental sustainability as a core goal.

The extent of policy innovativeness in a largely volunteer project like the AFB, however, depends on the energy and commitment levels of the individuals working on the project. It is also dependent on the extent to which the project recruits and integrates new ideas from new constituencies. On both counts, as the AFB project grew older, the amount of attention and priority directed to rejuvenating the project's base of volunteer researchers and writers, and continuing to expand and update its various policy formulations, diminished. In its last years, the AFB was influenced by the desire, partly motivated by ever-present funding difficulties, to "get the job done efficiently," in terms of preparing and producing the core deliverable documents. As a consequence, the AFB's functionality as a unique meeting place for creative progressive policy formulation was eroded.

viii. Structural measures

A similar trend is visible in the extent to which the respective AFBs were willing and able to formulate demands that went beyond simply allocating resources to ameliorate social and economic problems, to instead challenge the fundamental political-economic structures and practices that create and recreate those problems. The AFB was never very ambitious in this regard; it avoided calling for any significant expansion of public ownership or regulatory capacity, and implicitly accepted the dominant role of private business and private wealth in Canadian society.

Some attention was given, beginning in 1996, to a set of structural measures in the financial realm, which were advanced with the goal of supporting and sustaining the AFB's call for lower interest rates. In a globalized, deregulated financial context, it was argued, lower interest rates would be sustainable in the longer run only if the financial industry was reregulated through measures such as restrictions on foreign content in tax-subsidized pension funds, compulsory community investments by private banks, and the establishment of public investment banks. The AFB also challenged the orthodox treatment of private intellectual property rights in the field of pharmaceutical products, with demands for a relaxation of drug patent laws and the establishment of a national public drug-procurement network, both of which were designed to help make a public pharmacare programme more feasible. The last AFB in 2000 developed a new proposal for a National Infrastructure Investment Authority, to provide financing for badly needed infrastructure improvements at all levels of government. This proposal was motivated by opposition to the growing tendency for cash-strapped governments to turn to private capital markets to finance these projects.

In these generally small ways, the AFBs hinted at a challenge to the legitimacy and the efficiency of private enterprise and private property rights, in certain specific areas of the economy. In general, though, the AFB documents failed to engage in a deeper questioning of the current neo-conservative socio-economic order. Even some AFB proponents would not question this order of emphasis, arguing that the AFB did not have a mandate from its sponsors to branch into this deeper and perhaps more controversial realm of analysis, critique, and policy-making. But in retrospect many people will be disappointed that there was not more to show for the years of effort that went into the AFB, in terms of the development over time of a more sustained and holistic critique of the power structures that have shaped Canadian society.

IV. Evaluating the balancing act

The overall evolution in these various dimensions of AFB policy-making is summarized visually in Figures 5 and 6, which illustrate the extent to which each AFB was relatively more or less challenging to dominant neo-conservative policy approaches. These figures are hand-drawn depictions of the broad trends in the policy stance of the AFBs, as summarized more concretely and explicitly in Tables 2 through 4. A position that differs only slightly from the orthodox view would be located lower on these graphs, near the "gradualist" end of the Y-axis; a position that represents a striking break from orthodoxy would be located higher, near the "audacious" end of the Y-axis. Figure 5 illustrates the positioning of the various AFBs with respect to the three key macroeconomic variables they utilized: monetary policy, spending power, and aggregate taxation.[4] Figure 6 does the same for the more political dimensions: tax redistribution, the overall intensity of policy innovation, and the extent to which the AFBs proposed measures challenging the broader power of the private sector and private capital in Canadian society.

A project that emphasized incremental reforms would be described by lines located mostly in the lower parts of Figures 5 and 6. A project that focussed on more ambitious challenges to the status quo would feature many lines in the upper portions of these figures. Finally, a project that maintained a broad balance between incremental reforms and far-reaching visionary changes, would be described by lines running across both the upper and lower ranges of the graphs. By this simple visual mode of analysis, it seems clear that the main political thrust of the AFBs was highly gradualist, and, indeed, this gradualism came to increasingly dominate the AFB's general outlook as time went by. Consider, for example, that latter versions of the AFB accepted official budget targets, existing aggregate taxation levels, and the current stance of monetary policy. They proposed no significant challenge to the general power of private business and wealth, and featured only modest attempts at policy innovation and tax redistribution. Ironically, the most audacious aspect of these latter AFBs was visible along the dimension of aggregate spending levels which, it was suggested above, is the dimension most compatible with gradualistic politics. If the core reformist goal of the AFB project was to show that more resources could be located to support public programmes, then the 1999 and 2000 AFBs fulfilled this goal to an extreme. They proposed massive increases in programme spending financed from the large latent budget surpluses of the day with no general tax increases, only modest tax redistribution, and proposing virtually no dramatic policy or structural changes in society at all.

In the context of the political debates of the day, the incrementalism of the early AFBs was strategic, deliberate, and defensible. Early incarnations were motivated by a desperate effort to support the campaigns of grassroots activists and social advocates against coming deep cutbacks in important public services and income support programmes. Demonstrating in a credible, accessible manner that those cutbacks were avoidable was of great use to those campaigns, and a head-on challenge to the neo-liberal vision. Propagating and debating proposals for more far-reaching, structural change could be seen to dilute the effectiveness of this overarching and urgent priority.

Later AFBs faced a different political landscape. Fiscal policy-making was then preoccupied with a historic choice regarding how to allocate the surplus resources that were the legacy of the unduly and, in retrospect, unnecessarily aggressive spending cuts of the middle decade. The AFB's message in this debate was equally focussed: the federal government should spend its surpluses to rebuild decimated public programmes. The latter AFBs were nothing short of audacious in terms of the amount of money they dedicated to this goal. However, when combined with the continuing silence of the AFBs on deeper structural issues, the inadvertent implication of this focussed message seemed to be that there was nothing wrong in Canadian society that a lot of government money couldn't cure.

Most of the individuals who contributed to the AFB over the years would not be satisfied with this conclusion as a summary description of their vision for social change. Yet even though its architects spent many hundreds of hours together discussing social and economic problems over a multi-year period, the AFB did not evolve into a vehicle for promoting that more critical and ambitious political-economic vision. This was not for lack of interest; indeed, during a series of workshops organized in 2000 to consider future new directions for the AFB, many supporters emphasized the need to find space in the project for exploring and advocating longer run, more far-reaching policy directions. For example, one proposal was for the AFB document to feature Blue Sky Boxes. These would be sidebar discussions of broader, longer run problems in society, and would propose far-reaching solutions to those problems even if those solutions were not fully budgeted within the standard two-year AFB projections.

Unfortunately, however, this desire to develop a broader, multidimensional political-economic perspective was repeatedly overwhelmed by the more immediately pressing political and operational challenges facing the project: the need to assemble a complete and internally consistent budget within a short time frame, and the need for that budget to resonate within the political campaigns and struggles of the moment. The simple but difficult lesson for progressive policy thinkers would seem to be that a persistent and conscious effort must be made to create and protect the organizational and political space to discuss big-picture issues, or else they will drop off the table amid the chronic scramble of more immediate challenges and struggles.

V. Conclusion: reform and revolution, means and ends

One dimension of the AFB's work that was not considered in the preceding discussion was its process. Here too the project faced an ongoing challenge. It had to balance a longer run commitment to participatory practice and to the gradual enhancement over time of the political and analytical capacities of social justice campaigners, against the immediate preoccupations and constraints of putting together an annual budget on a short timeline, and never with sufficient resources. Here, too, the AFB's balancing act shifted over time, with its internal process becoming more instrumental even as its politics were becoming more incremental. More and more of the crucial decisions regarding the content of the AFB were made at a central table populated by a gradually declining population of mostly professional policy thinkers; less emphasis and resources were placed on the regional consultation and popular education components that were important in earlier incarnations of the AFB.

Ironically, this occurred as progressive activism in many countries was being rekindled by a commitment to participatory democracy (Rebick, 2000). One very influential experience in this context has been the experiment with participatory budget making in regions of Brazil, under the leadership of progressive local and regional governments (Löwy, 2000). It seems ironic that as worldwide interest was exploding in the participatory budget processes of Brazil, Canada's alternative federal budget community was retreating from its own limited agenda for a more participatory process. The initial alternative budget community in Manitoba had always stressed the centrality of a more popular-based model of budgeting to its overall political message, as part of its claim that budgets should not be left up to experts, but, rather, were a site for popular engagement and struggle (CHO!CES, 1998: Ch. 9). Again, AFB participants at the federal level were not unsympathetic to this goal, but it foundered predictably on the same rocks of lack of resources and a preoccupation with producing immediate deliverables that hindered the AFBs' ability to develop a more systematic and thorough critical content. The 2003 Alternative Federal Budget addressed this shortcoming, publishing a detailed survey of the practice of participatory budgeting in Canada and abroad (CCPA, 2003); project participants are considering strategies for incorporating forms of participatory practice into future incarnations.

In summary, on grounds of both content and process the experience of Canada's alternative budgeting movement is both impressive and sobering. Over its first years of existence, the project succeeded in generating impressive awareness of the range of options that could be counterposed to the neo-conservative fiscal policies of the day. However, by concentrating its energies on highly focussed messages countering dominant neo-liberal policies—first challenging the argument that spending cuts were inevitable, and then the view that tax cuts were essential—the AFB project ultimately missed the opportunity to use its unique assemblage of local and national resources to develop something bigger and perhaps more influential than just a budget that adds up. If future versions of this or similar projects want to maintain a better balance between the gradualist and the visionary, they will require a thoughtful and deliberate assignment of priorities and resources. Otherwise the time and space that could be used to think together outside the box to imagine creative social change will likely once again be conscripted into the more immediate political and organizational priorities of the project.

Footnotes

1   The author thanks the many researchers and activists who contributed to the development of the Alternative Federal Budgets described here, and more importantly the social justice campaigners who used the arguments of the AFBs in their struggles for a more humane society. The comments in this chapter regarding the strengths and weaknesses of the AFBs are offered in a spirit of comradely reflection, in hopes that our future work together can be even more creative and effective.

2 In practice, lower interest rates played an enormous role in the rapid elimination of the federal deficit, precisely as had been originally urged by the AFB, by generating job growth and economic expansion, and reducing the government's own debt service costs. Mainstream commentators suggest that the federal government's budget cutting was a necessary condition for the rate reductions engineered in the wake of that retrenchment, but this conclusion is debatable.

3 In this understanding, new spending is not stimulative if it is matched by an equivalent amount of new taxation. This oversimplifies the matter, of course. Most public spending is more stimulative than most types of taxation because there are more leakages from private income and expenditure flows, for savings and imports, than is typically the case in the public sector. Hence new spending can be stimulative even if fully matched by new taxation, through the so-called "balanced-budget multiplier." As a simple composite way of measuring the net stimulative impact of each consecutive budget, however, the approach described in the text is adequate.

4 It could be argued that the global budget target, reported in Table 1, also represented a macroeconomic decision point, but since the AFBs accepted the official targets of the federal government in this regard, this variable is not visually described in Figure 5.

Figure 1 Macroeconomic indicators, 1990–2001

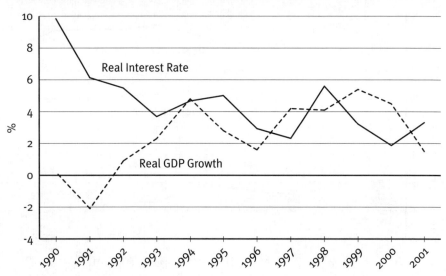

Source Author's calculations from Statistics Canada (2002b).
Real interest rate is nominal bank rate less growth in chain-linked GDP price deflator.

Figure 2 Fiscal balances in Canada, 1990–2001

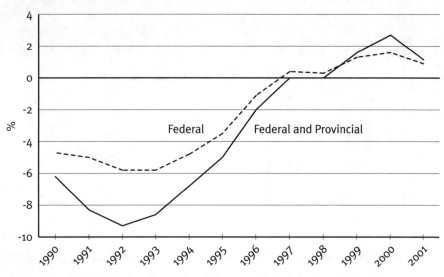

Source Author's calculations from Finance Canada (2001, 2002), Statistics Canada (2002a,b).

Figure 3 Federal budget flows, 1990–2001

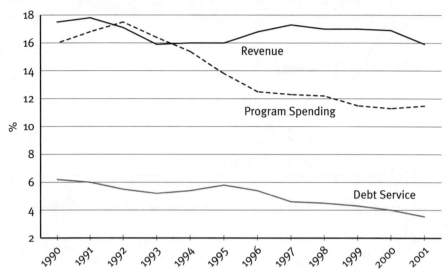

Source Author's calculations from Finance Canada (2001, 2002), Statistics Canada (2002b).

Figure 4 Net public debt, 1990–2001

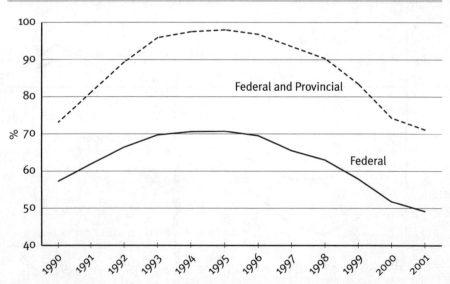

Source Author's calculations from Finance Canada (2001, 2002), Statistics Canada (2002a,b).

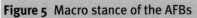

Figure 5 Macro stance of the AFBs

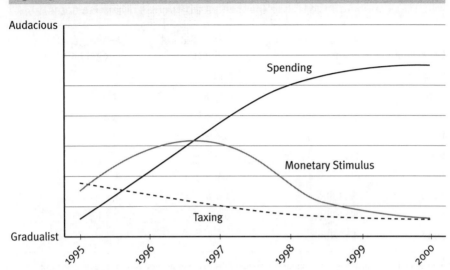

Figure 6 Policy stance of the AFBs

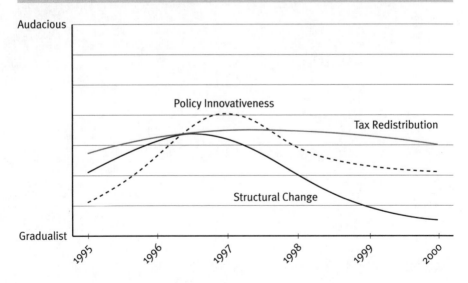

Stanford

Table 1 Budgetary targets and results
Federal government, 1994-2002 (per cent of GDP unless otherwise noted)

Fiscal year	Federal target budget balance	Actual federal balance	AFB target budget balance
1994		-4.8%	
1995		-3.5%	-4%
1996	-3%	-1.1%	-3%[1]
1997	-2%	0.4%	-2%
1998	-1%	0.3%	-1%
1999	0	1.3%	0
2000	+$3 billion	1.6%	0
2001	+$3 billion	0.9%	0
2002	+$3 billion		0

1 In 1996 the AFB also began to espouse a target for the net federal debt, pledging to reduce it to 60 per cent or lower by fiscal 2000; in fact, the AFB began to argue that year that a stable debt target was more important than particular annual budget balance targets.
Source Finance Canada (various years, 2001); CCPA and CHO!CES (various years).

Table 2 Key macroeconomic policy indicators,
Alternative Federal Budgets, 1995-2002

| Fiscal year | Monetary policy stance | Fiscal policy stance[1] | | Other job-creation measures |
		New programme spending ($billion)	Fiscal stimulus[2] (% GDP)	
1995	Moderate easing: reduce real interest rate one point.	$4.5 / $2.7	-1.2% / -0.8%	Spend $1.5 bn per year on job-creation programmes; set jobs target to create 1.2 mn new jobs over 3 years.
1996	Moderate easing: reduce real interest rate two points (one point lower nominal rate, one point higher inflation).	$6.7 / $6.3	-0.6% / -0.4%	Create 100-200,000 additional jobs per year through one point more real growth and a $3 bn annual job-creation programme.
1997	Moderate easing: reduce real interest rate one point (through higher inflation; nominal rate is unchanged).	$13.6 / $7.0	+0.2% / -0.4%	$3 bn per year spent on an Emergency Employment Investment Programme, to help create 930,000 extra jobs over 5 years; shorter work time in federal jurisdiction.
1998	Stronger easing: reduce nominal interest rates by 1¾ points, real by 2¼ points; increase Bank of Canada band by 1 point.	$12.9 / $9.0	+0.4% / +0.4%	Lower interest rates, more programme spending, and labour market measures create 800,000 extra jobs over 4 years; National Youth Job Strategy.
1999	Mild easing: interest rates are slightly reduced only starting in the second year.	$22.1 / $10.9	+1.7% / 0.4%	Strategy to create 600,000 additional jobs over 4 years through infrastructure spending, shorter work hours, and youth hiring.
2000	No change.	$16.1 / $9.1	+1.0% / +0.2%	Employment and spin-off benefits of increased programme spending not integrated into AFB projections.
2002[3]	No change.	$18.4 / $10.1	+1.0% / +0.2%	

1 The table summarizes the result in each of the first year and the second year of the AFB.
2 Fiscal stimulus equals change in programme spending as share of GDP less change in tax revenues as share of GDP.
3 Reports broad fiscal parameters described in CCPA (2001).
Source CCPA and CHO!CES (various years).

Stanford

Table 3 Tax policy indicators, Alternative Federal Budgets, 1995-2002

Fiscal year	AFB aggregate tax target[1]	Tax policy measures[3]
1995	+0.8% / 0	Collect back taxes owed ($1.4 bn); raise effective corporate tax rates; two new high-income PIT brackets; national wealth transfer tax; lower RRSP deduction limit; 2 low-income tax cuts.
1996	+0.5% / +0.3%	'Solidarity Tax' package includes: collect back taxes owed ($660 mn); excess profits tax on banks; corporate minimum tax; close corporate & personal loopholes; lower RRSP deduction limit; two new high-income PIT brackets; eliminate low-income surtax; abolish GST on reading materials.
1997	+0.8% / +0.2%	'Solidarity Tax' package includes: collect back taxes owed ($660 mn); excess profits tax on banks; corporate minimum tax; close corporate & personal loopholes; lower RRSP deduction limit; two new high-income PIT brackets; enhanced child benefit; end low-income surtax; expanded GST rebate; abolish GST on reading materials; carbon tax ($500 mn).
1998	+0.3% / -0.3%	Tax share of GDP frozen except for one-time excess profits tax on banks and enhanced enforcement ($600 mn); full inclusion of capital gains and dividends; close corporate and personal loopholes; wealth transfer tax; $9.7 bn targeted tax cuts (eliminate federal surtax, cut bottom tax rate, large expansion in child tax benefit and adult GST credit); two new high-income PIT brackets; carbon tax; eliminate oil & gas preferences; abolish immigration 'head tax'.
1999	0 / 0	Tax share of GDP frozen; full inclusion of capital gains and dividends; Mintz Committee business tax base-broadening measures; wealth transfer tax; $9.7 bn targeted tax cuts (eliminate federal surtax, cut bottom tax rate, large expansion in child tax benefit and adult GST credit); two new high-income PIT brackets; carbon tax; eliminate oil & gas preferences; abolish immigration 'head tax'.
2000	0 / 0	Tax share of GDP frozen; implement Campaign 2000 child poverty measures (redesign and expansion of child tax benefit); full indexing of the tax system; Mintz Committee business tax base-broadening measures; full inclusion of capital gains and dividends.
2002[2]	0 / 0	

1 Increase in overall tax collections as a share of GDP, first and second years of the AFB.
2 Reports broad fiscal parameters described in CCPA (2001).
3 PIT is personal income tax; RRSP is registered retirement savings plan; and GST is goods and services tax.
Source CCPA and CHO!CES (various years).

Table 4 Policy innovation and structural changes
Alternative Federal Budgets, 1995-2002[1]

Fiscal year	Proposed policy innovations	Proposed structural changes[2]
1995	Formal job-creation target for government; National Child Care programme; National Industrial Strategy; new Canada Post-Secondary Education Act; Human Security Fund replaces defense and development budgets.	Relax drug patent laws; reduce allowed foreign content in RRSPs to 10%; compulsory R&D spending by business; public Procurement Councils in health products and computers.
1996	Create 7 National Social Investment Funds; National Drug Plan; new Higher Education Act; more creative use of government bonds (Debt Victory bonds, real return bonds); Family Farm Support Program.	Bank of Canada refinances 10% of net debt over 5 years; phase out 20% foreign content on RRSPs and RPPs; RRSPs must hold some federal bonds; restore Bank of Canada regulation of chartered bank reserves; mandated community lending by chartered banks; creation of a public Enterprise Development Bank.
1997	Sets federal targets for unemployment and poverty, as well as fiscal targets; 13-point Frontal Assault on Poverty; 7 National Social Investment Funds; National Drug Plan; Community Action Program for Children; establish Canadian Council for Health; National Advance Maintenance Child Support System; Higher Education Act; Equity Participation Foundation; Common Security Fund; Family Farm Support Program.	Bank of Canada refinances 10% of net debt over 5 years; phase out 20% foreign content on RRSPs and RPPs; compulsory deposits by banks in public National Capital Funds; compulsory drug patent licensing.
1998	Engendered AFB; increase Bank of Canada inflation band to 2%–4%; government sets unemployment and poverty rate targets; establish RRSP-eligible CED corporations; National Youth Job Strategy; Canadian Atmospheric Fund; 7 National Social Investment Funds; National Drug Strategy; National Student Grants Program; Advance Maintenance Child Support System; revitalized federal role in training; Equity Participation Foundation.	Bank of Canada refinances 10% of net debt over 5 years; phase out 20% foreign content on RRSPs and RPPs; compulsory community reinvestment by banks, and compulsory deposits in a National Capital Investment Fund.
1999	Establish a separate UI budget; public home care programme; National Pharmacare plan; Canadian Atmospheric Fund; 7 National Social Investment Funds; Forest Investment Fund; Equity Participation Foundation.	Bank of Canada refinances 10% of net debt over 5 years; phase out 20% foreign content on RRSPs and RPPs; compulsory community reinvestment by banks, and compulsory deposits in a National Capital Investment Fund.
2000	8-point programme to support healthy families; National Priorities Capital Endowment (funded from 1999 surplus); separate UI budget; 7 National Social Investment Funds; public home care programme; National Pharmacare plan; National Post-Secondary Education Act; National Advisory Council on PSE; National Environmental Infrastructure Program; Climate Change Strategy; Forest Investment Fund.	National Infrastructure Investment Authority.

1 R&D is research and development; RRSP is registered retirement savings plan; RPP is registered pension plan; CED is community economic development; UI is unemployment insurance; PSE is post-secondary education. 2 A 'structural' change is defined here as anything which redefines or regulates private property rights, or significantly expands the realms of public or non-profit activity in the economy.

Chapter 19

ALTERNATIVE BUDGETING FOR AFRICA?

Lionel Cliffe

I. Africa influences the West: an episode of intellectual history

FROM an outsider's perspective, what is striking about the intellectual and ideological milieu from which the alternative budget (AB) approach has emerged are the echoes of particular dialogues within Africa a generation ago. Thus, it might be useful to sketch in that African intellectual context, which was central to the life and work of a generation of partisan scholars who entered into that milieu, and which shaped the ideas of certain individuals who have been involved in the development of the AB process in Canada. As I get more into old age, I feel that the setting out of such intellectual histories is more and more a necessary element in any political discourse. Awareness of the origins of contemporary discourses prevents new generations from forever having to reinvent the wheel. It also contributes to a living tradition of alternative thinking that has long and diverse roots. This is even more essential in contemporary discussions about Africa, for several reasons. First, at the policy level, the awareness of earlier debates can be a useful, sceptical corrective to whatever are the latest proposals for righting Africa's ills being put forward, mainly by outside agencies. So often what is offered as a new initiative is really just some old fad coming around again, not even always in new bottles. For instance, the new emphasis by the World Bank on governance looks just like the departing colonial powers' priorities of public administration in the early 1960s. Second, the fact that there have been rich traditions of discourse in Africa about African development is often not realised by following generations. There are many reasons for this, but one is the fact that the 1980s and

1990s saw a disjuncture in African discourses as a result of a *de facto* take-over of policy debate by the international financial institutions (IFIs). African contributions, including those that were part of a radical critique of economic and political neo-conservatism, tended to be confined to reactions to those external ideas rather than being proactive. Views of policy-makers and officials tended to be reactive to outsiders' proposals, and often focussed on short-term crisis management rather than longer term strategy. Third, what is striking to an old hand, and is perhaps hard for younger generations to accept, is that the present level of thinking about Africa's predicament and development options is generally at a level that is simplistic conceptually, narrow in disciplinary terms, and less well-informed compared with the awareness and analysis of a generation ago. If this is hard to swallow, just go and read the debates of the 1960s!

It is worth reiterating some of that earlier tradition. In the late 1960s and into the 1970s, one of the main arenas for debate about the "nature of Africa's underdevelopment"—which was the language often used—and of radical development alternatives was in Tanzania. There was a brief golden age of discourse among scholars and activists, who tried to live up to the values and methods of what Gramsci called "organic intellectuals." This hothouse climate led to a widespread familiarity with ideas and ideologies about imperialism, about notions of induced underdevelopment that had just burst onto the Latin American scene, about liberation, and about socialism. It also generated new perspectives on these issues, as attempts were made, not always successfully, to relate this left tradition to the specifics of African realities. Some of the published output of these intense debates can be found in the well-known work of Issa Shivji (1976), Anthony Rweyemamu (1970), Mahmood Mamdani (1976), Walter Rodney (1972), Tamás Szentes (1983), and Giovanni Arrighi and John Saul (1973). This output included collected volumes, presentations of collaborative work, and debates that contained fierce arguments. These were characteristic of the collective nature of the research and the intensity of dialogue.

The context that generated this intellectual climate and fostered the discourse was a product of a number of reinforcing factors. Most obvious was Tanzania's Arusha Declaration of 1967, committing the country to a path of socialism and self-reliance. This context, on the one hand, demanded debate and imaginative thinking about what concrete policies and political initiatives would best give expression to those goals, and scrutiny about the performance of the initiatives that began to be put in train. On the other hand, the commitment meant that Tanzania became a destination for radical activists and scholars from around the world. The remarkable Caribbean thinker CLR James said to me on a visit in 1969: "I never thought I would live to see the building of socialism in a black ex-colony, that was also English-speaking." There were many visitors like him, from socialists of all persuasions and continents, from the black power movement throughout the new world, and from liberation and solidarity movements. At the same time, there was also a resident set of people with similar backgrounds who came to work in teaching, in technical assistance, in non-governmental organizations (NGOs), and particularly in the University of Dar Es Salaam. There were even political refugees from the West who were given asylum!

The intellectual climate in the late 1960s and early to mid-1970s allowed a considerable openness. This reflected the relatively relaxed and tolerant indigenous culture and the absence of a detailed and explicit ideological definition of *ujamaa*, Tanzania's socialism. It was enhanced when Tanzania's ruling party came out in 1971 with the TANU Guidelines, which, for the first time, attacked commandism and rhetorically, at least, commended participation and bottom-up challenges to authority. This climate was reflected in the university and the intellectual networks in which it was involved and it allowed intense debate over everything from the nature of imperialism, to education policy and even the curriculum. What needs to be conveyed here is not simply the fact of ideas being put forward and challenged, but the widespread and intense nature of the dialogues. There was seldom an evening when there wasn't some seminar, rally, or visiting lecture occurring in the university — events outside classroom hours attended voluntarily by large numbers of students and by smatterings of the resident population of politicians, liberation movement personnel, and technical advisers in Dar Es Salaam. This intellectual and political climate, as seen from a Tanzanian perspective, has been captured in a recent memoir by Issa Shivji (2003).

The resident expatriate intellectual community grew up at the same time as the emergence of what was the first generation of young Tanzanian radical intellectuals. Up to the late 1960s, any genuine socialist commitment was confined to President Julius Nyerere and one or two of the people immediately around him. Even though he used his role as *Mwalimu* (teacher), and party-led political education activities were widespread, socialist ideas were not widely internalized. In 1966 the university was closed down after a student demonstration that was seen as reflecting the widespread elitism of students, and generally of the privileged few with higher education. A couple of years later, the student body threw up a group of self-taught revolutionary activists, among them several able Tanzanians and others from neighbouring countries, like Yoweri Museveni, who was to become President of Uganda. Their stance was broadly supportive of the Arusha initiatives but wanting more thoroughgoing and urgent implementation, and it was couched in the more scientific language of revolutionary and liberation movements than that of *ujamaa*.

One unsympathetic and external characterization of the different strands in this intellectual legacy, which was made at the time, referred to divisions between the Left, who were the democratic socialists associated with Nyerere, and the Ultra-Left, which referred to the Marxian intellectuals. The Canadian political scientist Cranford Pratt made a similar distinction between democratic socialists, in which he included himself and Nyerere, and the Marxists, among whom he included people such as fellow Canadians John Saul and John Loxley (Pratt, 1979). A later interpretation by a French neo-Marxist makes similar distinctions, seeing, however, three strands: partisans of Tanzanian socialism, reformists, and the "neo-marxist radicals which were never a homogenous group" (Copans, 1991). Given the character of the debates at the time, these categorizations were simplistic in many respects—not least in that the dominant voices even among the Marxian left were strongly democratic and anti-Stalinist, having come out of liberation movement mobilization and debates in western Marxism. Moreover, the attempt to offer a polarized view does not do justice to the extent to which the debates and generation of ideas were not just about fundamental, analytical issues such as imperialism and underdevelopment, accompanied as they often were by critiques of the post-colonial state, the Tanzania government, and the shortcomings of its policy commitment to socialism. While some were content simply to pitch their camp there, others were also concerned with what might be done practically in a country like Tanzania: what would a socialist formula for rural cooperatives, for higher education, or for public finance look like? Central to these debates about "what is to be done?" were views that underdevelopment meant loss of available surplus and that nationalization, especially of institutions of finance capital, could reverse this leaching of the wherewithal for investment in egalitarian development.

This oft-neglected feature of the intellectual legacy from Africa of a generation ago might be termed "radical pragmatism," and this legacy has directly informed the AB movement in Canada, as several people including, most notably, John Loxley, moved from Tanzania in the mid-1970s to Canada. Radical pragmatists in Tanzania sought to address simultaneously the practical matters as well as the big issues. This attempt to combine radical analysis of what needed to be done with practical concerns of how that might be done viewed the need for socialism as specifically the antidote to underdevelopment, and sought to offer policy suggestions to a state that could be an instrument for that project. With hindsight, of course, there was much delusion in that project. Today, such illusions would be totally unsustainable in any region: the world has moved on. However, in the current context of the supremacy of an increasingly globalized capitalism, the need for such radical pragmatism is even greater. Critiques of globalizing capitalism are all too obvious and easy to make, but those who make them either drift into an acceptance of its being the "only game in town," or posit a wholly unrealistic or indefinitely postponed alternative system. The search for realizable strategies for action that go beyond simple amelioration is thus an urgent necessity, and in this the AB approach may have an important role to play, not only in Canada, but in Africa.

II. The AB approach

It is not stretching parallels too far to see some carry over in thinking from these African debates to the AB initiatives in Canada. In essence the AB approach has three core elements: the articulation of alternative policy premises based on certain principles; the technical working out, with numbers, of these policy options within a credible fiscal framework; and broad participation in this exercise.

In terms of its general principles, the AB approach recognizes in the political economy the dominance of the aforementioned globalizing capitalism, and a state that, to a greater or lesser extent, depending on the complexion of the government of the day, is supportive of those interests. However, it promotes the argument that alternatives are possible, even in this context and even in the short run. More specifically, the approach tackles one of the prevalent arguments against policies for increased welfare provision, improved social services, and modest income redistribution. The rhetoric of the ruling politicians, especially of the centre-left, does not oppose such alternatives directly, but offer the excuse that there just isn't the money. The AB approach gainsays this in a manner that cannot be dismissed as impracticable within existing resource constraints, when, as is said in one document, "the [Alternative Federal] Budget itself casts our policy agenda within a credible fiscal framework, complete with numbers" (Canadian Centre for Policy Alternatives [CCPA] and CHO!CES, 1997).

Working within existing constraints to achieve a different set of outcomes seems an excellent example of the radical pragmatism practised in Tanzania in the 1970s by some of those who were later to become AB participants. The continuity of thinking can also be seen in more specific ways. For instance, another extract from the same document illustrates that, just as in the African debate three decades ago, the issue about how the surplus should be used is a central question. Forecasting a considerable budget windfall in the 1997 Canadian federal budget, the document argues:

> The bulk of this surplus [in the government budget] will likely go into deficit reduction, with small amounts being made available for the proposed infrastructure programme and for a new—and deeply flawed—integrated child benefit. The Alternative Federal Budget would use all of these funds to tackle Canada's pressing social problems, especially unemployment and poverty, reversing those federal government policies which have actually worsened these problems. But we should go further to argue that the government must do much more than this and cast off the fiscal straightjacket in which it has fettered itself. (CCPA and CHO!CES, 1997: 4)

This quotation also brings out another feature of the AB process in Canada: from an approach that focusses on the short term and on the quantification of priorities, it actually explores different policy options, and offers a fundamental challenge to the prevailing orthodoxies espoused by governments around the world. Again, from the 1997 document:

> [The] Alternative Federal Budget outlines a different approach, one which we believe is more responsive to both the needs and preferences of the people of Canada, and one which takes a positive, constructive and more humane approach to dealing with the se-

rious economic and social problems facing the country. It is rooted in basic principles agreed upon in advance by the many groups across the country participating in the AFB exercise. These consist of a commitment to:

- full employment,
- a more equitable distribution of income,
- the eradication of poverty,
- economic equality between men and women,
- the protection of civil, political, economic, social and cultural rights,
- improvement of the environment,
- the strengthening of social programs and public services, and
- the creation of a more just, sustainable and peaceful world order. (CCPA and CHO!CES, 1997: 4-5).

The participatory aspect of the AB approach, mentioned in the above extract, is another essential component, and what this means is also spelled out in the 1997 document:

> [The AFB] is the result of intense discussions over a six-month period around budget tables in Winnipeg and Ottawa; the result of consultations and budget schools in communities across the country; the result of Internet conferences and economists' roundtables. Twenty policy working groups have drafted and reworked many times the sections that together make up this document. The process has been open and inclusive. We asked only that participants subscribe to the fundamental values that underlie the exercise. The result is a consensus document—the product of a give-and-take in pursuit of common goals. (CCPA and CHO!CES, 1997: 1)

The AB approach is thus predicated upon an alternative vision. Using that vision, it seeks to demonstrate that choices are possible even within the context of a globalizing political economy. Moreover, in making those choices, the AB approach gives priority to participation. To this old Tanzania hand, it would appear that the radical pragmatism that informed much of our work in the late 1960s and early 1970s is alive and well in Canada.

An important caveat is, however, in order. The AB approach is not a single, well-defined method. Some definitions are necessary to clarify the different ways of approaching an AB process, the tasks that are involved in an AB, and what parts of the AB process might be possible in differing circumstances. The phrase "alternative budgets" can, it seems to me, be used in two broad senses:

• An alternative budgeting approach. This refers to the general perspective of realizing the importance of extra-parliamentary political mobilization around the government's budget process. It is predicated upon a commitment to certain alternative values, which might include poverty elimination, broad-based development, and equity of resource provision in terms of gender, race, region, and ethnic group. These values are applicable in many settings around the world, including Africa.

• An alternative budget. This is the preparation of a comprehensive and economically and fiscally consistent document, produced as an alternative to that produced by government.

Clearly, an alternative budget is part of an alternative budget approach. However, an alternative budget approach need not necessarily encompass the production of an alternative budget. In this light, it might help to distinguish two processes that form part of an alternative budget approach but which, if pursued alone, for technical or political reasons, can facilitate the emergence of an alternative budget process that falls short of a complete alternative budget:

• Budget scrutiny. This refers to any monitoring process conducted by popular forces, such as civil society organizations (CSOs) or opposition groups, which promotes awareness of the implications of budget provisions and actual expenditures. It thus involves using the budget as a means of advocacy and mobilization. Such mobilization might be informed by budget analysis of a specialist sort, as in Canada.

• Budget analysis. This refers to a systematic review of the government's budget, perhaps focussing on the implications for certain needs or special groups. It may be conducted by CSOs or opposition but requires a degree of technical expertise. An example would be gender budgets.

Again, budgetary analysis can be part of an overall process of budgetary scrutiny, but budgetary scrutiny does not necessarily involve a formal budgetary analysis.

Thus, there is a hierarchy of possibilities. At the one end, there is a full AB. Below that, there is the AB approach. Embedded within the latter can be a budget analysis, but this need not be the case. The AB approach adopted might simply consist of a process of budgetary scrutiny by CSOs and opposition groups.

Two other terms are now part of the discourse from within the AB network. If ABs offer a hierarchy of possibilities, these terms in some ways sit at the apex of the hierarchy, in that they mark a more complete process than that involved in producing a full AB:

- Participatory budgeting. To my mind, this refers to a range of processes distinct from the preparation of a full AB, with its implication of confrontation with a government document. Rather, participatory budgeting involves popular voices in the official budgetary process. One of the oft-quoted examples, from the city of Porto Alegre in Brazil, allows a certain percentage of the municipal budget to be determined by a "deliberative" process that allows participation by communities in the allocation of resources. Lesser degrees of consultation are occurring elsewhere in Brazil and in other countries (CCPA, 2003b).

- Democratic budgeting. This could represent the ideal, where the right for an extra-parliamentary, grassroots deliberative process, involving a share of actual projected expenditure and a range of policy choices, would be used to encourage popular control of the budgetary process. The participatory aspect of democratic budgets would, however, sit alongside formal parliamentary enactment and accountability. Thus, the institutional framework within which the budget would be designed, developed and implemented would be democratized (Loxley, 2003).

In light of these two, somewhat fuller, approaches, the AB process could be considered a dynamic towards the ideal, that of democratic budgets.

This definitional exercise has been more than just a semantic detour, because it can help specify what is appropriate and possible in different African circumstances. It is clear that ABs in Africa could take a variety of forms. It may be possible in some African countries to produce a full, formal AB document. In other settings, an AB approach might be helpful in encouraging popular participation and reducing conflict. Such an approach might involve formal budgetary analysis, or might involve greater or lesser degrees of budgetary scrutiny. Indeed, in many circumstances in Africa, including some of the most unlikely, budgetary scrutiny at the local level takes place, and this may be a fertile ground upon which to encourage further understanding of the tools and techniques of an AB approach.

III. The AB approach and African realities

Many people would accept the desirability of applying the basic concerns and fundamental values of the AB approach—critiquing underlying policy, articulating feasible alternative strategies, and encouraging popular mobilization around such ideas—to African countries. However, in order to develop ABs in Africa it is necessary to confront the different circumstances of Africa. For example, the list of fundamental values taken from the 1997 Alternative Federal Budget (CCPA and CHO!CES, 1997) has, at the top of the list, full employment. This, of course, is desirable for Africa and for Africans, but the meaning of full employment in Africa and prospects for achieving it may have to be very different from that in Canada. Similarly, the acknowledgement that current realities impose constraints on national policy that is central to Canada's AB may generate even less room to manoeuvre in most African conditions, subject as they are to structural adjustment programmes negotiated with the IFIs. Having said that, however, realizing that current African realities do not impose a completely demobilizing straightjacket is perhaps even more crucial for African countries. There is more room to navigate than is often appreciated. Notwithstanding this point, though, the key issue in thinking about how ABs could be used in Africa is to recognize that Africa's realities may result in the AB approach having different aims and different outcomes than that in developed market economies such as Canada.

It is instructive to look at some of these African realities. As Ryszard Kapuscinski cautions in his recent *The Shadow of The Sun: My Life in Africa* (2002: i), Africa "is too large to describe. It is a veritable ocean, a separate planet, a varied, rich cosmos. Only with the greatest simplification, for the sake of convenience, can we say 'Africa.' In reality, except as a geographical appellation, Africa does not exist." In this light, it is not surprising that the first reality is the tremendous variation in state structures, political organization, and socioeconomic conditions in Africa. There are collapsed states such as Somalia and the Congo. There are conflict-ridden states such as Sudan and Liberia. There are authoritarian states such as Eritrea and many smaller states in West Africa. There are partially democratized states such as Kenya and Nigeria. There are, finally, reasonably well-functioning capitalist democracies such as South Africa, Tanzania, and Uganda. This degree of variation means that the introduction of an AB process must reflect local realities, growing organically among those CSOs and political and social organizations that may exist.

A second fundamental feature of most African realities is widespread and endemic corruption. Fostering accountability, in the quite literal sense, and other measures to counter the corrupt use of public funds has thus to be a central and probably prior concern of an AB process, particularly because of its systemic consequences. Corruption produces a debilitating haemorrhaging of economic resources through capital flight, obscene conspicuous consumption, and speculation, particularly amongst the small elite, and can occur on a scale that seriously undermines development prospects. Indeed, capital flight and wasteful elite consumption, and the consequent lack of available surplus, were seen as central roots of underdevelopment in the Dar Es Salaam debates.

A third widespread African reality results from corruption and has a defining influence on the nature of politics. Diverted state funds form the basis of massive disbursements of patronage, and thus provide a central mechanism in shaping the political economy into a clientelist mould. In turn, the process of allocating resources becomes at best a regional or ethnic squabble over what is in the trough, and this, in turn, can obscure strategic issues such as poverty reduction and long-term development priorities. These tendencies have, if anything, become even more marked as some states have introduced civilian regimes and competitive elections in the 1990s. At worst, the clientelist struggle for spoils has degenerated into violent conflict and, in some cases, state failure has resulted (Doornbos, 2003).

One final, important dimension of African political realities in the 1990s that must be taken into account in considering ABs has been the trend towards democratization. The majority of countries on the continent have moved away from military rule to some form of civilian governance or from one-party states to some form of multiparty political system. There is debate about how far these trends have been externally driven by the imposition of political conditionality by donor governments and the IFIs, or by internal popular forces. The answer is probably not a simple either/or, but a more complex articulation of both. Certainly, external forces shape internal political forces, and not just the form of government and its policies. However, there is also clear evidence that Africans want to have a voice and, whatever the conclusion about original causes, there is a definite popular will for further democratization in many countries.

There are two implications of this particular reality. First, any AB initiative will be undertaken in a context where, in most situations, democratic institutional mechanisms are not yet established or deeply embedded. Even if the present government has been elected, only in a handful of cases has this meant a change of regime through the ballot box. As a consequence, the very notion of accountability may not even be rhetorically articulated, let alone internalized by those in power. At the same time, the amount of fiscal and economic data in the public domain is limited and officials are seldom cooperative in sharing what they have. This compounds the lack of accountability. Therefore, there will be practical difficulties and hard political struggles if there is to be any budget scrutiny, let alone accountability through a budget analysis or a more formal AB exercise. As a consequence, there is a second implication: the incompleteness and recentness of democratization efforts impose an imperative, that democratization become further embedded within the political economy. Ironically, in this light, an AB is worth considering precisely because it can be a tool in this broader process of embedding, particularly through its emphasis on participation and on scrutiny. Equally, the form and methods of any such AB initiative should ideally be seen as elements within a set of other, broader democratization initiatives. In short, the AB process may be even more vital in contexts where democratization is at an early and incomplete stage, rather than in Western countries where it gives long-existing democratic accountability an extra dimension and a new lease on life.

In circumstances of incomplete or partial democratization, a particular imperative is for civil society–based modes of accountability. The ongoing democratization process in much of Africa has been confined to some elements of parliamentary or representative democracy. The late Nigerian political analyst Claude Ake has argued that this form of democracy, further reduced to multiparty electoral competition and interest groups, is not the kind of democracy that Africa requires (Ake, 2000). He rejects this on the basis of principle, and from a practical concern with the interconnection of democracy and development. Ake shares the early, uncompromising conception of democracy offered by the ancients: direct rule by the people and not just representative government. Ake reminds us that even the authoritarian Aristotle saw democracy as meaning the "authority…of the poorer classes" (p. 8). Ake sees the principles of equality and of participation being eroded in the theory and emergence of the liberal democratic state in which democracy, by "being trivialized…is no longer threatening to political elites" (p. 30). The resulting patterns of competitive elitism and the apoliticization of civil society follow the parallel development of capitalism, so that the core values of democracy are presented as being essentially the same as those of the market:"egotism, property, formal freedom and equality" (p. 26). Ake further argues that the same "trivialization of democracy" in their own countries makes the developed Western governments and their international institutions wholly inappropriate as the means of delivering democratization to Africa, whether by political conditionality or intervention. In particular, Ake argued for an emphasis on participation, accountability, and the assertion of human rights as being more relevant than mere multiparty elections. Moreover, he insisted that what is required is attention to social and economic rights, and not just those of citizenship and political freedom.

Ake derives these imperatives from his more empirical discussion of the connection between democracy and development. He rejects any essentialist position of the inevitability of associating or, indeed, rejecting "democracy and development." Thus, he questions both the current fashion of seeing democracy as a necessary prerequisite for development, as well as the reverse, the necessity of authoritarian rule, which was in vogue among some theorists of both the right and the left in earlier decades. He argues for an approach that seeks "democratizing development" (p. 87). The practical advantage of the mass of the people's having a voice is the possibility that it may lead to a different kind of development path, which is not so outward-oriented and which stresses rural development. However, the need is for more than the people's having a say in policy formulation. A fundamental reversal of attitudes and a change in the basis of policy discourse are needed. Indeed, Ake gets at a fundamental but not always recognized issue in urging the need to get away from:

> Prevailing strategies [which] tend to assume that the people and their way of life are the "problem." But when people rather than development processes are problematised, development is derailed…Policy involves an assault on their culture in a misconceived battle against "backwardness" (Ake, 2000: 87).

There are echoes in this kind of concern for people-centred development with the principles that lie behind the AB approach, and which thus underscore its potential in Africa. However, in so doing, it is clear that in the African context, the challenge of contributing to the institutionalization, in civil society, of something beyond multiparty democracy must shape the forms and priorities of any AB initiative.

Given these realities, it might be considered a tall order to think about ABs. However, as the preceding makes clear, it is one that is consistent with the challenges facing much of Africa. The challenge in much of the continent is to find mechanisms for handling the allocation of revenues in a manner that not only exposes and limits corruption, but more fundamentally works against clientelist politics in a way that avoids degeneration into open conflict. In this, the AB process could have a role. Indeed, it could be argued that a minimum requirement for an anti-clientelist politics is a degree of transparency about spending, and that this is promoted by the AB approach. Transparency ensures that budgeted expenditures, even when allocated through some due process of reporting to a legislature, are devoted to public purposes and to the actual objectives specified for the expenditures. Contrary to the rhetoric of some of the IFIs, this is not just a technical and efficiency requirement. It is also essential politically, in that the capacity to undertake even minimal budgetary scrutiny, which can form part of an AB process, can assuage marginalized groups and can create revenue-sharing formulae that might be essential for peace building.

One vital institution that is needed to increase transparency would be an independent, effective—and, indeed, courageous—public accounts committee of an elected legislature. An outside observer might grant that an effective instrument of this kind has already been institutionalized in South Africa, with its sophisticated information networks and a constitution that provides for a number of parliamentary checks on the executive. However, even there it has only partially curbed corruption. Prospects in other countries would not be rated highly, especially given the prevalence of what might be termed a dominant party set-up in many of the now elected legislatures, where typically one party has a large, and seemingly semi-permanent, majority and is faced by a set of small opposition groups.

Clearly, there are reasons why Africa should be interested in subjecting the budget to scrutiny and perhaps to analysis, within, possibly, the framework of an AB approach, albeit one that is sensitive to African realities and which, as a consequence, might consider different aims from those adopted in other environments. The technical working out of a feasible fiscal framework, and thus the development of a more formal full AB, may be more challenging, although there are economists and other specialists who could be mobilized, and the numbers are arguably less complicated. Whatever the case, the participatory process used in an AB strategy would have to be organized on a quite different basis and in some of the most authoritarian states may be almost precluded. Notwithstanding this, however, ABs have the potential to act as an important tool in Africa.

IV. Alternative budgeting in Africa: experiences and possibilities
Africa already has some relevant experience in ABs. These could provide a foundation for initiatives in, and yield some lessons about, the appropriate forms of ABs in the African context. However, the great deal of variation in state structures, political organization, and socio-economic conditions are, not surprisingly, reflected in Africa's AB experience. The possibility exists for new initiatives, in light of the five-fold typology of state structures: capitalist democracy, partial democratization, authoritarian state, conflict-ridden state, and collapsed state. In each, ABs either have a role or have a potential role as a tool of accountability, advocacy, mobilization, and change.

i. Capitalist democracy: South Africa, Tanzania and Uganda
Not surprisingly, given its human, informational, and economic resources, and the breadth of its CSOs, South Africa has probably gone furthest in its embrace of AB initiatives. South Africa has a multiplicity of CSOs, a relatively sophisticated process that constitutionally provides for scrutiny of all legislation, including the budget, by parliament, which even publishes documents analyzing and critiquing government budgets.

A critical catalyst in the development of AB initiatives was the creation of a specialist Budget Information Service (BIS), that began work in the late 1990s, as an offshoot of the think-tank and activist resource network, the Institute for Democratic Alternatives in South Africa (IDASA). Dedicated to campaigning for "budgets responsive to the poor," it offers an e-mail service, called *Budget Briefings*, for people who want specific questions answered, and an informative website provides training and other services. It puts out a regular newsletter, *Budget Watch*, and has published special studies and analyses as well as a series of guide books. Its regular publications and training have tended to concentrate on how national and provincial budgets do or do not integrate and affect poverty, special groups like children, and basic services such as education and health, with the latter having a strong emphasis on HIV/AIDS.

A very significant aspect of its work has been its documentation of the wide range of implications of the budgetary process for women (Budlender, 1996, 1997, 1998, 1999). In this regard, the BIS has backed up initiatives initially taken within the newly elected, post-apartheid Parliament, where ideas about a gender budget were presented in the mid-1990s. One consequence of parliamentary and NGO activism was that the finance minister pledged to incorporate gender-budgeting methods into the official budgetary process in 1998. However, that commitment has since been withdrawn (Fleshman, 2002).

These extensive activities in South Africa provide a much-needed extra-parliamentary scrutiny of the complex processes of budgeting and their outputs, and a budget-based analysis of what this means for key social groups and issues. They have generated some transparency and helped to produce informed debate, both within parliament and other branches of government, and in civil society, where they have been a focus for some political mobilization. However, they have as yet to develop two of the three core features of alternative budgeting in Canada. Budget scrutiny and analysis have stopped short of producing a formal full AB document that could show the feasibility of different priorities and criteria. Nor has there emerged a participatory network that could be the basis of broad coalitions and that could thus focus campaigns on concrete, realizable, "radically pragmatic" alternatives. They are thus not fully fledged ABs. Development of the work of the BIS in this direction would be appropriate in South Africa. There are large and organized groups such as trade unions, women's groups, landless groups, and HIV/AIDS activists who clearly feel that their interests are, at best, marginalized in the allocation of resources by the state. There are also a multiplicity of special interest groups and CSOs that are taking up issues that have budgetary implications, but not always in a coherent way. A fully fledged AB could provide these groups with greater focus in their campaigning and advocacy efforts.

A prime concern of the BIS has been gender budgeting, and it is in this area that other capitalist democracies in Africa have developed similar initiatives. In Tanzania, for instance, a 1997 initiative by a group of members of parliament (MPs), women's groups, think-tanks, and NGOs formed the Feminist Activist Coalition (FEMACT) and organized a workshop to explain and demystify the budget process (Budlender, Elson, Hewitt, and Mukhopadhyay, 2002). They made a breakthrough in 1999 when the government invited FEMACT to participate in the official budgetary process and to sensitize officials to the necessary techniques. It has subsequently been asked to prepare analyses of key sectors such as health, education, and women and children's provision. In contrast to the experience of studies of other countries, these studies have been undertaken by teams involving NGOs, academics, and government participants. Perhaps this official sensitivity to such issues of equality, which has taken the Tanzanian government further in this direction than the South African, is testimony to the legacy of the socialist principles espoused and inculcated 30 years ago. However, like the actual experience of the 1960s and 1970s, the extent to which there can be an adjustment of spending priorities is severely restricted. Tanzania has a very limited revenue base and there are conditions on overall spending that are imposed by the development assistance necessary to balance the recurrent budget.

A similar coalition of women's advocacy groups, MPs, and government officials took initiatives in 1999 in Uganda. It regards the steps to involve parliament more, and at an earlier date in the budgetary process, as one of its contributions. It also considers the greater emphasis on local government as one of its achievements. It has also pointed out the fact that the national teaching hospital in the capital consumed 60 per cent of the total health budget, a pattern not dissimilar to those elsewhere in Africa (Fleshman, 2002).

Clearly, in functioning capitalist democracies in Africa, a fledging AB movement is emerging. Although the goals of AB proponents differ from country to country, and the tools they utilize therefore also differ, there is, in general, a clear understanding of the need to undertake budgetary scrutiny and analysis, even if there is not a full and formal AB.

ii. Partial democratization: Kenya

After the incomplete democratization process of the 1990s, there are many countries that share similar characteristics to those that typified Kenya up to the end of 2002. In these countries, despite competitive elections, the legislature and government are monopolized by a dominant party. This party is usually the single party that had ruled prior to competitive elections, or one formed by military or other rulers. It is common in these countries to find that freedoms of the media and to mobilize politically are curtailed. Government bodies often still act arbitrarily and without accountability, although in some cases, such as Kenya and Nigeria, there may be a degree of due legal process. In these countries there are often a multiplicity of CSOs that, as a result of the past decade's struggle for democratization, are politically concerned and used to networking with each other. However, in some, the vitality and range of CSOs may often be less advanced than that seen in Kenya or Nigeria.

Kenya is one example of a partially democratized country that has not yet attempted an AB analysis. However, it also exemplifies a number of other experiences that an AB process might build upon in an effort to increase accountability. In the mid-1990s the opposition MP and former director of the African Academy of Sciences, Professor Peter Anyang Nyong'o, managed to take over the chair of a moribund parliamentary Public Accounts Committee (PAC). The committee was invigorated and successfully tracked down some unsanctioned expenditure. It also acted as a forum for raising issues about the direction of overall policy. As a result, it got some external support. On one memorable occasion in 2001, one of the periodic International Monetary Fund (IMF) and World Bank delegations sent to consider whether to resume loans to Kenya, which had been suspended because of a lack of progress in anti-corruption measures, actually held meetings with the PAC. These meetings were in addition to those with the Treasury and other government ministries, and provoked much anger in President Daniel Arap Moi's government. An associated initiative activated the Public Investment Committee (PIC) of parliament, which, as a result, published annual reports in the years following the first multiparty elections that gave specific documentation of graft in awarding contracts for investment, consultancies, and the supply of materials. It also pointed to some underlying institutional weaknesses that allowed such activities. For instance, many parastatal corporations were, from the provisions of the State Corporation Act, subject to reduced political oversight and scrutiny. Similarly, the practices of the National Social Security Fund resulted in it utilizing its massive funds to "institutionalise corruption," as the 9th Report of the PIC put it (*East African Standard*, 13 April 2001). The effect of this parliamentary scrutiny was, unfortunately, limited, as the government refused to prosecute in any of the cases revealed by the two bodies. However, with a new government elected at the end of 2002 in Kenya, this is one area where some real accountability may emerge. Such accountability could serve as a precondition for the launch of an AB exercise by Kenya's wide range of CSOs.

Another specific anti-corruption initiative in Kenya also illustrates some of the constraints facing any attempt to set up an AB process. In the late 1990s, a law was passed, setting up a Kenya Anti-Corruption Authority (KACA), largely as a result of external pressure from the IFIs and donors. In particular, the IMF and the World Bank stipulated that measures along these lines were a precondition for the resumption of programme aid. The evidence from its few early months of operation suggests it was beginning to impose curbs. However, in late 2000 an appeal to the High Court was successful in getting the act declared unconstitutional, primarily on the grounds that appointing a judge as the KACA's head infringed on the principle of the separation of powers. Continued donor pressure led to the consideration of alternative legislation, but prior to the December 2002 presidential elections, no effective replacement for the KACA had been created, because of a lack of agreement between backbench MPs and the government. This illustrates that although there was, prior to the last presidential election, a numerically strong opposition, many MPs shared the government's wariness of any anti-corruption body with real teeth, for they too were part of the wealth-amassing clientelist game. Thus, in the political struggle to get an anti-corruption watchdog, pressure came not from parliament but from CSOs, donors, and international NGOs, most notably from a lively national branch of Transparency International. These bodies rightly argued that Kenya's mixed experience with the derailing of the KACA and the partial success of the PAC suggested that civil society mechanisms are essential to complement whatever scrutiny bodies there are within the different branches of government. This is the only basis on which there can be an effective anti-corruption watchdog, as the World Bank itself now acknowledges.

The role of CSOs in monitoring and scrutiny processes within government in Kenya has thus been substantial. The role of these organizations is often one of advocacy, although often they also have researchers. Advocacy groups are particularly strong in these areas:

1 **Women's groups:** The *Maendeleo ya Wanawake* (Development of Women) organization had been associated with the Moi regime, but its strong and reasonably independent base made it capable of raising concerns by itself, on issues such as constitutional reform and voter education. Other bodies have campaigned, educated, and informed, and offered legal and other services to women, notably the International Federation of Women Lawyers (Kenya), the National Council of Women of Kenya, and the Education Centre for Women and Democracy, among others.

2 **Environmentalists:** The Green Belt Movement and the Kenya Forestry Working Group have conducted vigorous, highly visible protests against the officially sanctioned encroachment into forest reserves, and the former has also campaigned on a wider range of non-forest environmental issues. Inevitably, these campaigns also raise issues of corruption.

3 **Human rights and constitutional reform:** Bodies like the Kenya Human Rights Commission, the *Elimu ya Sheria* (Education about Law), the Institute for Education in Democracy, the Law Society of Kenya, and the Citizens' Coalition for Constitutional Change have provided assistance to individuals and communities as well as undertaking investigations and campaigns on an ongoing basis. However, they have also joined forces with a network of organizations on constitutional reform, civic education, and election monitoring in the last decade.

There are also a number of institutions that do not have a specialist focus but that do have a support base and/or resources and a record of engagement on key issues to do with poverty and political reform. The most crucial are the trade unions, the churches—especially those affiliated with the National Christian Council of Kenya (NCCK)—as well as a range of local and international NGOs. The trade union movement has bargaining potential that is only as strong as one might expect from an economy with limited formal employment opportunities and a rapidly growing population, but it has had a continuous institutional existence since the 1960s and does get involved in broader political issues. The NCCK has conducted its own surveys on controversial public issues since the 1960s. It does not draw back from controversy, and also has extensive networks that report on food-security and conflict problems. Development NGOs have a widespread presence, and have become used to being involved in areas seemingly outside their specialist concerns, if only because anti-poverty programmes take them into rights issues, into conflict management, and, eventually, into democratization.

The work of CSOs, trade unions, the churches, and NGOs has been assisted by a number of think-tanks that grew up in the 1990s. These bodies continue to mobilize economists and other analysts to dig out and analyse data and to make alternative projections. These include the Institute of Economic Affairs, the International Centre for Economic Growth, the Series on Alternative Research in East Africa Trust, the Social Development Network, the Africa Centre for Technology Studies, and the already mentioned Transparency International (Kenya).

The success of the pressures mounted by popular organizations and movements is reflected in the scope of more recent political developments. By the end of the 1980s, there was little room for popular initiatives, although still there was more in Kenya than in most single-party systems. However, reform, when it came, was very much a result of a sustained period of popular pressure. This was spearheaded by the long-established CSOs, the churches, and some development NGOs, and was given support by some Western governments who, after the Cold War, began to see beyond the regime's anti-communism. This campaign intensified until it finally generated a single but critical political concession in 1991, the elimination of the one-party clause in the constitution.

The inability of the opposition parties that were formed to present a united front played into the cunning of the regime, so that no more fundamental reform came through the successive elections of the 1990s. However, during that period, pressures mounted on specific issues such as corruption, environmental decline, and poverty. These went alongside, although not always in tune with, periodic campaigns on broad-ranging political reform, and were led by a mushrooming set of CSOs that had a specific focus on governance and democratization. There were but a dozen or so in 1992, but by 1998 there were

over 150. However, the prospect of holding to account the then-existing, cyni-
cally corrupt regime, which had been built on a hierarchical web of clientelist
politics, was limited, as was the prospect of getting acceptance of wider political reform. The government's approach to such pressures was a strategy of frag-
menting the political opposition into two: the parliamentary and the popular.
Thus, in the long-drawn-out efforts to get some broader constitutional reform,
some steps were made, including a law that set out a procedure for it, but only
when parliamentary opposition parties made common cause with CSOs active
in the field. However, after the 1997 elections, when the regime kept control of
the presidency and parliament, collaboration between the ruling party and the
opposition led to the formation of an Inter-Party Parliamentary Committee
(IPPC). The IPPC saw the merits of considerable parliamentary control over
the process of constitutional reform, and from 1998 there was a two-track
dynamic at work, with many CSOs insisting on "people-driven constitution-
making," which culminated in the *Ufungamano* People's Commission of Kenya,
paralleling the Parliamentary Constitutional Review Commission (PCRC) set
up by a Parliamentary Select Committee. It is to the eternal credit of the chief
commissioner of PCRC, Professor Yash Ghai, who was another participant
in the Dar Es Salaam discourses of the 1960s and 1970s, that a dialogue was
maintained between these two processes, and that the *Ufunganamo* initiative
was kept active and visible. This was so despite efforts by people in government
to sabotage the latter's involvement. The PCRC was not quite successful in its
attempts to have draft constitutional proposals ready for discussion and enactment before the elections at the end of 2002. Even with a new government in
2003, the constitutional review is still unfinished business in Kenya, once again
contested between parliamentary groups and popular forces but its completion
is vital to further democratization and accountability.

The political context in Kenya has, of course, dramatically changed with
the electoral defeat of Moi's nominated successor and of the ruling party in
December 2002. The results of the elections permit some possible implications
for accountability and ABs. On the positive side, the constitutional review
process is continuing and it will be interesting to see what provisions there
will be for various forms of accountability, both within government and by
grassroots CSOs. More generally, there is, for the moment, a political climate
that is upbeat, although popular enthusiasm seems to be for the new political

conjuncture rather than necessarily for the new government. Demonstrations and statements are being made that implicitly say to the new government that much is expected of them, an attitude of healthy scepticism that bodes well for continuing demands for accountability and participation. This is welcome, as many figures in the new administration are politicians associated with the old politics of clientelism and tribalism, some having even served in previous governments. However, some observers have been surprised to see prominent critics of the old system, from within the party set-up, like Peter Anyang' Nyong'o, who made parliamentary accounting work, and from the CSO networks, like environmental campaigner Wangari Muthai, given posts within the government. This demonstrates the dilemma for participatory politics in Kenya, and hence for attempts at an AB process. The inclusion of more than just a few figures from the campaigning CSOs, which is one indicator of the potential for transformation, may, on the other hand, represent a process of incorporation and cooptation, and may at least deprive some of these bodies of their vitality. Given that any AB process would have to be rooted outside government, and not depend completely on parliamentary scrutiny, the present state-oriented focus of politics in Kenya may preclude sufficiently robust civil society initiatives designed to scrutinize government and thus enhance accountability.

Nevertheless, in Kenya the potential for extra-governmental scrutiny existed before the recent elections, and it continues to exist. The new government itself may confront the corruption of the previous regime—an investigation of the most notorious, the gold scandal of the early 1990s, has been set in motion—and may develop a more open political climate. In these circumstances some AB initiatives could help to realize some of the potential for ongoing scrutiny of government. In the first instance, of course, this should embrace some effective "corruption watch" mechanisms in both government and in civil society. These might combine efforts in appropriate political climates, like now, but the latter would be well advised to maintain some independent monitoring and dissemination capacity. A second stage might then be the more detailed scrutiny of budgets and of actual expenditure, and their evaluation in terms of criteria such as poverty alleviation, impact on women and children, and the like. Again, it would be healthy if the capacity to scrutinize and analyze the budget develops outside government, to complement the progress made under the old regime through parliamentary committees. The new political opening in Kenya could indeed lead to further democratization and a shift away from clientelist politics if steps were taken to go towards more formal ABs, because these entail the mobilization of political forces around alternative budget proposals, both from government and alternative grassroots organizations. In short, ABs have the potential to solidify democratization in Kenya by enhancing accountability and participation. Moreover, the network of CSOs needed to undertake ABs is already active, and has had influence in the political transformation that has recently taken place.

iii. Authoritarian states: Eritrea

There are many states in Africa with an autocratic regime remaining in place, few active CSOs or independent intellectual workers, and, in some instances, continuing, unresolved conflict. Nonetheless, there are some prospects for using key elements of the AB approach to challenge existing patterns of power and privilege. Eritrea is a good case in point.

From the days of its long liberation struggle from Ethiopian overrule and in the first few years of its statehood, Eritrea was noted as having an effective and disciplined organizational structure. This is still the case, but coinciding with the period of its war with Ethiopia between 1998 and 2000 and after that, the organizational core has lost the broad popular support it once had. Its discipline has turned into repression of opponents, the media, and all forms of dissent. Its fiscal and economic situation and its policies can no longer be considered benevolent to the people.

Part of Eritrea's security-conscious discipline has extended to the financial affairs of government. So far it has kept a tight watch on the first signs of corruption, through, it must be said, a number of fairly severe measures; but public finances are not clearly distinguishable from those of the ruling party and its extensive entrepreneurial activities. The budget and most economic and financial data are not publicly available. The most easily accessible sources of such information are web-based IMF and World Bank documents, in which the IFIs seek to make their own calculations of some of the key variables. Given, too, that the clampdown has restricted even further a very sparse civil society sector, there is clearly no obvious way any kind of standard AB process can be set in motion.

Or is there? One possible strategy could involve the sizeable diaspora and the emerging opposition forces, almost all of whom are in exile. A pure exile movement can usually do little to unseat an entrenched authoritarian regime. However, the exile movement could diversify its current critique of government to include issues of economic strategy and performance, and not just the denial of political rights. In the first instance, the emerging opposition could sharpen their criticism by documenting the economic, social, and fiscal impact of the war. Thus, as noted by the IMF (2003: 21), "growth has declined, inflation has risen, public expenditure (but on the military) has increased, the current account deficit has widened, and foreign reserves have been depleted." A budgetary analysis of actual estimated expenditures of military and civilian sectors, and in terms of other priorities, can be undertaken externally. With the web, and notwithstanding official attempts to curb it, that information can be made available to internal audiences. Moreover, budget monitoring and awareness can help direct a policy instrument that the exile movements and the diaspora have, in effect, in their hands. Remittances from the diaspora are on such a scale that they are what have kept the economy afloat, averaging 37 per cent of gross domestic product over the last 10 years (IMF, 2003: 24). A significant proportion of these remittances has been used to purchase government bonds, although, of course, most of it is transfers to families. The diaspora includes technically qualified people who can disseminate the information through networks and organizations. Its payment of remittances also gives it an incentive to keep an eye on budgets and expenditure, and through the power of targeting, withholding it has a possible weapon to gain some influence.

Thus, even in an authoritarian setting, an AB approach might have some role to play in fostering accountability. Granted, it could do little to change the nature of the regime. However, by offering an analysis of the budget and of the impact of remittances in sustaining authoritarianism, an AB initiative by the exile movement could contribute to a deeper understanding within the wider diaspora of why there is a need for change.

iv.   Conflict-ridden states: Sudan
Sudan is but one of several large and small countries that has experienced internal war, and specifically a conflict that, in part, is about the distribution of resources among regions and peoples with different histories and identities.

There are, in fact, many cultural and historical schisms. However, the most troubling is that between the state authorities, monopolized by political forces representing the mainly Arab northerners, which has been under an Islamist military regime for the last 14 years, and the southerners, who are more typical of sub-Saharan people in their customs and history. Sharp as those cultural fault lines are, they have been exacerbated by the discovery of oil in the south, and, in the last two years, with its exploitation and export.

Months of talks have taken place about a formula worked out in October 2002. The complex structure of these talks involved six committees that sought to come out with feasible and acceptable solutions to a set of issues outlined in the 2002 agreement. One of these was to do with sharing wealth, and, surprisingly, it was the one that seems to have made most headway. Of course, a formula for sharing oil and other revenues will depend on the constitutional structure, which is still to be spelled out but the peace agreement will involve a six-year transition period when the south will have some degree of regional autonomy. It will be crucial to the peaceful working of any wealth-sharing and power-sharing arrangements that such mechanisms be transparent. Here, the emergence of some elements of CSOs in the large areas of the south not under central government control might be an important starting point for developing budgetary awareness and ultimately scrutiny, if not actual analysis. Indeed, there would, of course, have to be monitoring of the formula governing the division of revenues and of the allocation of expenditure at the central and regional levels. If bodies outside government were allowed to contribute to this monitoring procedure, an embryonic AB process would, in effect, have been initiated.

If an acceptable and workable formula for distributing the key resources at the disposal of the government is agreed upon, and if later there is some public scrutiny of its working, there may be lessons for other resource-endowed countries seeking peace formulae, such as Angola, or for others where war goes on. The Sudanese could also benefit from reviewing the experiences of their neighbour Ethiopia, which, since the early 1990s, has developed a federal system based on ethnically defined regions. Its constitution provides for most major revenue collection to be the responsibility of the federal government, but it provides for a fixed formula for allocating a proportion of these revenues to the regions, depending on their population and their level of development. Studies (Love, 2002) have shown that this formula-based share-out is broadly equitable. However, that has not stopped opponents of the dominant ruling group, which comes from Tigray province, from accusing it of favouring its own regions. This political problem arises not from the formula's intrinsic elements but from the fact that it is opaque, and that there has not been any official or popular process of educating people on the budget or involving them in the process. There is, in this, a vital lesson for Sudan and other countries.

In many parts of Africa conflict is about the distribution or maldistribution of resources. In order to resolve this, it will be necessary to agree on their allocation. However, it will also require increased transparency within the state and increased accountability to popular movements. It is clear that this need to agree on resource allocation, transparency, and accountability is consistent with the AB process, and that, indeed, an AB process could contribute to a deepening of transparency and accountability, and, in so doing, contribute to conflict resolution.

v.   Collapsed states: Somalia

Since 1991 Somalia has experienced total state collapse. Many efforts at the macro and local levels to put something back together brings home the fact that (re)constructing a state is in large measure a matter of raising and allocating revenues (Green and Ahmed, 1999). However, beneath all the apparent anarchic chaos, there are structures, or at least informal understandings, designed to make some resources available for public services. These are often highly localized. A typical example was the set-up I observed in 1996 in the small, north-eastern port of Bossasso. This was not torn apart as much as other major cities and ports in the south, but an irregular militia controlled the harbour, levying a fee from all ships docking. This militia were themselves open on occasion to an armed challenge to their monopoly. Despite these circumstances, an Italian NGO, which ran the local hospital, used the good offices of local notables in the mid-1990s to get an agreement from the local militia leaders that they would give up a third of their levies to fund a medical service. Later these informal understandings were partly formalized with the formation of a state-like regional entity covering the entire region, known as Puntland. Thus, local agreements about revenue allocations have facilitated a degree of unrecognized state formation.

The most successful process of unrecognized state formation has been achieved in the northwest, where Somaliland has established a lasting peace between militias and clans, formed and run a government, and even held elections in 2003. A crucial part of this effort, and one that underpins much of the other initiatives, has consisted of finding some minimum revenues to cover the essentials of a state: salaries for a basic cadre of teachers, health workers, judges, police, and honest revenue collectors. The source of funding has to be easy to collect and virtually voluntary, ruling out any form of income tax. The most readily available has been an import duty. This piecemeal way of putting together the elements of local states, and the lessons it has for the more complete government of national reconciliation, under discussion in peace talks in Nairobi, are given little attention in the analysis of the collapse of the Somalian state. Nonetheless, making visible the role of revenue and expenditure in the construction of a viable local state is clearly important. So too, however, is ensuring that, as part of any eventual peace agreement, some public scrutiny of the collecting and disbursing of funds is possible. It can be argued that, as in the case of Sudan, the need to agree revenue-acquisition formulae and equitable distribution of expenditure requires transparency within whatever political formation emerges from the negotiations in Nairobi. It also requires accountability, and particularly to CSOs, so that communities and popular forces have a sense of understanding how revenues are collected and where they are allocated, and in so doing the potential for further conflict is reduced. This need is arguably an indirect example of where approaches derived from the practice of ABs might have something to offer even in collapsed states in Africa.

V. Conclusions: some programme ideas

What is appropriate and possible in terms of an AB approach depends upon the circumstances facing different African countries. Thus, in Kenya before the election of the new government, the conditions for framing an AB were present and might have enhanced the campaign for regime change and constitutional reform. The same possibilities may exist in other countries with some degree of political stability, a thriving CSO sector even with a government that resists any fiscal accountability. In post–election Kenya, given past efforts through parliament to build in anti–corruption and accountability mechanisms, it may be more appropriate for forces in civil society to expend their energies on trying to get a partially receptive government to institutionalize some elements of alternative or participatory budgeting. Likewise, the way forward in South Africa, where there has been budget analysis and scrutiny from civil society, plus some consultation through parliament, might be to seek to broaden and institutionalize those processes. Having said that, some worker, anti–poverty, and gender activists are increasingly losing faith in official development strategies, and for these people a critiquing of existing strategies via the framing of an AB would be more of an immediate priority.

In the many other, less promising, countries where authoritarian rule, conflict, or state failure makes the prospects of ABs or any other steps toward democratizing budgetary processes far less obvious, there is still a potential role for budget analysis. This could be done by exile groups, as in Eritrea or Somalia. Alternatively, budget analysis could be part of a search for alternative, non–violent modes of distribution of resources and, as such, budgetary analysis from CSOs could be conducted as part of a monitoring exercise designed to ensure that agreements to maintain the peace are being honoured.

How might AB initiatives be promoted? Clearly they should not be imposed. Indeed, even a technical assistance programme from outside the continent faces obvious contradictions. The international financial institutions and bilateral donors from the Western powers are shaping budgets through processes that are not in any way democratic or accountable, nor developmental. They are part of the problem in charting inappropriate strategies and obfuscating the possibility of accountability by nationals, so their involvement in providing a solution is problematic, to say the least. On the other hand NGOs, as an alternative channel for disseminating the experience of Canada, Brazil, and other countries, are limited in resource terms. More fundamentally, whether alternative, participatory, or democratic budgeting is to be pursued should be a matter of choice by the peoples and organizations of Africa, based on their reading of the needs and priorities.

Nonetheless, for an informed choice to be made, information about ABs has to be made available. The spread of the idea itself is, of course, part of the answer. The availability of both the technical dimensions of budget analysis and the framing of an AB, and the political experience of mobilizing for such initiatives, took an important step forward with the publication of the Technical Papers from the Canadian Alternative Federal Budget (CCPA and CHO!CES, 1997, 1998; CCPA, 2003a), as well as by John Loxley's book (2003). The latter starts with a chapter entitled "Budgets: The Technical Side Made Easy." There are also think-tanks geared to provide information, notably the International Participatory Budget Project, and Canadian and other bodies ready to share their experiences.

African CSOs must seek out this information for themselves as the key starting point. If that process and the spontaneous dissemination of the approach by its international advocates are not sufficient, then an outreach programme might be considered. International conferences and workshops could make the idea and its feasibility more widely known and help train trainers in the techniques. National seminars in countries where there is even a minimal commitment, whether confined to some elements of civil society or also including official circles, could develop projects and then be supported with technical papers and training. Some of the latter might be delivered through the array of distance-learning modalities now available. However, as mentioned above, the source of funding and institutional base of such technical assistance and capacity building would be crucial in determining its acceptability and its appropriateness. The locus of such initiatives is a controversial issue if democratizing development goals are not to be subverted. Perhaps building on the initiatives and studies on such topics as gender budgets, embarked upon by the United Nations Development Programme and other United Nations agencies, may offer a point of departure that avoids some of these possible contradictions. If western donors are to have any role, some of the Scandinavian countries or others — even Canada? — with a tradition of accountable democracy might prove more acceptable.

This chapter has argued that some of the ideas that have informed the AB approach have been applied in some worthwhile experiments in a few African countries. At the same time, other dimensions of the AB approach could be taken up in many others, including some countries that seem very unpromising. Moreover, in African conditions such initiatives could contribute to more than just popular debate about underlying government strategies and priorities and the enhancement of accountability. Initiatives concerning ABs could also provide popular mechanisms for exposing corruption, dampening down clientelist politics, strengthening formative democratization processes, and resolving and preventing resource-based internal conflicts. Clearly, ABs in Africa are a potential tool for the future. However, this should not be surprising, because they are rooted in a radical pragmatism that was central to Africa's post-colonial intellectual renaissance in the late 1960s and early 1970s.

Chapter 20

NEO-CONSERVATIVE IDEOLOGY, THE STATE AND DEMOCRACY

A Haroon Akram-Lodhi

I. Introduction

IN 1979 Margaret Thatcher was elected Prime Minister of the United Kingdom. In 1980 Ronald Reagan was elected President of the United States[1]. These two elections signalled the beginning of the dismantling of post-war capitalist social democracy around the non-communist world, and particularly in the advanced capitalist countries. Capitalist social democracy had drawn heavily upon the ideas of John Maynard Keynes, who, in *The General Theory of Employment, Interest and Money*, first published in 1936, had shown that the state had the capacity to moderate the business cycle through its ability to spend and tax. The effect of the Keynesian revolution in economic policy-making in the post-war period was profound, in both the advanced capitalist and developing economies, as the role of the state expanded dramatically. This expansion was witnessed in the increased provision of social benefits and public goods, the nationalization of significant numbers of capitalist enterprises, the regulation of market activity, and some attempts at indicative economic planning. Overall economic performance in the advanced capitalist countries and in the developing economies was fairly impressive, and it is for this reason that many refer to this period as the "golden age" of capitalism (Marglin and Schor, 1990). However, in the mid-1960s capitalist social democracy began to witness systemic imbalances driven by declining profitability and chronic disproportionalities in production. This was a result of costs of production rising faster than prices or productivity. Systemic imbalances precluded growth and fostered relatively high rates of inflation (Wolff, 2003; *The Economist*, 8

December 2001; Dumenil and Lévy, 2000; Brenner, 1998; Shaikh and Tonak, 1994; Armstrong, Glyn and Harrison, 1991; Moseley, 1988; Weisskopf, 1979). As popular discontent grew and anti-systemic movements challenged capitalism, most notably in the developing economies but also in the countries of advanced capitalism, neo-conservative intellectuals and politicians began to articulate an alternative vision rooted in a wholesale rejection of capitalist social democracy.

This chapter has five purposes. First, it will critically discuss the ideas of neo-conservatism, and will suggest that these ideas are, in essence, a reification of the hierarchies of actually existing capitalism. Second, it will, in this context, distinguish the key differences between neo-conservatism and neo-liberalism, arguing that the role of the state demonstrates the central doctrinal difference. Third, the chapter will consider the issue of globalization, arguing that neo-conservatives seek a deepening of global hierarchies and that globalization, from a political perspective, is consistent with this. Fourth, it will discuss how neo-conservatism has sought to restructure the state, particularly in developing economies, in order to deepen global hierarchies, suggesting that this effort represents an attempt at the depoliticization of economic decision making. Finally, the chapter will note the implications of this for democracy, suggesting that popular responses to neo-conservative interventions have sought to articulate alternatives predicated upon an informed and participatory democratization of economic decision-making.

II. Neo-conservative ideology

For some readers, it might seem odd to locate the origins of neo-conservatism in the 1960s because, outside of Canada, it has been discussed and debated only since the election of George W Bush to the presidency of the United States. The rise to prominence of figures such as Paul Wolfowitz, Richard Perle, Elliot Abrahms, Abram Shulsky, Steve Cambone, Doug Feith, "Scooter" Libby, and John Bolton within the US government, Robert Kagan within the American intellectual community, William Kristol and the *Weekly Standard* within US journalism, and the American Enterprise Institute as the leading neo-conservative think-tank, can make it appear as if many principal politicians and policymakers within the US administration are neo-conservative, and have, at the very least, the attention of George Bush. However, neo-conservatism has been a powerful force in politics and economics over the last 25 years. Long before the current recognition of neo-conservatism as a coherent political and economic ideology, figures such as Irving Kristol in the US broke with the left wing of the Democratic Party and started to systematically espouse the need for ideological "rearmament." Early allies included Ronald Reagan, who employed Richard Perle and Elliot Abrahams in his first adminstration. In the United Kingdom, figures such as Keith Joesph, Enoch Powell, Roger Scruton, Maurice Cowling and Rhodes Boyson were developing neo-conservative propositions in the late 1960s and early 1970s, supported by the Adam Smith Institute, academic research, and influential media voices such as *The Times* of London. Neo-conservatism is thus not new, although it has been called other things, including Thatcherism, Reaganism, monetarism, and even, quite mistakenly, neo-liberalism.

A defining belief of neo-conservatives is that the world and its people are not equal, and are shaped by hierarchies between and within societies (Strauss, 1990b). According to neo-conservatives, only the elite at the apex of the hierarchy can understand this "natural" truth about human society and history (Strauss, 1990a). This gives the elite insights into how the political economy operates, as well as power over its operation. It also gives the elite a moral clarity that is not held by those who are subordinate, who, while not capable of understanding it, are capable of questioning their subordination and in so doing challenging civil order and structures of power. There is, therefore, a need, within this model, for authority. As a consequence neo-conservatives can be critical of individualism, because it can upset hierarchy and authority relations. They similarly believe in the essential fragility of representative democracy: it has the potential to challenge hierarchy and upset order. Indeed, in its capacity to engender what neo-conservatives would deem the social decadence arising from a lack of order and authority, democracy can damage public and private morality and civil life (Bloom, 1988). Armed with their clarity and their belief that they can identify both order and decadence, it is not surprising that neo-conservatives believe that the world can be viewed in terms of good and evil, which only they are capable of defining. Neo-conservatism is thus rooted in authentically conservative themes of morality, civil authority, and hierarchy.

These themes are then articulated with a classically liberal emphasis on the need for a free economy. The neo-conservative economic vision sought to re-establish the dominance of the market through internal deregulation and privatization, external trade and financial liberalization, the opening up of economies to inflows of foreign direct investment, and the realignment of exchange rates in accordance with market priorities, while at the same time reshaping the role of the state through lower corporate taxes, fiscal discipline, and monetary rigour. This vision represented an attempt to restore the rate of profit in the advanced capitalist economies by, in essence, cutting real wages and, more particularly, the social wage.

There are, in this articulation, clear echoes of the politics of Ronald Reagan from the 1960s and Margaret Thatcher from the 1970s. Both portrayed politics in terms of a struggle between good and evil, with good being represented by the patriarchal family and market fundamentals and evil being represented by internal dissent to their policies and the external threat of the Soviet Union (Dallek, 2000; Young, 1993). Both Reagan and Thatcher reasserted the role of a particular conception of morality in civic life; for example, when efforts were made to reclaim civil authority over "enemies within." These enemies could be striking air-traffic controllers or coal miners, rebellious students or the sanctuary movement. In reasserting their version of morality Thatcher and Reagan privileged private property as a bulwark of civil authority, and portrayed public provision as responsible for the emergence of a decadent mediocrity. Finally, despite making noises about equality, both, in their pursuit of market fundamentalism, deepened inequality and promoted social divisions. It is thus not too difficult to paint Reagan and Thatcher as having ideas that thoroughly endorsed neo-conservative philosophy.

Neo-conservatives reject capitalist social democracy, but not the social relations of capitalism. In their defence of private property and social inequality the natural hierarchy of neo-conservatism is implicitly the hierarchies of class in general and capitalism in particular. Those who sit at the apex of the hierarchy are the capitalist class, who understand that, as a consequence of the class relations emerging out of the separation of the direct producers from the means of production, there are limits to understanding and knowledge amongst the labouring classes, and hence their capacity to take action. Moreover, the knowledge that the capitalist class holds gives its members clarity about the essential reality of class relations, and authority over enemies within: those who would challenge the pattern of class relations. Authority must, for the capitalist class, be translated into civil order, which sustains capitalist social relations, requiring the extraction of surplus value and thus the dominance of the capitalist class over labour and other social forces (Marx, 1982). If the crisis of capitalist social democracy fostered declines in the rate of profit the restoration of the social authority of capital would allow capital to extract more unpaid labour from their workers and increase the rate of exploitation. The social authority of capital is thus clearly rooted in economic relations, but it also extends into social and cultural life (Gramsci, 1971). It operates by fostering the emergence of an individualized consumerist culture that uses the celebration of a commodity fetishism-based mediocrity to trivialize the public provision of social needs and reduce the popular appeal of participatory democracy as an alternative means of organizing social and economic affairs. Therefore, despite neo-conservative claims that they have unique insights into the operation of the political economy, and notwithstanding the point that neo-conservatism offers in many ways a modernist rereading of 19th century ideas, this cursory examination of neo-conservative philosophy demonstrates that it is, in essence, untrammelled capitalist ideology (Worsthorne, 1971).

Thus, for neo-conservatives capitalism is how the economic system should be organized, and institutions that sustain capitalist activity are vital to the defence of capitalism. However, under capitalist social democracy the role of two key capitalist institutions had been weakened. As a consequence, neo-conservatives sought to reinvigorate these two institutions. The first was markets. Neo-conservatives sought the removal of obstacles to markets because of their capacity to use dispersed and fragmented information to enhance the efficiency of capital. In this emphasis on institutions, information and markets, neo-conservatives place their economic philosophy in a vein that is similar to that of Fredrich Hayek (2001). However, the Austrian economist, as a liberal apologist of capitalism, saw the existence of markets and free competition as an end in itself (Hayek, 1996). By way of contrast, for neo-conservatives markets and competition are a means to an end. That end is the maintenance of the dominance of the hierarchical capital/labour relation, and hence the social authority of capital, an authority that had been undermined within civil society, intellectuals, and culture by capitalist social democracy (Worsthorne, 1971).

The second institution that neo-conservatives sought to reinvigorate was the state. According to neo-conservative political philosophy the state must be strong in order to fulfill four key functions. First, it must continue to undermine residual commitment within communities to the collectivism of capitalist social democracy and, in so doing, continue to sustain capitalist social relations. Second, it must be capable of governing the market, ensuring that the coercive discipline of competition that is so central to capitalism's dynamic of accumulation is sustained. Third, it must be capable of facilitating the generalization of the productivity gains arising from coercive competition across the economy as a whole. Thus, for neo-conservatives the priority is the capitalist system as a whole, and not, as is the case for neo-liberals, individual capitals. Fourth, the state must be capable of upholding the social dominance of the capital/labour relation. However, for neo-conservatives these functions are not equally important. The maintenance of the dominance of the capital/labour relation, and hence the social authority of capital, outweighs the other responsibilities of the state.

These functions have certain implications for neo-conservative ideology. The first implication is that capitalism, in its need for the state, depends on social institutions that are not the creation of markets. Hence, the market is an outcome of social relations, and not the producer of social relations. The second implication is that the importance of markets is not in their relationship to democracy but because they offer the best means of allocating resources, providing incentives, and stimulating the accumulation upon which capitalism depends. The third implication, which follows from this emphasis on markets, is that policies are not about social welfare and public need but rather the private efficiency of capital. The last implication is, in some ways, the most important. It is clear that for neo-conservatives both markets and states are a means to an end: the sustenance of capitalist social relations. Thus, despite their emphasis on the need for markets, neo-conservatives take a fairly pragmatic view about the relationship between states and markets. Neo-conservatives do not take issue with the need for the state to be interventionist in its efforts to sustain capitalist social relations, albeit interventionist in ways that, as shall be shown below, differ significantly from those undertaken under capitalist social democracy.

In offering these views, neo-conservatives had to vigorously contest and, indeed, undermine capitalist social democracy. They did this by undertaking a wide-ranging and diverse intellectual struggle in the 1970s to change the dominant set of ideas held by people and thus reshape the social fabric (Hall and Jacques, 1983). In some places, such as the US, Australia, New Zealand and the Netherlands, this struggle was undertaken on reasonably friendly terrain. In other places, such as the UK and Canada, the terrain was less friendly. A critical variable in this struggle was the harnessing of popular discontent with capitalist social democracy. This discontent concerned the way the economy operated, relations within civil society, and cultural values. Discontent cut across a number of social divisions, and neo-conservative ideology bonded with certain aspects of popular experience. However, capturing popular discontent also required taking a clear leading position about the cause of discontent, even if it was, at the time, a minority position. The neo-conservative position most clearly articulated was, of course, that to do with the management of the economy and the need to restructure the way in which the state intervened in the management of the economy. Here, neo-conservative market fundamentalist prescriptions became, over time, widely accepted, and popular hostility became directed towards the state rather than the capitalist class. In this way, neo-conservatives, in Stuart Hall's (1988) evocative phrasing of Gramsci, "remade common sense": that which is simply taken for granted and which, invisibly and unconsciously, forms the basis from which individuals engage with each other in their social life. Indeed, in the Canadian province of Ontario the neo-conservative leader of the 1990s, Mike Harris, explicitly spoke of a "common sense revolution" (Jeffrey, 1999). This allowed neo-conservatives, critically, to win a strategic measure of popular consent as well as sufficiently deep social authority. By the late 1970s they had established a complex, heterogeneous composition of social power and social domination that was predicated upon the dominance of capital but which cut across class lines in its popular support; neo-conservatism achieved a measure of hegemony over advanced capitalist society. This hegemony did not end social contradictions such as class, gender, ethnicity, age, sexuality, and the like, because the maintenance of hegemony was and is an ongoing struggle. Indeed, in many cases these social contradictions intensified during the 1980s and the 1990s. Nonetheless, in this struggle the strongest way to sustain hegemony is to restructure common sense, and neo-conservatives cemented their acquisition of the true commanding heights of the capitalist economy: cultural, intellectual and indeed moral leadership.

III. Neo-conservatism or neo-liberalism?

It is in their reasonably pragmatic view of the relationship between the state and the market that the doctrinal differences between neo-liberals and neo-conservatives are clear. These differences have been apparent since the mid 1980s, and were cogently laid out by Andrew Gamble (1988). Gamble argued that neo-liberals and neo-conservatives together formed what was called in the 1970s the "New Right." In several areas these two strands of the New Right shared common interests, and this allowed them to unite behind the political project of Thatcher, Reagan and a host of other political leaders across the advanced capitalist world that were articulating New Right ideas. In particular, both neo-liberalism and neo-conservatism sought the overthrow of capitalist social democracy, believing that the growth of state intervention in the economy had had pernicious effects on the operation of capitalism and its social outcomes since the 1940s. In this, they shared the position that there was a need to cut state spending on services to labour and other popular and democratic forces, and to cut taxes on capital. This position was predicated upon a shared respect for the sanctity of capitalist property relations, and moreover suggested a need to direct popular hostility towards the state, and away from the capitalist class.

Nonetheless, neo-liberals and neo-conservatives diverged dramatically in their conception of the role of the state. Neo-liberals sought a smaller, more efficient state, with powers limited to policing the market and enforcing laws so that individual capitals had greater freedom to shape the operation of the political economy. Neo-conservatives, as has been noted, took quite a different view: that free markets require strong states to sustain the overarching dominance of the capital/labour relation and hence the social authority of capital as a whole. Indeed, in acting as a buttress to the free economy, the state is able to ensure its own legitimacy and the legitimacy of capitalist social relations. Gamble (1988) neatly encapsulated neo-conservative ideology when he coined the maxim "the free economy and the strong state."

If the key difference between neo-liberals and neo-conservatives is their conception of the role of the state, then an examination of the extent of the role of the state since the mid-1970s should be sufficient to resolve empirically whether neo-liberal or neo-conservative is a more appropriate appellation. Such an examination can be made using World Bank (2002d) data, which demonstrates that, whether in terms of state consumption expenditure or state current revenues, on a global scale the state was larger in the mid 1990s than it was in the mid-1970s. In the mid-1970s some 16 per cent of global GDP was dedicated to state consumption expenditure, whereas by the mid-1990s this figure stood at 17 per cent. In terms of state current revenue, in the mid-1970s some 20 per cent of global GDP was collected by the state, whereas in the mid-1990s the figure was 25 per cent. Of course, there has been some variation around this trend. Thus, in terms of state consumption expenditure, the state was, at 17 and 18 per cent respectively, very slightly smaller in the mid-1990s than in the mid-1970s in high income countries. Similarly, in terms of state current revenue, the state was, at 18 and 22 per cent respectively, somewhat smaller in the mid-1990s than in the mid-1980s in middle income countries. Nonetheless, empirical evidence suggests that rather than downsizing the state, which capitalist intellectuals and politicians such as Reagan and Thatcher claimed as their objective throughout the 1980s, the state retains a pivotal, if different, role in the operation of the political economy, which will be explored later. Thus, there is a degree of continuity in the role of the state over the past quarter century. If there is continuity, it is not sensible to think that a period of neo-liberalism in the 1970s and 1980s is now giving way to a period of neo-conservatism, as has been suggested in the media.

In this light, recent developments in economic policy become more consistent with the broad thrust of policy over the past quarter century. The advanced capitalist economies ran an overall budget deficit of more than 4 per cent of gross domestic product (GDP) in 2003 (*The Economist*, 23 August 2003). In the US the budget deficit may reach 6 per cent of GDP, in Japan the budget deficit was 8 per cent of GDP, while in the UK and the Euro area the budget deficit was around 3 per cent of GDP. However, the advanced capitalist countries ran budget deficits throughout the 1980s and early and mid 1990s, even under politicians such as Thatcher and Reagan. It was the temporary emergence of budget surpluses in the late 1990s that represented a discontinuity in the budgetary policies of the advanced capitalist economies during the last quarter century. Clearly, neo-conservatives are willing to countenance budgetary deficits and significant public spending, in particular in areas such as security or populist initiatives designed to sustain a strategic measure of popular consent.

Akram-Lodhi

The reason neo-conservatives countenance budgetary deficits is straight-forward—state spending can benefit capital at the expense of labour and other popular and democratic forces. Comparative research has demonstrated that state spending in the UK and the US brings less benefit to labour than to capital and to the state. Labour, through tax payments, has undertaken a net transfer to capital and to the state in the UK and the US in excess of that which labour received from the state (Akram-Lodhi, 1996). Comparative research also demonstrates that in some years in Canada the state and capital together received a net transfer of resources from labour (Sepehri and Chernomas, 1992). This finding can be generalized as typical of the capitalist state (Shaikh and Tonak, 2000). Thus, the state can bring direct benefits to capital at the expense of labour, through its redistributive activities.

Nonetheless, there can be little doubt that the activities of the state have changed significantly since the heyday of capitalist social democracy. For example, whereas during the golden age a significant aspect of intervention was the creation of state-owned enterprises, under neo-conservatism intervention comprises the web of regulatory control over markets enforced by state-sanctioned quasi-autonomous intermediary non-governmental organizations and the establishment of quasi-markets in health, education and other public goods. If anything, this redefinition represents a deepening of state intervention in market activity compared with that in the golden age, in that micro-management is now the rule rather than the exception. However, two aspects of the changing role of the state over the 1980s and 1990s stand out in particular, and these aspects are especially consistent with neo-conservative acceptance of a deepening role for the state in the market. The first is that since the early 1980s the state has increased its involvement in shaping individual activities and lifestyles. Indeed, the capitalist state in the early years of the 21st century can be thought of as being "neo-paternalist" (*The Economist*, 17 July 2003). This is seen in social policy changes, and particularly cuts in the public goods and transfers, that had previously comprised a significant proportion of the social safety net in the advanced capitalist economies. These changes, which have brought a number of benefits to capital, date from the early 1980s, but have been most fully realized only since the mid 1990s in the advanced capitalist countries. A classic work ethic lies at the heart of this social policy counterrevolution, which is predicated upon individuals assuming full private

406

responsibility for meeting their social needs. The privatization of social need has resulted in reinforcing the dominance of the market as the principle means of provisioning for social need even as redistributive transfers from capital to labour have been cut. Both aspects of the privatization of social need brings benefits to capital: the role of the labour market in sustaining access to social needs has been enhanced, while concomitantly social needs have been integrated into the culture of mass consumerism. What currently remains is that those who cannot meet their social needs privately through the use of markets receive minimal provision. Cumulatively, the effect has been to not only reproduce capitalist social relations but, indeed, to deepen them by deepening the commodification of labour.

The second area where the role of the state has changed is security. Despite the end of the Cold War, and well before the events of September 11 2001, there has been increased spending on internal and external security. While protection against the external threat posed by communism and more recently Wahhabism (Frum and Perle, 2004) is central to state security measures, the state has also increasingly used its coercive power against its "enemies within," whether they be strikers, alternative globalization activists, or asylum seekers. Indeed, the state is, as it always had been, prepared to use its coercive power against any that seek to systematically challenge the effort to privatize social need. This is because for neo-conservatives "the use of the state's coercive power is justified when it is used to defeat or contain those interests, organizations and individuals that threaten…the free economy by flouting the rules or resisting the outcomes of market exchanges" (Gamble, 1988: 31).

IV. Neo-conservatism and the globalization question

Neo-conservative ideology assumes an acceptance of class hierarchies and inequalities. This applies both within countries and between countries. To that end, neo-conservative policy-makers have sought, from the advanced capitalist centre of the world economy, to use the international financial institutions (IFIs) that they control and bilateral state-to-state relations to weaken the position of the state in the developing and transition economies. The reason is straightforward: weaker states in developing and transition economies are less capable of resisting neo-conservatism and the global class hierarchies and inequalities that it fosters. In doing this, neo-conservatism has, in effect, shaped the introduction of neo-liberalism in Latin America, Asia and Africa, and it is in these regions of the world economy that it is appropriate to use the appellation "neo-liberal." The International Monetary Fund (IMF) and the World Bank in particular have been responsible for the development and implementation of structural adjustment programmes and, more recently "poverty reduction strategies" in Latin America, Africa and Asia. These programmes and strategies, by strengthening the role of the market and weakening the role of the state within the political economy of these regions, have enhanced the capacity of capital to control the global economy and have deepened the hierarchies of the world capitalist system. Both institutions readily accepted the main tenets of the neo-conservative counter-revolution, promoting a vision based on markets and incentives that placed particular emphasis on the role of the private sector at the expense of the state in developing and transition economies. However, neither institution did so in order to give developing and transition countries the capacity for autonomous development. Indeed, the activities of both institutions demonstrate their implicit accession to the need for a hierarchically ordered global economy, in which capital in the advanced capitalist core, through its control of global production, markets and technology, is able to shape the destiny of the global economy and thus by implication the destinies of the developing and transition countries. This accession is witnessed in the fact that both institutions, whether under adjustment programmes or under poverty reduction strategies, used their financial power to promote state compression in the developing world and in so doing fostered the emergence of neo-liberal regimes that were both unable and unwilling to challenge the logic of advanced capitalism.

It might be suggested that the data noted in the previous section does not demonstrate a neo-liberal compression of the state in low income countries. However, there is a key difference in state expenditures between high, middle and low income countries. That difference is debt servicing. In 1990 and 1995 low income countries paid 5 per cent of their gross national income to service short- and long-term debt acquired from the IFIs and global financial institutions (World Bank, 2002d). These payments have altered the role of the state in developing and transition economies by reducing its effective capacity, and, along with the enhanced capacity of capital and the restructuring of the state in the advanced capitalist economies, deepened global hierarchies.

The implication of a deepening of global hierarchies is that the improvements in social equity achieved on a global scale during the period between 1945 and 1973 have been decisively eroded. It might be thought by some that this erosion represents a setback on the road to development. However, a longer term view would suggest that the record of global capitalism of the past 150 years is an increasingly well documented rise in relative inequality across and within nations over time (Milanovic, 2003; Wade, 2004). The only break in this long wave of increasing inequality is precisely the period between 1945 and 1973. Then, the response to the challenge of the Soviet Union and the economic collapse of the 1930s was the creation of capitalist social democracy. It was, as already noted, the contradictions of capitalist social democracy, as well as the diminution of the Soviet Union as an external threat to capitalism, that formed the terrain on which the neo-conservative counterrevolution could be set.

The current context for neo-conservatism is globalization. However, despite the extent to which the phenomena of globalization has penetrated the culture of the advanced capitalist countries, the internationalization of trade, production and finance are not as great as has been suggested (Akram-Lodhi, 2000a). Rather, if anything the role of globalization has been to allow capital and the state to reshape society by reducing constraining regulations on capital, cutting taxes on capital, while all the while re-regulating labour so as to reduce labour resistance. In this, capital, however, has been only partially successful. There has been, no doubt, a continued capacity of capital to extract surplus value at the point of production. However, there has only been a partial recovery in the rate of profit, and it is not clear whether this partial recovery is sustainable (Brenner, 2004; Wolff, 2003; *The Economist*, 8 December 2001; Dumenil and Lévy, 2000; Shaikh and Tonak, 2000).

The enhanced capacity of capital from the advanced capitalist countries in general, and US capital in particular, to control the development of the global economy through their control of the IFIs (Wade, 2002) has been reinforced by the militarization of international relations that has followed the collapse of the Berlin Wall. The US is increasingly using its military power to shape the world in a way that not coincidentally opens up new markets for goods and services produced by US capital. This capacity is also consistent with efforts to sideline the United Nations. Although the UN has increasingly sought to accommodate American interests, and in so doing has become an accomplice to neo-conservatism, it nonetheless still represents the vestiges of an alternative economic order in which the hegemony of capital can be challenged and US military power limited. The current US administration in particular, shaped as it is by neo-conservative influence, sees a unique American right to crusade against evil, spread truth, justice and the American way, whether the world wants it or not, and remake the world according to the dictates of neo-conservative ideology.

These efforts have been accompanied by economic collapse in some parts of the developing world, as declines in total domestic investment over three decades in, for example, Africa, have not been corrected. With economic collapse there has been state failure, and the rise of conflict, particularly in Africa, where the combined impact of war and disease has cost millions of lives. This is not unrelated to the increasing affluence of a few, which has, as its corollary, large increases in the numbers of people living in absolute poverty (Milanovic, 2003; Wade, 2002) as debt repayments are made to financiers, tax incentives to transnational capital deplete resources for social spending, and inflows of transnational investment fail to be translated into jobs that pay a living wage. At the end of 2000 80 countries had per capita incomes lower than those they had at end of the 1980s (Tabb, 2003).

Clearly, neo-conservatism cannot be shown to have succeeded in terms of its economic goals. It has only generated a partial recovery in the trend rate of profit across the global capitalist economy, and it is not, as yet, clear whether this partial recovery is sustainable. It has not been able to obviate the cycles of capitalism by increasing the capacity of capital to extract absolute and relative surplus value at the point of production. However, as a class project of capital, designed to restore and sustain the dominance of the hierarchical capital/labour relation and hence the social authority of capital, neo-conservatism has unambiguously succeeded. It has increased the power of transnational capital, the neo-conservative state, international finance capital, and client elites in developing and transition economies, while concurrently managing to direct popular hostility towards the state and not the capitalist class. Neo-conservative power is thus ultimately rooted in capital's control of the means of production, but expressed and sustained in its capacity to shape an individualistic common sense that is dominated by the commodity fetishism that maintains the capitalist economy.

V. Neo–conservatism, state reform and democracy

The neo–conservative response to the only partial recovery in the rate of profit has been to blame states in the advanced capitalist world for continuing to hold on to residual remnants of capitalist social democracy, particularly in European attitudes towards the regulation of labour markets and continued social provisioning, while blaming states in the developing world for a lack of ownership over and implementation of adjustment programmes and poverty reduction strategies, which, they argue, are a consequence of poor governance by the client elite that they have fostered. The way forward, for neo–conservatives, is further liberalization and reform of the rules of the national and international economy through the World Trade Organization. However, in that this would result in the depoliticization of economic decision–making through a further reduction of the limited capacity of representative democracies to regulate the operation of the capitalist economy, the effective governance reforms that neo–conservatives currently advocate are consistent with the class interests of global capital.

The governance agenda has two public faces. In the advanced capitalist economies, following the crisis in corporate governance typified by Enron, significant fractions of transnational capital are now seeking to reform the public face of its operations by changing structures of private sector governance. Such changes are nonetheless predicated upon sustaining the social authority of capital. In the developing economies governance is supposed to be about seeking greater support for adjustment policies and poverty reduction strategies. However, in practice governance reforms seek to remove politics from policy–making in those areas that most directly affect capital, leaving decisions to unelected technocrats. Governance reforms also promote a selective deconcentration of state functions to the local level. However, decentralization reforms do not challenge local patterns of class relations and do not devolve financial control, resulting in a transfer of responsibility but not power. Indeed, if anything the governance agenda accedes to local patterns of power and privilege, reinforces hierarchies between the central and the local state, and redistributes authority in the central state from the elected to the unelected.

The governance agenda thus demonstrates a neo-conservative conception of democracy which is predicated upon restricting the voice of citizens in a fashion that further limits the capacity of people to challenge the dominance of capital.

In this light, a range of alternatives to neo-conservatism has begun to coalesce over the past 15 years. These alternatives have been found in the factories and in the universities, amongst peasants and on the streets. These alternatives challenge neo-conservatism on its own ground, undertaking struggles to control the "common sense" of the day (Klein, 2001). These alternatives are predicated upon popular and democratic movements making a fresh commitment to create more participatory forms of democracy that are not based upon the power of capital but are rather rooted in accountability, social equality, and giving people more control over their lives by "reclaiming the state" (Wainwright, 2003). Of course, the capacity to achieve a more democratic development of economic policy-making is constrained by the neo-conservative "common sense" need to maintain balanced budgets while reducing corporate taxes to internationally acceptable levels, thereby maintaining an acceptable climate for capital. This reality might suggest to some that the scope for a more democratic approach to economic policy-making may be narrow. However, as one activist put it in 1997, "when there's less money, all the more reason to be democratic" (Ngwane, 2003). This approach has been reflected in a variety of oppositional activities that seek to reshape the politics of economic decision-making. For example, during the mid-1980s the Greater London Council offered citizens consultations on budgetary allocations. In Johannesburg following municipal elections in the mid 1990s citizens were given decision-making power over shares of budgetary expenditure (Ngwane, 2003), and this approach has been replicated in parts of Brazil, most notably Porte Alegre, since the late 1990s (Wainwright, 2003). Thus, despite the climate, a range of initiatives have been launched by activists to audit or indeed seek to alter the impact of state economic policies on the poor, on women, on children and youth, on the aged, and on other marginalized and disenfranchised groups in society. These interventions represent, in some ways, a return to the ideals of European forms of Marxist social democracy of the 19th century, which advocated the need for both political and economic democratization. Clearly, democracy is only partially about elections, and largely about the social relations that structure what is politically possible. Social need should not be subordinate to the market, and capital should not be able to override the requirements of labour and other popular and democratic forces. Class power and the global logic of capital are the key social relations faced by people in the global economy, and it is these social relations that popular resistance increasingly seeks to challenge, in order to create a more just political and economic system.

VI. Conclusion

This chapter has argued that neo-conservatism has clear limits as an economic ideology. It has sought to use the state to undertake a set of structural economic reforms that strengthen the dominance of the hierarchical capital/labour relation and hence the social authority of capital, at the expense of labour and other popular and democratic forces, around the world. As a consequence of these reforms, neo-conservatives believed that the falling rate of profit that has characterized global capitalism since the late 1960s would be reversed. However, the economic reforms have led to only a partial recovery in the rate of profit. Therefore, neo-conservatism has attempted to restructure the operation of the state itself. Using the language of governance neo-conservatives have sought to remove economic decision-making from the purview of representative institutions such as parliaments. The shift towards a technocratic approach to economic decision-making was meant to be deeply depoliticizing. However, as the global citizenry witnessed an increasing inability to have any control over their own lives, popular movements of resistance to the class project of the neo-conservatives has arisen, designed to weaken the relationship between the state and capital. An expansion of popular initiatives to deepen participatory democratic practices has the potential to challenge and perhaps even transform those social relations. In this way, the politics and economics of neo-conservatism has promoted, in a true dialectic, the very antithesis of what it set out to do: the possibility of an alternative, more democratic and humane, future.

Footnotes

1 My thanks to Peter Lawrence, Robert Chernomas, Ardeshir Sepheri, Martin Doornbos and Wicky Meynen for their comments on an earlier draft of this chapter.

BIBLIOGRAPHY

Abdel Aal, M. 2002. Agrarian reform and tenancy in Upper Egypt. In *Counter-revolution in Egypt's countryside: Land and farmers in the era of economic reform*, edited by Ray Bush. London: Zed Books.

Abdel-Khalek, G. 2001. *Stabilization and adjustment in Egypt: Reform or de-industrialisation.* Cheltenham, England: Edward Elgar.

———. 2002. Stabilization and adjustment in Egypt: Sequencing and sustainability. In *Counter-revolution in Egypt's countryside: Land and farmers in the era of economic reform,* edited by Ray Bush. London: Zed Books.

Agarwal, A., and S. Narain. 2000. Community and household water management: the key to environmental regeneration and poverty alienation [cited 14 January 2002]. Available from http:/www.undp.org/seed/pei/publication/water.pdf.

Agarwal, B. 1992. The gender and environment debate: Lessons from India. *Feminist Studies* 18 (1): 119-158.

———. 1994. *A field of one's own: Gender and land rights in South Asia.* Cambridge: Cambridge University Press.

Agenor, P.R. 1991. Output, devaluation and the real exchange rate in developing countries. *Weltwirtschaftliches Archiv,* Band 127, 18-40.

Agosin, M., and R. Mayer. 2000. *Foreign investment in developing countries: Does it crowd in domestic investment?* UNCTAD Discussion Paper, 46. Geneva: United Nations Conference on Trade and Development.

Agrawal, A., and C. Gibson. 1999. Enchantment and disenchantment: The role of community in natural resource conservation. *World Development* 27 (4): 629-47.

———. 2001. *Communities and the environment.* New Jersey: Rutgers University Press.

Agrawal, A., and J. Ribot. 2000. Analyzing decentralization: A framework with South Asian and West African environmental cases. Digital Library of the Commons Working Paper [cited 25 January]. Available from http://dlc.dlib.indiana.edu/documents/dir0/00/00/04/40/dlc-00000440-01/agrawalribot440.pdf.

Ahluwalia, M. 1997. Representing communities: The case of a community-based watershed management project in Rajasthan, India. *IDS Bulletin* 28 (4): 23-34.

Ake, C. 2000. *The feasibility of democracy in Africa.* Dakar: Council for the Development of Social Science Research in Africa.

Akram-Lodhi, A. 1996. The public finances of the United Kingdom: A reinterpretation. *International Review of Applied Economics* 10 (2): 173-193.

Akram-Lodhi, A.H. 2000a. The agrarian question in an age of "new capitalism." In *Political Economy and the New Capitalism: Essays in Honour of Sam Aaronovitch*, edited by J. Toporowski. London: Routledge.

———. 2000. *An introduction to policy analysis.* Paper presented at the National Committee for the Advancement of Women Research Analysis and Policy Workshop, June 16, Hanoi.

Al Ahali (various issues).

Al Ahram Weekly (various issues).

Alderman, H. 1991. *Downturn and economic recovery in Ghana: Impacts on the poor* (Monograph 10). Cornell Food and Nutrition Policy Program.

Alderman, H., and V. Lavy. 1996. Household responses to public health services: Cost and quality tradeoffs. *World Bank Research Observer* 11 (1): 3-22.

Álvarez, L. 1997. Introduction. In *Participación y democracia en la ciudad de México. México D.F.,* edited by L. Álvarez. Mexico City: La Journada Ediciones/Centro de Investigaciones Interdisciplinarias en Ciencias y Humanidades de la UNAM.

Al Waft (various issues).

Amin, S. 1998. *Spectres of capitalism.* New York: Monthly Review Press.

———. 1990. *Delinking.* London: Zed Books.

Arestis, P., and P.O. Demetriades. 1997. Financial development and economic growth: Assessing the evidence. *Economic Journal* 107 (May): 783-799.

Armstrong, P., A. Glyn, and J. Harrison. 1991. *Capitalism since 1945.* Oxford: Blackwell Publishers.

Armstrong, R. 1996. *Ghana country assistance review: A study in development effectiveness.* Washington, DC: The World Bank.

Arrighi, G., and J. Saul. 1973. *Essays on the political economy of Africa.* New York: Monthly Review Press.

Aryeetey, E., J. Harrigan, and M. Nissanke, eds. 2002. *Economic reforms in Ghana: The miracle and the mirage.* London: James Curry Ltd.

Austen, R. 1987. *African economic history.* London: James Curray.

Azam, J.-P. 1999. Dollars for sale: Exchange rate policy and inflation in Africa. *World Development* 27 (10): 1843-1859.

Bach, K.H. 2002. Rural Egypt under stress. In *Counter-revolution in Egypt's countryside: Land and farmers in the era of economic reform,* edited by R. Bush. London: Zed Books.

Bakker, I. 1994. Introduction: Engendering macro-economic policy reform in the era of global restructuring and adjustment. In *The strategic silence: Gender and economic policy,* edited by I. Bakker. London: Zed Books.

Bakker, I., and D. Elson. 1998. Towards engendering budgets. *Alternative federal budget papers 1998.* Ottawa: Canadian Centre for Policy Alternatives and CHO!CES.

Baldwin, J.R., T.M. Harchaoui, and J.-P. Maynard. 2001. Productivity growth in Canada and the United States. In *Productivity growth in Canada,* edited by J.R. Baldwin, D. Beckstead, N. Dhaliwal, R. Durand, V. Gaudreault, T.M. Harchaoui, et al.. Ottawa: Statistics Canada.

Bank for International Settlements. 1998. *68th annual report.* Basle: The Author.

Barber, C.L. 1979. Some implications of declining birth rates in developed countries. In *The Collected Economic Papers of C.L. Barber,* edited by A.M.C. Waterman, D.P. J. Hum, and B.L. Scarfe. Winnipeg: ISER.

Barr, N. 1994. The role of government in a market economy. In *Labour markets and social policy in central and eastern Europe: The transition and beyond*, edited by N. Barr. New York: Oxford University Press.

Bauer, P.T. 1976. *Dissent on development*. London: Weidenfeld and Nicolson.

———. 1981. *Equality, the third world, and economic delusion*. Cambridge: Harvard University Press.

Baumann, P. 1998. *Panchayati raj* and watershed management in India: Constraints and opportunities. Overseas Development Institute Working Paper, 114. London: Overseas Development Institute.

———. 2000. Sustainable livelihoods and political capital: Arguments and evidence from decentralisation and natural resource management in India. Overseas Development Institute Working Paper, 136. London: Overseas Development Institute.

Beck, T., R. Levine, and N. Loayza. 2000. Finance and the sources of growth. *Journal of Financial Economics* 58 (1-2): 261-300.

Beckman, B. 1992. Empowerment or repression? The World Bank and the policies of African adjustment. In *Authoritarianism, democracy and adjustment: The politics of economic reform in Africa*, edited by P. Gibbon, Y. Bangura, and A. Ofstad. Uppsala, Sweden: Scandinavian Institute of African Studies.

Begg, D., S. Fischer, and R. Dornbusch. 1994. *Economics*. 4th ed. London: McGraw-Hill Book Company.

Berg, E. 1993. *Rethinking technical cooperation: Reforms for capacity-building in Africa*. New York: United Nations Development Programme.

Berry, S. 1993. *No condition is permanent: The social dynamics of agrarian change in sub-Saharan Africa*. Madison, WI: The University of Wisconsin Press.

———. 1997. Tomatoes, land and hearsay: Property and history in Asante in the time of structural adjustment. *World Development* 25 (8): 1225-1241.

Bhaskar, R. 1975. *A realist theory of science*. Leeds: Leeds Books.

Blair, H.W. 1996. Democracy, equity and common property resource management in the Indian subcontinent. *Development and Change* 27 (3): 475-499.

Blau, F.D., M.A. Ferber, and A.E. Winkler. 1998. *The economics of women, men, and work*. 3rd ed. Upper Saddle River, NJ: Prentice Hall.

Bleaney, M., N. Gemmell, and D. Greenaway. 1995. Tax revenue instability, with particular reference to sub-Saharan Africa. *Journal of Development Studies* 31 (6): 883-902.

Bleaney, M., and D. Greenaway. 2001. The impact of terms of trade and real exchange rate volatility on investment and growth in sub-Saharan Africa. *Journal of Development Economics* 65 (2): 491-500.

Bloom, A. 1988. *The closing of the American mind*. New York: Simon and Schuster.

Bloom, G., and X. Gu. 1997. Introduction to health sector reform in China. *IDS Bulletin* 28 (1): 1-11.

Bloom G., S. Lucas, J. Gao, and X. Gu. 1995. *Financing health services in poor rural areas: Adapting to economic and institutional reform in China*. Institute of Development Studies Research Report, 30. Brighton, UK: Institute of Development Studies.

Bogg, L., D. Hengjin, W. Keli, C. Wenwei, and V. Diwan. 1996. The cost of coverage: Rural health insurance in China. *Health Policy and Planning* 11 (3): 238-252.

Boltho, A. 2003. What's wrong with Europe? *New Left Review*, 2d ser., 22: 5-26.

Borosage, R. 1999. The battle in Seattle. *The Nation*. 6 December.

Boyer, R. 1996. The convergence hypothesis revisited: Globalization but still the century of nations? In *National diversity and global capitalism,* edited by S. Berger and R. Dore. Ithaca, NY: Cornell University Press.

Brandt Commission. 1980. *North-south: A programme for survival.* London: Pan Books.

Brenner, R. 1998. Uneven development and the long downturn: The advanced capitalist economies from boom to stagnation, 1950-1998. *New Left Review* 229: 1-265.

———. 2004. New boom or new bubble? *New Left Review,* 2d ser., 25: 57-100.

Bromley, D.W., et al., eds. 1972. *Making the commons work: Theory, practice and policy.* San Francisco: Institute for Contemporary Studies Press.

Brown, P.L. , ed. 1998. *Finding our collective voice: Democratizing the social union.* Ottawa: Canadian Centre for Policy Alternatives.

Bruno, M. 1979. Stabilization and stagflation in a semi-industrialized economy. In *International economic policy, theory, and evidence,* edited by R. Dornbusch, and J.A. Frenkel. Baltimore: The Johns Hopkins University Press.

Bryceson, D., C. Kay, and J. Mooij. 2000. *Disappearing peasantries? Rural labour in Africa, Asia and Latin America.* London: Intermediate Technology Publications.

Buchanan, J. 1989. The public-choice perspective. In *Essays on the political economy,* edited by J. Buchanan. Honolulu: University of Hawaii Press.

Budlender, D. 1996. *The women's budget.* Cape Town: Institute for Democracy in South Africa.

———. 1997. *The second women's budget.* Cape Town: Institute for Democracy in South Africa.

———. 1998. *The third women's budget.* Cape Town: Institute for Democracy in South Africa.

———. 1999. *The fourth women's budget.* Cape Town: Institute for Democracy in South Africa.

———. 2000. The political economy of women's budgets in the south. *World Development* 28 (7): 1365-1378.

Budlender, D., D. Elson, G. Hewitt, and T. Mukhopadhyay. 2002. *Gender budgets make cents: Understanding gender responsive budgets.* London: Commonwealth Secretariat.

Budlender, D., and R. Sharp, with K. Allen. 1998. *How to do a gender-sensitive budget analysis: Contemporary research and practice.* London: Commonwealth Secretariat.

Bush, R. 1999. *Crisis and the politics of reform in Egypt.* Boulder, Colorado: Westview.

———, ed. 2002. *Counter-revolution in Egypt's countryside: Land and farmers in the era of economic reform.* London: Zed Books.

———. 2002a. More losers than winners in Egypt's countryside: The impact of changes in land tenure. In *Counter-revolution in Egypt's countryside: Land and farmers in the era of economic reform,* edited by R. Bush. London: Zed Books.

Butter, D. 1992. Egypt: Special Report. *Middle East Economic Digest.* Egypt.

Cagatay, N., D. Elson, and C. Grown. 1995. Introduction to gender, adjustment and macroeconomics. *World Development* 23 (11): 1827-1836.

Cagatay, N., M. Keklik, R. Lal, and J. Lang. 2000. *Budgets as if people mattered. Democratizing macroeconomic policies.* New York: United Nations Development Programme, Social Development and Poverty Elimination Division.

Caledonian Blue Book 1997: National Accounts for Scotland, 1951-1996. Glasgow: Glasgow Caledonian University.

Cameron, R., with O. Crisp, H.T. Patrick, and R. Tilley. 1967. *Banking in the early stages of industrialisation: A study in comparative economic history.* New York: Oxford University Press.

Campbell, B. 1997a. La Banque mondiale prône un État efficace: Pour quoi faire? *Revue Québécoise de Droit International* 10: 189-199.

———. 1997b. Quelques enjeux conceptuels, idéologiques et politiques autour de la nation de gouvernance. In *Good governance and development*. Dakar: Institut Africain pour la Démocratie.

———. 2000a. New rules of the game: The World Bank's role in the construction of new normative frameworks for states, markets and social exclusion. *Canadian Journal of Development Studies* 21 (1): 7-30.

———. 2000b. Governance, réformes institutionnelles et redéfinition du rôle de l'État: Quelques enjeux conceptuels et politiques soulevés par le projet de governance décentralisée de la Banque mondiale. In *Governance, réformes institutionnelles et l'émergence de nouveaux cadres normatifs dans les domaines social, politique et environnemental*, edited by B. Campbell, F. Crépeau, and L. Lamarche. Montréal, PQ: Cahiers du Centre d'études sur le droit international et la mondialisation, Université du Québec à Montréal.

Canada. Department of Finance. Various years. *The budget plan*. Ottawa: The Author.

———. 2001. *Fiscal reference tables*. Ottawa: The Author.

———. 2002. *The fiscal monitor*. Ottawa: The Author.

———. Statistics Canada. 2001a. *Canadian economic observer: Historical statistical supplement 2000/01*. Cat. # 11-210-XPB. Ottawa: The Author.

———. Statistics Canada. 2001b. *Financial statistics for enterprises*. Cat. # 61-008. Ottawa: The Author.

———. Statistics Canada. 2002a. *Canadian economic observer*. Cat. #11-010. Ottawa: The Author.

———. Statistics Canada. 2002b. *Canadian economic observer: Historical statistical supplement*. Cat. # 11-210. Ottawa: The Author.

———. Statistics Canada. 2002c. CANSIM II. Available from http://cansim2.statcan.ca.

———. Statistics Canada. 2002d. *The Daily*, 12 July.

Canadian Centre for Policy Alternatives. 2001. *Economic and fiscal statement*. Ottawa: The Author.

———. 2003a. *Alternative federal budget 2003*. Ottawa: The Author.

———. 2003b. Democracy counts! Participatory budgeting in Canada and abroad. Alternative Federal Budget Technical Paper, 4. Available from http://www.policyalternatives.ca.

Canadian Centre for Policy Alternatives and CHO!CES. 1997. *The 1997 alternative federal budget framework document*. Ottawa: Canadian Centre for Policy Alternatives.

———. 1997, 1998, and various years. *Alternative federal budget papers*. Ottawa: The Author.

Canadian International Development Agency (CIDA). 2001. *Strengthening aid effectiveness: New approaches to Canada's international assistance program*. Ottawa: The Author.

Canetti, E., and J. Greene. 1991. Monetary growth and exchange rate depreciation as causes of inflation in African countries: An empirical analysis. International Monetary Fund Working Paper, WP/91/67. Washington: International Monetary Fund.

Carney, D., and J. Farrington. 1998. *Natural resource management and institutional change*. New York: Routledge.

Cashel-Cordo, P., and S.G. Craig. 1990. The public sector impact on international resource transfers. *Journal of Development Economics* 32 (1): 17-42.

Caufield, C. 1996. *Masters of illusion: The World Bank and the poverty of nations*. London: Pan.

Chang, H. 1998. Globalization, transnational corporations, and economic development: Can the developing countries pursue strategic industrial policy in a globalizing world economy? In *Globalization and progressive economic policy*, edited by D. Baker, G. Epstein, and R. Pollin. Cambridge: Cambridge University Press.

Chen, J. 1997. The impact of health sector reform on county hospitals. *IDS Bulletin* 28 (1): 48-52.

Chenery, H.B., and A.M. Strout. 1966. Foreign assistance and economic development. *American Economic Review* 56 (4): 679-733.

Cherry, R., C. D'Onofrio, C. Kurdas, T.R. Michl, F. Moseley, and M.I. Naples, eds. 1987. *The imperiled economy, book 1: Macroeconomics from a left perspective*. New York: The Union for Radical Political Economics.

Chhibber, A., and N. Shafik. 1991. The inflationary consequences of devaluation with parallel markets: The case of Ghana. In *Economic reform in sub-Saharan Africa,* edited by A. Chhibber, and S. Fischer. Washington, DC: World Bank.

CHO!CES: A Coalition for Social Justice and Canadian Centre for Policy Alternatives. 1998. *Show us the money! The politics and process of alternative budgets.* Winnipeg: Arbeiter Ring.

Cleaver, F. 2000. Moral ecological rationality, institutions and the management of common property resources. *Development and Change* 31 (2): 361-383.

Clements, M.P., and D. Hendry. 1995. Macroeconomic forecasting and modelling. *Economic Journal* 105 (431): 1001-1031.

Cohen, G.A. 1988. Freedom, justice, and capitalism. In *History, labour and freedom: Themes from Marx*. Oxford: Clarendon Press.

Collier, P. 1999. Learning from failure: The international financial institutions as agencies of restraint in Africa. In *The self-restraining state: Power and accountability in new democracies,* edited by A. Schedler, L. Diamond, and. M.F. Plattner. Boulder, Colorado: Lynne Rienner Publishers.

Commonwealth Secretariat. 1999. *Gender budget initiative: A commonwealth initiative to integrate gender in national budgetary processes*. London: The Author.

Cooper, I. and E. Kaplanis. 1994. Home bias in equity portfolio, inflation hedging, and international capital market equilibrium. *Review of Financial Studies* 7 (1): 45-60.

Cooper, R.N. 1971. Currency devaluation in developing countries. *Essays in International Finance* 86.

Copans, J. 1991. Some debates within the debates. In *Re-thinking the Arusha Declaration*, edited by J. Hartmann. Copenhagen: Centre for Development Research.

Cottani, J.A., D.F. Cavallo, and M.S. Khan. 1990. Real exchange rate behavior and economic performance in LDCs. *Economic Development and Cultural Change* 39 (1): 61-76.

Courchene, T.J. 1981. A market perspective on regional disparities. *Canadian Public Policy* 7 (Autumn).

————. 1994. Potholes in the road to social policy reform. In *A new social vision for Canada? Perspectives on the federal discussion paper on social security reform*, edited by K. Banting, and K. Battle. Montreal: McGill-Queen's University Press.

Craig, S.G., and R.P. Inman. 1986. Education, welfare, and the "new" federalism: State budgeting in a federalist public economy. In *Studies in state and local public finance*, edited by H. Rosen. Chicago: University of Chicago.

Cullenberg, S., J. Amariglio, and D.F. Ruccio, eds. 2001. *Postmodernism, economics and knowledge*. London: Routledge.

Culpeper, R., and J. Serieux. 2000. *Journeys just begun: From debt relief to poverty reduction*. Ottawa: The North-South Institute.

Dahl, R. 1971. *Polyarchy: Participation and opposition*. New Haven: Yale University Press.

————. 1989. *Democracy and its critics*. New Haven: Yale University Press.

Dallek, M. 2000. *The right moment: Ronald Reagan and the decisive turning point in American politics*. New York: The Free Press.

Dante, I. 2002. *Aid co-ordination and donor reform*. Prepared for North-South Institute Workshop on Ownership and Partnership in Africa's Development Strategy, April, Nairobi.

Dao, M. 1995. Determinants of government expenditures: Evidence from disaggregative data. *Oxford Bulletin of Economics and Statistics* 57 (1): 67-76.

De Bruijne, A. 2001. Globe, oikoumene en oikos. Reflecties over human geography. Valedictory address, November 30, University of Amsterdam, Amsterdam, The Netherlands.

Deidda, L., and B. Fattouh. 2002. Non-linearity between finance and growth. *Economics Letters* 74 (3): 339-345.

Demery, L. 1997. Gender and public social spending: Disaggregating benefit incidence. Washington, DC: Poverty and Social Policy Department, The World Bank. Mimeographed.

Demetriades, P.O. and K.A. Hussein. 1993. Financial development and economic growth: cointegration and causality tests for 12 countries. Department of Economics Working Paper Series 93.15. Keele University, UK: Department of Economics.

————. 1996. Does financial development cause economic growth? Time-series evidence from 16 countries. *Journal of Development Economics* 51 (2): 387-411.

Demetriades, P.O. and K. Luintel. 1996a. Financial development, economic growth and banking sector controls: Evidence from India. *Economic Journal* 106 (March): 359-374.

————. 1996b. Banking sector policies and financial development in Nepal. *Oxford Bulletin of Economics and Statistics* 58 (2): 355-372.

————. 1997. The direct costs of financial repression: Evidence from India. *Review of Economics and Statistics* 79 (2): 311-320.

————. 2001. Financial restraints in the South Korean miracle. *Journal of Development Economics* 64 (2): 459-479.

Deolalikar, A. 2000. Health sector. In *Vietnam: Managing public resources better—public expenditure review 2000.* Vol. 2. Hanoi: Vietnam Development Information Center.

Dercon, S. 1998. Wealth, risk and activity choice: Cattle in western Tanzania. *Journal of Development Economics* 55 (1): 1-42.

Desai, J. 2000. Vietnam through the lens of gender: five years later—results from the second Vietnam Living Standards Survey. Report prepared for the Food and Agricultural Organization of the United Nations, Regional Office for Asia and the Pacific, Bangkok, Thailand.

Devarajan, S., A.S. Rajkumar, and V. Swaroop. 1998. What does aid to Africa finance? Unpublished paper commissioned by the African Economic Research Consortium, Nairobi, Kenya.

Diamond, L. 1997. *Prospects for democratic development in Africa.* Palo Alto, CA: Hoover Institution on War, Revolution and Peace.

Diamond, L., J.J. Linz, and S.M. Lipset, eds. 1990. *Politics in developing countries: Comparing experiences with democracy.* Vol. 2. Boulder, Colorado: Lynne Rienner.

Do, N.P. 2000. Issues of equity and effectiveness in health care in Vietnam. In *Efficient, equity-oriented strategies for health: International perspectives—focus on Vietnam,* edited by M. H. Pham, I. H. Minas, Y. Liu, G. Dahlgrem, and W. C. Hsiao. Melbourne, Australia: Centre for International Mental Health, University of Melbourne.

Doherty, J., E. Graham, and M. Malek, eds. 1992. *Postmodernism and the social sciences.* London: MacMillan.

Domínguez, Jorge I., and Abraham F. Lowenthal. 1996. Introduction: constructing democratic governance. In *Constructing democratic governance: Latin America and the Caribbean in the 1990s: Themes and issues,* edited by Jorge I. Domínguez and Abraham F. Lowenthal. Baltimore: Johns Hopkins University Press.

Doornbos, M. 2001. Research-led policy deliberation in Eritrea and Somalia: Searching to overcome institutional gaps. In *African pastoralism: Conflict, institutions and government,* edited by M.A. Mohamed Salih, T. Dietz, and A.G. Mohamed Ahmed. London: Pluto Press.

Doornbos, M. 2003. State collapse and fresh starts: some critical reflections. In *State failure, collapse and reconstruction,* edited by Jennifer Milliken. Oxford: Blackwell Publishing.

Doornbos, M., and L. Gertz. 1994. Sustainability, technology and corporate interest: Resource strategies in India's modern dairy sector. *The Journal of Development Studies* 30 (3): 916-950.

van Doorslaer, E., and A. Wagstaff. 1992. Equity in the delivery of health care: Some international comparisons. *Journal of Health Economics* 11 (4): 389-411.

van Doorslaer, E., et al. 2000. Equity in the delivery of health care in Europe and the US. *Journal of Health Economics* 19 (4): 553-584.

Dordunoo, C.K., and D. Njinkeu. 1997. Foreign exchange rate regimes and macroeconomic performance in sub-Saharan Africa. *Journal of African Economies* 6 (3): 121-149.

Dow, A., S.C. Dow, and A. Hutton. 1997. The Scottish political economy tradition and modern economics. *Scottish Journal of Political Economy* 44 (4): 368-383.

————. 2000. Applied economics in a political economy tradition. *History of Political Economy* 32 (annual supplement): 177-198.

Dow, A., and C. Kirk. 2000. The numbers of Scottish businesses and economic policy. *Fraser of Allander Institute Quarterly Economic Commentary* 25 (4): 28-34.

Dow, S.C. 1990. Beyond dualism. *Cambridge Journal of Economics* 14 (2): 143-158.

————. 1991. Are there any signs of postmodernism within economics? *Methodus* 3 (1): 81-85.

————. 2001. Modernism and postmodernism: a dialectical analysis. In *Postmodernism, economics and knowledge,* edited by S. Cullenberg, J. Amariglio, and D.F. Ruccio. London: Routledge.

Duménil, G., M. Glick, and D. Lévy. 2001. Brenner on competition. *Capital and Class* 74: 61-77.

Duménil, G., and D. Lévy. 2000. The profit rate: Where and how much did it fall? Did it recover (USA 1948-1997). Paris: CEPREMAP. Mimeographed.

Dung, P.H. 1996. *Study on health and health systems in Vietnamese transitional economy.* Paper prepared for the final meeting sponsored by the Asian Development Bank on Social Sector Issues in Asian Transition Economies, June 20-21. Manila.

Dunlop, D. 1999. Situation review of health financing and health insurance in Vietnam. Paper prepared for the Asian Development Bank Rural Health Project TA, Hanoi.

Dunning, J. 1997. The advent of alliance capitalism. In *The new globalism and developing countries,* edited by J. Dunning and K. Hamdani. New York: United Nations University Press.

Dwivedi, R. 2001. Environmental movements in the global south. *International Sociology* 16 (1): 11-31.

Dymski, G., and D. Isenberg. 1998. Housing finance in the age of globalization: From social housing to life-cycle risk. In *Globalization and progressive economic policy,* edited by D. Baker, G. Epstein, and R. Pollin. Cambridge: Cambridge University Press.

Economist Intelligence Unit. 2000. *Egypt country report.* London: The Author.

Economist, The. (various issues).

————. 1995. The myth of the powerless state. 7 October.

————. 2000. Globalisation and tax survey. 29 January.

Edwards, C. 1985. *The fragmented world: Competing perspectives on trade, money and crisis.* London: Methuen.

Egypt. Central Agency for Public Mobilisation and Statistics. 1991. *Statistical yearbook 1991.* Cairo: Arab Republic of Egypt.

————. Central Agency for Public Mobilisation and Statistics. 1998. *Household income and expenditure survey 1995.* Cairo: Arab Republic of Egypt.

————. Central Bureau of Statistics. (various issues). *Quarterly Digest of Statistics.* Accra: Central Bureau of Statistics.

Elbadawi, I., and N. Majid. 1996. Adjustment and economic performance under a fixed exchange rate: A comparative analysis of the CFA Zone. *World Development* 24 (5): 939-951.

Elbadawi, I., and R. Sota. 1997. Real exchange rates and macroeconomic adjustment in sub-Saharan Africa and other developing countries. *Journal of African Economies* 6 (3): 74-120.

Elson, D. 1998. Integrating gender issues into national budgetary policies and procedures: Some policy options. *Journal of International Development* 10: 929-941.

Elson, D., and N. Cagatay. 1999. Engendering macroeconomic policy and budgets for sustainable human development. Paper presented to the First Global Forum on Human Development, 29-31 July, at United Nations, New York.

Elson, D., B. Evers, and J. Gideon. 1996. Concepts and sources. University of Manchester Genecon Unit Working Paper, Manchester, UK: University of Manchester Genecon Unit.

Elson, D., and R. Pearson. 1981. The subordination of women and the internationalisation of factory production. In *Of marriage and the market: Women's subordination internationally and its lessons,* edited by K. Young, C. Wolkowitz, and R. McCullagh. London: RKP.

Ensor, T., and P.B. San. 1996. Access and payment for health care: The poor of northern Vietnam. *International Journal of Health Planning and Management* 11: 69-83.

Evans, R. 1984. *Strained mercy: The economics of Canadian health care.* Toronto, ON: Butterworths.

Everhart, S., and M. Sumlinski. 2000. *Trends in private investment in developing countries: Statistics for 1970-2000 and the impact on private investment of corruption and the quality of public investment.* World Bank Discussion Paper, 44. Washington: The World Bank.

Faini, R. 1994. The output and inflationary impact of devaluation in developing countries: Theory and empirical evidence from five African low-income countries. In *From adjustment to development in Africa,* edited by G. Andrea, A. Cornia, and G.K. Helleiner. New York: St. Martin's Press.

Fairholm, R., et al. 1999. North American monetary union—debate. *Canadian Business Economics* 7 (4): 1-33.

Faris, M.M., and M.H. Khan, eds. 1993. *Sustainable agriculture in Egypt.* Boulder: Lynne Rienner.

Felix, D. 1998. Asia and the crisis of financial globalization. In *Globalization and progressive economic policy,* edited by D. Baker, G. Epstein, and R. Pollin. Cambridge: Cambridge University Press.

Fergany, N. 2002. Poverty and unemployment in rural Egypt. In *Counter-revolution in Egypt's countryside: Land and farmers in the era of economic reform,* edited by R. Bush. London: Zed Books.

de Ferranti, D. 1985. Paying for health services in developing countries: An overview. World Bank Staff Working Paper, 721. Washington, DC: The World Bank.

Feyzioglu, T., V. Swaroop, M. Zhu. 1998. A panel data analysis of the fungibility of foreign aid. *World Bank Economic Review* 12 (1): 29-58.

Fforde, A., and S. de Vylder. 1996. *From plan to market: The economic transition in Vietnam.* Boulder: Westview Press.

Fielding, D. 1997. Modelling the determinants of government expenditure in sub-Saharan Africa. *Journal of African Economics* 6 (6): 377-390.

Fielding, D., and M. Bleaney. 2000. Monetary discipline and inflation in developing countries: The role of the exchange rate regime. *Oxford Economic Papers* 52 (3): 521-538.

Financial Times. (various issues).

Fleetwood, S., ed. 1999. *Critical realism in economics.* London: Routledge.

Fleshman, M. 2002. "Gender budgets" seek more equity. *Africa Recovery* 16 (1): 4.

Fletcher, L.B., ed. 1996. *Egypt's agriculture in a reform era.* Ames: Iowa State University Press.

Food and Agriculture Organization of the United Nations (FAO). 1999. *Comparative advantage and competitiveness of crops, crop rotations and livestock products in Egypt.* Cairo: FAO Regional Office.

Folbre, N. 1997. Gender coalitions: Extrafamily influences on intrafamily inequality. In *Intrahousehold resource allocation in developing countries: Models, methods and policy,* edited by L. Haddad, J. Hoddinott, and H. Alderman. Baltimore: Johns Hopkins University Press.

————. 2001. *The invisible heart: Economics and family values.* New York: New Press.

Fortin, P. 2001. Interest rates, unemployment and inflation: The Canadian experience in the 1990s. In *The longest decade: Canada in the 1990s,* edited by K. Banting, A. Sharpe, and F. St.-Hilarie. Montréal, PQ: Institute for Research on Public Policy.

Fosu, A.K. 1996. The impact of external debt on economic growth in sub-Saharan Africa. *Journal of Economic Development* 21 (1): 93-117.

————. 1999. The external debt burden and economic growth in the 1980s: Evidence from sub-Saharan Africa. *Canadian Journal of Development Studies* 20 (2): 307-318.

————. 2001. A proposal for alleviating the African external debt problem. Unpublished preliminary report submitted to the Organization of African Unity. Addis Ababa, Ethiopia.

Frank, A.G. 1967. *Capitalism and underdevelopment in Latin America.* New York: Monthly Review Press.

Frum, D., and R. Perle. 2004. *An end to evil: How to win the war on terror.* New York: Random House.

Fry, M.J. 1995. *Money, interest and banking in economic development.* Baltimore: Johns Hopkins University Press.

Gamble, A. 1998. *The free economy and the strong state: The politics of Thatcherism.* London: Macmillan.

Gang, I.N., and H.A. Khan. 1990. Foreign aid, taxes and public investment. *Journal of Development Economics* 34 (1-2): 355-369.

Gauld, R. 2000. Maintaining centralized control in community-based forestry: Policy construction in the Philippines. In *Forests: Nature, people, power,* edited by M. Doornbos, A. Saith, and B. White. Oxford: Blackwell Publishers.

Gellert, G. 1995. The influence of market economies on primary health care in Vietnam. *Journal of the American Medical Association* 273 (19): 1498-1505.

George, S., and F. Sabelli. 1994. *Faith and credit: The World Bank's secular empire.* Harmondsworth: Penguin Books.

Gerschenkron, A. 1962. *Economic backwardness in historical perspective: a book of essays.* Cambridge, MA: Belknap Press of Harvard University Press.

Ghana. 1995. *Ghana—Vision 2020. Presidential report to parliament on the co-ordinated program of economic and social development policies.* Accra: Office of the President. Mimeographed.

Ghura, D., and T. Grennes. 1993. The real exchange rate and macroeconomic performance in sub-Saharan Africa. *Journal of Development Economics* 42 (1): 155-174.

Giddens, A. 1979. *Central problems in social theory.* London: Macmillan.

Gilson, L. 1995. Management and health care reform in sub-Saharan Africa. *Social Science and Medicine* 40 (5): 695-710.

Girishankar, N., and B. Levy. n.d.. Addressing governance and institutional issues in the poverty reduction strategy process: An approach for country teams in the Africa region. Background paper for World Bank, 2000. *World development report 2000/2001: Attacking poverty.* Washington, DC: World Bank.

Globe and Mail, The. 19 July 2002.

Glover, D. 1991. A layman's guide to structural adjustment. *Canadian Journal of Development Studies* 12 (1): 173-186.

Goldsmith, R. 1969. *Financial structure and development.* New Haven: Yale University Press.

Goldstein, M., and P. Montiel. 1986. *Evaluating Fund stabilization programs with multicountry data: Some methodological pitfalls.* International Monetary Fund Staff Papers, 33 (2): 304-344. Washington, DC: International Monetary Fund.

Gordon, D.M. 1980. Stages of accumulation and long economic cycles. In *Process of the world system,* edited by T. Hopkins and I. Wallerstein. Beverly Hills, CA: Sage Publications.

Graff, M. 2002. Causal links between financial activity and economic growth: Empirical evidence from a cross-country analysis, 1970-1990. *Bulletin of Economic Research* 54 (2): 119-133.

Gramsci, A. 1971. *Selections from prison notebooks.* London: Lawrence and Wishart.

Green, R. and I. Ahmed. 1999. Rehabilitation, sustainable peace and development: Towards reconceptualisation. *Third World Quarterly* 20 (1): 179-206.

Griffin, C. 1987. *User charges for health care in principle and practice.* World Bank Economic Development Institute Seminar Paper, 37. Washington, DC: World Bank.

Gronow, C.J.V. 1995. Shifting power, sharing power: Issues from user-group forestry in Nepal. In *Power and participatory development,* edited by N. Nelson and S. Wright. London: Intermediate Technology Publications.

Grown, C., D. Elson, and N. Cagatay. 2000. Introduction to growth, trade, finance and gender inequality. *World Development* 28 (7): 1145-1156.

Guldner, M. 1995. Health care in transition in Vietnam: Equity and sustainability. *Health Policy and Planning* 10 [suppl.]: 49-62.

Guldner, M. and S. Rifkin. 1993. *Sustainability in the health sector: Vietnam case study.* Report for the Save the Children Fund (UK), London.

Gulhati, R., S. Bose, and Atukorala, V. 1986. Exchange rate policies in Africa: How valid is the scepticism? *Development and Change* 17: 399-423.

Gurley, J., and E.S. Shaw. 1960. *Money in a theory of finance.* Washington, DC: Brookings Institute.

Haddad, L., J. Hoddinott, and H. Alderman, eds. 1997. *Intrahousehold resource allocation in developing countries: Models, methods and policy.* Baltimore: Johns Hopkins University Press.

Hall, S. 1988. *The hard road to renewal: Thatcherism and the crisis of the left.* London: Verso.

Hall, S., and M. Jacques, eds. 1983. *The politics of Thatcherism.* London: Lawrence and Wishart.

Hamdani, K. 1997. Introduction to *The new globalism and developing countries,* edited by J. Dunning and K. Hamdani. New York: United Nations University Press.

Hamner, L. 1994. What happens to welfare when user fees finance health care? The impact of gender on policy outcomes—theory and evidence from Zimbabwe. Institute of Social Studies Working Paper Series 180. The Hague: Institute of Social Studies.

Hamner, L., and A.H. Akram-Lodhi. 1998. In "the house of spirits": towards a post-Keynesian theory of the household? *Journal of Post-Keynesian Economics* 20 (3): 415-434.

Hamner, L., G. Pyatt, and H. White. 1997. *Poverty in sub-Saharan Africa: What can we learn from the World Bank's poverty assessments.* The Hague: Institute of Social Studies Advisory Services.

Hardin, G. 1968. The tragedy of the commons. *Science* 162: 1243-1248.

Hassan, G., and C. Warhurst, eds. 1999. *A different future: A modernisers' guide to Scotland.* Edinburgh: Centre for Scottish Public Policy.

———, eds. 2000. *The new Scottish politics: The first year of the Scottish Parliament and beyond.* Norwich: Stationary Office.

Hayek, F. 1996. *Individualism and economic order.* Chicago: University of Chicago Press.

———. 2001. *The road to serfdom.* London: Routledge.

Hayek, F.A. 1975. Full employment at any price. *Hobart Paper* 45. London: Institute of Economic Affairs.

Helleiner, G.K., ed. 1994. *From adjustment to development in Africa.* New York: St. Martin's Press.

Helleiner, G.K. 1999. Changing aid relationships in Tanzania. (December 1997 through March 1999). Report prepared for the Government of the United Republic of Tanzania. Re-published in *NEPAD at country level: Changing aid relationships in Tanzania,* edited by S. Wangwe. Dar Es Salaam: Mkuki na Nyota Publishers, 2002.

————. 2000. Markets, politics and globalization: Can the global economy be civilized? The Tenth Raúl Prebisch Lecture, 11 December. Geneva.

————. 2000a. External conditionality, local ownership, and development. In *Transforming development: Foreign aid for a changing world,* edited by J. Freedman. Toronto, ON: University of Toronto Press.

————. 2000b. Towards balance in aid relationships: Donor performance monitoring in low-income developing countries. *Cooperation South* 2: 21-35. Re-published in *Development economics and structuralist macroeconomics: Essays in honour of Lance Taylor,* edited by Amitava Khrishna Dutt and Jaime Ros. Cheltenham, England: Edward Elgar, 2003.

Helleiner, G.K., T. Killick, N. Lipumba, B. Ndulu, and K.E. Svendsen. 1995. *Report of the group of independent advisors on development cooperation issues between Tanzania and its aid donors.* Copenhagen: Royal Danish Ministry of Foreign Affairs.

Heller, P.S. 1975. A model of public fiscal behavior in developing countries: Aid, investment and taxation. *American Economic Review* 65 (3): 429-445.

Helmsing, A.H., and T. Kolste, eds. 1993. *Small enterprises and changing policies.* London: Intermediate Technology Publications.

Hicks, J. 1969. *A theory of economic history.* Oxford: Clarendon Press.

Hilferding, R. [1910] 1985. *Finance capital: A study of the latest phase of capitalist development,* edited by T. Bottomore. London: Routledge and Kegan Paul.

Hill, A., and E. King. 1995. Women's education and economic well-being. *Feminist Economics* 1 (2): 21-46.

Hirst, P., and G. Thompson. 1999. *Globalization in question: The international economy and the possibilities of governance.* 2d ed. Cambridge: Polity Press.

Hobley, M., and K. Shah. 1996. What makes a local organisation robust? Evidence from India and Nepal. *ODI Natural Resource Perspectives,* No. 11 [cited 2 May 2000]. Available from http://www.oneworld.org/odi/nrp/11.html.

Hodgson, G.M. 2001. *How economics forgot history: The problem of historical specificity in social science.* London: Routledge.

Holmes, M., S. Knack, N. Manning, R. Messick, and J. Rinne. 2000. Governance and poverty reduction. Background paper for World Bank, 2000. *World development report 2000/2001: Attacking poverty.* Washington, DC: World Bank.

Hoogvelt, A., ed. 1987. *Multinational enterprise.* Basingstoke, England: Macmillan.

Hopkins, N.S. 1993. Small farmer households and agricultural sustainability. In *Sustainable agriculture in Egypt,* edited by M.M. Faris and M.H. Khan. Boulder: Lynne Rienner.

Horsman, M., and A. Marshall. 1994. *After the nation state.* London: HarperCollins.

Hossain, S. 1997. *Tackling health transition in China.* World Bank Working Paper, 1813. Washington, DC: World Bank.

Hsiao, W. 1994. Marketisation—the illusory magic pill. *Health Economics* 6 (3): 351-358.

Ibrahim, S.E., and H. Löfgren. 1996. Successful adjustment and declining governance? The case of Egypt. In *Governance, leadership and communication*, edited by L. Frischk and I. Atiyas. Washington, DC: The World Bank.

Inman, R.P. 1979. The fiscal performance of local governments: An interpretative review. In *Current issues in urban economics*, edited by P. Mieszkowski and M. Straszheim. Baltimore: Johns Hopkins University Press.

Institute of Statistical Social and Economic Research (Various issues). *The state of the Ghanaian economy*. Accra: University of Ghana Institute of Statistical Social and Economic Research.

International Development Association and International Monetary Fund. *Review of the poverty reduction strategy paper (PRSP) approach: Main findings* [cited 15 March 2002]. Available from http://www.imf.org/external/np/prspgen/review/2001/index.htm.

International Monetary Fund. (Various issues). *Balance of payments yearbook*. Washington, DC: The Author.

———. (Various issues). *Exchange arrangements and exchange restrictions*. Washington, DC: The Author.

———. (Various issues). *International financial statistics yearbook*. Washington, DC: The Author.

———. 1993. *International capital markets, part 1: Exchange rate management and international capital flows, April*. Washington, DC: The Author.

———. 1997. *Annual report of the executive board for the financial year ended April 30 1997*. Washington, DC: The Author.

———. 1999. *World economic outlook, October*. Washington, DC: The Author.

———. 2003. *Eritrea: Selected issues and statistical appendix*. International Monetary Fund Country Report, 03/166. Washington, DC: The Author.

International Monetary Fund and World Bank Development Committee. 2002. *Poverty reduction strategy papers (PRSP)—progress in implementation*. Washington: International Monetary Fund and World Bank.

Isham, J., D. Narayan, and L. Pritchett. 1995. Does participation improve performance? Establishing causality with subjective data. *The World Bank Economic Review* 9 (2): 175-200.

Jackson, A., D. Robinson, B. Baldwin, and C. Wiggins. 2002. *Falling behind: The state of working Canada, 2000*. Ottawa: Canadian Centre for Policy Alternatives.

Jackson, C. 1997. Actor orientation and gender relations at a participatory project interface. In *Getting institutions right for women in development*, edited by A. Goetz. New York: Zed Books.

Jeffrey, B. 1999. *Hard right turn: The new face of neo-conservatism in Canada*. Toronto: HarperCollins.

Jesperson, E. 1992. External shocks, adjustment policies and economic and social performance. In *Africa's recovery in the 1990s*, edited by G. Cornia, R. van der Hoeven, and T. Mkandawire. New York: St. Martin's Press.

Johnson E., and H. Johnson. 1978. *The shadow of Keynes: Understanding Keynes*. Oxford: Blackwell.

Kamin, S.B. 1988. Devaluation, external balance, and macroeconomic performance: A look at the numbers. *Princeton Studies in International Finance* 62. Princeton, NJ: Princeton University.

———. 1995. Contractionary devaluation with black markets for foreign exchange. *Journal of Policy Modeling* 17 (1): 39-57.

Kant, S., and R. Cooke. 1998. *Complementarity of institutions: A prerequisite for the success of joint forest management. A comparative case of four villages from India*. International Workshop on Community-Based Natural Resource Management, Washington, DC [cited 2 May 2000]. Available from http://www.worldbank.org/wbi/conatrem/India-01-Paper.htm.

Kapur, I., M.T. Hadjimichael, P. Hibert, J. Schiff, and P. Szymczak. 1991. *Ghana: Adjustment and growth, 1983-1991.* International Monetary Fund Occasional Paper, 86. Washington, DC: International Monetary Fund.

Kapuscinski, R. 2002. *The shadow of the sun: My life in Africa.* Harmondsworth: Penguin Books.

Kenen, P.B. 1985. Macroeconomic theory and policy: How the economy was opened. In *Handbook of international economics.* Vol. 2, edited by R.W. Jones and P.B. Kenen. Amsterdam: North-Holland.

Kennedy, P. 1998. *African capitalism.* Cambridge: Cambridge University Press.

Kesselman, J.R. 2001. Policies to stem the brain drain—without Americanizing Canada. *Canadian Public Policy* 27 (1): 77-93.

Keynes, J.M. [1967] 1970. *The general theory of employment, interest and money.* Reprint, London: Macmillan and Company Ltd.

Khan, M.S. 1990. The macroeconomic effects of fund-supported programs: An empirical assessment. *International Monetary Fund Staff Papers* 37 (2): 195-231.

Killick, T. 1978. *Development economics in action: A study of economic policies in Ghana.* New York: St. Martin's Press.

Kimei, C.S. 1992. A perspective on exchange-rate policies and their results: The experience of Tanzania. In *Instruments of economic policy in Africa,* edited by African Center for Monetary Studies. Dakar: African Center for Monetary Studies.

Kindleberger, C. 1984. *A financial history of western Europe.* London: Allen and Unwin.

King, R.G., and R. Levine. 1993. Finance and growth: Schumpeter might be right. *Quarterly Journal of Economics* 108 (3): 717-737.

Kitchen, H. 1983. *United States interests and Africa.* New York: Praeger.

Kitchen, R.L. 1986. *Finance for the developing countries.* Chichester: John Wiley.

Klein, N. 2001. *No logo.* London: Flamingo.

Klooster, D. 2000. Institutional choice, community, and struggle. A case study of forest co-management in Mexico. *World Development* 28 (1): 1-20.

Krueger, A.B., and M. Lindahl. 2001. Education for growth: why and for whom? *Journal of Economic Literature* 39 (4): 1101-1136.

Krugman, P. 1998. The return of demand-side economics. Lecture at the Free University of Berlin, 4 December, Berlin, Germany.

Krugman, P., and L. Taylor. 1978. Contractionary effects of devaluation. *Journal of International Economics* 8 (3): 445-456.

Kuhn, T.S. 1962. *The structure of scientific revolutions.* Chicago: University of Chicago Press.

Kurian, M. 2001. Farmer managed irrigation and governance of irrigation service delivery. Analysis of experience and best practice. Institute of Social Studies Working Paper, 351. The Hague: Institute of Social Studies.

Kurien, J. 1992. Ruining the commons and the response of the commoners: Coastal overfishing and fishworkers' actions in Kerala State, India. In *Grassroots environmental action: Participation in sustainable development,* edited by D. Ghai and J. Vivian. London: Routledge.

Laidler, D., and Aba, S. 2002. Productivity and the dollar: Commodities and the exchange rate connection. *C.D. Howe Institute Commentary* 158.

Land Center for Human Rights. 2002. Farmer struggles against law 96 of 1992. In *Counter-revolution in Egypt's countryside: Land and farmers in the era of economic reform,* edited by R. Bush. London: Zed Books.

Lash, S., and J. Urry. 1987. *The end of organized capitalism.* Cambridge: Polity Press.

Lawrence, P. 2002. Household credit and saving: Does policy matter? Keele Economics Research Papers 2002/04. Keele, Staffordshire, UK: Keele University Economics Department.

Lawson, T. 1997. *Economics and reality*. London: Routledge.

Lazar, H. 2000. The social union framework agreement and the federal budgetary process. In *The 2000 federal budget: Retrospect and Prospect*, edited by P.A.R. Hobson and T.A. Wilson. Kingston, Ontario: John Deutsch Institute.

Leach, M., R. Mearns, and I. Scoones. 1997. Institutions, consensus and conflict: Implications for policy and practice. *IDS Bulletin* 28 (4): 90-95.

———. 1999. Environmental entitlements: Dynamics and institutions in community-based natural resource management. *World Development* 27 (2): 225-247.

Lee, R. 1994. Modernization, postmodernism and the Third World. *Current Sociology* 42 (2): 1-63.

Leechor, C. 1994. Ghana: Frontrunner in adjustment. In *Adjustment in Africa: Lessons from country case studies*, edited by I. Hussein and R. Faruqee. Washington, DC: The World Bank.

Leeuwis, C. 2000. Reconceptualizing participation for sustainable rural development: Towards a negotiation approach. *Development and Change* 31 (5): 931-960.

Left Business Observer. 1998. The U. S. boom. 81 (3).

Leite, S.P., A. Pellechio, L. Zanforlin, G. Begashaw, S. Fabrizio, and J. Harnack. 2000. Economic development in a democratic environment. International Monetary Fund Occasional Paper, 199. Washington, DC: International Monetary Fund.

Lélé, S.M. 1991. Sustainable development: A critical review. *World Development* 19 (6): 607-621.

Levine, R. 1997. Financial development and economic growth: Views and agenda. *Journal of Economic Literature* 35 (2): 688-726.

Leys, C. 1978. Capital accumulation, class formation and dependency: The significance of the Kenyan case. In *The socialist register 1978*, edited by R. Miliband and J. Savile. London: Merlin Press.

Li, T.M. 1996. Images of community: Discourse and strategy in property relations. *Development and Change* 27 (3): 501-527.

Lim, D. 1983. Instability of government revenue and expenditure in less developed countries. *World Development* 11 (5): 447-450.

Lipietz, A. 1992. *Towards a new economic order: Postfordism, ecology and democracy*. Oxford: Polity Press.

Lipumba, N.H.I. 1992. The exchange rate in structural adjustment and economic growth in sub-Saharan Africa: Policy issues. In *Instruments of economic policy in Africa*. Dakar: African Center for Monetary Studies.

Liu, X., and W. Hsiao. 1995. The cost escalation of social health insurance plans in China: Its implication for public policy. *Social Sciences and Medicine* 41 (8): 1095-1101.

Lizondo, J.S., and P.J. Montiel. 1989. Contractionary devaluation in developing countries. *International Monetary Fund Staff Papers* 36 (1): 182-227.

Ljunggren, B. 1993. Market economies under communist regimes: Reform in Vietnam, Laos, and Cambodia. In *The challenge of reform in Indochina*, edited by B. Ljunggren. Cambridge: Harvard Institute for International Development.

Lonnroth, K., M. Thuong, D. Linh, and K. Diwan. 1998. Risk and benefit of private health care: Exploring physicians' views on private health care in Ho Chi Minh City, Vietnam. *Health Policy* 45: 81-97.

Love, R. 2002. Political economy of the coffee *filiere* in Ethiopia. Ph.D. diss., University of Leeds, UK.

Löwy, M. 2000. A "red" government in the heart of Brazil. *Monthly Review* 52 (6): 16-20.

Loxley, J. 1966. The development of the monetary and financial system of the East African currency area 1950 to 1964. Ph.D. diss., University of Leeds, United Kingdom.

———. 1981. The great northern plan. *Studies in Political Economy* 6: 151-182.

———. 1986. *Debt and disorder: External finance for development*. Ottawa, Ontario: North-South Institute.

———. 1989. The devaluation debate in Tanzania. In *Structural adjustment in Africa*, edited by B.K. Campbell and J. Loxley. Hampshire, UK: Macmillan Press, Ltd.

———. 1990. Economic planning under social democracy. In *The political economy of Manitoba*, edited by J. Silver, D. Cook, and J. Hull. Regina, SK: Great Plains Press.

———. 1990b. Structural adjustment in Africa: Reflections on Ghana and Zambia. *Review of African Political Economy* 47: 8-27.

———. 1991. *Ghana: The long road to recovery 1983-1990*. Ottawa, ON: The North-South Institute.

———. 1993. Democratizing economic policy formulation: The Manitoba experience. In *A different kind of state? Popular power and democratic administration*, edited by G. Albo, D. Langille, and L. Panitch. Toronto, ON: Oxford University Press.

———. 1998. *Interdependence, disequilibrium and growth*. Ottawa, ON: London International Development Research Centre and Macmillan.

———. 1999. Financial fragility, global capital markets and global governance. In *Out of control: Canada in an unstable financial world*, edited by B. MacLean. Toronto, ON: James Lorimer and Co. Ltd.

———. 2003. *Alternative budgets: Budgeting as if people mattered*. Halifax, NS: Fernwood Press.

Lubker, M., G. Smith, and J. Weeks. 2002. Growth and the poor: A comment on Dollar and Kraay. *Journal of International Development* 14 (5): 555-571.

Lucas, R.E. Jr. 1988. On the mechanics of economic development. *Journal of Monetary Economics* 22 (1): 3-42.

Lukes, S. 1985. *Marxism and morality*. Oxford, UK: Oxford University Press.

MacEwan, A. 1999. *Neo-liberalism or democracy? Economic strategy, markets and alternatives for the 21st century*. London, UK: Zed Books.

Maddison, A. 1995. *Monitoring the world economy, 1820-1992*. Paris: Development Centre of the Organisation for Economic Cooperation and Development.

Malhotra, K. 1999. Basic health services for vulnerable families in Vietnam: Should user fees be the way forward? Paper prepared for the International Save the Children Alliance and Unicef, Hanoi, Vietnam.

Mamdani, M. 1976. *Politics and class formation in Uganda*. New York: Monthly Review Press.

Manor, J. n.d.. Democratic decentralisation in two Indian states: Past and present. Draft paper [cited 23 September 2002]. Available from http://www.livelihoodoptions.info/papers/htm.

Manser, M.E., and G. Picot. 1999. Self-employment in Canada and the United States. *Perspectives on Labour and Income* 9 (3): 37-44.

Marglin, S., and J. Schor, eds. 1990. *The Golden Age of Capitalism: Reinterpreting the Postwar Experience*. Oxford: Clarendon Press.

Martinussen, J. 1997. *Society, state and market: A guide to competing theories of development*. New York: Zed Books.

Marx, K. [1894] 1959. *Capital: A critique of political economy*. Vol. 1. Reprint, Moscow: Progress Publishers.

———. [1894] 1959. *Capital: A critique of political economy*, edited by Frederick Engels. Vol. 3. Reprint, Moscow: Progress Publishers.

Marx, K. [1894] 1982. *Capital: A critique of political economy*. Vol. 2. Translated by Ben Fowkes. Harmondsworth, England: Penguin Books.

Matose, F. 1997. Conflicts around forest reserves in Zimbabwe: What prospects for community management? *IDS Bulletin* 28 (4): 69-78.

May, E. 1985. *Exchange controls and parallel market economies in sub-Saharan Africa: Focus on Ghana.* World Bank Working Paper, 711. Washington, DC: The World Bank.

Mayoux, L. 1995. Beyond naivety: Women, gender inequality and participatory development. *Development and Change* 26 (2): 235-258.

McCay, B.J., and Acheson, J.M. 1987. Human ecology of the commons. In *The question of the commons: The culture and ecology of communal resources,* edited by B.J. McCay and J.M. Acheson Tucson: The University of Arizona Press.

McGiffen, S.P. 2001. *The European union: A critical guide.* London: Pluto Press.

McGuire, G. 2000. Physician agency. In *Handbook of Health Economics*. Vol. 1A. Edited by A. Culyer and J. Newhouse. Amsterdam: North-Holland.

McKinnon, R.I. 1973. *Money and capital in economic development.* Washington, DC: Brookings Institute.

McLain, R., and E. Jones. 1998. Whose mushrooms? Dealing "outsiders" into communal management of common natural resources [cited 5 May 2000]. Available from http://www.id21.org.

Mehta, L., M. Leach, and I. Scoones. 2001. Editorial: Environmental governance in an uncertain world. *IDS Bulletin* 32 (4): 1-9.

Meinzen-Dick, R, and M. Zwarteveen. 1997. *Gendered participation in water management: Issues and illustrations from water users' associations in south Asia* [cited 9 October 2001]. Available from http://www.jar.ubc.ca/centres/cisar/MEINZEN-DICK/MD1.html.

Meltz, N., and A. Verma. 1997. *Developments in industrial relations and human resource practices in Canada: An update from the 1980s.* In *Employment relations in a changing world economy,* edited by R. Locke, T. Kochan, and M. Piore. Cambridge, MA: MIT Press.

Meynen, W. 1989. Fisheries development, resource depletion and political mobilization in Kerala: The problem of alternatives. *Development and Change* 20 (4): 735-770.

Mick, M. 1993. Declining to learn from the East? The World Bank on "governance and development." *IDS Bulletin* 24 (1): 39-49.

Middle East Times. 2000. Egypt's clampdown [cited 18 August 2002]. Available from www.metimes.com/2K/issue2000-28/eg/egypts_clampdown_on.htm.

Milanovic, B. 2003. The two faces of globalization: Against globalization as we know it. *World Development* 31 (4): 667-683.

Milliken, Jennifer, ed. 2003. *State failure, collapse and reconstruction.* Oxford: Blackwell Publishing.

Mitchell, T. 1998. The market's place. In *Directions of change in rural Egypt,* edited by N.S. Hopkins and K. Westergaard. Cairo: American University in Cairo Press.

———. 1999. No factories, no problems: The logic of neoliberalism in Egypt. *Review of African Political Economy* 26 (82): 455-456.

Mohan, G., and K. Stokke. 2000. Participatory development and empowerment: The dangers of localism. *Third World Quarterly* 21 (2): 247-268.

Moore, K.M., M.K. Bertelsen, L. Diarra, A. Kodio, S. Cissé, and P. Wyeth. 2000. Natural resource management institution building in the decentralized context of west Africa: The SANREM CPRS approach. Paper prepared for the IFSA Symposium, November 2000, Santiago, Chile [cited 9 October 2001]. Available from http://www/oird.vt.edu/sanremcrsp/workpapers/0102.pdf.

Moore, M., and J. Putzel. 1999. Politics and poverty. Background paper for World Bank, 2000. *World development report 2000/2001: Attacking poverty.* Washington, DC: World Bank.

Moseley, F. 1988. The Marxian macroeconomic variables and the postwar US economy: A critique of Wolff's estimates. *American Economic Review* 78 (1): 298-303.

————. 1997. The rate of profit and the future of capitalism. *Review of Radical Political Economics* 29 (4): 23-41.

————. 1999. The United States economy at the turn of the century: Entering a new era of prosperity. *Capital and Class* 67: 25-45.

Mosley, P., J. Hudson, and S. Horrell. 1987. Aid, the public sector, and the market in less developed countries. *Economic Journal* 97 (387): 616-641.

Mosley, P., T. Subasat, and J. Weeks. 1995. Assessing adjustment in Africa. *World Development* 23 (9): 1459-1473.

Mosely, P., and J. Weeks. 1993. Has recovery begun? Africa's adjustment in the 1980s revisited. *World Development* 21 (10): 1583-1606.

Mosse, D. 1995. The symbolic making of a common property resource: History, ecology and locality in a tank-irrigated landscape in south India. *Development and Change* 28 (3): 467-504.

Nassar, S. 1993. The economic impact of reform programs in the agricultural sector in Egypt. Cairo: Ministry of Agriculture, Livestock and Fishery Wealth and Land Reclamation, Economic Affairs Sector. Mimeographed.

Nelson, N., and S. Wright, eds. 1995. *Power and participatory development.* London: Intermediate Technology Publications.

Nelson, P. 2002. *Access and influence: Tensions and ambiguities in the World Bank's expanding relationship with civil society organizations.* Ottawa, ON: The North-South Institute.

Newlyn, W.T. 1977. *The financing of economic development.* Oxford: Clarendon Press.

Newlyn, W.T., and D.C. Rowan. 1954. *Money and banking in British colonial Africa: A study of the monetary and banking systems of eight British African territories.* Oxford: Oxford University Press.

Ngirumpatse, P. 2004. L'initiative d'allègement de la lettre des payes pauvres très endettés: adéquation entre allègement de la dette et réduction de la pauvreté: le cas du Rwanda. Master's thesis, Department of Political Science, Université du Québec à Montréal, Montréal, PQ.

Nguyen, V.T., N.P. Dao, N.H. Nguyen, and V.T. Ngo. 2000. Changes in the health sector during renovation in Vietnam (1997-1998). In *Efficient, equity-oriented strategies for health: International Perspectives—focus on Vietnam,* edited by I.H. Pham, Y. Minas, G. Liu, G. Dahlgrem, and W.C. Hsiao. Melbourne, Australia: Centre for International Mental Health, University of Melbourne.

Niblock, T. 1993. International and domestic factors in the economic liberalisation process in Arab countries. In *Economic and political liberalisation in the Middle East,* edited by T. Niblock and E. Murphy. London: British Academic Press.

Nissanke, M., and E. Aryteerey. 1998. *Financial integration and development: Liberalization and reform in sub-Saharan Africa.* London: Routledge.

Nkrumah, G. 2002. Jostling for position in the Africa union jive. *Al-Ahram Weekly,* 18 July.

North, D.C. 1990. *Institutions, institutional change and economic performance.* Cambridge: Cambridge University Press.

Nowak, M. 1984. Quantitative controls and unofficial markets in foreign exchange: A theoretical framework. *International Monetary Fund Staff Papers* 31 (2): 404-431.

Nurkse, R. 1953. *Problems of capital formation in underdeveloped countries.* New York: Oxford University Press.

Nwana, G.I. 1987. Devaluation, unanticipated inflation and output growth: A comparative aggregate analysis. *Economia Internazionale* 40: 329-344.

Obstfeld, M. 1998. The global capital market: Benefactor or menace? *Journal of Economic Perspectives* 12 (4): 9-30.

Ocampo, J.A. 2001. Rethinking the development agenda. *Cambridge Journal of Economics* 26: 393-407.

Odedokun, M.O. 1997. Dynamics of inflation in sub-Saharan Africa: The role of foreign inflation, official and parallel market exchange rates, and monetary growth. *Applied Financial Economics* 7 (4): 395-402.

O'Donnell, G. 1999. Horizontal accountability in new democracies. In *The self-restraining state: Power and accountability in new democracies*, edited by A. Schedler, L. Diamond, and M.F. Plattner. Boulder, Colorado: Lynne Rienner Publishers.

Ohmae, K. 1990. *The borderless world*. New York: Collins.

Organization for Economic Cooperation and Development (OECD). 1994. *DAC principles for effective aid*. Paris: The Author.

———. 1995. *Development cooperation, efforts and policies of the members of the development assistance committee, 1994*. Paris: The Author.

———. 1996. *Shaping the 21st century: The contribution of development cooperation*. Paris: The Author.

———. 1998. *OECD economic outlook, June*. Paris: The Author.

Osberg, L., and P. Fortin, eds. 1995. *Unnecessary debts*. Toronto, ON: James Lorimer and Company.

Ostrom, E. 1990. *Governing the commons: The evolution of institutions for collective action*. New York: Cambridge University Press.

———. 1992. *Crafting institutions for self-governing irrigation systems*. San Francisco: Institute for Contemporary Studies.

Oxfam (GB). 1999. *A participatory poverty assessment: Duyen Hai and Thanh districts, Tra Vinh Province, Vietnam*. Hanoi: The Author.

Palmer, I. 1995. Public finance from a gender perspective. *World Development* 23 (11): 1981-1986.

Pantana, P., M. Real, and B. Resurreccion. n.d. Officializing strategies: Participatory processes and gender in ADB's capacity building in Thailand's water resources sector. Perspective Paper, Mekong Regional Environmental Governance, REPSI-WRI, 2000-2001. Bangkok: Asian Development Bank.

Parpart, J.L. 1995. Deconstructing the development "expert:" Gender, development, and the "vulnerable groups." In *Feminism, Postmodernism, and Development*, edited by M.H. Marchand and J.L. Parpart. London: Routledge.

Patel, I.G. 1971. Aid relationships for the seventies. In *The widening gap: Development in the 1970s*, edited by B. Ward, L. d'Anjou, and J.D. Runnalls. New York: Columbia University Press.

Pathak, A. 1994. *Contested domains: The state, peasants and forests in contemporary India*. London: Sage Publications.

Pham, T. 2002. User fees and fees exemption mechanism in public health facilities: The case of Quang Ngai Province. Master's thesis, University of Economics, Ho Chi Minh City.

Pinto, B. 1990. Black market premia, exchange rate unification, and inflation in sub-Saharan Africa. *World Bank Economic Review* 3 (3): 321-338.

Poffenberger, M. 1996. The struggle for forest control in the jungle *mahals* of West Bengal, 1750-1990. In *Village voices, forest choices: Joint forest management in India*, edited by M. Poffenberger, and B. McGean. Delhi: Oxford University Press.

Poffenberger, M., and B. McGean, eds. 1996. *Village voices, forest choices: Joint forest management in India*. Delhi: Oxford University Press.

Poffenberger, M., and C. Singh. 1996. Communities and the state: Re-establishing the balance in Indian foreign policy. In *Village voices, forest choices: Joint forest management in India*, edited by M. Poffenberger and B. McGean. Delhi: Oxford University Press.

Polak, J.J. 1995. Fifty years of exchange rate research and policy at the International Monetary Fund. *International Monetary Fund Staff Papers* 42 (4): 734-761.

Popov, Y. 1977. *The developing countries from the standpoint of Marxist political economy*. Moscow: Progress Publishers.

Pratt, C. 1979. *Tanzania's transition to socialism: Reflections of a democratic socialist*. In *Towards socialism in Tanzania*, edited by B. Mwansasu and C. Pratt. Toronto, ON: University of Toronto Press.

Preker, A., and R. Feachem. 1994. Health and health care. In *Labour markets and social policy in central and eastern Europe: The transition and beyond*, edited by N. Barr. New York: Oxford University Press.

Prescott, N. 1997. *Poverty, social services, and safety nets in Vietnam*. World Bank Discussion Paper, 376. Washington, DC: World Bank.

President's Information Technology Advisory Committee. 1999. *Information technology research: Investing in our future*. Washington: Executive Office of the President of the United States.

Quan, D. 1999. The state and social sector in Vietnam: Reforms and challenges for Vietnam. *ASEAN Economic Bulletin* 16 (3): 373-393.

Rao, S. and A. Sharpe, eds. 2002. *Productivity issues in Canada*. Calgary, AB: University of Calgary Press.

Rao, S., and J. Tang. 2001. The contribution of ICTs to productivity growth in Canada and the United States in the 1990s. *International Productivity Monitor* 3: 3-18.

Rashed Un Nabi. 1998. *The inland capture fisheries in Bangladesh: Institutions and endowments*. Master's research paper, Institute of Social Studies, The Hague.

Razzak, W.A. 1995. Are devaluations effective in inducing real depreciations in sub-Saharan Africa? *Applied Economics Letters* 2 (11): 437-439.

Rebick, J. 2000. *Imagine democracy*. Toronto, ON: Stoddart.

Reich, R. 1992. *The work of nations*. New York: Vintage.

Riddell, C.W. and A. Sharpe, eds. 1998. *Canadian public policy* 24 (S1).

Riddell, J. 1992. Things fall apart again: Structural adjustment programs in sub-Saharan Africa. *The Journal of Modern African Studies* 30 (1): 53-68.

Robinson, J. 1952. *The rate of interest and other essays*. London: Macmillan.

Robinson, L. 1995. Monetizing the debt. *Studies in Political Economy* 48 (Autumn): 137-147.

Rocheleau, D., and D. Edmunds. 1997. Women, men, and trees: Gender, power, and property in forest and agrarian landscapes. *World Development* 25 (8): 1351-71.

Rodney, W. 1972. *How Europe underdeveloped Africa*. Dar Es Salaam, Tanzania: Tanzania Publishing House.

Rodrik, D. 1999. *The new global economy and developing countries: Making openness work*. Washington, DC: Overseas Development Council.

Romer, P.M. 1990. Endogenous technological change. *Journal of Political Economy*, part two, 98 (5): 71-102.

Rouis, M., W. Razzak, and C. Mollinedo. 1994. The supply response to exchange rate reform in sub-Saharan Africa. World Bank Policy Research Working Paper, 1311. Washington, DC: The World Bank.

Rubin, J. and J. Lester. 1996. *When will the fiscal brake be released?* CIBC Wood Gundy Occasional Report, 15. Toronto, ON: CIBC Wood Gundy.

Rugman, A. 2000. *The end of globalisation*. London: Random House.

Runge, C.F. 1986. Common property and collective action in economic development. *World Development* 14 (5): 623-635.

Rweyemamu, A.H., ed. 1970. *Nation-building in Tanzania: Problems and issues*. Nairobi, Kenya: East African Publishing House.

Saad, R. 2002. Egyptian politics and the tenancy law. In *Counter-revolution in Egypt's countryside: Land and farmers in the era of economic reform*, edited by R. Bush. London: Zed Books.

Saito, K., and D. Spurling. 1992. Developing agricultural extension for women farmers. World Bank Discussion Paper, 156. Washington, DC: The World Bank.

Salanti, A. and E. Screpanti, eds. 1997. *Pluralism in economics*. Cheltenham, England: Edward Elgar.

Sarel, M. 1996. Nonlinear effects of inflation on economic growth. *International Monetary Fund Staff Papers* 43 (1): 199-215.

Sarin, M. 1996. From conflict to collaboration: Institutional issues in community management. In *Village voices, forest choices: Joint forest management in India*, edited by M. Poffenberger and B. McGean. Delhi: Oxford University Press.

Schedler, A., L. Diamond, and M. F. Plattner, eds. 1999. *The self-restraining state: Power and accountability in new democracies*. Boulder, Colorado: Lynne Rienner.

Schmidt, R. 2002. *Impact assessment for macroeconomic poverty policy*. Paper prepared for the UNDP regional programme, Macroeconomics of Poverty Reduction. New York: United Nations Development Programme.

Scottish Council Foundation. 2001. Out of the ordinary: the power of ambition in an uncertain world. Paper 19 [cited 29 January 2002]. Available from http://scottishpolicynet.org.uk.

Scottish Executive. 2000. *The way forward: A framework for economic development in Scotland*. Edinburgh: Scottish Executive.

Seddon, D. 1990. The politics of adjustment: Egypt and the IMF, 1987-1990. *Review of African Political Economy* 47 (Spring): 95-104.

Seers, D. 1963. The limitations of the special case. *Bulletin of the Oxford Institute of Economics and Statistics* 25 (2): 77-98.

Segall, M., G. Tipping, V. Dao, and H. Dao. 1999. *Economic reform, poverty and equity in access to health care: Case Studies in Vietnam*. Research Report 34. Brighton, UK: Institute of Development Studies at the University of Sussex.

Sen, A. 1999. *Development as freedom*. Oxford: Oxford University Press.

Sen, G. 2000. Gender mainstreaming in finance ministries. *World Development* 28 (7): 1379-1390.

Sepehri, A., and R. Chernomas. 1992. Who paid for the Canadian welfare state between 1955-1988? *Review of Radical Political Economics* 24 (1): 71-88.

Sepehri, A., R. Chernomas, and A.H. Akram-Lodhi. 2002. Penalizing patients and rewarding health providers: User charges and health care utilization in Vietnam. Winnipeg, MB: Department of Economics, University of Manitoba. Mimeographed.

————. 2003. If they get sick, they are in trouble: Health care restructuring, user charges, and equity in Vietnam. *International Journal of Health Services* 33 (1): 137-161.

Serieux, J. 2001. The enhanced HIPC initiative and poor countries: Prospects for a permanent exit. *Canadian Journal of Development Studies* 21 (2): 527-547.

Sfakianakis, J. 2002. In search of bureaucrats and entrepreneurs: The political economy of the export agribusiness sector in Egypt. In *Counter-revolution in Egypt's countryside: Land and farmers in the era of economic reform*, edited by R. Bush. London: Zed Books.

Shafaeddin, S. M. 1992. The effectiveness of nominal devaluation: The influence of the level of development. In *Industrial and trade policy reform in developing countries*, edited by R. Adhikari, C. Kirkpatrick, and J. Weiss. Manchester, England: Manchester University Press.

434

————. 1993. Import shortages and the inflationary impact of devaluation in developing countries. *Industry and Development* 32: 19-37.

Shah, M.K., and P. Shah. 1995. Gender, environment and livelihood security: An alternative viewpoint from India. *IDS Bulletin* 26 (1): 75-82.

Shaikh, A., and E.A. Tonak. 1994. *Measuring the wealth of nations: The political economy of the national accounts.* Cambridge: Cambridge University Press.

————. 2000. The rise and fall of the US welfare state. In *Political economy and contemporary capitalism: Radical perspectives on economic theory and policy*, edited by R. Baiman, H. Boushey, and D. Saunders. Armonk, NY: M.E. Sharpe.

Shan, J.Z., A.G. Morris, and F. Sun. 2001. Financial development and economic growth: An egg-and-chicken problem? *Review of International Economics* 9 (3): 443-454.

Sharaf, M., and J. Gleeson. 1999. *Land tenure study phase II.* Agricultural Policy Reform Program. Cairo: Government of Egypt Ministry of Agriculture and Land Reclamation and USAID.

Sharp, R. 1995. A framework for gathering budget information from government departments and authorities. Adelaide: Research Centre for Gender Studies, University of South Australia. Mimeographed.

Sharp, R. and R. Broomhill . 1990. Women and government budgets. *Australian Journal of Social Issues* 25 (1): 1-14.

Sharpe, A. 2002. Recent productivity developments in the United States and Canada: Implications for the Canada-US productivity and income gaps. *International Productivity Monitor* 4: 3-14.

Shaw, E.S. 1973. *Financial deepening in economic development.* New York: Oxford University Press.

Shepsle, K.A. 1979. Institutional arrangements and equilibrium in multidimensional voting models. *American Journal of Political Science* 23: 27-59.

Shivji, I. 1976. Class struggles in Tanzania. Dar Es Salaam, Tanzania: Tanzania Publishing House.

————. 2003. The life and times of Babu: The age of liberation and revolution. *Review of African Political Economy* 95: 109-118.

Shrybman, S. 1999. *The World Trade Organization: A citizen's guide.* Toronto, ON: James Lorimer and Co. Ltd.

Sidel, V. 1993. New lessons from China: Equity and economics in rural health care. *American Journal of Public Health* 83 (12): 1665-1666.

Sinha, S., S. Gururani, and B. Greenberg. 1997. The "new traditionalist" discourse of Indian environmentalism. *Journal of Peasant Studies* 24 (3): 65-99.

Skinner, A.S. 1965. Economics and history: the Scottish enlightenment. *Scottish Journal of Political Economy* 32 (1): 1-22.

Solow, R. 1956. A contribution to the theory of economic growth. *Quarterly Journal of Economics* 70: 65-94.

Sowa, N. 1994. Fiscal deficits, output growth and inflation targets in Ghana. *World Development* 22 (8): 1105-1117.

Stanford, J. 1995. The economics of debt and the remaking of Canada. *Studies in Political Economy* 48 (Autumn): 113-135.

————. 1997. Interest, growth and debt: Canada's fall from the knife-edge. In Canadian Centre for Policy Alternatives and CHO!CES: A Coalition for Social Justice, *Alternative federal budget papers 1997.* Ottawa, ON: Canadian Centre for Policy Alternatives.

————. 1999. *Paper boom: Why real prosperity requires a new approach to Canada's economy.* Toronto, ON: Canadian Centre for Policy Alternatives and James Lorimer and Co. Ltd.

435

————. 2001. The economic and social consequences of fiscal retrenchment in Canada in the 1990s. In *The longest decade: Canada in the 1990s*, edited by K. Banting, A. Sharpe, and F. St.-Hilarie. Montreal: Institute for Research on Public Policy.

van Staveren, I. 2002. Beyond rhetoric: Assessing government's commitment to women's small and medium enterprises through gender budget analysis. Paper presented to the Women, Gender Relations and Enterprise Development in Vietnam Summer School, Institute of Social Studies, September 20, The Hague.

van Staveren, I., and Akram-Lodhi, A.H. 2002. Women SME entrepreneurs and VAT in Vietnam: An exercise. Paper read at the Women, Gender Relations and Enterprise Development in Vietnam Summer School, Institute of Social Studies, 20 September, The Hague.

Steins, N.A., V.M. Edwards, and N. Röling. 2000. Redesigned principles for CPR theory. *The Common Property Digest* 53 (June).

Stiglitz, J.E. 1997. The role of government in the economies of developing countries. In *Development strategy and management of the market economy*, edited by E. Malinvaud, I.P. Szekely, and R. Sabot. Oxford: Clarendon Press for the United Nations.

Stiglitz, J.E. and A. Weiss. 1981. Credit rationing in markets with imperfect information. *American Economic Review* 71 (3): 383-410.

Strauss, L. 1990a. *An introduction to political philosophy: Ten essays by Leo Strauss*. Detroit: Wayne State University Press.

————. 1990b. *Natural right and history*. Chicago: University of Chicago Press.

Streeten, P. 1987. Structural adjustment: A survey of the issues and options. *World Development* 15 (12): 1469-1482.

Structural Adjustment Participatory Review Initiative Network. 2002. The policy roots of economic crisis and poverty. Available from http://www.saprin.org/SAPRI_Findings.pdf.

Subramanian, A. 1997. The Egyptian stabilisation experience: An analytical perspective. Working Paper, 18. Cairo: Egyptian Centre for Economic Studies. October.

Sundar, N. 2000. Unpacking the "joint" in joint forest management. In *Forests: Nature, people, power*, edited by M. Doornbos, A. Saith, and B. White. Oxford: Blackwell Publishers.

Szentes, T. 1983. *The political economy of underdevelopment*. 4th ed. Budapest: Akadémiai Kiadó.

Tabb, W. 2003. After neoliberalism? *Monthly Review* 55 (2): 25-33.

Tanzi, V. 1989. The impact of macroeconomic policies on the level of taxation and the fiscal balance in developing countries. *International Monetary Fund Staff Papers* 36 (3): 633-656.

Taylor, L. 1979. *Macro models for developing countries*. New York: McGraw-Hill Book Company.

————. 1981. IS/LM in the tropics: Diagrammatics of the new structuralist macro critique. In *Economic stabilization in developing countries*, edited by W.R. Cline and S. Weintraub. Washington, DC: The Brookings Institution.

————. 1993. *The rocky road to reform: Adjustment, income distribution and growth in the developing world*. London: The MIT Press.

Thomas, C.Y. 1974. *Dependence and transformation: The economics of the transition to socialism*. New York: Monthly Review Press.

Thurow, L. 1996. *The future of capitalism*. New York: Penguin Books.

————. 1999. Building wealth. *The Atlantic Monthly*, June, 57-69.

Tibaijuka, A. 1994. The cost of differential gender roles in African agriculture: A case study of smallholder banana-coffee farms in the Kagera region, Tanzania. *Journal of Agricultural Economics* 45 (1): 69-81.

Tipping, G., D. Troung, T. Nguyen, and M. Segall. 1994. Quality of public health services and household health care decisions in rural communes in Vietnam. Research Report, 27. Brighton, UK: Institute of Development Studies.

Toulmin, C. 1991. Bridging the gap between top-down and bottom-up in natural resource management. In *When the grass is gone*, edited by P. T. W. Baxter. Uppsala, Sweden: The Scandinavian Institute of African Studies.

Tran, T. 2001. The health system in rural Vietnam: Community-based evidence and comments. Paper presented at the NEU-ISS seminar series in Development Economics, 4 December, at The World Bank, Hanoi, Vietnam.

Tsikata, Y. M. 2001. Successful reformers: Ghana. In *Aid and reform in Africa: Lessons from ten case studies*, edited by S. Devarajan, D. Dollar, and T. Holmgren. Washington, DC: The World Bank.

Tullock, G. 1971. Public decisions as public goods. *Journal of Political Economy* 79 (4): 913-918.

Tyson, L. 1991. They are not us: Why American ownership still matters. *The American Prospect*, Winter, 37-49.

UNIFEM. 2000a. Gender-sensitive budget initiatives for Latin America and the Caribbean: A tool for improving accountability and achieving effective policy implementation. Paper read at the 8th Regional Conference on Women of Latin America and the Caribbean, 8-10 February, Lima, Peru.

————. 2000b. *Progress of the world's women 2000*. New York: United Nations.

United Kingdom. Actuary's Department. 2000. Projected population of Scotland (2000-based). Available at http://www.groscotland.gov.uk/grosweb/grosweb.nsf

————. Department for International Development (DFID). 2001. *Making government work for poor people: Building state capability*. London: United Kingdom Department for International Development.

————. Her Majesty's Treasury. 2001. Productivity in the UK: 3. The regional dimension. November. London: The Author.

United Nations. 1988. *Transnational corporations in world development: Trends and prospects*. New York: United Nations Center on Transnational Corporations.

————. 1992. *World investment report 1992: Transnational corporations as engines of growth*. New York: The Author.

————. 1998. *World investment report 1998: Trends and determinants*. New York: The Author.

————. 2001. *World investment report 2001*. New York: The Author.

United Nations Centre on Multinational Corporations. 1989. *Multinational corporations in world development*. New York: United Nations.

United Nations Conference on Trade and Development. 2002. *Economic development in Africa: From adjustment to poverty reduction—what is new?* New York: United Nations.

United Nations Development Programme. 1995. *Human development report, 1995*. Oxford: Oxford University Press.

United Nations Development Programme. 2000. *Gender-sensitive budgets* [cited January 2000]. Available from http://www.undp.org/poverty/resources/gender_budgets.htm

United Nations Research Institute for Social Development (UNRISD). 2000. *What choices do democracies have in globalizing economies?* Report of the UNRISD International Conference, 27-28 April, Geneva.

United Republic of Tanzania. 1998. *National poverty eradication strategy*. Dar Es Salaam: Government of Tanzania.

United States Embassy. 1991. *Foreign economic trends, April*. Cairo: United States Embassy in Egypt.

United States Department of Commerce, Bureau of Economic Analysis. 2002. *National accounts data*. From http://bea.doc.gov.

United States Agency for International Development (USAID). 1997. *The land tenure policy study*. Report No. 21. Agricultural Policy Reform Program, Reform Design and Implementation Unit. Cairo: The Author.

———. 1999. *Agriculture: Vision for 2003*. Agricultural Policy Reform Program, Reform Design and Implementation Unit. [policy brief]. Cairo: The Author.

———. 2000. *Agriculture sector*. Available from http://www.usaid.gov/eg/proj-agr.htm.

Uphoff, N. 1998. Community-based natural resource management: Connecting micro and macro processes, and people within their environments. International Workshop on Community-Based Natural Resource Management, Washington, DC [cited 6 May 2001]. Available from http://www.frameweb.org/pdf/CBNRM_micro_macro_processes.pdf.

Utting, P. 1993. *Trees, people and power: Social dimensions of deforestation and forest protection in Central America*. London, England: Earthscan Publications Ltd.

———. 2001. An overview of the potential and pitfalls of participatory conservation. In *Forest policy and politics in the Philippines: The dynamics of participatory conservation*, edited by P. Utting. Honolulu, Hawaii: University of Hawaii Press.

Van Arkadie, B. 1986. Some realities of adjustment: An introduction. *Development and Change* 17 (3): 371–386.

———. 1990. The role of institutions in development. *Proceedings of the First Annual World Conference on Development Economics*. Washington, DC: World Bank.

Van Arkadie, B., and M. Karlsson. 1992. *Economic survey of the Baltic States*. London: Francis Pinter.

Van Arkadie, B., and H. Mule. 1996. Some comments on recent developments in donor conditionality. In *Aid: Dialogue or domination*, edited by K. Haavnevik and B. Van Arkadie. Uppsala, Sweden: Nordic Institute of African Studies.

Van Wijinbergen, S. 1986. Exchange rate management and stabilization policies in developing countries. *Journal of Development Economics* 23 (2): 227–247.

Veit, P.G. 1996. Place-based environmental management: The role of local government [cited 9 October 2001]. Available from http://www.melissa.org/English/publications/Proceedings1996/role96.htm.

Veit, P.G., A. Mascarenhas, and O. Ampadu-Agyei. 1995. *Lessons from the ground up: African development that works*. Washington: World Resources Institute.

Vietnam. General Statistical Office. 1993. *Vietnam living standards survey 1993*. Hanoi: The Author.

———. 1998. *Vietnam living standards survey 1998*. Hanoi: The Author.

———. Ministry of Health. 1996. *Orientation for people's health care and protection 1996-2000*. Hanoi: The Author.

———. Ministry of Health. 1998. *Health statistics yearbook*. Hanoi: Health Statistics and Information Division, Ministry of Health.

Vilias, C. 1997. Inequality and the dismantling of citizenship in Latin America. *NACLA Report on the Americas* 31 (1): 57–63.

Wachtel. P. 2001. Growth and finance: What do we know and how do we know it? *International Finance* 4 (3): 335–362.

Wachtel, P., and P. Rousseau. 1995. Financial intermediation and economic growth: A historical comparison of the US, UK and Canada. In *Anglo-American financial systems: Institutions and markets in twentieth-century North America and United Kingdom*, edited by M.D. Bordo and R. Sylla. Homewood, Illinois: Irwin.

Wade, R. 1988. *Village republics: Economic conditions for collective action in south India*. Cambridge: Cambridge University Press.

———. 1996. Globalization and its limits: Reports of the death of the national economy are greatly exaggerated. In *National diversity and global capitalism*, edited by S. Berger and R. Dore. Ithaca, NY: Cornell University Press.

———. 2002. US hegemony and the World Bank: The fight over people and ideas. *Review of International Political Economy* 9 (2): 215-243.

———. 2004. Is globalization reducing poverty and inequality? *World Development* 32 (4): 567-589.

Wainwright, H. 2003. *Reclaim the state: Experiments in popular democracy*. London: Verso.

Wallerstein, I. 1980. *The modern world system*. Vol. 2. New York: Academic Press.

Warren, B. 1980. *Imperialism: Pioneer of capitalism*. London: New Left Books.

Waterbury, J. 1983. *The Egypt of Nasser and Sadat: The political economy of two regimes*. Princeton: Princeton University Press.

Watson, W., et al.. 1999. The brain drain / L'exode des cerveaux. *Policy Options* 20 (7): 3-43.

Webster, D. 2000. The political economy of Scotland's population decline. *Fraser of Allander Institute Quarterly Economic Commentary* 25 (2): 40-70.

Webster, N. 1995. Democracy, decentralized government, and NGOs in Indian rural development. *Journal Für Entwicklungspolitil, XI* (2): 187-212.

Weiss, L. 1997. Globalization and the myth of the powerless state. *New Left Review* 225: 3-27.

———. 1999. Managed openness: Beyond neoliberal globalism. *New Left Review* 238: 126-140.

Weisskopf, T. 1979. Marxian crisis theory and the rate of profit in the postwar US economy. *Cambridge Journal of Economics* 3: 341-378.

Wheelock, J. 1996. People and households as economic agents. In *Economics and changing economies*, edited by M. Mackintosh, V. Brown, N. Costello, G. Dawson, G. Thompson, and A. Trigg. London: International Thompson Business Press.

White, T.A., and C.F. Runge. 1995. The emergence and evolution of collective action: Lessons from watershed management in Haiti. *World Development* 23 (10): 1683-1698.

Willoughby, J. 1993. Toward a neo-institutionalist theory of imperialism. *Review of Radical Political Economy* 25 (3): 60-67.

Witter, S. 1996. *Doi moi* and health: The effect of economic reforms on the health system in Vietnam. *International Journal of Health Planning and Management* 11: 159-172.

Wolfenson, J. 1999. *A proposal for a comprehensive development framework: A discussion draft*. Washington, DC: Office of the President of the World Bank.

Wolff, E.N. 2003. What's behind the rise in profitability in the US in the 1980s and 1990s? *Cambridge Journal of Economics* 27 (4): 479-499.

World Bank. 1981. *Accelerated development in sub-Saharan Africa: An agenda for action*. Washington, DC: The Author.

———. 1985a. *Ghana: Towards structural adjustment*. Vol. 2. Washington, DC: The Author.

———. 1985b. *World development report*. New York: Oxford University Press.

———. 1987a. *Financing health services in developing countries: An agenda for reform*. Washington, DC: The Author.

———. 1987b. *Ghana: Policies and issues of structural adjustment*. Washington, DC: The Author.

———. 1988. *World debt tables*. Washington, DC: The Author.

———. 1989. *World debt tables*. Washington, DC: The Author.

———. 1991. *World development report*. New York: Oxford University Press.

———. 1992a. *African development indicators*. Washington, DC: The Author.

———. 1992b. *Arab Republic of Egypt: An agricultural strategy for the 1990s.* Report No. 11083-EAT, 11 December. Agricultural Operations Division, Country Department, II, Middle East and North African Region. Washington, DC: The Author.

———. 1992c. *Governance and development.* Washington, DC: The Author.

———. 1992d. *Vietnam: Population, health and nutrition—sector review.* World Bank Report No. 10289-VN. Washington, DC: The Author.

———. 1993. *The east Asian miracle: Economic growth and public policy.* Oxford: Oxford University Press.

———. 1994a. *Adjustment in Africa: Reforms, results, and the road ahead.* New York: Oxford University Press.

———. 1994b. *Governance: The World Bank's experience.* Washington, DC: The Author.

———. 1995a. *Strengthening the effectiveness of aid: Lessons for donors.* Washington, DC: The Author.

———. 1995b. *Towards gender equality: The role of public policy.* Washington, DC: The Author.

———. 1996a. *African development indicators.* Washington, DC: The Author.

———. 1996b. *Partnership for capacity building in Africa.* Washington, DC: The Author.

———. 1996c. *World development report 1996: From plan to market.* Oxford: Oxford University Press.

———. 1997. *World development report 1997: The state in a changing world.* Oxford: Oxford University Press.

———. 1999a. *Global development finance.* Washington, DC: The Author.

———. 1999b. *Vietnam: Attacking poverty.* Joint Report of the Government-Donor-NGO Working Group. Hanoi: The Author.

———. 1999c. *World development report 1999/2000: Entering the 21st century.* Oxford: Oxford University Press.

———. 2000a. *African development indicators.* Washington: The Author.

———. 2000b. *Can Africa claim the twenty-first century?* Washington, DC: The Author.

———. 2000c. *Comprehensive development framework: Mid-term progress report* [executive summary]. Washington, DC: The Author.

———. 2000d. Memorandum of the President of the International Development Association and the International Finance Corporation to the Executive Directors on a Country Assistance Strategy of the World Bank Group for the Republic of Mozambique, Executive Summary, Report 20521 MOZ, Document of the World Bank, 1–79 [cited 12 June 2000]. Available from http://www-wds.worldbank.org/servlet/WDS_Ibank_Servlet?pcont=detailsandeid=000094946_00072005323687.

———. 2001a. *Engendering development: Through gender equality in rights, resources and voice.* Oxford: Oxford University Press.

———. 2001b. *Ghana: International competitiveness, opportunities and challenges facing non-traditional exports.* Report No. 22421-GH. Washington, DC: The Author.

———. 2001c. *Vietnam economic monitor, Spring 2001* [cited 7 June 2001]. Available from http://www.worldbank.org.vn/rep30.

———. 2001d. *World development report, 2002.* Washington, DC: The Author and Oxford University Press.

———. 2002a. *African development indicators.* Washington, DC: The Author.

———. 2002b. *Assessing central government policy making institutions in cabinet government* [cited 17 June]. Available from http://wbin0018.worldbank.org/prem/ps/iaamarketplace.nsf/075c69a32615405f8525689c0051fb88/a37fable36f89376852568a10083aa2c?OpenDocument.

———. 2002c. Autonomy and revenue boards [cited October 2002]. Available from http://www1.worldbank.org/publicsector/tax/autonomy.html.

———. 2002d. *World development indicators 2002*. Washington, DC: The Author.

———. 2003. *World development indicators 2003*. Washington, DC: The Author.

World Bank et al. (SIDA, AusAID, Royal Netherlands Embassy, and Ministry of Health of Vietnam). 2001. *Growing healthy: A review of Vietnam's health sector*. Hanoi: World Bank.

Worsthorne, P. 1971. *The socialist myth*. London: Cassell.

Yiheyis, Z. 1997a. Export adjustment to currency depreciation in the presence of parallel markets for foreign exchange: The experience of selected sub-Saharan African countries in the 1980s. *Journal of Development Studies* 34 (1): 111-130.

———. 1997b. Output and price adjustment to devaluation in sub-Saharan Africa. *Canadian Journal of Development Studies* 18 (1): 93-117.

———. 2000. Fiscal adjustment to currency devaluation in selected African countries: An empirical analysis. *African Development Review* 12 (1): 1-23.

Yoder, R. 1989. Are people willing and able to pay for health services? *Social Science and Medicine* 29 (1): 35-42.

Young, H. 1993. *One of us*. London: Pan Books.

Younger, S.D. 1992. Testing the link between devaluation and inflation: Time series evidence from Ghana. *Journal of African Economies* 1 (3): 369-394.

Yu, H., S. Cao, and H. Lucas. 1997. Equity in the utilization of medical services: A survey in poor rural China. *IDS Bulletin* 28 (1): 16-23.

Zanfei, A. 2000. Transnational firms and the changing organisation of innovative activities. *Cambridge Journal of Economics* 24 (5): 515-542.

Zeleza, P. 1993. *A modern economic history of Africa: The nineteenth century*. Oxford: Codesria.

Zhao, J., D. Drew, and T.S. Murray. 2000. Brain drain and brain gain: The migration of knowledge workers to and from Canada. *Education Quarterly Review* 6 (3): 8-35.

Zwarteveen, M. 2001. Thinking about user based irrigation organisations from a feminist perspective: Access, participatory parity and democracy. Paper read at the Institute of Social Studies Rural Development Seminar, 29 January, The Hague.

INDEX

Germany, 115; in India, 113; industrialization and, 116; in Nepal, 113; in Scotland, 116; in US, 115

Bank of Canada, 52, 58, 59, 336, 337, 346

Bank of England, 292

Bank of Ghana, 146

bankruptcies, 23, 55

banks, 108, 109-10; borrowers' interest rates, 110; central, 324, 325-6; choice of customers, 109; and corruption, 110; defaulted loans, 110, 111; in ex-colonial countries, 109-10. *See also* financial institutions

Barber, Clarence, 299

Bauer, P.T., 69

Beck, T., 113-14

Bencivenga, V.R., 117

Benin, 166

Berry, S., 270

Bhaskar, R., 289

biotechnology, 38

Blair, Tony, 321

Bleaney, M., 89, 95, 102

Bossasso (Somalia), 391

Botswana: debt service rate in, 165; education expenditure in, 166

Brazil, 354. *See also* Porto Alegre (Brazil)

Bretton Woods institutions, 31, 207, 241, 247, 260, 332, 333

Britain. *See* England; Scotland; United Kingdom

budget analysis, 372; in Africa, 376; in Kenya, 387-8; in South Africa, 380

budget deficits, 345, 405-6; in Canada, 338, 344-5, 347, 360; in Egypt, 152; in EU, 405; in Ghana, 132; in Japan, 405; and public programmes, 339, 348; tax increases and, 339, 348; in UK, 405; in US, 405

budgets: balanced, 325, 340, 344-5; in Canada, 340, 344, 353; choices in, 324, 342; and civil society organizations, 324; consultations on, 412; democratic, 373, 393; education expenditure as share of, 169-71; external aid in, 170; and gender relations, 318; gender (*see* gender budgets); interest groups and, 324; NGO audit of, 326; participatory, 354-5; as political documents, 342; PRSPs and, 331; surpluses, 340, 344, 353, 405

budget scrutiny, 169, 372; in Africa, 373-4, 376; in Kenya, 387-8; in South Africa, 380

Bush, George W., 398

business cycles, 19-20, 47, 48, 50-1, 54, 307, 397

Business Monitor International, 149

business sector: in Canada, 347-8; defined, 44-5; and GDP, 45; productive workers in, 45; and surplus value, 45, 58; in US, 20. *See also* corporations; private sector

Cameron, R., 116

Canada: AFB in (*see* Alternative Federal Budget(s)); anti-inflation policy, 22, 52; balanced budgets, 340, 344-5; brain drain from, 43; budget deficits, 338, 344-5, 360; budget surpluses, 340, 344, 353; business cycles, 50-1, 52; business sector, 347-8; capital accumulation, 44, 54-5, 58, 59-60; cutbacks in programme spending, 339, 342, 353; debt service costs, 338; dollar exchange rate, 43, 337; economic growth, 337, 339-40; economic performance, 43, 337; employment, 52-3, 56; exchange rate, 43, 60n1; 1995 federal budget, 339; financial industry, 348; financial restructuring, 338; fiscal balances, 339-40; fiscal federalism, 59; fiscal policy, 59; fiscal position, 337-8; fiscal problems, 343; fiscal retrenchment, 336; GDP growth rates, 43, 337; government expenditures, 73; high-income households in, 348; income security programmes, 338; indirect business taxes in, 53-4, 57-8, 67 fig.; infrastructure in, 347, 351; interest rates, 57-8, 337, 338, 339-40, 346, 351; job creation, 345, 346; labour in, 53, 57, 347; monetary policy, 52, 58, 59, 345-6; neo-conservatism in, 58; poverty rate, 345; productivity in, 43, 50, 64 fig.; profit rate in, 49, 51-2, 58; public debt in, 54, 340; radical pragmatism in, 371; rate of profit in, 46-8; recessions in, 52, 54, 55, 58, 337; revenue flows in, 339; social consequences of cutbacks, 339, 340; social problems, 343; social programmes, 52, 59; taxes in, 339, 347-9; tax revenues, 59, 337-38; technological change in, 55; trade, 55, 58; transformation of labour in, 55-6; unemployment in, 43, 338, 339,

345, 346; value of output in, 49-50, 64 fig.; wage–productivity gap, 51, 55, 66 fig.; wage-productivity ratio, 50, 61 table; welfare state in, 59

Canada Health and Social Transfer (CHST), 339, 349

Canada–US Free Trade Agreement, 55, 336

Canadian Centre for Policy Alternatives (CCPA), 341-2, 394

Canadian International Development Agency (CIDA), 248-9, 316

Canadian Labour Congress (CLC), 341, 342

Canetti, E., 97, 102-3

capital: circulating vs. fixed, 116-17; control of global economy, 408; controls, 31, 33; destruction of, 23; diminishing marginal productivity of, 52; flight, 21, 22, 375; footloose, 36, 296, 297; for infrastructure, 117; internationalization of, 32; liberalization of, 31; mobility, 27-8; neo-conservatism and, 410-11; organic composition of, 49, 51, 53, 54-5, 57, 58, 59, 66 fig.; short-term movement of, 34; social authority of, 401, 413; strikes, 21-2, 22; transfer of resources from labour, 406; transfers to labour, 407; value of stock, 47

capital accumulation, 111; and cross-border financial flows, 33; in developing countries, 69; and financial systems, 109; Keynesianism and, 70; by poor, 243; SAPs and, 70; state and, 72

capital flows, 28; and economic convergence, 296, 298

capital investment: in goods, 52; in manufacturing, 117; and reinvestment of profits, 117. See also investment

capitalism, 44, 70; African countries and, 72, 79, 81, 82-3; casino, 34; and colonialism, 72; dependence on social institutions, 402; economic crisis phase, 19; economic slowdown, 3, 20; and falling profit rates, 48; global, 369, 409; golden age of, 397; individual styles of, 331; and profits, 20; property relations, 404; and state intervention, 404

capitalist class, 400-1

capitalist social democracy, 397-8, 401-3, 404,

409

Caribbean: financial sector share in GDP, 119

Cashel-Cordo, P., 166

Catagay, N., 331

causality, 107, 113, 114, 115, 290

Cavallo, D.F., 95

CDFs. *See* Comprehensive Development Frameworks

Chad, 166

charter of economic and human rights, 39-40

Chenery, H.B., 123n3

Chhibber, A., 104

China: financial development and economic growth in, 114; health care utilization and fee-for-service systems in, 185; hospitalization costs in, 193; one-party rule in, 217; poverty reduction in, 221

CHO!CES, 341-2, 394

Chrétien, Jean, 321

citizens' expectations, 21

civil service. *See* public service

civil society, 215, 219, 316; apoliticization of, 377; and budgetary impact on gender relations, 318; NGOs and, 215-16; organizations of, 318

civil society organizations (CSOs): AB approaches and, 394; budget process and, 324; budget scrutiny by, 372; and economic policy-making, 326; in Kenya, 382, 383, 384, 385-6, 387, 388, 392-3; in Nigeria, 382; in Somalia, 392; in South Africa, 379, 380-1; in Sudan, 390

clientelist politics, 378; in Kenya, 386, 388

climate change, 350

Clinton, Bill, 321

Cole, W.A., 117

Collier, Paul, 263

colonialism: African countries as neo-colonial, 71; and banking, 107, 108, 109-10; and capitalism, 72; developing countries' emergence from, 70; early post-colonial years, 204; and governance, 365

commons, 268

Commonwealth Secretariat, 316

community development approach, 217

Comprehensive Development Frameworks (CDFs), 204, 227, 240, 244-5

Congo (Democratic Republic): as collapsed state, 374; debt service rate in, 165

Consensus Economics Inc., 43

consultations: conflict and, 220; by donors, 215-17; with NGOs, 215-16; with stakeholders, 220

corporations: governance of, 202, 203; low-profit, 22; tax cuts for, 22; WTO rules and, 35. *See also* business sector; multinational corporations (MNCs)

corruption, 110, 255; in Africa, 375, 378; bureaucratic, 207; in Eritrea, 388; in Kenya, 383, 386, 387; and patronage, 375; in revenue allocation, 375, 378; in South Africa, 378

cost reduction, 37; extensive/intensive methods, 21

Cottani, J.A., 89, 95

Craig, S.G., 166

credit, 107, 109, 111; informal sources of, 121; rationing, 110, 111; restrictions on, 22. *See also* lending

critical realism, 288, 289-91, 301

crony capitalism, 210

Crow, John, 336, 337

CSOs. *See* civil society organizations

Dahl, R., 254, 255, 316-17

Dao, M., 170

Deane, P., 117

debt: of African countries, 78; circumventing of, 176; crisis, 70, 74, 76; and development, 262; and economic growth, 166; and education expenditures, 6, 166; and exports, 262; government, 22; and government expenditures, 166; illiteracy and, 262; and institutional weaknesses, 262; net, and external debt, 171; and poverty reduction, 240

debt relief: criteria for access to, 264; and Enhanced HIPC Initiative, 258-63; and institutional reforms, 258-63, 264; manoeuvrability in, 262-3; NGOs and, 327; and poverty reduction, 327; and restrictions on governments, 260; and sovereignty, 258, 260, 263

debt servicing, 4, 167-8, 169-70, 408; and ability to pay vs. prevailing debt levels, 171;

arrears of, 165; and education expenditures, 175-6; and exports, 165; and government expenditure, 171-5; and liquidity constraints, 165, 171, 176; and net debt, 171; predicted, 171, 175; and structural adjustment programmes, 165; in sub-Saharan Africa, 165

decentralization: and administrative devolution, 276; boundary setting in, 281; and decision-making, 274, 284; democratic, 283; and empowerment, 278; and fiscal savings, 275; and higher vs. lower level bodies, 274; in India, 276-80, 281; and local communities, 275; NRM and, 267, 268, 270, 271, 272, 283-5; and policy conflicts, 273-4; policy inconsistencies in, 273, 283; and poverty alleviation, 218; and privatization, 275, 283; sectoral approaches, 281; of services delivery, 244; and state, 274-5, 284-5; and subsidiarity, 274-5; in west Africa, 274-5

decision-making: civil liberties and, 316; decentralization and, 274, 284; devolution in India, 276; gender in, 313-14, 316, 317; local, 219; stakeholders in, 220; women in, 317

decolonization, 70, 71, 82

Deidda, L., 114, 119

demands, and stability, 256

Demetriades, P.O., 112-13, 113-14, 115

democracy/-ies, 323; accountability and, 377; in Africa, 376; characteristics of, 316-17; classical, 255; and decentralization, 283; and development, 376, 377; in economic policy, 2, 12, 412; engendering of, 319; gender and, 317; gender budgets and, 316-20; and global markets, 323; local leadership and, 331; and market, 377; parliamentary, 376-7; participatory, 350, 354, 401, 412, 413; as political, vs. economic and social, 256; and polyarchy, 256; representative, 376-7; social, 412; technocratic approach to, 263; third-wave, 253

democratization, 323; in Africa, 375-6; and authoritarian government, 218; authoritarian government and, 218; of economic policy-making, 322-3; embedding of, 376; of global governance, 332-3; and globalization, 249-50; in Kenya, 382, 388; in Nigeria, 382; PRSPs and, 330; technocracy and, 249-50, 251 demos, political authority from, 254-5

Denmark: Danish International Development Agency, 231; and Tanzania, 224

depreciation, 87, 88, 92, 93, 94, 96, 100, 104, 146

deregulation, 78-9; neo-conservatism and, 400; in Vietnam, 177

devaluation(s), 4, 85, 207; and aggregate economic activity, 87; and aggregate output, 86, 87-96; and balance of payments, 87; before-after approach and, 87, 88, 92, 100; contractionary, 85, 86, 87, 104, 105; control-group approach, 92-3, 100; and domestic economic activity, 85, 86, 87; econometric methods, 93; estimating approaches, 87; and exchange rates, 96-103; as expansionary, 86, 104; and external competitiveness, 85; and external sector, 85; in Ghana, 135; and inflation, 85, 86-7, 96-103, 104, 105; and output, 103-4, 105; and real depreciation, 87; and SAPs, 86; and stabilization programmes, 86; as stagflationary, 86, 87-103; and stagnation, 105; in sub-Saharan Africa, 86, 87

developing countries: aid to, 166; banks in, 109; capital accumulation in, 69; economic collapse in, 410; economic growth in, 321; economic policies, and IMF and World Bank, 77; emergence from colonial rule, 70; external inflows into, 166; fiscal policy in, 325; global economy and, 408; governance in, 202, 411; government budget scrutiny in, 169; government expenditures in, 74; government intervention in monetary and financial systems, 109; government revenues and spending in, 165; individual styles of capitalism, 331; institutions in, 210; interest rates in, 111; investment projects in, 69; legal origins of, 114; loans to, 166; macroeonomic mismanagement in, 69; market economy in, 321-2; MNC investment in, 30-1; national development plans, 70; national sovereignty for, 216; neo-conservatism in, 77; non-capitalist path of development, 75; poverty in, 321-2; private sector in, 408; public sectors in, 69; SAPs in, 76-7, 85; share of FDI in gross fixed capital formation, 81; stabilization programmes, 85; state in, 407; state role in,

74; Western alliances with, 72; and world economy, 26

development: democracy and, 376, 377; economists, 321; and indebtedness, 262; people-centred, 378; postmodernism in, 287-8; rural, 377; theory, 69. *See also* economic development

Diamond, Larry, 262-3

donors. *See* aid donors

Dordunoo, C.K., 89, 95

Dymski, G., 32

East African countries: banking sector in, 119-20; lending in, 119, 120-1; local vs. expatriate enterprises in, 120; mobile banking units, 119; savings and credit societies, 121

East Asian countries: economic success in, 322; economies of, 208; education in, 221; and international economy, 26; poverty reduction in, 221; range of economic governance mechanisms in, 221

economic convergence, 296

economic crises, 19-20, 115, 321; in Asian countries, 34, 122, 178, 325; of debt, 70, 74, 76; in Ghana, 127, 132-4; in Mexico, 34, 305, 337; oil, 26, 114, 133, 151, 153, 205, 207

economic development: basic needs, 204, 205; governance and, 202, 204-5, 208, 218; investment in, 69; Keynesianism and, 72; long-term, and banks, 109; long-term, and state, 110; new approaches to, 322; particularity vs. generality in, 291; partnerships in, 204; poverty-focussed, 205; state in, 72-3. *See also* development

economic distortions, 206

economic growth, 69; and authoritarian government, 218; authoritarian government and, 218; in Canada, 337, 339-40; in developing countries, 321; education and, 176, 296; and external debt, 166; financial deepening and, 113; financial development and (*see* financial development and economic growth); financial institutions and, 108; and financial intermediaries, 112, 113-14; financial markets and, 108-9, 121, 122; financial policies for, 122; financial sector and, 108-9, 118; functionalism and, 258;

governance and, 242; and government intervention, 109; and government regulation, 109; and human capital investment, 166; IMF role in, 247, 248; incentives and, 69; inflation and, 22; interest rates and, 59; and investment, 108; markets and, 69; and population growth, 298; and poverty alleviation, 220-1, 247; role of private sector in, 69; systemic imbalances and, 397-8; technological innovation and, 116; unequal patterns of, 221; in US, 337; World Bank role in, 247-8

economic interdependence, 23, 24

economic laws, 289-90

economic performance: governance and, 202, 203; over-optimism of targets, 230; postwar, 397; in Tanzania, 224

economic planning, 323

economic policy: accountability in, 323; alternative, 325; autonomy of experts in, 323; critical realism and, 289-91; democracy in, 2, 12, 412; democratization and, 322-3; detachment of, 324; gender and, 314-15, 319; and global markets, 324-5; governance and, 202, 203, 205-12; impact on women, 318; and multilateral organizations, 324; NGOs and, 326-7; ownership of, 327, 328, 330, 332; political commitment and, 210; and private sector, 325; role for theory in, 288; technocratic approaches to, 250; and transparency, 323

economic reform: commitment to, 210-11; and governance, 205, 206; market-based, 205; NRM and, 267; and social equity, 7

economic theory: modernism in, 301; postmodernism in, 287

The Economist, 36

economy/-ies: borderless, 23; centrally planned, 177, 205, 244; closed, 289-90; new, 48, 54; productive vs. unproductive sectors of, 45; remote, 296, 297. *See also* global economy

ecosystems, 279, 281

education, 21; of children, 309; in east Asia, 221; and economic growth, 176, 296; in England, 116; and poverty reduction, 243; privatization of, 36; in Scotland, 116; state vs. private sector investment in, 38; of women, 309; and workforce quality, 207; and WTO agreement, 35. *See also* training

education expenditure, 167-8, 169; debt service payments and, 175-6; and external debt, 6, 166; and per capita GNP, 170; share of government budget, 169-71; in sub-Saharan Africa, 166

efficiency: in banking sector, 110; and cross-border financial flows, 33; gender inequalities and, 308

Egypt: after World Trade Center attack, 150-1; Agrarian Reform Law, 157; agricultural data, 155; agricultural liberalization, 149; agricultural modernization, 156-7, 160, 162; agricultural production, 154-5, 161; agricultural reform, 6, 154-6, 161; agriculture, 149; banking sector, 150, 152; black market, 153; bread prices/subsidies, 151, 155; and Britain, 78; budget deficits, 152; children in, 160; class interests in, 153; commodity exports in, 154; crops in, 154, 156, 157; devaluations, 153; diversification in, 156; dollarization of, 153; economic accounting in, 155; economic growth, 149, 162, 163; economic history, 78; Economic Reform and Structural Adjustment Program (ERSAP), 151-2, 154, 159; economic reform in, 149, 159; employment in, 153, 154, 156; energy costs in, 151; exchange rate, 150, 152; exchange vs. production in, 153-4; exports, 155, 156; farm incomes, 154, 156; as food-deficit, 153, 155; food subsidies, 154; free market in, 151, 152, 161; GDP, 154; government deficit, 152; idle capacity, 153; and IFIs, 150, 152, 153, 159, 160, 162, 163; and IMF, 150, 151, 152; imports, 155; incomes in, 156; inequalities in, 162; *infitah* in, 151; inflation in, 152; interest rates, 151; Islamist Labor Party, 150; Land Center for Human Rights (LCHR), 158; landowners in, 157-8, 159, 160-1, 162, 163; land tenure reform, 157-60, 161, 162-3; Law 96, 157-60, 162; living standards, 160; macroeconomic indicators, 162; military, 153; Ministry of Agriculture, 158, 162; Muslim Brotherhood, 150; National Democratic Party, 150, 157; and oil, 153; opposition to Law 96, 158; poor in, 149; population increases in, 154; pound, 153; poverty in, 149,

156, 163; price and marketing controls, 154; and privatization, 152; privatization, 149-50, 152; reconciliation committees in, 159; rich in, 149; rural violence in, 160; SDR (special drawing right) in, 151; Shura Council, 156; social costs of reforms, 152-3; Social Fund for Development (SFD), 153; social unrest, 150; socio-economic differentiation in, 161; stabilization of economy, 152-3; state and agriculture, 161, 162; state in, 151; state ownership in, 154; state-sponsored projects vs. free market reform, 151; street protests, 151; structural adjustment in, 149; structural reforms, 153; subsidies in, 152, 155-6; and Suez Canal, 153; tax revenue, 152; tenant farmers in, 149, 157-8, 159, 160, 161, 162; tourism, 150; trade, 155; urban growth, 156; and US, 152, 153; USAID in, 154-5, 159, 161; wheat production, 155; women in, 160; and World Bank, 150, 151; youth unemployment, 150

Elbadawi, I., 90, 93, 97, 100, 101

elections, 217; participation in in local vs. national, 219; and polyarchy, 256

electorate, right of, 246

employment: in Africa, 374; in African countries, 374; in Canada, 52-3, 56; in Egypt, 153, 154, 156; interest rates and, 59; in Scotland, 292. *See also* unemployment

England: banking in, 116; education in, 116; and Egypt, 78; industrial revolution in, 116-17. *See also* United Kingdom

Enhanced HIPC initiatives, 241, 258, 264; in Ethiopia, 261; and institutional reform, 262; in Mali, 261; in Mozambique, 259; and poverty reduction, 261; in Rwanda, 259-60; in Uganda, 261

Ensor, T., 194

entrepreneurship, 69

environment: in Kenya, 384; legislation, and WTO agreement, 36; protection, and NRM, 275, 279; state role in, 38; sustainability of, 350

equality: of opportunities, 257; and polyarchy, 256-7; rural, 221; in Tanzania, 381

equity: and economic reform, 7; gender, 309; and good governance, 220-2

Eritrea: AB process in, 388-9, 393; as authoritarian state, 374, 393; conflict in, 388; corruption in, 388; debt service rate in, 165; diaspora remittances to, 389; exiles from, 389, 393; government financial affairs in, 388; IMF on, 389; opposition, 389; organizational structure, 388; repression in, 388; war with Ethiopia, 388

Ethiopia: constitution, 390-1; education expenditure in, 166; Enhanced HIPC in, 261; federal system in, 390-1; resource allocation in, 390-1; war with Eritrea, 388

Europe: agricultural subsidies in, 162; banking and industrialization in, 116; collapse of centrally planned economies, 177; decline of economic left in, 78; eastern, 177, 180; economic growth, 21; unemployment in, 19

European Union (EU): budget deficit in, 405; FDI in, 30; Growth and Stability Pact, 306, 325; trade flows in, 26

exchange markets, turnover on, 31-2

exchange rate(s): adjustment, 85, 86; devaluation and, 96-103; and inflation, 101-2; volatility in, 34

exploitation rates, 44, 46, 51, 52, 53, 55, 56, 57-8, 59, 66 fig., 401

exports: debt service payments and, 165; Egyptian, 154, 155, 156; and FDI, 28; Ghanaian, 132, 133, 134, 140; and indebtedness, 262; Rwandan, 259; as share of GNP, 26; Vietnamese, 178

external aid. *See* aid

external debt. *See* debt

Faini, R., 90, 93, 97, 102

farmers: credit for, 121; in Egypt, 149, 157-8, 159, 160, 161, 162

Fattouh, B., 114, 119

fee-for-service systems. *See* user charges

Fergany, N., 156

Fielding, D., 102, 169

finance ministries: IMF in, 123n4; technocratic approaches to, 306-7; World Bank in, 123n4

financial crises. *See* economic crises

financial deepening, 110-11, 112, 113

financial development and economic growth, 5; bidirectional relationship, 107, 112-13, 114;

case-study work in, 123; causal relationship, 113, 114; correlation between, 113; and deregulation, 114; directions of causation, 107, 113, 114, 115; and financial repression, 114, 115; in history, 115-19; in industrial revolution, 118; intercountry variation in, 115-16; and investment credit, 120; and liberalization of markets, 122; in low- vs. high-income countries, 114; periodicity in, 114; relationship between, 108, 112; and repressionist policies, 113; time-series techniques, 115

financial flows, 31-4, 39

financial institutions: and economic growth, 108; informal vs. formal, 120-1; regulation of, 122. *See also* banks

financial markets: deregulation of, 33; and economic growth, 108-9, 121, 122; globalization of, 32; government regulation of, 109; and industrialization, 117-18; liberalization, 5, 33, 107, 111; regulation, 122

financial repression, 5, 109-10, 112, 113, 114, 115

financial sector: development of, 248; and economic growth, 108-9, 118; global expansion, 122; share in GDP, 118-19

financial systems: cross-country variations in, 114; functions of, 111; international, 23

firms. *See* corporations

fiscal policy, 243; of AFB, 336; in Canada, 59; in developing countries, 325; experts in, 322-3; gendered impact of, 309-10; in Ghana, 138-9; humane, 336; managed by independent financial agencies, 306; progressive, 336; public objectives through, 325

foreign direct investment (FDI), 22-3; in developing countries, 80-1; and exports, 28; and fixed capital formation, 30; flows into US, 29; geographic distribution of, 30-1; and globalization, 28; neo-conservatism and, 400; in sub-Saharan Africa, 80-1; in tertiary sector services, 30; and trade, 28; within trading blocks, 30, 39. *See also* investment

France: foreign asset investment in, 33; government expenditures in, 73

free markets. *See* markets

Fry, M.J., 112

functionalism, 251, 258, 269

Gambia, 165

Gamble, Andrew, 404

G7 countries: deficits in, 338; growth in real GDP, 43

gender: and allocation of resources, 313; audit, 314-15; blindness, 307-9; in decision-making, 313-14, 316, 317; and democracy, 317; division of labour, 308-9, 313; and economic policy, 319; and fiscal envelope, 315; in macroeconomic policy, 307-9; in macromodels, 315; and policy, 314-15, 317; and poverty, 317; and productivity, 309; public services and, 312-13; subsidies and, 311; and taxation, 312

gender budgets, 11-12, 310, 315-16, 319-20, 350, 372, 394; and democracy, 316-20; and public spending, 311-12; in South Africa, 380, 381; in Tanzania, 381

gender inequalities: economic impacts, 308; in households, 308; markets and, 308; and microeconomic policy, 310; in political economy, 316; redistribution and, 308

gender relations, 310; budgets and, 318; in NRM, 270; and political parties, 318; and public services delivery, 311; and public spending, 311, 317-18; and transfer payments, 311

General Agreement on Tariffs and Trade (GATT), 23, 34, 35

Germany: banking sector in, 115; economic growth, 20-1; foreign asset investment in, 33; government expenditures in, 73; stock market in, 115

Ghai, Yash, 386

Ghana: agriculture in, 132-3, 140, 144, 146, 147; Ashanti Goldfields Company, 140, 145; balance among sectors, 144; banking system, 140; Bank of Ghana, 138; borrowing costs in, 147; budget deficit, 132; capacity building, 140-1; capital formation in, 133; civil service refor, 140-1; Cocoa Board, 140; cocoa in, 127, 132, 133-4, 135, 138, 140; construction industry, 145; Consultative Assembly, 141; corporate taxes, 139, 140; debt servicing, 135, 165; devaluation, 105n2,

135; diversification in, 132, 133; dividends remitted overseas, 140; domestic borrowing, 139; donor dependency, 147; Dutch auction system in, 135; earnings in, 132; economic crisis, 127, 132-4; economic growth, 127, 132, 141, 144-5, 146; economic indicators, 128-31, 142-3; Economic Recovery Program (ERP), 134-46, 148; economy, 127-32; education expenditure in, 166; electric power generation, 145; exchange rate, 133, 135, 147; exports, 132, 133, 134, 140; financial reform, 127, 134; fiscal policy, 138-9; food shortage, 133; foreign corporations in, 140, 146; foreign exchange in, 127, 134, 146, 147; foreign investment in, 139, 140; GDP per capita, 132, 144; gold in, 132, 145; government budgets, 132; government deficits, 133, 146; guaranteed minimum prices for maize and rice, 140; and IMF, 127, 134; imports, 132, 133, 135, 147; income per capita, 146; independence of, 127; industry in, 132, 144, 145, 147; inflation in, 132, 133, 145-6; infrastructure, 134, 139, 144; institutional reforms, 140-1; interbank market system, 135; interest rates, 145-6, 147; investment in, 135, 139, 140, 145-6, 147; *kalabule* in, 134; lending rates, 145-6; living standards, 134; long-term sustainability in, 147; manufacturing in, 133, 134, 140, 147; mining in, 145; monetary growth, 133; monetary policy, 138; National Commission for Democracy (NCD), 141; National Development Planning Commission (NDPC), 141; petty trading in, 134; population growth in, 133; poverty alleviation in, 135; prices in, 134, 139; private sector, 135, 145-6; Private Sector Advisory Group, 140; Produce Buying Company, 140; productive sector, 133, 147; Program of Action to Mitigate the Social Costs of Adjustment (PAMSCAD), 141; Provisional National Defence Council (PNDC), 127; public sector, 133, 145, 147; Public Service Investment Programme, 139; roads, 144; savings in, 135, 139, 145-6, 147; services sector, 132, 144, 147; small business in, 134; staple foods output, 132, 133; Statistical Service, 141; structural adjustment in, 5-6, 134, 146, 148, 305;

structural reforms, 140; structural weaknesses in economy, 132-3; tariff rates, 139, 140; tax reforms, 139; tourism in, 147; trade, 133, 134, 139, 140, 146, 147; transportation, 144; Tripartite Committee, 139; Value Added Tax (VAT), 139; Vision 2020, 141; wages and salaries in, 134, 139, 146; and World Bank, 127, 134

Ghura, D., 90, 95, 98, 100

Global Development Finance (World Bank), 171

global economy: capital control of, 408; control by IFIs, 409; democratization of, 332-3; and developing countries, 26, 408; growth of, 19; and international trade, 25-6; and NRM, 283; in transition economies, 408; women in, 316

globalism, new, 23

globalization, 2, 3, 24; Asianization vs., 27; and democratization, 249-50; Europeanization vs., 26; FDI and, 28; of financial markets, 32; of financial sector, 122; and imperialism, 76; in India, 276; and interest groups, 274; internationalized world vs, 24-5; as myth, 23-5; and neo-conservatism, 407-11; NRM and, 278-9; and poverty alleviation, 249; of production, 28-30; and rate of profit, 34; regionalization vs, 25-34; and Scotland, 294-6; strong/weak hypotheses of, 23-5

Glover, D., 77

gold standard, 25, 26, 33

Gorbachev, Mikhail, 76

governance: agenda, 7-8; of corporations, 202, 203; decentralized, 257; defined, 201-2; in developing economies, 411; and development, 202, 204-5; and economic development, 208, 218; and economic growth, 242; and economic performance, 202, 203; and economic policy, 202, 203, 205-12; and economic reform, 205, 206; effective, 257, 264; emphasis on, 213; engendering of, 319; and ethical behaviour, 202; good, 208, 217, 218, 264, 271; hierarchy in, 318; and importance of institutions, 209-10; and market economy, 209; political ends of, 203-4; poor, 203; and poverty, 242, 243, 245; and property rights, 243; repoliticization of, 257; and social responsibility, 202; weak, 243, 245; World Bank and, 365 government deficits, 22, 133, 146; in Egypt, 152; in Ghana, 133, 146

government expenditures: and gender budgets, 311-12; and gender division of labour, 313; and gender relations, 311, 317; and household survey data, 312; inequalities in, 310-11; and time use, 313; transparency about, 378

government(s): accountability to representative institutions, 214; consultations with civil society, 215; control of programs, 212; debt, 22, 33; decline in capacity, 206-7, 214; donor partnerships with, 229-31; donors and, 213-14; expenditures, 165, 166, 167-8, 405, 406; external assistance, and reform, 208; and external debt, 166; external loans and aid, 165; and financing of health expenditure, 191; intervention in monetary and financial systems, 109-10; ownership of policies, 212; performance overloading, 230; poor performance of, 203; as provider of health care services, 191; reform, 208; relationship with donors, 212; restraints on, 253; restrictions on debt relief, 260; revenues, 165, 167-8, 169; role of, 205-6; self-restraint, 253, 264; and trade agreements, 324; women's representation in, 316. *See also* state(s)

Graff, M., 114, 119

Grameen Bank, 121

Gramsci, A., 366, 403

Granger causality tests, 94, 97, 98, 102-3, 113, 114

Great Depression, 23

Greenaway, D., 89, 95

Greene, J., 97, 102-3

Greenspan, Alan, 325

Grennes, T., 90, 95, 98, 100

gross domestic product (GDP): business sector and, 45; central government expenditure and, 73-4; financial sector share in, 118-19; growth rates, 43, 62 fig.; non-business sector share of, 45-6

gross national product (GNP), 25; and education spending, 170; share of exports and imports in, 26

Gulf War, 152, 336

Hall, Stuart, 403

Hardin, G., 268

Harris, Mike, 403

Hayek, Fredrich, 401

health, 21; state role in, 38

health care: accessibility to, 194; affordability ratio, 191; costs, 191; equitable access to, 178; free health cards in, 194; government in, 191; insurance for, 192, 194; monitoring of, 178; overprovision of, 185, 195; privatization of, 36; rational utilization of services, 184-5; reform of, 194; regulatory framework for, 178; safety net, 178; user charges for, 178, 181; and WTO agreement, 35

health care providers: cost of accessing, 187; government as, 191; moral hazard of, 184, 192, 196; as perfect agents, 184-5

Heavily-Indebted Poor Countries (HIPC), 215, 240, 326-7

Helleiner, G.K., 332-3

Heller, P.S., 168-9

Hicks, J., 116

Hilferding, R., 123

Hirst, P., 25, 31

Hobley, M., 278-9

Hong Kong, one-party rule in, 217

horizontal accountability, 252-4, 255, 264

Horrell, S., 168-9

hospitals: admissions to, 187-9, 191-3, 192; financial burden of use, 191-4, 195-6; and insured vs. uninsured patients, 188-9; intensity of servicing in, 192-3, 195; length of stay in, 188, 189, 192, 193; patient revenues, 184, 192, 194-5; revenues, 183, 191-2; staff bonuses in, 183-4, 195; use by poor, 191; user charges, 191, 192; utilization rate, 192

households: gendered character of, 315; gender inequalities in, 308; hospital costs for, 190, 191-3; maintenance activities, 310, 313, 315; and public revenue data, 312; public spending data and, 312

Hudson, J., 168-9

human capital investment, 221; and economic growth, 166; state and, 208

human rights, 377; in Kenya, 384

Hussein, A., 112-13

illiteracy, and indebtedness, 262

455

Mohan, G., 273
Moi, Daniel Arap, 382, 386
monetarism, 204, 399
monetary policy, 243, 325-6; of AFB, 346;
  of Bank of Canada, 52; in Canada, 345-6;
  experts in, 322-3; and Keynesianism, 325; and
  profitability, 59
money: internationalization of, 32; restrictions
  on, 22; short-term movement of, 34
Morris, A.G., 114
Mosley, P., 88, 90, 92, 168-9
Mozambique, 259
Mubarak, Hosni, 150, 151, 152, 153, 159, 163
multilateralization, of poverty reduction
  strategies, 247-9, 264
multinational corporations (MNCs), 23, 24,
  294-5; and African countries, 72-3, 74-5, 82;
  demands for concessions, 39; home bases, 31;
  institutional support system, 31; investment
  in Asian economies, 30; investment in
  developing economies, 30-1; investment
  in OECD countries, 31; in manufacturing
  production, 28-30; parent operations of, 31;
  state support for, 31; in three trading blocks,
  30; as transnational, 31; and WTO agreement,
  36
multiparty electoral systems, 214, 217
Museveni, Yoweri, 368
Muthai, Wangari, 387
Mwinyi, Ali Hassan, 223

Nasser, Gamal Abdul, 153, 154, 157
nationalization, 369, 397
nation building, 204
natural resource management (NRM):
  and access to resources, 268, 269, 281,
  284-5; anthropological perspectives, 268;
  community-based, 271-2, 283; community
  groups in, 279, 280; conflicts in, 268;
  decentralization of, 267, 268, 270, 271, 272,
  283-5; deregulation of, 283; devolution to
  local user groups, 272-3; ecological, 268;
  and economic reform, 267; and ecosystems,
  279; and environmental protection, 275, 279;
  equitable, 267, 268, 275; gender relations in,
  270; global economic forces and, 283; and
  globalization, 278-9; grassroots participation

in, 267, 284; IFIs and, 283; in India, 276-80;
and institutional boundary conflicts, 279-
80; institutional restructuring for, 267, 270,
283; and international donor agencies, 274;
local communities and, 268, 282-3; local
government in, 280-1; local inequalities and,
271, 281, 284; market forces and, 278-9;
NGOs in, 271; participation in, 270, 272, 273,
279; power relations in, 270; privatization in,
270; and property rights, 268, 276, 282-3,
284; representation in, 281-3; and resource
development, 268; sectoral approaches, 272,
276, 277; state in, 271; sustainable, 9-10, 267,
268, 279, 280, 281; traditional communities
in, 271-2; and use of resources, 269; user
groups in, 279; women's exclusion from, 281-
2, 283
needs: basic, 204, 205, 257, 305; social, 401, 407
Nelson, P., 329, 330
neo-conservatism, 1-2, 204; and AFB, 351-
4, 359; alternatives to, 2, 412-13; in Canada,
58; and capital, 410-11; and capitalist
social democracy, 400; and common sense,
403, 411, 412; and deregulation, 400; and
devaluation, 85; in developing countries, 77;
in development theory, 69; and economic
convergence, 299; elites and, 399; and
"enemies within," 400, 407; and foreign
direct investment, 400; and free economy,
399-400; globalization and, 407-11; good
and evil in, 399, 400; governance agenda,
411-12; hegemony of, 403; hierarchies
in, 399, 400, 407, 413; and IMF, 408; and
individualism, 399; and inequalities, 400, 407;
limits of, 413; and market, 400; and media,
399; moral clarity in, 399; neo-liberalism
vs., 1-2, 404-7; origins of, 398-9; popular
support for, 403; and privatization, 400; and
representative democracy, 399; and research
and development, 37, 38; rise of, 2-3, 321;
and SAPs, 76; and skilled labour, 38; and
social divisions, 400; and social sector, 306;
and Soviet Union, 400; and states, 1-2, 401-2,
411; subordinates in, 399; success vs. failure of,
410-11; and UN, 410; in US, 36-7; and wages,
400; and World Bank, 408; and World Trade
Organization, 411

neo-liberalism, 399, 408; neo-conservatism vs., 1-2, 404-7
Nepal, 113
Netherlands Ministry of Development Cooperation, 316
Newlyn, W.T., 107, 108-9
New Partnership for African Development (NEPAD), 78, 83-4
New Right, 404
Nicaragua, 335
Nigeria: CSOs in, 382; debt service rate in, 165; democratization in, 374, 382; education expenditure in, 166
Nissanke, M., 121, 122
Njinkeu, D., 89, 95
Nkrumah, Kwame, 71
Non-Aligned Movement, 71, 76
non-business sector, 45-6
non-capitalist path of development, 72, 75
non-governmental organizations (NGOs): and AB approaches, 393; and civil society, 215-16; constituency of, 216; and debt relief, 327; donor consultations with, 215-16; and economic policy, 326-7; governance of aid, 216; in India, 276; international, 216; in NRM, 271
North, Douglass, 322
North America: decline of economic left in, 78; FDI in, 30; trade flows in, 26
North American Free Trade Agreement (NAFTA), 324
Northern Ireland Assembly, 293
North-South Institute: Debt Sustainability Analyses, 260-1
NRM. *See* natural resource management (NRM)
Nurske, R., 76
Nwana, G.I., 91, 93
Nyerere, Julius, 219, 223, 367-8

Obeid, Atef, 163
Ocampo, J.A., 325
Odedokun, M.O., 98, 102
O'Donnell, G., 254-6
Official Development Assistance (ODA), 170
oil: in Egypt, 151, 153; prices, 26, 114, 133, 205, 207; in Scotland, 297, 300; in Sudan, 390

one-party rule, 217
Ontario, public debt burden in, 338
Organization for Economic Cooperation and Development (OECD): capital flows, 28; Development Assistance Committee (DAC), 225; economic performance, 337; financial development and economic growth in, 114; financial sector share in GDP, 119; government expenditures in, 74; Millennium Development Goals, 327; MNC investment in, 31; trade flows among, 26, 27; unemployment in, 300
Organization of African Unity, 83
Ostrom, E., 269
output: devaluation and, 86, 87-96, 103-4, 105; profit share of, 49, 63 fig.; value of, 49-50, 64 fig.
owner-operators, 45
ownership: of economic policies, 327, 328, 330, 332; of programmes, 224-5, 226, 229, 231-2, 236, 327

Pakistan, 221
Paris Club, 78, 152
parliaments, 258
participation: and accountability, 319; in Kenya, 387, 388; in local vs. national elections, 219; in NRM, 270, 272, 273, 279; political, 244; and polyarchy, 255
participatory budgeting, 373
participatory democracy, 354, 401, 412, 413
Pearson, Lester, 204
Peru, 282
pharmaceutical industry, 178, 181, 194
Picot, G., 56
pluralistic society, 217
Polak, J.J., 105n1
policy: compromises regarding, 211-12; consensus for, 211; gender and, 314-15, 317; internal vs. external origins of, 212. *See also* economic policy; social policy
policy-making: people's say in, 377-8; policy implementation and, 251; and service delivery, 251
political parties, 254
political processes: donor intrusion into, 214; effectiveness of, 206; in good society,

217; model for institutional reforms, 252; public control over, 253-4; stability of, 263; technification and, 258; and technocracy, 249-51; World Bank concepts of, 257-8

polyarchy, 254-6

poor: capital accumulation by, 243; economic participation, 252; empowerment of, 243; exemptions from user fees for, 193-4; and interest groups, 215; pro-poor coalitions, 252; public services for, 243; quality of health care for, 187; use of hospitals, 191. *See also* poverty

Porto Alegre (Brazil), 373, 412

postmodernism, 287-8, 301

poverty: in Africa, 410; and aid, 239; analysis of, 247; in Canada, 345; and civil liberties, 317; in developing countries, 321-2; in Egypt, 149, 156, 163; gendered nature of, 317; and governance, 242, 243, 245; and health service contacts, 186, 187; illness and, 189, 193, 195; technification of, 251; in Vietnam, 178, 186, 187, 221. *See also* poor

poverty alleviation, 204, 205; and aid agencies, 205; decentralization and, 218; economic growth and, 220-1; in Ghana, 135; globalization and, 249; good governance and, 242; growth and, 247; and market economy, 220-1; and political decentralization, 218; in Tanzania, 205

poverty reduction: in China, 221; debt and, 240; and debt relief, 260-1, 327; in East Asia, 221; education and, 243; and Enhanced HIPC initiatives, 261; and external debt, 240; governance and, 243, 245; and HIPC initiatives, 241; and infrastructure, 243; institutional framework for, 239, 247; institutional reforms, 241, 242-5, 264; multilateralization of strategies, 247-9, 264; and policies, 239-40; resource flows for, 262; strategies, 408; in Tanzania, 234; technocratic approaches, 249-51; World Bank and, 239-41

Poverty Reduction Strategy Papers (PRSPs), 215, 227, 240-1, 247, 263, 323, 327-8; and AFB model, 331; and alternative macroeconomic policy, 331; capacity needed for, 329-30; challenges posed by, 328-9; content of, 329; and democratization, 330; and economic decision-making, 331; groups excluded from, 329; in Mozambique, 259; and national budgets, 331; ownership vs. donor impositions, 328, 330; and policy formulation, 327-8; process of, 329; reviews of, 328-30; in Rwanda, 259-60; in Senegal, 259-60; and structural adjustment, 329; in Tanzania, 233

Pratt, Cranford, 368

prices, 397; aggregate levels, 49; controlled, 111; lowering of, 22; oil, 26, 114, 133, 205, 207

private property. *See* property rights

private sector: in developing countries, 408; economic policy and, 325; investment in education, 38; investment in training, 38; and property rights, 242; savings, 135; short-run time frame of, 37-8; in transition economies, 408; in Vietnam, 177; women in, 316; and WTO agreement, 35. *See also* business sector; corporations

privatization, 78-9; decentralization and, 275, 283; of education sector, 36; of health sector, 36; and institutional reform, 267; of medical practices, 178; neo-conservatism and, 400; in NRM, 270; of public sector, 22; of social needs, 407

production: capital intensity of, 49; costs of, 3, 19, 397; disproportionalities in, 397; globalization of, 28-30; internationalization of, 23; productivity and costs of, 19

productivity, 397; in Canada vs. US, 43; and costs of production, 19; gender equity and, 309; growth rates, 50, 52, 64 fig.; labour (*see* labour productivity)

profitability: business sector and, 45; capital strike and, 21-2; decline in, 3, 47-8, 49, 397, 401, 413; depression in, 58; interest rates and, 59; monetary policy and, 59; and own-account workers, 56-7; pro-cyclical nature, 47; and productivity slowdown, 50; and rates of exploitation, 51; as return on capital employed (ROCE), 46-7, 62 fig.; as return on equity (ROE), 46-7, 62 fig.; taxes and, 59

profit rates, 44; and business cycles, 47, 48, 54; in Canada, 46-8; in Canadian business sector, 47-8, 63 fig.; defined, 46; equation for, 48-9; globalization of, 34; and labour productivity, 57; and recessions, 52, 54; recovery in, 58, 409, 413; restoration of, 400

profits: capitalism and, 20; defined, 46; and surplus value from worker production, 53
project management, 228
property rights, 210, 242, 351; and civil authority, 400; governance and, 243; and NRM, 268, 276, 282-3, 284
PRSPs. *See* Poverty Reduction Strategy Papers
public accounts committees, 378
public debt burden: in Canada, 338, 340; in Italy, 338; in Ontario, 338
public-expenditure incidence analysis, 312
public goods, 2, 3, 206, 305, 313, 397, 406. *See also* public services
public programmes: and budget deficits, 339, 348; resources for, 342-3, 352; restructuring of, 343; spending on, 346-7. *See also* public services
public revenue incidence analysis, 312
public sector: in developing countries, 69; and legal institutions, 210; privatization of, 22; in Vietnam, 177; and WTO agreement, 35
public service, 206; donors and, 208-9; in good society, 217; salaries, 207, 208-9; structural adjustment and, 207
public services: delivery of, 244, 250; and gender, 312-13; for poor, 243; role of state in, 206, 207; and unpaid economy, 311. *See also* public goods; public programmes
Puntland (Somalia), 391

radical economic pragmatism, 322, 369; in Canada, 371; in Tanzania, 370
railways, 117
Razzak, W.A., 99, 100
Reagan, Ronald, 204, 321, 325, 397, 399, 400
real estate, 28
recessions, 33; 1982, 52, 55, 58, 76; 1991, 54, 55, 58; 2001, 43; in Canada, 337; and new technologies, 60
rentier class, 34, 59
rent-seeking, 134, 162, 207, 210, 220
research and development, 37-8
resource allocation: and AB process, 391; and AFB, 353, 370; in Ethiopia, 390-1; by free markets, 111; in Sudan, 390
return on capital employed (ROCE), 46-7, 62 fig.

return on equity (ROE), 46-7, 62 fig.
Robinson, Joan, 107
Rodrik, D., 332
Rosenstein-Rodan, P., 322
Rouis, M., 91, 94, 98, 99, 100, 103
Rowan, D.C., 107, 108
Rubin, J., 339
rural society: development in, 377; donor vision of, 218-19; equality, 221
Russia: demodernization of, 19. *See also* Soviet Union
Rwanda: Chamber of Commerce, 259; coffee export tax, 259; Enhanced HIPC Initiative in, 259-60; Internal Trade Act, 259; Poverty Reduction and Growth Facility (PGRF), 259; privatizations in, 259-60; PRSP, 259-60

Saad Eddin, Ibrahim, 150
Sadat, Anwar, 151, 153, 159
San, P.B., 194
SAPs. *See* structural adjustment programmes (SAPs)
Saul, John, 368
savings, 110, 111; decentralization and, 275; in East African countries, 121; in Ghana, 135, 139, 145-6, 147
scarcities, 207
Schreyer, Ed, 289
Schumpeter, J., 123
science: and fixed capital, 117; and technological innovation, 118
Scotland: analysis of economy, 294, 300-1; banking and industrialization in, 116; budget, 293; civic society in, 299-301; Constitutional Convention, 299; depopulation of, 298-9; development disparities in, 288; devolution in, 292-3, 300; economic development, 291, 295, 300; economic growth, 292, 298, 299; economic performance, 292, 293; economic power, 293; economic transformation, 293-4; education in, 116, 295-6; electronic industries, 295-6, 300; employment in, 292; financial sector, 297-8; globalization and, 294-6; Government Actuary, 298; health standards in, 299; Highlands and Islands Enterprise, 294, 300; indigenous industry, 295, 300; job creation in, 295; liquidity preference

in economy, 298; manufacturing in, 292, 296; Ministry for Enterprise and Lifelong Learning, 294, 295; natural resource sector in, 296; neo-conservatism in, 295, 299; nursery education in, 300; oil and gas in, 297, 300; out-migration from, 298; per capita income in, 292; peripherality in, 296-8; political economy, 292-3; public expenditure, 293; public sector in, 292; Registrar General, 298; services in, 292; small business in, 300; social transformation, 288, 292, 293, 300; structural transformation, 10-11; tax powers, 293; technological innovation in, 295-6; transport infrastructure, 296-7; unemployment in, 292, 300

Scottish Development International, 295

Scottish Enterprise, 293, 294, 295, 299, 300

Scottish Executive, 292, 293, 294, 295

Scottish Office, 292, 293

Scottish Parliament, 288, 292, 293, 297, 300

security, spending on, 407

Seers, Dudley, 321, 322

Senegal, 165, 260

September 11, 2001. See World Trade Center attack

Serieux, J., 261, 262

Shafaeddin, S.M., 99, 100-1

Shafik, N., 104

Shah, K., 279

Shah, M.K., 280

Shah, P., 280

Shan, J.Z., 114

shareholders, 37-8

Sharp, R., 311

Shaw, E.S., 110, 111

Shivji, Issa, 367

Sierra Leone, 166

Singapore: one-party rule in, 217; poverty reduction in, 221; welfare state in, 221

Smith, Adam. The Wealth of Nations, 220

Smith, R.D., 117

social dumping, 39

socialism, 366; African countries and, 72

social justice, 1, 13, 15, 257, 354

social movements, 254, 257

social policy: of AFB, 336; under capitalism, 406; as residual, 306; technocratic approaches, 250

social sector, and neo-conservatism, 306

social stability, 256, 257, 263

social welfare, 21, 167-8, 251, 257, 322-3, 370, 402. See also welfare state

Somalia: accountability in, 392; as collapsed state, 374; CSOs in, 392; debt service rate in, 165; education expenditure in, 166; elections in, 392; public services in, 391; revenues in, 391-2; state collapse in, 391, 392, 393; transparency in, 392

Soto, R., 97, 100

South Africa: AB approach in, 380; budget analysis in, 380, 393; Budget Briefings, 380; Budget Information Service (BIS), 379, 381; budget scrutiny in, 380, 393; Budget Watch, 380; as capitalist democracy, 375; constitution, 378; corruption in, 378; CSOs in, 379, 380-1; gender budgets in, 315, 380, 381; Institute for Democratic Alternatives in South Africa (IDASA), 379-80; interest groups in, 380-1. See also Johannesburg

South Korea, 115, 217, 221

sovereignty, and debt relief, 258, 260, 263

Soviet Union, 70, 72, 76; aid to Vietnam, 177; demise of, 78; neo-conservatism and, 400; subsidized drugs from, 180. See also Russia

speculation: and corruption, 375; financial, 33-4

stagflation, and devaluation, 86, 87-103

stagflationary hypothesis, 85-7, 103, 105

stagnation, 20, 21, 55, 105

stakeholders, 219-20; dialogue among, 275-6; in institutional reform, 245-6, 248-9; women as, 276

Stanford, J., 58

Starr, R.M., 117

state(s): and application of "rules", 209; and business cycles, 397; and capital accumulation, 72; changing role, 406; consumption expenditure, 405; decentralization and, 274-5, 284-5; in developed vs. developing countries, 74; devolution to local groups, 272-3; distrust of, 254; and economic infrastructure, 208; employees, 21; enterprises, 110; and environment, 38; expansion of, 397; expenditures, 22; expenditures and

intellectuals in, 367-8; radical pragmatism in, 370; socialism in, 366, 367-8; stabilization, 224; structural adjustment policies, 224; TA in, 232-3; TANU Guidelines, 367; *Tanzania National Development Vision 2025,* 228; *ujamaa,* 219, 367, 368; University of Dar Es Salaam, 367, 368, 375

taxes; and AFB, 348-9, 362; budget deficits and, 339, 348; in Canada, 53-4, 57-8, 67 fig., 339, 347-8, 348-9; corporate, 22, 139, 140; gender and, 312; in Ghana, 139, 140; indirect business, 53-4, 57-8, 67 fig.; and profitability, 59; redistribution of, 348-9; in Scotland, 293

tax revenues: in Canada, 59, 337-38; in Egypt, 152

technical assistance (TA), 228; and AFB-PRSP partnerships, 331; in African countries, 225; in Tanzania, 232-3; World Bank assessments of, 233

technocracy: costs of regulation, 250-1; and democratization, 249-50, 251; and economic policy, 250; and political processes, 249-51; and resource distribution, 250, 251

technocratic approaches: to economic decision-making, 413; to finance ministries, 306-7

technological change, 69; and cost of capital equipment, 55; and growth, 116

technology/-ies: and capital flight, 21; new, 31, 48, 58, 60; transfer, and economic convergence, 296

tertiary sector services, 30

Thailand, 179

Thatcher, Margaret, 204, 321, 324, 325, 332, 397, 400

Thiessen, Gordon, 337

Thomas, Clive, 291

Thompson, G., 25, 31

threshold regression models, 114

Thurow, Lester, 37-8

Toulmin, C., 275

trade: agreements, 27, 34-5, 324; among OECD countries, 26, 27; of Canada, 55, 58; concentration among trading blocks, 26, 39; of Egypt, 155; in EU, 26; FDI and, 28; flows, 26-7; of Ghana, 133, 134, 139, 140, 146, 147; internationalization of, 409; of Japan, 26-7; liberalization, 248, 400; sanctions, 35-6.

See also Canada-US Free Trade Agreement; international trade; North American Free Trade Agreement (NAFTA)

trading blocks: FDI within, 30, 39; MNCs within, 30; trade concentration among, 26, 39

training: state vs. private sector investment in, 38. *See also* education

transcendental realism, 289, 290

transfer payments, 339; AFB on, 349; and gender relations, 311; and unpaid economy, 311

transition economies: fee-for-service systems in, 185; global economy in, 408; health care utilization, 185; institutions in, 209-10; private sector in, 408; state in, 407

transparency: and AB process, 391; accountability and, 319; in African countries, 391; in economic policy, 323; in Somalia, 392; in spending, 378

Transparency International, 383

Tyson, L., 31

Uganda: AB in, 381; as capitalist democracy, 375; Enhanced HIPC in, 261; health budget in, 381; local government in, 381

underdevelopment, and loss of surplus, 368-9, 375

unemployment: AFB on, 345; in Canada, 43, 338, 339, 345, 346; in Europe, 19; in OECD countries, 300; in Scotland, 292, 300; in US, 43; in US vs. Canada, 43. *See also* employment

UNIFEM, 316

unionization, of workers, 51, 53

United Kingdom: budget deficit in, 405; Department for International Development (DFID), 201-2; foreign asset investment in, 33; government expenditures in, 73; Labour Party, 293; neo-conservatism in, 399; state spending in, 406. *See also* England; London (Eng.); Scotland

United Nations: Conference on Trade and Development, 71, 331; Development Programme, 153, 394; Food and Agriculture Organization (FAO), 159; neo-conservatism and, 410; Research Institute on Social Development (UNRISD), 249-51; and United States, 409-10

United States: agricultural subsidies in, 162; banking sector in, 115; budget deficit in, 405; dollar exchange rate, 43; economic growth, 20-1, 337; economic slowdown, 336; and Egypt, 152, 153; exchange rate, 60n1; FDI flows into, 29; Federal Reserve, 22, 336; foreign asset investment in, 33; in global economy, 409; government expenditures in, 73, 406; growth in real GDP, 43; IT research funding in, 37; Japanese trade with, 27; manufacturing in, 20, 31; mergers and acquisitions in, 29; and neo-conservatism, 36-7, 398-9, 410; President's Information Technology Advisory Committee (PITAC), 37; private business sector, 20; profits in, 20, 48; research and development in, 37; reverse causality in, 115; stock market in, 115; and UN, 409-10; unemployment rates, 43; and WTO agreement, 35

USAID, in Egypt, 154-5, 159, 161

user charges, 178, 181, 185, 191, 192, 193-4

Vector Autoregression model, 97, 102, 114

Veit, P.G., 280-1

vertical accountability, 253, 254, 255, 256

Vietnam: agricultural production cooperatives in, 177; central planning in, 177-8, 194; commune health centres (CHCs), 179, 187; commune health workers, 180; Commune People's Committees, 180; community nurses in, 180; consensus for market reforms in, 211; deregulation in, 177; district health system in, 179; doctors in, 181-82; drugs from eastern Europe, 180; economic performance, 180; economic reforms, 177; exports, 178; farm cooperatives in, 179, 180; fee structures in, 182; financial sector reform, 177; foreign aid to, 180; GDP growth in, 178; health budget, 180, 183; health care in, 7; health care providers in, 178, 184, 196; health care reform in, 181-5, 194; health care services in, 179-81; health care spending, 187; health care utilization in, 184-94; health expenditure in, 180; health insurance in, 181, 192, 194; health service contacts in, 186-7; hospitals in, 179, 183-4, 185, 186-9, 191-3, 194-5; illness in, 189-91, 193; Living Standards

Surveys, 186, 189, 191, 193; macroeconomic stabilization, 177-8; microinstitutional change in, 177; Ministry of Health, 182, 183; nurses in, 182; one-party rule in, 217; overprovision of services in, 184, 185, 187, 195; patient revenues in, 184, 192, 194-5; payments by patients, 182-3, 190, 191-3; pharmaceutical industry, 178, 180, 181, 186, 194; physicians in, 186; poverty in, 178, 186, 187, 221; preventive care services in, 180; primary care, 180-1; private clinics in, 182, 186-7; private health sector, 181-2, 194; private health spending in, 181; private medical practice in, 182, 194; private sector in, 177; public health expenditure, 181, 183; public health sector, 179, 181-2; public sector in, 178; revenues in, 183; salaries in, 184, 192; social sector in, 178; SOEs in, 177; Soviet aid to, 177; staff bonuses, 183-4, 195; transition period in, 179-80; user charges in, 178, 181, 182, 183, 184, 191, 194-5

Wachtel, P., 123n5

wages and salaries: in Ghana, 134, 139, 146; growth in, 50-1, 61 table; indexation of, 104; and labour productivity, 50-1, 61 table, 65 fig.; lowering of, 22; neo-conservatism and, 400; of own-account workers, 56-7; of part-time and self-employed workers, 53, 56; productivity gap, 51-2, 55; public service, 207, 208-9; social, 59, 400; in Vietnam, 184, 192

Wali, Yusef, 149

Washington Consensus, 204, 249

The Wealth of Nations (Smith), 220

Weeks, J., 88, 90, 92

Weiss, L., 23, 36, 111, 115

welfare state, 21, 22, 59, 72, 221. *See also* social welfare

Welsh Assembly, 293

West African countries: authoritarian states in, 374; decentralization in, 274-5

Willoughby, J., 77-8

women: access to government services, 310; access to natural resources, 281-2, 283; budgetary process for, 380; in care economy, 309, 310, 316; committees for, 318; in decision-making, 317; education of, 309; in

463

global economy, 316; groups in Kenya, 384; impact of economic policy on, 318; in labour force, 53; ministries for, 317-18; organizations of, 319; and political parties, 318; in private sector, 316; representation in government, 316; as stakeholders, 276

workers: expectations of, 21, 22, 53; number of, and value of capital stock, 49; "own-account" self-employed, 45, 56-7; part-time, 53, 56; real output per, 49; and 1972 recession, 52; self-employed, 53, 56; unionization of, 51; value added per, 49-50, 64 fig.; and wage-productivity gap, 51-2. *See also* labour

work ethic, 406-7

workplace: capital-labour struggle in, 52, 57, 59-60; restructuring, 58, 59

World Bank, 4, 40, 69, 74, 85, 324; *Addressing Governance and Institutional Issues in the Poverty Reduction Strategy Process,* 243; *African Development Indicators,* 171; assessments of TA, 233; Comprehensive Development Frameworks (CDFs). *See* Comprehensive Development Frameworks (CDFs); concepts of institutional reforms, 263, 264; Development Committee, 240, 241; and economic policies, 77; and Egypt, 150, 151; and expansion of capital, 122; in finance ministries, 123n4; on financial development, 107; and financial repression, 115; and Ghana, 127, 134; *Global Development Finance,* 171; and governance, 365; *Governance and Development,* 240; *Governance and Poverty Reduction,* 242, 245, 252; health system modernization project, 194; and HIPC initiative, 240; and

institutional reforms for poverty alleviation, 239-40; International Development Association, 328; in Kenya, 382, 383; and multilateralism, 249; and neo-conservatism, 408; on ownership of programmes, 224-5; on political processes, 257-8; and poverty-focussed development, 205; and poverty reduction, 239-41; and public vs. private investment, 79-80; role in economic growth, 247-8; *World Debt Tables,* 171; *World Development Report 2000/2001: Attacking Poverty,* 239, 242, 245, 247, 249, 252; *World Development Report 1999/2000: Entering the 21st Century,* 240, 258; *World Development Report 1997: The State in a Changing World,* 240, 257

World Debt Tables (World Bank), 171

World Employment Program, 205

World Trade Center attack, 42, 150-1

World Trade Organization (WTO), 27, 34-7, 326, 411

Yiheyis, Z., 88, 91, 92, 99, 100

youth: in labour force, 53; unemployment in Egypt, 150

Zaire, 166

Zambia, 105n2

Zanzibar, 230

Zeleza, P., 78

Zimbabwe, 165

Zwarteveen, M., 282